T
Crusade
of Jerusalem

A Dynastic History 1099-1125

ALAN V. MURRAY

P&G

Prosopographica et Genealogica

2000

Occasional Publications of the Linacre Unit for Prosopographical Research, vol. 4.
General Editors, K. S. B. Keats-Rohan, Christian Settipani

ISBN 1-900934-03-5

Published by the Unit for Prosopographical Research,
Linacre College, Oxford, OX1 3JA.
Printed in Great Britain by Oxford Print Centre, 36 Holywell, Oxford

Contents

Acknowledgements

Many people have helped in the making of this book in a great many ways. In 1999 I was awarded a research scholarship from the Faculty of Arts in the University of Leeds, and I am grateful to all those within and outwith the University who made this possible, especially Professor Ian Wood for his encouragement. I would like to express my appreciation to colleagues in the International Medieval Institute, particularly Rhiannon Lawrence-Francis and Josine Opmeer, who shouldered additional responsibilities during my absence from my normal duties. Much of the writing was done at the Institut for Historie, Kultur og Samfundsbeskrivelse at the University of Southern Denmark at Odense, and I would like to thank the Institute for providing me with work space and computer facilities, and Dr Kurt Villads Jensen in particular for his part in facilitating my stay in Denmark. The product of that stay now appears in an innovative series published by the Oxford Unit for Prosopographical Research, and I am grateful to the General Editors, Dr Katharine Keats-Rohan and Dr Christian Settipani, for making this possible.

The book has benefited from the suggestions, criticism and expertise of many scholars at various stages. Professor Hans Eberhard Mayer of the University of Kiel unfailingly answered correspondence and offered much detailed comment. My colleague Dr Graham Loud read the entire manuscript and made many helpful suggestions. Dr Heather Tanner of the University of Oregon provided me with extracts from her unpublished doctoral thesis on the comital family of Boulogne and discussed several problems with me. Dr Ann Williams offered valuable comments in reply to queries regarding Anglo-Saxon England, while Mr Malcolm Davis of the Brotherton Library advised on medieval Hebrew. Dr Donald Jackman of Pennsylvania State University was a source of advice on matters genealogical as well as technical. Like many other historians of the crusades, I am indebted to Dr Susan Edgington of Huntingdonshire College for information on the history and manuscripts of Albert of Aachen. I was encouraged to develop many ideas on the prosopography of the Franks by an invitation to participate in a seminar on the government of the Kingdom of Jerusalem in 1999 organised by the Institute for Advanced Studies at the Hebrew University of Jerusalem, and I am grateful to the

Institute for its generous support, and to Professor Benjamin Z. Kedar for his hospitality. The book has also profited from discussions with Professor Hugh Kennedy (University of Leeds), Professor Bernard Hamilton (University of Nottingham), Professor Jonathan Riley-Smith (University of Cambridge), Herr Rolf Götz (Weilheim an der Teck) and Mr Ian Moxon (University of Leeds). Any errors are, of course, mine. My former colleague Dr Romy Günthart, now of the University of Zürich, tracked down many publications which would have been otherwise difficult to obtain, and Katherine Fenton of Leeds Electronic Text Centre provided assistance in scanning the cover illustration.

Parts of the text of Chapter V were originally published in an article, 'Baldwin II and his Nobles: Baronial Factionalism and Dissent in the Kingdom of Jerusalem, 1118-1134', *Nottingham Medieval Studies* 38 (1994), 60-85, and I am grateful to the publishers, especially Professor Michael Jones, for permission to reproduce these. I also thank Brepols Publishers for permission to reproduce passages from the Corpus Christianorum edition of William of Tyre.

This book is dedicated to my wife Martina, who, from Bouillon to Jerusalem, has been with me on many of the geographical and intellectual journeys that went into its making.

Leeds ALAN MURRAY

Abbreviations

AA	Albert of Aachen, *Historia Hierosolymitana*, RHC Occ. 4: 265-713.
BD	Baldric of Dol, *Baldrici episcopi Dolensis Historia Jerosolimitana*, RHC Occ. 4: 1-111.
Cantatorium	*La chronique de Saint-Hubert dite Cantatorium*, ed. K. Hanquet (Brussels, 1906).
C. Hosp.	J. Delaville Le Roulx, *Cartulaire général de l'ordre des Hospitaliers de Saint-Jean de Jérusalem 1100-1310*, 4 vols (Paris, 1894-1906).
FC	Fulcher of Chartres, *Fulcheri Carnotensis Historia Hierosolymitana (1095-1127)*, ed. H. Hagenmeyer (Heidelberg, 1913).
GF	*Gesta Francorum et aliorum Hierosolimatorum*, ed. R. Hill (London, 1962).
GN	Guibert of Nogent, *Historia quae dicitur Gesta Dei per Francos*, RHC Occ. 4: 113-263.
JGLGA	*Jahrbuch der Gesellschaft für lothringische Geschichte und Altertumskunde / Annuaire de la Société d'histoire et d'archéologie de la Lorraine.*
LL	Laurence of Liège, *Laurentii de Leodio Gesta episcoporum Virdunensium et abbatum s. Vitoni*, ed. G. Waitz, MGH SS 10: 486-516.
MGH	Monumenta Germaniae Historica (Hannover, 1826-):
MGH SS	Scriptores in folio, 32 vols (1826-1934)
MGH Const.	Constitutiones et acta publica imperatorum et regum (1893-)
MGH DD	Diplomata Regum et Imperatorum Germaniae (1879-) K.I, H.I, O.I = 1. *Conradi, Heinrici I et Ottonis I Diplomata*; O.II = 2/1. *Ottonis II* Diplomata; O.III = 2/2. *Ottonis III Diplomata*; H.II = 3. *Heinrici II et Arduini Diplomata*; K.II = 4. *Conradi II Diplomata*; H.III = 5. *Heinrici III Diplomata*; H.IV = 6. *Heinrici*

	IV Diplomata; L.III = 8. *Lotharii III Diplomata nec non Richenzae Imperatricis Placita*; F.I = 11. *Friderici I Diplomata*
PL	J. P. Migne, Patrologia cursus completus. Series latina, 221 vols (Paris, 1844-64).
PSHIGDL	*Publications de la Section historique de l'Institut Grand Ducal de Luxembourg.*
PT	Peter Tudebode, *Petri Tudebodi seu Tudebovis sacerdotis Sivracensis historia de Hierosolymitano itinere*, RHC Occ. 3: 1-117.
RA	Raymond of Aguilers, *Raimundi de Aguilers canonici Podiensis historia Francorum qui ceperunt Iherusalem*, RHC Occ. 3: 231-309.
RBPH	*Revue belge de philologie et d'histoire / Belgisch Tijdschrift voor Filologie en Geschiedenis.*
RHC	Recueil des historiens des croisades, ed. Académie des Inscriptions et Belles-Lettres (Paris, 1841-1906):
RHC Occ.	Historiens occidentaux, 5 vols (1844-95)
RHC Or.	Historiens orientaux, 5 vols (1872-1906)
RHC Lois	Les Assises de Jérusalem, 2 vols (1841-43)
ROL	*Revue de l'Orient latin*
RRH	R. Röhricht, *Regesta Regni Hierosolymitani* (Innsbruck, 1893) and *Additamentum* (Innsbruck, 1904).
WT	Guillaume de Tyr, *Chronique,* ed. Robert B. C. Huygens, Corpus Christianorum, Continuatio Mediaevalis, 63-63A, 2 vols (Turnhout, 1986).

Introduction

In the city of Jerusalem in July 1099 the leaders of the First Crusade elected Godfrey of Bouillon, duke of Lower Lotharingia, as the first ruler of the newly established Frankish state in Palestine. On his death after a reign of just under a year, Godfrey was succeeded by his younger brother Baldwin, who assumed the title of king of Jerusalem, and reigned for eighteen years. Their elder brother, Eustace III, count of Boulogne, who had returned to Europe in 1099 on the completion of his pilgrimage, was expected by many in Jerusalem to succeed to the kingdom in turn, but on the death of Baldwin I in 1118 Eustace's claims were defeated by those of a rival candidate, Baldwin of Bourcq, count of Edessa. Thus for the first nineteen years of the existence of the kingdom of Jerusalem these three brothers were in turn monarchs or, in the case of Eustace, prospective monarch of the Frankish state. The aim of this book is to investigate the process by which this dynastic interest acquired, maintained and finally lost the rulership of the kingdom.

Each of the three brothers acquired a different reputation for posterity, and consequently, has been quite differently treated in scholarship. Within a few years of his untimely death, Godfrey of Bouillon was regarded as the great hero of the crusade; by the end of the Middle Ages he figured as the central figure of a cycle of epic poetry, descendant of the Swan Knight, and he was one of the select members of the Nine Worthies, the literary and artistic pantheon of medieval chivalric virtue.[1] This reputation has been reflected in the great number of studies devoted to Godfrey in modern scholarship.[2] By contrast, the eighteen-year reign of his brother

---

[1] The Nine Worthies were three triads of chivalric heroes, which by the later Middle Ages were generally regarded as comprising three Jews (Joshua, King David and Judas Maccabaeus), three pagans (Hector, Alexander and Julius Caesar), and three Christians (King Arthur, Charlemagne and Godfrey of Bouillon). The composition of the Nine, especially that of the Christian triad, tended to vary according to different national traditions.

[2] Apart from general works on the history of Lotharingia and the First Crusade, these include: K. Breysig, 'Gottfried von Bouillon vor dem Kreuzzuge', *Westdeutsche Zeitschrift für Geschichte und Kunst* 17 (1898), 169-201; Ch. Moeller, 'Godefroid de Bouillon et l'avouerie du Saint-Sépulcre', in *Mélanges Godefroid Kurth: Recueil de mémoires relatifs à l'histoire, à la philologie et à l'archéologie*, 2 vols (Liège, 1908), 1: 173-83; H. Vanderlinden, 'La date de la nomination de Godefroid de Bouillon comme duc de

Baldwin, which saw the major territorial expansion of the kingdom, has been less well-served.[3] Furthermore, with the notable exceptions of Andressohn and Mayer, most historians have generally tended to deal not with the complete careers of Godfrey and Baldwin, but to restrict themselves to either the period before or after their departure on crusade. This dichotomy is unfortunate, since some scholarship has held that important institutional characteristics of the early kingdom, particularly the relationship between monarchy and nobility, derived from conditions obtaining in Godfrey's duchy of Lower Lotharingia before the crusade.[4]

Lotharingie (1087)', *Bulletin de la Commission Royale d'Histoire* 90 (1926), 189-92; M. Lobet, *Godefroid de Bouillon: Essai de biographie antilégendaire* (Brussels, 1943); J. C. Andressohn, *The Ancestry and Life of Godfrey of Bouillon* (Bloomington, 1947); H. Dorchy, 'Godefroid de Bouillon, duc de Basse-Lotharingie', *RBPH* 26 (1948), 961-99; G. Despy, 'La date de l'accession de Godefroid de Bouillon au duché de Basse-Lotharingie', *RBPH* 36 (1958), 1275-84; G. Hagspiel, *Die Führerpersönlichkeit im Kreuzzug* (Zürich, 1963). P. Knoch, *Studien zu Albert von Aachen: Der Erste Kreuzzug in der deutschen Chronistik* (Stuttgart, 1966), pp. 126-46; G. Waeger, *Gottfried von Bouillon in der Historiographie* (Zürich, 1969); J. S. C. Riley-Smith, 'The Title of Godfrey of Bouillon', *Bulletin of the Institute of Historical Research* 52 (1979), 83-86; J. France, 'The Election and Title of Godfrey de Bouillon', *Canadian Journal of History* 18 (1983), 321-29; Despy, 'Godefroid de Bouillon, mythes et réalités', *Académie Royale de Belgique, Bulletin de la Classe des Lettres et des Sciences morales et politiques*, ser.5, 71 (1985), 249-75; Pierre Aubé, *Godefroy de Bouillon* (Paris, 1985). A. V. Murray, 'The Title of Godfrey of Bouillon as Ruler of Jerusalem', *Collegium Medievale* 3 (1990), 163-78; M. Menzel, 'Gottfried von Bouillon und Kaiser Heraclius', *Archiv für Kulturgeschichte* 74 (1992), 1-21.

[3] On Baldwin there exist two short German dissertations, A. Wolff, *König Balduin I. von Jerusalem* (Königsberg, 1884) and P. Gindler, *Graf Balduin I. von Edessa* (Halle an der Saale, 1901). Although not conceived as a biography, the best work on the life of Baldwin I is H. E. Mayer, *Mélanges sur l'histoire du royaume latin de Jérusalem*, Mémoires de l'Académie des Inscriptions et Belles-Lettres, n.s. 5 (Paris, 1984). R. Hiestand, 'König Balduin und sein Tanzbär', *Archiv für Kulturgeschichte* 70 (1988), 343-60, offers further interesting perspectives on Baldwin's time as king.

[4] J. Richard, *Le royaume latin de Jérusalem* (Paris, 1953), pp. 62-63, especially p. 63: 'Nous avons déjà montré que Godefroy devenu "roi" restait aux yeux de ses vassaux duc de Basse-Lorraine et leur seigneur naturel. Son frère Baudouin jouit du même prestige'; Joshua Prawer, *Crusader Institutions* (Oxford, 1980), p. 8: 'As Jean Richard has pointed out, the court of Godfrey of Bouillon was overwhelmingly composed of people who were his vassals in Lower Lotharingia. The political tradition of those vassals could not have been that of strong aristocratic opposition against the *Advocatus* who was their sovereign as duke of Lotharingia'. See also Prawer, *Histoire*

It seems therefore that any investigation of how Godfrey's dynasty acquired, held and lost the kingdom of Jerusalem needs to deal not only with all three brothers, but also with their ancestry and careers before the crusade, particularly the role of Godfrey as duke of Lower Lotharingia. The overall conception of the present study is, however, not biographical, but prosopographical. To put it simply, although Godfrey of Bouillon and Baldwin I acquired and ruled the kingdom of Jerusalem, they did not do this by themselves. As well as presenting a narrative of crusading history, this study aims to identify the personal basis of dynastic power, by identifying individuals and groups who were the instruments of the acquisition and exercise of power up to the end of the dynasty's rule, and clarifying the nature of the bonds between them and the monarchs.

The origins of the nobility and higher clergy of the kingdom have long been recognised as playing a crucial role in its political and institutional development. Historians of the Latin East have almost unanimously stressed the composition of the First Crusade as the decisive factor in determining the character of the early Jerusalem nobility, having an importance far beyond that of any subsequent immigration from the west. In 1953, Jean Richard argued that the knights of the first two monarchs originated largely from the duchy of Lower Lotharingia and the county of Boulogne.[5] Shortly afterwards Joshua Prawer, the doyen of Israeli historians of the Frankish period, made a similar point, while also highlighting the role of individuals who entered the service of Godfrey's family during the crusade.[6] Subsequent work has been able to clarify the origins of numerous individuals in Godfrey's contingent during the

du royaume latin de Jérusalem, 2 vols (Paris, 1969), 1: 467-70; H. E. J. Cowdrey, 'The Latin Kingdom of Jerusalem', *History* 57 (1972), 228-34 (here 230); W. Zöllner, *Geschichte der Kreuzzüge* (Berlin, 1977), p. 175.

[5] Richard, *Le royaume latin de Jérusalem*, pp. 62-63: 'A quelques exceptions ... les premiers chevaliers établis dans le royaume venaient du nord de la France, et, par leurs mouvances féodales et leurs parentés, se rattachaient aux ducs de Basse-Lorraine et aux comtes de Boulogne dont Godefroy était issu'.

[6] J. Prawer, 'La noblesse et le régime féodal du royaume latin de Jérusalem', *Le Moyen Age* 65 (1959), 41-74 (here 42): 'La majorité de ces chevaliers appartenaient aux vassaux européens de la maison de Bouillon ou était entrée au service de cette famille pendant la croisade'.

course of the crusade and early years of the kingdom.[7] The most wide-ranging study of participation in the crusade has been made by Riley-Smith, based especially on the consultation of a vast number of charters. He has provided the most comprehensive listing of crusaders to date, and has emphasised the importance of continuing settlement in the Holy Land after the completion of the First Crusade.[8] Nevertheless, there is evidently still a great uncertainty in both academic and popular writing concerning the extent of participation in the crusade and the identities and origins of crusaders. Even Riley-Smith's work is concerned primarily with questions of motivation rather than origins, and in many cases gives little information about the individual participants listed. This book seeks to do something different from these works, in examining the formation and working of the dynastic interest of the crusader kingdom from its origins in Lotharingia and Boulogne through to the circumstances of its loss of the throne after the death of Baldwin I, with a particular stress on the identity and origins of those crusaders and settlers whose ties to Godfrey and Baldwin were important in the crusade and the early years of the kingdom.[9]

This subject-matter raises several issues of nomenclature and terminology which require clarification at the outset. Eustace III of Boulogne, Godfrey of Bouillon and Baldwin I of Jerusalem were the offspring of a marriage contracted in the third quarter of the eleventh century, between Count Eustace II of Boulogne, and Ida, daughter of Godfrey II ('the Bearded'), count of Verdun. The maternal ancestry of the three brothers has been designated by a sometimes bewildering variety of names in modern historiography: Ardenne(s) (*Ardennergrafen*), Verdun, Ardenne(s)-Verdun or Bouillon. The term 'Ardennes' on its own is unsatisfactory, since in most recent scholarship it has been mostly used to refer to an interrelated family network which also included the lineages of the counts

[7] J. S. C. Riley-Smith, 'The Motives of the Earliest Crusaders and the Settlement of Latin Palestine', *English Historical Review* 98 (1983), 721-37; A. V. Murray, 'The Army of Godfrey of Bouillon, 1096-1099: Structure and Dynamics of a Contingent on the First Crusade', *RBPH* 70 (1992), 301-29.

[8] J. S. C. Riley-Smith, *The First Crusaders, 1095-1131* (Cambridge, 1997).

[9] Individual crusaders and settlers are treated in the Prosopographical Catalogue, 'The Personal Basis of Bouillon-Boulogne Power'.

of Luxembourg and the counts of Bar.[10] The term 'Verdun' is perhaps almost as inappropriate, considering how tenuous the family's hold on the county of Verdun was during much of the period under discussion here. In this work, therefore, Godfrey of Bouillon's maternal ancestry is designated by the name 'Ardennes-Bouillon', highlighting the core allodial possession of the dynasty, while the term 'Bouillon-Boulogne' is used to refer to the three sons of Eustace II of Boulogne and Ida of Bouillon in the context of the kingdom of Jerusalem.

A further source of confusion in writing on the crusader period has been the name of the duchy held by Godfrey before the crusade, to which English-speaking historians have frequently referred as 'Lower Lorraine'. In modern French historical writing the name *Lorraine* is predominantly applied to the later medieval duchy, which corresponded to only part of the southern half of the ancient *regnum Lotharii*; Godfrey's ducal authority applied to the northern half. The two duchies into which Lotharingia was divided in the tenth and eleventh centuries are more usually known in French as *Basse-Lotharingie* (cf. German *Niederlothringen*) or *Lothier* for the northern circumscription, and *Haute-Lotharingie* (cf. German *Oberlothringen*) for the southern one. It therefore seems preferable to use the names Lower Lotharingia and Upper Lotharingia respectively as the most accurate English equivalents.

[10] See, for example, M. Parisse, 'Généalogie de la Maison d'Ardenne', *PSHIGDL* 95 (1981), 9-42.

Chapter I

The Origins of the Bouillon-Boulogne Dynasty (951-1095)

The Ancestral Heritages

The three brothers who belonged to the first ruling dynasty of crusader Jerusalem were the sons of Eustace II, count of Boulogne, and Ida of Bouillon, daughter of Godfrey II 'the Bearded', count of Verdun and duke of both Upper and Lower Lotharingia. The eldest brother, Eustace, was named after his father and was intended to succeed to the county of Boulogne. There was also the prospect of a maternal inheritance. Ida's brother Godfrey III ('the Hunchback') had no children, and it was therefore likely that at some point his lands would pass to one of his sister's sons. Before he died, Godfrey III adopted as heir his sister's second son, Godfrey, who – significantly – had been given the leading name (*Leitname*) of his maternal ancestry.[1] The third son, Baldwin, was destined for the church. Thus the dynastic heritage of the first ruling dynasty of the kingdom of Jerusalem consisted of two distinct components, that of the Ardennes-Bouillon family, and that of the counts of Boulogne.

The Ardennes-Bouillon Dynasty

Prior to the First Crusade, Godfrey of Bouillon was the lord of various territories in Lotharingia which were an inheritance of his maternal ancestry. The founder of that line was his ancestor Godfrey, known as 'the Captive'. Godfrey was a son of a Count Gozlin (†942/943), brother of Bishop Adalbero I of Metz, and Uda, who was a daughter of Gerard, count of Metz, and Uda of Saxony. Through his paternal grandparents, the Count of the Palace Wigeric and his wife Cunigunde, Godfrey the Captive was connected to a vast interrelated network which included the houses of Bar, Salm and Luxembourg, and which has been described as

[1] LL p. 495; *Cantatorium*, p. 100.

the 'Mid-Moselle Clan'.[2] This designation is somewhat misleading in that it implies a group identity common to the entire network, but it is doubtful whether its members were aware of such a unity. The varying and at times competing landed interests of each family as well as the evidence of name-giving habits suggest that dynastic consciousness was in fact centred on the individual branches. In the Ardennes-Bouillon branch this separate identity was expressed in the use of the characteristic names Godfrey and its derivative form Gozelo, which were repeatedly bestowed on male family members over several generations.

The Emperor Otto I granted the county of Verdun to Godfrey the Captive at some time between 944 and 951. Godfrey died after 997, and his sons came to acquire important dignities and possessions in Lotharingia. The eldest, Frederick (†1022), inherited the county of Verdun on his father's death. Adalbero became bishop of Verdun (984-88). Hermann became margrave of Eename. Godfrey I became duke of Lower Lotharingia (1012-23). His younger brother Gozelo I (†1044) succeeded him, and became duke of Upper Lotharingia in 1033. Around 1005 Frederick had become a monk, entering the abbey of St Vanne at Verdun; at that time the county of Verdun probably passed to Godfrey I, and on his death to Gozelo I.[3] By 1033 a single member of the lineage, Gozelo I, held the duchies of Upper and Lower Lotharingia as well as the margraviate of Antwerp and the county of Verdun. When Gozelo died in 1044 the Emperor Henry III attempted to break up this concentration of ducal power through a division of offices between two of his sons, and granted Upper Lotharingia to Godfrey II and Lower Lotharingia to Gozelo II. Godfrey, however, disputed the settlement and after two unsuccessful revolts against the monarchy was deprived of his duchy and numerous fiefs; when Gozelo died in 1046 the duchy of Lower Lotharingia was given to Frederick of Luxembourg (1046-65), a member

---

[2] W. Mohr, *Geschichte des Herzogtums Lothringen,* 3 vols (Saarbrücken, 1976-79), 1: 51-60; Parisse, 'Généalogie de la Maison d'Ardenne', 9-42; H. Renn, *Das erste Luxemburger Grafenhaus* (Berlin, 1941), pp. 23ff; G. Tellenbach, 'From the Carolingian Imperial Nobility to the German Estate of Imperial Princes', in *The Medieval Nobility: Studies on the Ruling Classes of France and Germany*, ed. T. Reuter (Amsterdam, 1979), p. 211. Godfrey's surname derived from a lengthy period of imprisonment in West Francia after his capture by King Lothar at Verdun in 985.

[3] J.-P. Evrard, 'Les comtes de Verdun aux Xe et XIe siècles', *PSHIGDL* 95 (1981), 153-82.

of one of the other main branches of the Ardennes kin group. Since he had once more been disappointed in his ducal aspirations, Godfrey's interests now shifted to Italy where he spent most of the rest of his life. In 1054 he married Beatrix, widow of the Marquis Boniface of Tuscany; with the help of Godfrey's growing influence his younger brother Frederick was elected pope in 1065 as Stephen IX (†1022). Although restored as duke of Lower Lotharingia in 1065, Godfrey clearly regarded Italy as the more promising sphere of interest. Mathilda, daughter of Boniface and Beatrix, was the heiress to her father's extensive lands in northern Italy, and in the hope of securing this inheritance for his own descendants, Godfrey arranged a marriage between Mathilda and Godfrey III ('the Hunchback'), his own son by his first marriage. This dynastic match proved to be spectacularly unsuccessful, breaking up soon after the death of the elder Godfrey. Mathilda became the major lay supporter of the Papacy during the Investiture Contest; her estranged husband returned to Lower Lotharingia and loyally served the Emperor Henry IV as duke until he was assassinated during a conflict with Robert I of Flanders in 1076.[4] On his death-bed Godfrey III formally designated as heir his nephew Godfrey, the son of his sister Ida and Eustace II of Boulogne. This Godfrey (IV), generally known to history simply as 'Godfrey of Bouillon', shortly afterwards took up his inheritance under the guardianship of his kinsman Henry of Verdun, bishop of Liège.[5]

The Inheritance of Godfrey of Bouillon

The landed possessions of the Ardennes-Bouillon family in Lotharingia were a heterogenous accumulation of fiefs, rights and allodial properties whose character varied considerably in the course of the one and a half centuries between the time of Godfrey the Captive and the departure of his great-great-grandson on crusade. The core consisted of the county of Verdun and various allodial possessions in the area of the middle Meuse. After the initial period of acquisition, expansion and consolidation under Godfrey the Captive and his sons, losses to the patrimony resulted owing to three main factors. The first of these was the conventional piety of the age which encouraged gifts of property to the church. Among donations

---

[4] Mohr, *Geschichte des Herzogtums Lothringen,* 2: 41-63; Andressohn, *Ancestry and Life of Godfrey of Bouillon,* pp. 9-18.
[5] LL p. 495; *Cantatorium*, pp. 90-92.

known were those of allods at Longlier, given by Godfrey II to the abbey of Florennes around 1056, and lands at Bellevaux, alienated by Godfrey III in 1074 or 1075.[6] Secondly, properties were regularly given as dowries to female members of the family on their marriage. Gozelo I gave his daughter Regelindis the allodial complex of Durbuy on her marriage to Albert II of Namur.[7] A fairly extensive dowry for Ida, sister of Godfrey III, can be deduced from transactions made by her to raise funds for the crusade in 1095-96. Such alienations were common to practically all noble families of the period and cannot therefore be considered as major losses.

Much more serious were the results of the two revolts against the German monarchy by Godfrey II in 1045-46 and 1049. The Emperor Henry III took severe punitive action in depriving Godfrey of offices and lands. Adam of Bremen reports that in 1047 the emperor gave to the church of Hamburg the *comitatum Fresiae ... quem ante Gotafridus habuit*. This would appear to be identical with the county of Fivelgo, described by Adam as the largest county in Friesland, which brought the archbishop an annual income of 1000 pounds of silver.[8] The county of Drenthe, formerly held by Godfrey's father Gozelo I, was granted to the church of Utrecht in 1046.[9] Further south, Godfrey's castle at Böckelheim on the Nahe was destroyed by the king: this is the last mention of any Ardennes-Bouillon holdings in the Rhineland.[10] The picture that emerges from the aftermath of Godfrey's rebellions is somewhat fragmentary, but it suggests that while the core possessions on the middle Meuse remained intact, the monarchy carried out considerable punitive confiscations beyond these holdings. While the holdings of the Ardennes-Bouillon dynasty as a whole have been relatively well researched in scholarly literature, any attempt to assess the landed resources of Godfrey IV on

[6] MGH DD H.III, no. 408; J. Bertholet, *Histoire ecclesiastique et civile du duché du Luxembourg et du comté de Chiny* 3 (Luxembourg, 1743), preuves, xxviii.

[7] M. Van Rey, *Die Lütticher Gaue Condroz und Ardenne im Frühmittelalter* (Bonn, 1977), p. 291.

[8] Adam of Bremen, 'Gesta Hammaburgensis ecclesiae pontificum', in *Quellen des 9. und 11. Jahrhunderts zur Geschichte der hamburgischen Kirche und des Reiches*, ed. W. Trillmich and R. Buchner (Darmstadt, 1961), pp. 334, 384.

[9] MGH DD H.III, no. 152. On the evidence of D.II, no. 504 and D K.II, no. 43, it would seem that the county had previously been granted to the church of Utrecht, although it was in Gozelo's possesion by the 1040s.

[10] Hermann of Reichenau, *Chronicon*, MGH SS 5: 125.

the eve of the First Crusade must confine itself to the period after the revolts of his grandfather, that is to say, the second half of the eleventh century.[11]

BOUILLON AND ITS TERRITORY

The castle of Bouillon, towering on rocky heights above the River Semois in the Ardennes, is first mentioned in a letter of Adalbero, archbishop of Rheims, to his brother Godfrey the Captive in 988.[12] It seems to have been the original patrimonial possession of the Ardennes-Bouillon family and remained the focal point of its holdings, functioning as its principal refuge and repository of its treasury. The settlement around the castle was also important as it constituted the only real urban centre under Godfrey's control, housing artisans and merchants; it was also the site of a ducal mint.[13] On the right bank of the Semois was the church of St Peter, which was established as a priory of the abbey of Saint-Hubert by Duke Godfrey II as he lay dying in 1069.[14] The status of Bouillon and its surrounding territory has been frequently misinterpreted as a result of confusion in nomenclature. In the twelfth century it was common for lords to be known by the name of their most important, often allodial property, which then became confused with other titles. Thus a series of dukes of Lower Lotharingia whose main territorial holdings were centred on Bouillon later gave rise to the notion of a 'duchy' or 'county' of Bouillon for which there is no justification in the eleventh century.[15]

---

[11] For the lands of the dynasty from the mid-tenth to the late eleventh centuries, see Ch. Dupont, 'Les domaines des ducs en Basse-Lotharingie au XIe siècle', *PSHIGDL* 95 (1981), 217-40, and M. Werner, 'Der Herzog von Lothringen in salischer Zeit', in *Die Salier und das Reich*, 1: *Salier, Adel und Reichsverfassung*, ed. S. Weinfurter and H. Kluger (Sigmaringen, 1991), 367-473.

[12] F. Weigle, *Die Briefsammlung Gerberts von Reims*, MGH Briefe der deutschen Kaiserzeit 2 (Berlin, 1966), no. 129.

[13] Werner, 'Der Herzog von Lothringen in salischer Zeit', p. 463.

[14] *Cantatorium*, p. 59; W. Peters, 'Zur Gründung und zur frühen Geschichte des Benediktinerpriorats St Peter in Bouillon', *Revue Bénédictine* 109 (1999), 341-58.

[15] E. Poncelet, 'Les droits souverains de la principauté de Liège sur le duché de Bouillon', *Bulletin de la Commission Royale d'Histoire* 108 (1943), 257-58. Andressohn, *Ancestry and Life of Godfrey of Bouillon*, p. 31, mistakenly refers to a 'county' of Bouillon.

The territory was a complex of allodial properties and rights, the basis of which had been part of the fisc of Paliseul. It included the villages of Bellevaux, Mogimont, Sensenruth and Assenois.[16] The castle of Bouillon was in the charge of a castellan, whose office was hereditary, while most of the surrounding villages were assigned as fiefs to the knights who provided the principal military resources of the Ardennes-Bouillon family.[17] In 1069 Godfrey III, supported by his vassals, refused to carry out some of the bequests to the monastery of Saint-Hubert made by his dying father, on the grounds that too many of these fiefs would thereby be lost.[18] The bishop of Liège had previously granted to Godfrey II the advocacy of this monastery situated at *Andaginum* in the Ardennes forest, about 35 kilometres north-east of Bouillon. His son and grandson in turn inherited this office.[19] The advocate had the duty of protecting the monastery and representing it in temporal affairs, but his office also offered numerous opportunities to exploit the resources of the monastery. Thus at one point Godfrey II intended to force its workers to perform labour services to repair the fortifications of Bouillon.[20] It is likely that some of the properties of the Bouillon complex had been acquired by usurpation of monastic holdings by the advocates. For example, the allod of Tellin was included among the possessions of the abbey in 817/825. However, at some point it was acquired by the lords of Bouillon and was only restored by Godfrey IV in 1076 at the urging of his kinsman Bishop Henry of Liège.[21]

To the south, and contiguous to the allodial territory of Bouillon proper, lay a fief held by the lords of Bouillon from the archbishop of

[16] *Cantatorium,* pp. 64-65; Giselbert of Mons, *Chronicon Hanoniense*, ed. L. Vanderkindere (Brussels, 1904), p. 43; Van Rey, *Die Lütticher Gaue,* pp. 709-10, 716-17, 720-30; Dupont, 'Les domaines des ducs en Basse-Lotharingie', pp. 219-20. MGH DD H.III, no. 51 (1040) shows that for a time Paliseul was held illegally by Hermann of Eename, brother of Godfrey I and Gozelo I.

[17] *Cantatorium,* p. 59: *erant vero ipse possessiones fere omnes militum stipendiarie.*

[18] *Cantatorium,* pp. 64-65.

[19] H. Müller-Kehlen, *Die Ardennen im Frühmittelalter* (Göttingen, 1973), pp. 50-54; A. Laret-Kayser, 'La fonction et les pouvoirs ducaux en Basse-Lotharingie au XIe siècle', *PSHIGDL* 95 (1981), 133-52 (here 146-48); Werner, 'Der Herzog von Lothringen in salischer Zeit', p. 414.

[20] Laret-Kayser, 'La fonction et les pouvoirs ducaux en Basse-Lotharingie', p 145.

[21] *Cantatorium,* pp. 11-15, 91-93.

Rheims. It was described in a treaty of 1127 as the *beneficium quod Remensis ecclesie ab antiquo esse dinoscitur quod etiam ad Bullionem pertinere nulli dubium est.*[22] Although situated within the kingdom of Germany, the fief was a temporal possession of the cathedral church of Rheims and seems to have been created from land originally belonging to the abbey of Mouzon, of which several members of the Ardennes-Bouillon family had been advocates. It lay between the Forêt de Bouillon and the Rivers Chiers and Meuse. In the twelfth century it included the villages of Sedan, Givonne, Douzy, Villers-Cernay and Pouru-aux-Bois.[23]

THE COUNTY OF VERDUN

The county of Verdun in Upper Lotharingia was held by the Ardennes-Bouillon dynasty from the mid-tenth century up to 1096. The county was contiguous with the entire diocese of Verdun, except where it extended into the bishopric of Rheims to the west to take in the Argonne, an area which had originally been a march of the empire. The Argonne ridge formed a natural frontier protecting Verdun from the west, and included the mountain strongholds of Montfaucon-en-Argonne and Vienne-le-Château.[24]

A diploma issued by the Emperor Frederick I in 1156 suggests that towards the end of the tenth century the German monarchy had conferred on Bishop Haimo of Verdun the right to grant out the *beneficium comitatis et marchiae.*[25] In practice the bishops were frequently unable to

---

[22] S. Bormans, E. Schoolmeesters and E. Poncelet, *Cartulaire de l'église de Saint-Lambert de Liège* (Brussels, 1893-1933), 1, no. 35; *Cantatorium,* pp. 244-45.

[23] C. Zoller-Devroey, 'Feodalité et economie dans les Ardennes médiévales: le fief de Bouillon en Sedanais', in *Centenaire du Seminaire d'Histoire médiévale de l'Université libre de Bruxelles* (Brussels, 1977), pp. 21-57.

[24] L. Clouët, *Histoire de Verdun et du pays verdunois* (Verdun, 1868), 1: 402; M. Parisse, *La noblesse lorraine XIe-XIIIe siècle* (Lille, 1976), pp. 14-15. The toponym and location of Montfaucon-en-Argonne have caused some confusion among historians. The stronghold, whose Latin name was *Falconis Mons* (cf. LL p. 498), was referred to without any precise identification as 'Schloß Falkenstein' by Breysig, 'Gottfried von Bouillon vor dem Kreuzzuge', a misnomer followed by R. Röhricht, *Geschichte des Ersten Kreuzzuges* (Innsbruck, 1901), p. 60, Andressohn, *Ancestry and Life of Godfrey of Bouillon,* p. 51, and J. France, *Victory in the East: A Military History of the First Crusade* (Cambridge, 1994), p. 84.

[25] MGH DD F.I, no. 149.

assert their right to nominate the count in the face of a tendency towards hereditary succession pursued by the counts themselves. Thus after the death of Godfrey the Captive, the succession to the county passed in turn to his sons Frederick, Godfrey I and Gozelo I. Soon after Gozelo's accession, Bishop Rambert attempted to nominate his own choice as count, Louis of Chiny, who was subsequently defeated and killed in battle by Gozelo.[26] This was the only serious challenge to the counts until the first rebellion of Godfrey II (1044-46). Henry III deprived Godfrey of the county and ordered Bishop Richard to re-grant it.[27] There is no evidence that the county was ever granted out by him. His successor Theoderic eventually restored the county to Godfrey after he had done penance and made restitution for the capture and burning of the city in 1047.[28] However, taken in conjunction with the intervention of Henry III, the charter evidence suggests that this restoration may have been made on terms far less favourable to Godfrey than had been the case prior to 1044. Under the bishops Berengar, Wigfrid, Haimo and Rambert the importance of the count was signalled in episcopal documents by his name being listed in the first place among the lay witnesses.[29] During the episcopates of Theoderic (1047-89) and Richer (1089-1107) the name of the count disappears from episcopal documents completely, figuring neither in the witness list nor in the dating formula, which usually names only the bishop and the reigning emperor.[30]

This development can be understood in the wider context of political power in Lotharingia. On the western frontier of the German kingdom the monarchy supported the bishoprics as institutions that were amenable to central authority and could be relied upon as bulwarks against the forces of local particularism. In the dioceses of Liège, Cambrai, Verdun, Toul and Metz the emperors tended to install bishops of their own

---

[26] Clouët, *Histoire de Verdun*, 2: 26; Parisse, *Noblesse lorraine*, p. 15.

[27] LL p. 492: *hunc idem imperator inter multa alia comitatum huius urbis, quem a praedecessoribus suis tenebat, iam in curia sua exheredavit, ipsumque comitatum Richardo urbis episcopo manu dederat, ut alteri, quem idoneum iudicasset, illum traderet.*

[28] LL pp. 492-93.

[29] J.-P. Evrard, 'Les actes des évêques de Verdun' (unpublished dissertation, Univ. of Nancy, 1973), nos. 15, 22, 23, 24, 37, 45. No. 46 is an exception to this pattern, although Godfrey II is named in the dating formula immediately after Duke Frederick.

[30] Evrard, 'Les actes des évêques de Verdun', nos. 55-88.

choosing, usually of non-Lotharingian origin, and gave them powers and lands to strengthen the church as a counterweight to the less accountable hereditary dynasties.[31]

One can gain an impression of the respective powers of bishop and count in the time of the episcopate of Theoderic of Verdun by examining contemporary developments in the neighbouring and better documented bishopric of Toul. There, on the death of Count Rainald II (1052), Bishop Udo granted the county to a different dynasty in the person of Arnulf of Sorcy, whom he deposed in 1069. In the same year Udo issued a document setting out the respective rights of the bishop and the new count, Frederick of Astenois.[32] The count's authority was excluded from the episcopal city; the bishops had exclusive rights of coinage and commanded a force of knights. One third of the profits of justice went to the count and two-thirds to the bishop. The main duties of the count were the surveillance of highways and frontiers, but outside the city he was entitled to no rights of justice, service or hospitality. This evidence, and the equally tractable position of the counts of Metz, suggests that after the revolts of Godfrey II the balance of power in Verdun had swung in favour of the bishop. The bishop had a force of knights at his command, and during the wars between Godfrey of Bouillon and Theoderic the vassals of Verdun were mostly on the side of the bishop.[33] The only later evidence of comital activity comparable to the period before 1044-46 is to be found in a charter probably issued in 1065 or 1066, in which Godfrey II regulated the rights and duties of the lay advocates of the Verdun abbeys.[34] Yet, as the document itself states, this act was in fact a renewal of regulations issued jointly by Bishop Richard, Gozelo I and Godfrey himself in the period 1039-44; therefore the apparent evidence of this document is actually a reflection of a time when comital authority was considerably stronger.

---

[31] A. Cauchie, *La querelle des investitures dans les diocèses de Liège et de Cambrai* (Louvain, 1890), pp. viii-x; A. Danzer, 'La querelle des investitures dans les évêchés de Metz, Toul et Verdun de 1075 à 1122', *Annales de l'Est* 16 (1902), 85-100.

[32] A. Calmet, *Histoire de la Lorraine* (Nancy, 1728), 1: 466-67.

[33] Evrard, 'Les actes des évêques de Verdun', nos. 67, 69; Laurence of Liège, pp. 494-97.

[34] H. Bloch, 'Die älteren Urkunden des Klosters S. Vanne zu Verdun', *JGLGA* 14 (1902), 48-150, no. 54.

STENAY AND MOUZAY

The allods of Stenay and Mouzay, situated midway between Bouillon and Verdun on the right bank of the Meuse, were more recent acquisitions of the Ardennes-Bouillon line. The *caput* of this cluster of possessions was the former royal castle of Stenay above the Meuse, the scene of the murder of the Merovingian king Dagobert II and site of a church dedicated to him.[35] Stenay and Mouzay had come to Godfrey II as part of the dowry of his second wife, Beatrix (†1076), daughter of Frederick II of Bar, duke of Upper Lotharingia.[36] This meant that the Ardennes-Bouillon claim to the allods was open to question; as Beatrix had no children by Godfrey, they could also be claimed by Mathilda, the daughter of Beatrix and her first husband, Boniface of Tuscany.[37]

DISPERSED POSSESSIONS IN BRABANT AND HESBAYE

In addition to these three main blocs, the existence of a number of smaller allodial domains further to the north is revealed by the documents recording sales of property in 1095-96 to raise money for the crusade. These properties formed two groups. One lay in Brabant, and included the allods of Baisy-Thy and Genappe.[38] The other group lay in the Hesbaye (Haspengouw) district, mostly on the west bank of the Meuse around the town of Maastricht. Here the Ardennes-Bouillon family had land in the villages of Brekhout, Herderen, Riemst, Rijkhoven, Reek, Leten, Martenslinde, Asserbeek, Bilzen, Wijlre, Gellik, Repen, Eigenbilzen, Guigoven, Langerlo, Rotem and Amelsdorp.[39] This group of lands appears to have belonged principally to Godfrey IV's mother Ida, although he may have also held properties in the area himself; in 1096 Bishop Otbert of Liège disposed of two mills near Maastricht formerly in the possession of Godfrey.[40] There was probably a similar pattern of tenure in the case of the Brabant cluster. The settlement of Baisy itself

---

[35] Clouët, *Histoire de Verdun*, 1: 167.

[36] R. Parisot, *Les origines de la Haute-Lorraine et sa première maison ducale 959-1033* (Paris, 1909), pp. 177-79.

[37] The claim of Mathilda is mentioned in MGH DD H.IV, no. 373 (1085).

[38] MGH DD H.IV, no. 459;.

[39] S. P. Ernst, *Histoire du Limbourg*, 7 vols (Liège, 1837-52), 6: 113-15.

[40] A. Wauters, *Table chronologique des chartes et diplômes imprimés concernant l'histoire de la Belgique*, 1 (Brussels, 1866), 601.

belonged to Ida, who gave its church to the abbey of Saint-Hubert on the eve of the crusade.[41] Another donation made by Ida to the abbey of Affligem shows that both she and her son held lands in and around Genappe.[42] Ida's properties in both the Brabant and Hesbaye groups seem to have been regarded as part of the inheritance of her second son Godfrey, since the surviving documents relating to sale or donation usually include the consent of Godfrey, rather than that of Eustace, her eldest son.[43]

GODFREY'S STRUGGLE FOR HIS INHERITANCE

It is difficult to establish with certainty the extent to which Godfrey was in actual control of the lands discussed above during the twenty years between his succession to them in 1076 and his departure on crusade in 1096. He had been designated heir by his uncle but was by no means the only claimant. Mathilda of Tuscany claimed the inheritance of her mother Beatrix of Bar: Stenay and Mouzay and parts of the territory of Bouillon (e.g. Longlier).[44] The remainder of the Ardennes-Bouillon lands were claimed by Albert III, count of Namur, who was a son of Regelindis, a daughter of Gozelo I.[45] In addition to his hereditary county of Namur,

---

[41] *Cantatorium,* pp. 205-6: *ipsa Ida comitissa matrem ecclesiam in Baseio villa, que propria ab antiquo sui patrimonii in Brabante erat sita, juxta Nivigellam...*

[42] A. Miraeus, *Opera diplomatica et historica*, ed. J.-F. Foppens, 4 vols (Brussels, 1723-48), 1: 77: *Filius quoque meus dux Godefridus in eadem villa Genapia quinque mansos terrae donavit iisdem fratribus, ad quos postea in augmentum concessi quasdam partes circumiactentes.* Godfrey's donation may be the same as that mentioned in the *Chronicon Affligemense* (MGH SS 9: 415), which also comprised five *mansi.*

[43] In the three documents in question Eustace is mentioned in only one, that for Affligem, where his consent is given after that of Godfrey.

[44] Parisot, *Les origines de la Haute-Lorraine*, 177-79; Mohr, *Geschichte des Herzogtums Lothringen,* 2: 63.

[45] Considerable confusion exists concerning Regelindis and the Namur claim. Mohr, *Geschichte des Herzogtums Lothringen,* 2: 63, following Breysig, 'Gottfried von Bouillon vor dem Kreuzzuge', p.183, claims that Albert III married an elder sister of Godfrey IV's mother Ida. In that case his claim would presumably have been better than Godfrey's own, but Mohr is mistaken. Both the *Fundatio ecclesiae s. Albani Namucensis*, MGH SS 15: 962, and the *Genealogia ex stripe s. Arnulfi*, MGH SS 25: 384 indicate that it was Albert III's father, Albert II, who married a daughter of Gozelo I. Thus the marriage connection was two generations removed from Godfrey of Bouillon. Andressohn, *Ancestry and Life of Godfrey of Bouillon*, p. 34, confuses the two Alberts

Albert had acquired extensive lands to the north-east of Bouillon on his marriage to Ida, widow of Frederick of Luxembourg, duke of Lower Lotharingia (1046-65). These territories, which later formed the county of Laroche, threatened the neighbouring lands of Saint-Hubert, of which Godfrey was advocate.[46] Further claims on the territory of Bouillon were raised by Theoderic *Flamens*, count of Veluwe on the lower Rhine, who also held lands at Graide, to the north of Bouillon.[47] These claimants were joined by other local dynasts keen to share in the spoils: Waleran, count of Arlon and Limburg, and Arnulf II of Chiny, whose county of Chiny and domains at Warcq and Givet lay adjacent to the territory of Bouillon.[48] The crucial link in this hostile coalition was provided by Theoderic, bishop of Verdun, who perceived a chance to end the hereditary succession in the county of Verdun. He bestowed the county on Mathilda of Tuscany, who in turn granted it to Albert of Namur as guardian of her interests in Lotharingia. Mathilda's influence with Pope Gregory VII further persuaded Manasses I, archbishop of Rheims, to grant to Albert the *beneficium quod Remensis ecclesie ab antiquo esse dinoscitur.*[49]

In one of the earlier stages of the struggle, probably soon after Godfrey's accession, Albert of Namur laid siege to Bouillon but was repulsed by Godfrey.[50] Fighting evidently continued at least until 1081-82; at some point during this time Theoderic *Flamens* was taken prisoner, dying after a captivity of six months in the castle of Bouillon.[51] During this period Godfrey seems to have been unable to gain a foothold in the

---

and mistakenly identifies Regelindis with Ida of Saxony, widow of Frederick of Luxembourg and wife of Albert III. According to Bernold of St Blasien, *Chronicon*, MGH SS 5: 457, Ida of Bouillon did have a sister, Wiltrudis, who married Count Adalbert of Calw, but there is no evidence of any claim from that quarter.

[46] F. Rousseau, *Actes des comtes de Namur de la première race 946-1196* (Brussels, 1937), pp. xciv-xcvi.

[47] P. C. Boeren, 'Overzicht der dynastie van Wassenburg-Gelre en verwante geslachten gedurende de elfde eeuw', *Bijdragen en Mededelingen van de Vereeniging Gelre* 41 (1938), 1-23; Boeren, *De oorsprong van Limburg en Gelre en enkele naburige heerschappijen* (Maastricht, 1938), pp. 71-86.

[48] Mohr, *Geschichte des Herzogtums Lothringen,* 2: 64; H. Goffinet, 'Les comtes de Chiny', *Annales de l'Institut archéologique de Luxembourg* 9 (1877), 317-42.

[49] Evrard, 'Les actes des évêques de Verdun', no. 73; Rousseau, *Actes des comtes de Namur,* p. lxxxv.

[50] LL p. 494. For the dating, see Mayer, *Mélanges*, pp. 23-24.

[51] *Cantatorium,* pp. 104-6.

county of Verdun. Most of the Verdun barons including his own kinsmen Rainald III of Toul and Peter of Dampierre served in the episcopal army. This explains why Godfrey prevailed upon one of his captives, Count Henry-Hezelin II of Grandpré, to change sides, sending him 'as an enemy to the territory of Verdun'.[52]

Godfrey's main support came from the imperialist bishop of Liège, Henry of Verdun, who purchased the stronghold of Mirwart from the Countess Richilda of Hainaut to prevent it being used as a base against Bouillon and Saint-Hubert by Albert of Namur, whose lands lay at the centre of the temporal possessions of the bishopric.[53] By 1082 Bishop Henry had succeeded in establishing a truce in his diocese.[54] Conditions were different in the diocese of Verdun. Henry IV felt it necessary to take action against Mathilda because of her support for Pope Gregory VII; after several years of sitting on the fence, Bishop Theoderic was persuaded to join the imperial camp, and on 1 June 1085 the emperor granted him Stenay and Mouzay, confiscated from the countess.[55] The most intensive period of fighting seems to have occurred during 1086. In that year Theoderic of Verdun and Albert of Namur launched an expedition against Stenay, which Godfrey had fortified. A major but indecisive battle occurred on 12 September, in which many of the knights of Verdun were killed. The siege of Stenay was raised after Godfrey's brothers Eustace and Baldwin arrived with reinforcements. Peace between Godfrey and the bishop of Verdun was eventually established through the intervention of Henry, bishop of Liège, who was not only a former archdeacon of Verdun but also a kinsman of Godfrey and of two of the principal Verdun barons, Rainald of Toul and Peter of Dampierre.[56] Yet there is evidence that hostilities between Godfrey and his enemies continued after this date. The confirmation of the grant of the priory of St Dagobert near Stenay made by Godfrey to the abbey of

---

[52] LL pp. 494-97.

[53] *Cantatorium,* pp. 106-8.

[54] H. Vanderlinden, 'Le tribunal de Paix de Henri de Verdun (1082) et la formation de la principauté de Liège', in *Mélanges Henri Pirenne*, 2 vols (Brussels, 1926), 2: 589-96.

[55] MGH DD H.IV, no. 373.

[56] LL p. 494; Ch. Aimond, 'La nécrologe de la cathédrale de Verdun', *JGLGA* 21 (1910), 132-314 (here 313); J.-P. Evrard, 'Les comtes de Verdun aux Xe et XIe siècles', *PSHIGDL* 95 (1981), 153-82 (here 164, 182).

Gorze states that after the death of his uncle (i.e. Godfrey III) the church was pillaged and laid waste by his enemies; and now that it had been recovered he wished to make provision for the monks. The document survives in two versions dating from 1093 and 1096, which suggests that Godfrey's possession of Stenay was only consolidated by a relatively late date.[57] The earlier charter names Count Arnulf (that is to say of Chiny) as the usurper of Stenay, and lays great stress on the legality of Godfrey's title to it. Further evidence for a continuation of hostilities into the 1090s can be found in the Annals of Mouzon, which mention an *incensio Mosomi et devastatio* in the year 1092.[58] The destruction of the castle of Mouzon (midway between Bouillon and Stenay) was still a bone of contention between Godfrey and Arnulf in 1095.[59]

Godfrey's position in the county of Verdun appears to have been much more tenuous than in his other territories. Unlike his predecessors he is not known to have issued any documents as count.[60] A final settlement with the bishop was not reached until his departure for the Holy Land, and its terms throw considerable light on the respective positions of bishop and count at this stage. Stenay and Mouzay were purchased by Bishop Richer 'for many pounds of gold of silver', but in exchange for surrendering his rights to the county Godfrey received nothing. In fact, as part of the general settlement he was obliged to raze the fortifications of

[57] Miraeus, *Opera diplomatica et historica*, 1: 390, 395. For dating see Wauters, *Table chronologique*, 1: 581.

[58] *Annales Mosomagenses*, MGH SS 3: 162.

[59] *Cantatorium*, p. 192.

[60] A donation of property at Varnencourt to the abbey of St Ageric (Saint-Airy) in Verdun by Godfrey in 1095 is cited by Wauters, *Table chronologique*, 1: 591, and Breysig, 'Gottfried von Bouillon vor dem Kreuzzuge', p. 196. The text, reproduced by François de Rosières, *Stemmatum Lotharingiae ac Barri ducum* (Paris, 1580), describes the issuer as *Godefridus filius Domini Eustachii Comitis Bollonei, ac Dominae Idae filiae Domini Godefridi Barbati Ducis Lotharingiae, Dux Lotharingiae superioris ac Mosellanae, ac Marchio Brabantiae, Hasbaniae, Buillon, sacri Imperii Marchio et Virdunensis.* Godfrey was never duke of Upper (Mosellan) Lotharingia. During his lifetime Brabant was held by Godfrey of Louvain, who became duke of Lower Lotharingia in 1106, while the Hesbaye was part of the principality of Liège. As the text also incorrectly names Godfrey of Bouillon as founder of the abbey this document can be regarded only as a most primitive forgery.

Montfaucon. This suggests that Godfrey's only foothold in the county was the march of Argonne, which lay outside the diocese.[61]

The county of Verdun, Bouillon and its dependent territories, and the allods of Stenay and Mouzay formed the principal domains which constituted the inheritance of Godfrey of Bouillon in 1076. Concentrated in central Lotharingia, on the frontiers of the empire, these lands had a strategic position. The strongpoints of Bouillon, Stenay and Montfaucon-en-Argonne controlled communications along a considerable section of the Meuse valley and lay across two important trade-routes; one running from Liège via Sedan to the Ile-de-France and another from Flanders via Huy and Verdun to Basel and the Upper Rhine.[62] However, Godfrey of Bouillon's possession of his hereditary lands was insecure for much of the period 1076-96, and in the case of the county of Verdun it would appear that he never exercised effective authority outside the western border area.

Godfrey of Bouillon as Duke of Lower Lotharingia

In 1012, at the instigation of the bishops of Cambrai and Liège, the Emperor Henry II established a new duchy of Lower Lotharingia, conferring it on Godfrey I, son of Godfrey the Captive.[63] From that time until the death of Godfrey III in 1076, the duchy was held almost continuously by members of the Ardennes-Boulogne family, albeit with a major break after the revolt of Godfrey II when it was granted to Frederick of Luxembourg (1046-65). As his uncle had served the emperor loyally until his death, Godfrey of Bouillon could have had a reasonable expectation of succeeding to this office. However, in 1076 Henry IV conferred the duchy on his own infant son Conrad, and since Conrad could not exercise the ducal functions in person, Albert III of Namur was made vice-duke.

---

[61] LL p. 498: *Ipse Godefridus sanctum iter meditans arma quae in nos moverat abiuravit, pacem cum episcopo Richero composuit, Mosacum et Sathanacum cum castro quod in nos firmaverat, cum omnibus appenditiis sanctae Mariae in perpetuum tradidit. Unde episcopus auri et argenti pondera plurima ... ei in sumptum sacrae expeditionis contulit ... idem dux castrum Falconii-montis, quod in episcopio firmaverat ... abiens fecit everti.* Andressohn (*Ancestry and Life of Godfrey of Bouillon*, p. 51) misinterprets this key passage, claiming that the castle of 'Falkenstein' was *sold* by Godfrey to the bishop.

[62] *Cantatorium*, pp. 106-8, 217-18; J. L. Charles, *La ville de Saint-Trond en Moyen Age* (Paris, 1965), pp. 242-43.

[63] Werner, 'Der Herzog von Lothringen in salischer Zeit', p. 469.

Only when Conrad was crowned king of Germany in 1087 was the duchy at last conferred on Godfrey.[64] The one title bestowed on Godfrey by Henry IV in 1076 was that of margrave of Antwerp; this office appears to have been specially created out of certain ducal powers exercisable within a limited area, and was evidently meant as a consolation prize.[65] Nevertheless, there is little evidence of any activity of Godfrey as margrave, which is hardly surprising in view of the struggles over the Ardennes-Bouillon inheritance that raged throughout this period.[66] There was therefore a clear distinction between the hereditary lands to which Godfrey succeeded in 1076 (although his title to these was of course contested) and the ducal office which he assumed only eleven years later.

The powers and functions of the dukes in the German kingdom depended on the character of each individual duchy. In duchies with a pronounced ethnic identity, such as Swabia or Saxony, there existed at least a latent right of the nobility as representatives of the *populus* to appoint or install the duke, who was regarded as leader of the tribe.[67] Lotharingia, however, had no separate ethnic identity; its origins were political. The *regnum Lotharii* was originally the portion assigned to Lothar II in the division of the Frankish empire in 855.[68] It was first organised as a duchy when it was incorporated into the East Frankish kingdom on the death of its last king, Zwentibold (900), and during the third quarter of the tenth century it was split into two administrative circumscriptions, Upper and Lower Lotharingia, roughly corresponding to the ecclesiastical

---

[64] Vanderlinden, 'La date de la nomination de Godefroid de Bouillon comme duc de Lotharingie', 189-92; Despy, 'La date de l'accession de Godefroid de Bouillon au duché de Basse-Lotharingie', 1275-84.

[65] E. Boshof, 'Lothringen, Frankreich und das Reich in der Regierungszeit Heinrichs III', *Rheinische Vierteljahrsblätter* 42 (1978), 79-84.

[66] Charters of Godfrey I of Brabant (1124) and Burchard (1124) and Lietard of Cambrai (1135) allude to the donation by Godfrey of two-thirds of the tithes of the parish of Antwerp to the chapter of St Michael in Antwerp. G. Despy, 'Les actes des ducs de Basse-Lotharingie du XIe siècle', *PSHIGDL* 95 (1981), 65-132.

[67] B. S. Schlotterose, *Die Besetzung der deutschen Herzogtümer bis zum Jahre 1125* (Halle, 1912), pp. 16-17; H. Maurer, *Der Herzog von Schwaben: Grundlagen, Wirkungen und Wesen seiner Herrschaft in ottonischer, salischer und staufischer Zeit* (Sigmaringen, 1978), pp. 133-35.

[68] Mohr, *Geschichte des Herzogtums Lothringen,* 1: 7-9; U. Nonn, *Pagus und comitatus in Niederlothringen: Untersuchungen zur politischen Raumgliederung im früheren Mittelalter* (Bonn, 1983), pp. 52-53; Werner, 'Der Herzog von Lothringen in salischer Zeit', p. 368.

provinces of Trier and Cologne.[69] Its inhabitants were considered to be part of the Frankish tribe; nevertheless they were culturally diverse, being divided among speakers of French, Frisian and various High and Low German dialects.[70]

Although both Lotharingian duchies were held at various times by members of the Ardennes-Bouillon family, the duke was regularly appointed and installed by the king.[71] The king could depose the duke (as in the case of Godfrey II) or even keep the ducal function in effective abeyance by appointing an absentee (as in the case of the infant Conrad). The two Lotharingian duchies, then, were not hereditary principalities, but offices bestowed by the monarchy.[72] The *ducatus*, as the office was designated, and which it would perhaps be better to translate as 'ducal authority', referred not to the territory itself, but rather to the delegated powers and functions exercised within the limits of that territory.[73]

The original function, implicit in the title *dux*, was a military one, which was also reflected in the more specific designation *magister militiae Lotharingiae*, applied to the duke by a Lower Lotharingian chronicler.[74] In time of war the duke acted as leader of the troops of the duchy, both within and outside its borders.[75] The duke was obliged to keep the peace, defend the frontiers and police the highways. He also had a general obligation to

---

[69] Mohr, *Geschichte des Herzogtums Lothringen,* 1: 51; Werner, 'Der Herzog von Lothringen in salischer Zeit', pp. 375-76.

[70] J. Ficker, *Vom Reichsfürstenstande* 2/3 (Graz, 1911), 5-9; G. Läwen, *Stammesherzog und Stammesherzogtum: Beiträge zur Frage der Rechtstellung von Herzog und Stamm im Mittelalter* (Berlin, 1935), pp. 18ff; Tellenbach, 'From the Carolingian Imperial Nobility to the German Estate of Imperial Princes', p. 215.

[71] *Gesta episcoporum Cameracensium*, MGH SS 7: 468; Sigebert of Gembloux, *Chronica*, MGH SS 6: 355, 357, 359; *Annales Altahenses maiores*, MGH SS 20: 799, 802, 821; Hermann of Reichenau, pp. 126, 128; Lambert of Hersfeld, *Annales*, MGH SS 5: 243; *Annales s. Iacobi Leodiensis*, MGH SS 16: 639.

[72] Werner, 'Der Herzog von Lothringen in salischer Zeit', pp. 397-98; H-W. Goetz, 'Das Herzogtum im Spiegel der salierzeitlichen Geschichtsschreibung', in *Die Salier und das Reich*, 1: *Salier, Adel und Reichsverfassung*, ed. S. Weinfurter and H. Kluger (Sigmaringen, 1991), pp. 253-71.

[73] G. Despy, 'La fonction ducale en Lotharingie, puis en Basse-Lotharingie de 900 à 1100', *Revue du Nord* 48 (1966), 107-9; M. Parisse, 'Les ducs et la duché de Lorraine au XIIe siècle, 1048-1206', *Blätter für deutsche Landeskunde* 111 (1975), 86-102.

[74] *Triumphus s. Remacli de Malmundariensi coenobio*, MGH SS 11: 443.

[75] Werner, 'Der Herzog von Lothringen in salischer Zeit', pp. 381-88.

maintain justice, but his precise powers of jurisdiction are unclear, and seem to have largely depended on the actual power, and in particular comital authority of individual dukes, for it was the counts and bishops who were the principal sources of jurisdiction in the duchy.[76]

By the time of Godfrey of Bouillon ducal power in Lower Lotharingia had decreased considerably in favour of other sources of public authority. This process had begun a century before. In 980 Otto II confirmed to Bishop Notger of Liège all previous donations to his church with the important additional concession that no-one except the bishop might exercise jurisdiction or raise taxes within the temporal possessions of the bishopric.[77] These privileges may have been fairly modest in extent at this stage, but with this general immunity they formed the nucleus of the future ecclesiastical principality.[78] Soon after this, Notger received a complete county (Huy), and in the course of the eleventh century the monarchy added the counties of Brugeron and Hesbaye as well as numerous other territories.[79] The defence of this territorial structure was consolidated by a policy of construction and acquisition of strongholds, which received a new impetus in the 1090s as a result of the Investiture Contest and the departure of important lords on the crusade.[80] The growth of the power of the prince-bishops was reflected in the military forces of Liège. Bishop Notger had been expected to provide Otto II with 60 armed horsemen; in 1071 Bishop Theoduin pledged himself to aid the countess of Hainaut with 500 *milites* should they be required. In the period 1076-1127 the bishop could deploy 700 knights. In the entire duchy of Lower Lotharingia only the count of Hainaut and the duke of Brabant among the lay princes had comparable numbers at their

---

[76] Läwen, *Stammesherzog und Stammesherzogtum*, pp. 28-53; Werner, 'Der Herzog von Lothringen in salischer Zeit', pp. 389-96.

[77] MGH DD O. II, no. 210.

[78] Vanderkindere, *La formation territoriale,* 2: 187; J.-L. Kupper, *Liège et l'église imperiale. XIe-XIIe siècles* (Paris, 1981), pp. 421-26, 440-41.

[79] MGH DD O.III, no. 16; Kupper, *Liège et l'église imperiale*, pp. 425-26.

[80] R. Deprez, 'La politique castrale dans la principauté de Liège du Xe au XIVe siècle', *Le Moyen Age* 65 (1959), 501-38.

disposal.[81] In addition to these professional mounted soldiers the bishop could also call on urban militias from Liège, Huy and Saint-Trond.[82]

These developments in the bishopric of Liège were paralleled elsewhere in Lower Lotharingia. As early as 1007 the Emperor Henry II had transferred comital rights in Cambrai to its bishop.[83] In the north of the duchy, the bishops of Utrecht acquired the counties of Teisterbant, Groningen, Drenthe, Hamaland, Oostergo and Westergo as well as the *comitatus Agridiogensis* on the eastern shore of the IJsselmeer.[84] The county of Fivelgo in Friesland had been granted to the church of Hamburg.[85] The imperial policy of creating ecclesiastical principalities by grants of comital powers and immunities to the bishops thus effectively excluded ducal authority from well over half of Lower Lotharingia. Even then it is difficult to establish to what extent this existed in the remainder. It would be wrong to regard the duke as suzerain of Lower Lotharingia; there is no evidence that the counts were regarded as vassals of the duke,[86] apart from one exceptional case. In 1071 the Countess Richilda of Hainaut sought imperial protection from the encroachments of Robert I, count of Flanders. In return she surrendered Hainaut, Valenciennes and all her allodial possessions, which she then received back as fiefs. They were to be held by the countess in the first instance from Duke Godfrey III, who in turn was to hold them from the bishop of Liège. The status of the count of Hainaut as vassal of the duke lapsed in 1076 on the death of Godfrey III, as had been specified in the treaty.[87] The only area where Godfrey of Bouillon had a legal right to exercise jurisdiction was in the

81 *Indiculus loricatorum*, MGH Const. 1 (Hannover, 1893), 633; Giselbert of Mons, p. 14; Kupper, *Liège et l'église imperiale*, pp. 449-51.

82 A. Joris, *La ville de Huy en Moyen Age* (Paris, 1959), pp. 110, 124, 450-52; Joris, 'Remarques sur les clauses militaires des privilèges urbains liégeois', *RBPH* 37 (1959), 297-316.

83 Nonn, *Pagus und comitatus in Niederlothringen*, p. 121.

84 MGH DD K.II, no. 64; DD H.III, nos. 45, 99, 152, 164; DD H.IV, no. 402.

85 Adam of Bremen, p. 384.

86 Werner, 'Der Herzog von Lothringen in salischer Zeit', p. 387.

87 MGH DD H.IV, no. 242; *Infeodatio comitatus Hanoniae*, MGH Const. 1, no. 441; A. Hansay, 'L'inféodation du comté de Hainaut à l'église de Liège en 1071', *Bulletin de la Société de l'art et l'histoire du diocèse de Liège* 13 (1902), 45-58.

march of Antwerp; otherwise he did not possess a single county within the borders of his *ducatus*.[88]

The diminution of the public authority of the duke was accompanied by inroads into the traditional military functions of the *magister militiae Lotharingiae*. In the first half of the eleventh century the duke often acted to defend the frontier and maintain the peace on royal orders.[89] Yet during the revolts of Godfrey II against the monarchy in 1044-47 the main resistance to him and his allies came not from the Dukes Gerard of Alsace (of Upper Lotharingia) and Frederick of Luxembourg (of Lower Lotharingia), but from the bishops Theoduin of Liège, Bernold of Utrecht and Adalbero III of Metz.[90] As duke, Godfrey III is known to have led the troops of the duchy during the Saxon campaigns of Henry IV, although there is no hard evidence of any similar activity by Godfrey IV. William of Tyre claims that he fought on the side of Henry IV at the battle of the Elster (Grüna) in Saxony (15 October 1080) against the anti-king Rudolf of Swabia, while Albert of Aachen mentions his presence on the Italian campaign of 1081-84.[91] Yet as he did not become duke until 1087, neither instance provides evidence for him exercising the ducal function of military leader. Furthermore it is difficult to see why he should have wished to take part in distant expeditions considering that he was still engaged in the war of succession over the Ardennes-Bouillon inheritance. By contrast, local sources attest to his activity in Lotharingia during this period.[92]

One of these activities was his participation in the movement known as the Peace of God. In the final quarter of the eleventh century Lower Lotharingia was increasingly affected by lawlessness and violence, resulting from numerous feuds and acts of brigandage, the struggle over the Bouillon inheritance and above all, the Investiture Contest, especially after the election of Hermann of Salm as anti-king in 1081 in succession to Henry IV's opponent Rudolf of Rheinfelden, duke of Swabia. Significantly it was Henry of Verdun, bishop of Liège, who proclaimed the

[88] Läwen, *Stammesherzog und Stammesherzogtum*, pp. 36-41. The county of Verdun, in the ecclesiastical province of Trier, lay in Upper Lotharingia.

[89] Anselm, *Gesta episcoporum Leodiensium*, MGH SS 7: 207; *Gesta episcoporum Cameracensium*, p. 471; Werner, 'Der Herzog von Lothringen in salischer Zeit', pp. 381-82.

[90] E. Dupréel, *Histoire critique de Godefroid le Barbu* (Uccle, 1904), p. 52.

[91] WT IX.8, pp. 429-30; AA p. 440.

[92] Dorchy, 'Godefroid de Bouillon duc de Basse-Lotharingie', pp. 970-77.

peace in March of that year. Both Albert III of Namur as vice-duke and later Godfrey remained content to leave the initiative to the bishop who exercised both the direction and jurisdiction of the peace.[93] This tendency contrasted sharply with neighbouring Flanders where the peace rapidly developed into a comital institution.[94]

The administration of the peace can hardly be considered a surprising phenomenon considering the military strength of the bishop. In theory the duke could command the king's vassals in order to maintain the peace; this was clearly impossible in cases where they were his personal enemies. An illuminating passage in the Chronicle of Saint-Hubert, referring to Godfrey III, suggests that the *militia sui ducaminis* consisted of the knights of the territory of Bouillon: the only reliable force available to the duke was his personal military retinue.[95]

The working of the Peace of God is merely one facet of the feeble nature of ducal authority in Lower Lotharingia by the end of the eleventh century. Another illustration is the policy of the monarchy in appointing dukes. The tribal duchies with their separatist tendencies were normally given to men originating from outside the duchy, frequently relatives of the royal family, but in Lotharingia the monarchy was content to appoint natives.[96] From the mid-eleventh century the ecclesiastical principalities were more than a counterweight to ducal power. Thus there is little justification to speak of a 'sovereign as duke of Lotharingia' or an 'effective feudal lordship of Lower Lorraine' as some historians of the crusades have done.[97] Whereas he disposed of his landed properties on the eve of the First Crusade, Godfrey remained duke, at least in name, after 1096; at least no successor was appointed until late 1101, when Henry IV gave the duchy to Henry, count of Limburg.[98] Nevertheless, the office of duke had little effective authority unless the incumbent also had substantial lands and comital powers within the duchy.

---

[93] Vanderlinden, 'Tribunal', pp. 589-96; Kupper, *Liège et l'église imperiale*, pp. 458-60.
[94] R. Monier, *Les institutions centrales du comté de Flandre de la fin de XIe siècle à 1384* (Paris, 1943), pp. 18-19.
[95] *Cantatorium,* pp. 64-65.
[96] Tellenbach, 'From the Carolingian Imperial Nobility to the German Estate of Imperial Princes', pp. 214-15.
[97] Prawer, *Crusader Institutions*, p. 8; Cowdrey, 'The Latin Kingdom of Jerusalem', p. 230.
[98] Mohr, *Geschichte des Herzogtums Lothringen,* 2: 74.

The Counts of Boulogne

The House of Boulogne originated as a cadet branch of the family of the counts of Flanders. The first count, Adelolf (918-33), was a younger son of Baldwin II of Flanders (879-918), inheriting from him the Boulonnais and Ternois.[99] The counts of Boulogne were descended from Charlemagne through Baldwin's mother Judith, daughter of the Emperor Charles the Bald. More Carolingian blood was acquired on the marriage of Eustace I (1024-46) with Mathilda, daughter of Lambert I of Louvain, who was herself descended from Charlemagne on both sides. The consciousness of the particular quality of the Boulogne ancestry was expressed in one of the earliest surviving genealogies of any comital family, the *Genealogia comitum Boloniensium*. The earliest versions, composed in the closing years of the eleventh century, trace the dynasty's descent from Merovingian times through Charlemagne down to the three sons of Eustace II of Boulogne and Ida of Bouillon.[100] The life of St Ida, written by a monk of Le Wast in the Boulonnais in the 1130s, refers to Eustace as *heros quidam genere nobilissimus, Carolo etiam regi consanguinitate proximus*.[101] The fact that the author of neither work thought it necessary or advantageous to mention Ida's own Carolingian ancestry is itself a silent but eloquent testimony to the well-developed dynastic consciousnesses of the counts of Boulogne. The principal possession of the dynasty was the county of Boulogne, which occupied the greater part of the former *pagus Bononiensis* and was held from the king of France.[102] The detached *territorium Mercatii* to the north, consisting of the settlements of Marck, Calais and their hinterland, was separated from the main body of the county by the neigh-

---

[99] Vanderkindere, *La formation territoriale*, 1: 333-34; P. Héliot, *Histoire de Boulogne et du Boulonnais* (Lille, 1937), p. 68; J. Lestocquoy, *Histoire des territoires ayant formé le département du Pas-de-Calais* (Arras, 1946), p. 41.

[100] *Genealogia comitum Buloniensium*, pp. 300-1.

[101] *Vita Beatae Idae*, p. 439.

[102] H. J. Tanner, 'Between Scylla and Charybdis: The Political Role of the Comital Family of Boulogne in Northern France and England (879-1159)' (unpublished Ph.D. dissertation, Univ. of California at Santa Barbara, 1993), pp. 28-29, 49-57; Tanner, 'The Expansion of the Power and Influence of the Counts of Boulogne Under Eustace II', in *Anglo-Norman Studies, XIV: Proceedings of the Battle Conference, 1991*, ed. M. Chibnall (Woodbridge, 1992), pp. 251-86.

bouring county of Guînes.[103] To the south lay the Ternois, an area which had been inherited by Count Adelolf, but which was a constant object of Flemish expansion. Baldwin IV of Flanders (988-1037) was able to establish control of the northern half of the Ternois, including Thérouanne, Fauquembergues and Saint-Omer. The southern half came to form the county of Saint-Pol, whose counts held it as vassals of the count of Boulogne.[104] By the early tenth century the counts of Boulogne were also in possession of the county of Lens (*comitatus Scribiu*), although this county came under Flemish overlordship in the time of Count Baldwin V of Flanders (1037-67). Associated with the tenure of Lens was the advocacy of the fisc of Harnes, which was a domain of the abbey of St Peter at Ghent. Lens passed to a younger son of Eustace I of Boulogne, Lambert, but on his death in battle in 1056 the county reverted to his elder brother Eustace II. Thereafter Lens was administered by a castellan answerable to the count of Boulogne.[105]

The prospects of landward expansion for the counts of Boulogne were severely restricted by the wealthy and powerful counts of Flanders. By contrast, the geographical position of Boulogne on the English Channel indicated England as a potential sphere of interest. Eustace II's first marriage, to Godgifu (Goda), sister of Edward the Confessor, was probably an expression of this policy and his presence in England as an envied favourite of the king is attested in the period before 1066.[106] However, it was Eustace's participation in the Norman Conquest of

---

[103] A. Longnon, *Etudes sur les pagi de la Gaule*, 2 vols (Paris, 1869-72), 1: 25-38.

[104] Lestocquoy, *Histoire des territoires ayant formé le département du Pas-de-Calais*, p. 51; P. Feuchère, 'Les origines du comté de Saint-Pol', *Revue du Nord* 35 (1953), 125-49; Tanner, 'Between Scylla and Charybdis', pp. 70-71; Tanner, 'The Expansion of the Power and Influence of the Counts of Boulogne', p. 251.

[105] Vanderkindere, *La formation territoriale,* 1: 326; Lestocquoy, *Histoire des territoires ayant formé le département du Pas-de-Calais*, pp. 53ff; Tanner, 'Between Scylla and Charybdis', pp. 70-71, 105-15. Orderic Vitalis, *The Ecclesiastical History of Orderic Vitalis*, ed. and trans. M. Chibnall, 6 vols (Oxford, 1969-80), 2: 206, remarks that Eustace II was ruler of three counties: Boulogne, Guînes and Thérouanne. However, Guînes was never held directly by him, although Tanner, 'Between Scylla and Charybdis', suggests that he had gained control of some territory there; Thérouanne was in the Flemish half of the Ternois. Therefore the three counties meant by Orderic are more likely to have been Boulogne, Lens and Saint-Pol.

[106] Vanderkindere, *La formation territoriale,* 1: 333; *Anglo-Saxon Chronicle*, ed. B. Thorpe (London, 1861), 1: 313ff, 2: 144ff.

England that brought the most significant gains. Eustace took part in William the Conqueror's invasion as an ally working on a free enterprise basis. Not only could Eustace provide troops and ships, but his contacts and experience in England undoubtedly gave him valuable specialist knowledge of the political and military situation there.

William rewarded Eustace with a vast fief, made up of numerous non-contiguous holdings, which came to be known as the Honour of Boulogne. A quarrel between the two men led to an abortive attack on Dover by Eustace in 1067 and resulted in the confiscation of his lands, which were, however, subsequently restored to him.[107] By the time of the Domesday Survey these comprised holdings in Essex, Suffolk, Hertfordshire, Somerset, Kent, Surrey, Bedfordshire, Cambridgeshire, Huntingdon, Norfolk, Oxfordshire and Hampshire. In Essex and Hertfordshire Eustace was the greatest lay landholder. This fief received the service of 120 knights, most of whom seem to have originated in the Boulonnais. In addition Eustace's wife Ida had English holdings of her own.[108]

As a result of his participation in the Norman Conquest Eustace II was transformed into one of the greatest landholders and tenants-in-chief in England. The Conquest furthermore acted as a catalyst to the economic potential inherent in Boulogne's geographical situation. In this period Calais, Dunkirk and Oostende had not yet been developed as ports. The comital harbours of Boulogne and Wissant came to handle most of the cross-Channel traffic, including a large proportion of the lucrative English wool trade on its way to the cloth industry of Flanders. Thus the strategic position of the county of Boulogne gave it a political and economic importance out of all proportion to its size. In contrast to the apanage mentality which on one previous occasion had threatened to split the inheritance (the case of Lambert of Lens) the Boulogne possessions on both sides of the Channel were regarded as a whole, and passed in their entirety to Eustace's eldest son Eustace III (1088-1125).[109] The younger

---

[107] Tanner, 'The Expansion of the Power and Influence of the Counts of Boulogne', p. 271.

[108] J. H. Round, *Studies in Peerage and Family History* (Westminster, 1901), pp. 147-64.

[109] There is no agreement as to the date of the death of Eustace II. Mayer, *Mélanges*, pp. 17-18 argues that Eustace II died soon after 1070, whereas Tanner, 'The Expansion of the Power and Influence of the Counts of Boulogne', p. 276, indicates that he died in 1087, although both agree that Eustace III had succeeded to Boulogne by 1088.

Eustace contracted a marriage to Mary, daughter of Malcolm III of Scotland and Margaret of Hungary. Thus, as well as being a king's daughter, Mary was also a representative of the old Anglo-Saxon royal house. This alliance reflected both the insular interests and the growing prestige of the counts of Boulogne. Eustace III was probably wealthier than his brother Godfrey. Unlike him there are no indications that Eustace was obliged to sell or mortgage property in order to finance the crusade.[110]

Baldwin of Boulogne Before the Crusade

The inheritances of Eustace II of Boulogne and his wife Ida of Bouillon were maintained as separate entities, being eventually transmitted to their two sons Eustace III and Godfrey of Bouillon respectively. The youngest son, Baldwin, was apparently intended to receive no part of either paternal or maternal inheritance. To make provision for him the family resorted to a practice common among the nobility of western Europe. According to William of Tyre, Baldwin studied the liberal arts and trained for the priesthood, obtaining prebends in the episcopal churches of Cambrai, Rheims and Liège.[111] To judge from the locations of these benefices their acquisition was probably the result of family influence. It would certainly have been understandable for Godfrey to exercise influence on the bishop of Liège, his kinsman and ally Henry of Verdun. The provision of a benefice for his younger brother may have been a *quid pro quo* for such acts as the donation of Tellin to the abbey of Saint-Hubert in 1076.[112]

At some point before the crusade Baldwin left the church in order to become a knight.[113] This decision may have been made as early as the 1080s; during the siege of Stenay, one of the struggles in the dispute over the Ardennes-Bouillon inheritance, which is dated by Laurence of Liège

---

[110] Héliot, *Histoire de Boulogne*, pp. 73ff.

[111] WT X.1, p. 453: *Hic in adolescentia sua liberalibus disciplinis convenienter imbutus, clericus, ut dicitur, factus est et in Remensi, Cameracensi, Leodiensi ecclesiis beneficia, que vulgo prebende dicuntur, gratia generositatis, qua singulariter preminebat, obtinuit.* Albert of Aachen (AA p. 547) says that he was a *vir litteris eruditus,* which presumably refers to his clerical training.

[112] *Cantatorium,* pp. 91-93.

[113] WT X.1, p. 453: *Tandem ex causis nobis occultis arma capescens militaria, deposito clerici habitu miles effectus est...* .

to the fortieth year of the episcopate of Theoderic of Verdun (1086), Baldwin and Eustace organised military support for their brother Godfrey, an activity more appropriate to the lifestyle of a knight than that of a cleric.[114] Baldwin's motivation for reverting to lay status is unclear; it is possible that reformist sentiment in the dioceses of Cambrai and Rheims made it difficult for him to hold on to multiple prebends.[115] Nevertheless, his clerical training and knowledge probably proved of crucial importance during his disputes with the church as king of Jerusalem.

After leaving the church, Baldwin married Godehilde (Godevere), daughter of the Norman lord Ralph II of Tosny.[116] This was a brilliant alliance for a younger son. The origins of the Tosny family date back to around 943 when a certain Hugh became archbishop of Rouen and made over to his brother Ralph I the domain of Tosny in Normandy, previously part of the estates of the church. Ralph's son Roger fought the Muslims in Spain and founded the abbey of Conches. His son Ralph II was banner-bearer of Normandy and lord of Tosny and Conches, an honour in eastern Normandy comprising 50 knights' fiefs. Although he was deprived of his lands and banished by Duke William they were restored to him in 1063. Three years later Ralph fought at Hastings and was awarded lands in Berkshire, Gloucestershire, Herefordshire, Hertfordshire, Norfolk and Worcestershire. By his wife Isabella, daughter of Simon of Montfort-l'Amaury, Ralph had three children: Roger, who died young; Ralph III, who inherited his lands; and Godehilde. Baldwin's wife was therefore not an heiress. However, the marriage offered prospects of advancement both in Normandy itself, but even more so in England, where Eustace III and Ida were already important landholders. Robert of Stafford, a younger brother of Roger I, and a cousin of theirs also called Robert had both obtained English lands after the conquest. Thus, through his Boulogne and Tosny connections Baldwin probably could have looked forward to a successful career in the Anglo-Norman realm.[117] The importance of the English holdings of the Tosny family explains

[114] LL p. 494.

[115] Mayer, *Mélanges*, pp. 14-15.

[116] WT X.1, pp. 453-54; Orderic Vitalis, 3: 128.

[117] L. Musset, 'Aux origines d'une classe dirigente: les Tosny, grands barons normands du Xe au XIIIe siècle', *Francia* 5 (1977), 55-80; Mayer, *Mélanges*, pp. 15-18.

William of Tyre's description of Baldwin's marriage partner: *uxorem ex Anglia duxit illustrem et nobilem dominam Gutueram nomine.*[118] Baldwin's marriage therefore was not merely an alliance between two dynasties in Flanders-Picardy and Normandy, but between two of the greatest landed interests in England. The alliance was consolidated in 1103, when Godehilde's brother Ralph III married Alice, the daughter of Waltheof, earl of Northumberland, and his wife Judith, herself a daughter of Lambert of Lens (brother of Eustace II of Boulogne) and Alice, sister or half-sister of William the Conqueror.[119]

This alliance was consistent with the policy of the counts of Boulogne in looking towards England as their most profitable sphere of interest. Certainly for most of the period prior to the crusade Baldwin appears to have been associated with Boulogne and Normandy rather than with Lotharingia. Orderic Vitalis mentions his frequent presence at the castle of Conches before 1090; his marriage may therefore have dated from around this time. Significantly, his one appearance in Lotharingia during this time was in the company of his brother Eustace.[120] However, in the period immediately preceding the crusade his presence in Lotharingia became more frequent, and it is possible that it was concerned with his status within the family.

On the eve of the First Crusade Godfrey of Bouillon and his mother Ida either sold or gave to the church all of their lands in Lotharingia. Baldwin figured as a witness to several of these transactions. The abbey of Saint-Hubert claimed to have a charter of Godfrey issued at Bouillon which detailed his donation of the church of Baisy to the abbey's priory of St Peter at Bouillon. This document survives only in a sixteenth-century paper copy, and is puzzling in several respects.[121] The date given (1084) conflicts with the indiction (1094), while a phrase in the arenga referring to Godfrey's intention to go to Jerusalem would indicate a date after the crusade was proclaimed in November 1095.[122] This document is interesting from the point of view of Baldwin's status as he is named as a

118 WT X.1, p. 453.

119 D. C. Douglas, *William the Conqueror* (London, 1964), p. 380.

120 Orderic Vitalis, 4: 216-218; LL p. 494.

121 MS. Arlon, Archives de l'Etat, fonds Saint-Hubert 10.A.4; G. Kurth, *Chartes de l'abbaye de St.-Hubert* 1 (Brussels, 1903), no. 48, pp. 59-61.

122 Kurth, *Chartes de l'abbaye de St.-Hubert*, 1: 61: *Sed quia Jherusalem ire disposui, defensionem hujus mee advocacionis committo in manu omnipotentis Dei* ...

witness before his elder brother Eustace. Kurth was suspicious of this ordering, and concluded that the surviving early modern copy derived from a twelfth-century fabrication whose scribe wrongly placed Baldwin's name first as a reflection of his subsequent importance as king of Jerusalem, as well as mistaking the date of the original transaction. However, Despy's study of the document suggests that the original donation of the church of Baisy was made by Ida of Bouillon rather than Godfrey, but that the scribe who wrote the 'pseudo-original' some time after the crusade wanted to maximise the effect of the donation and consequently the abbey's title, and preferred to attribute it to the famous ruler of Jerusalem rather than his mother. He achieved this, Despy argues, by utilising a genuine document of Godfrey's dating from 1096, and interpolating into it a section concerning Baisy; the rest of the text and the witness list can be regarded as genuine.[123]

The order of the names of Baldwin and Eustace in this document may be an actual indication of their status in Lotharingia, particularly as there is corroborative evidence in other documents issued by Godfrey around this time. Two of these concern the donation by Godfrey of the church of St Dagobert at Stenay to the abbey of Gorze, documented in 1093 and again in 1096.[124] The text of this later version twice uses the formula *ego ... et frater meus Balduinus*, and in the witness list Baldwin also appears immediately after his brother.[125] It would seem that Godfrey, the abbey community or both thought it desirable to have his original donation confirmed before he left Lotharingia with the crusade, and that it was also important for Baldwin's consent to be included. The charter recording the sale by the Countess Ida of the allods of Genappe and Baisy to the abbey of St Gertrude at Nivelles in 1096 survives in a transumpt in a diploma of Henry IV issued at Aachen in 1098. The excerpted text uses the formula *dux Godefridus et frater eius Balduinus*, both in the subscription and in the witness list.[126]

---

[123] Despy, 'Les actes des ducs de Basse-Lotharingie', pp. 99-105.

[124] A. D'Herbomez, *Cartulaire de l'abbaye de Gorze: Ms. 826 de la Bibliothèque de Metz* (Paris, 1898), no. 139, pp. 242-44.

[125] Miraeus, *Opera diplomatica et historica*, 1: 365. For commentary see D'Herbomez, *Cartulaire*, pp. 541-42.

[126] DD H.IV, no. 459, pp. 619-20. Since the transumpt states that the Abbess Richeza acquired the allods from Countess Ida, these estates may actually have been part of

Up to this time Godfrey had spent most of his adult life in defending his inheritance from rival claimants. It is unlikely that during this period he had given no thought to the succession to these lands in the event of his death. Since he was not married and had no legitimate children, his heir presumptive can only have been one of his two brothers, Eustace and Baldwin. Yet as count of Boulogne, Eustace III was a vassal of the king of France and thus unlikely to be acceptable either to the German monarchy or to the bishops of Lower Lotharingia. This must have been obvious to Godfrey and his brothers because of a famous test case a quarter-century previously in which their uncle Godfrey III had been involved, which related to the succession to the county of Hainaut. Count Baldwin VI of Flanders (†1070) had married Richilda, the widow and heiress to Count Hermann of Hainaut (†1050). Their eldest son, Arnulf III, was intended to succeed to both Flanders and Hainaut. However, when Baldwin VI died his younger brother Robert I the Frisian (†1093) rose up against Arnulf, who was killed at the battle of Cassel in 1071. This revolt left Robert in control of Flanders, while Richilda and her younger son Baldwin (†1098) were able to maintain control of Hainaut. The Emperor Henry IV and his chief vassals wished to prevent the possibility of the county of Hainaut passing into the hands of the count of Flanders, who already had substantial possessions in what was known as 'Imperial Flanders', east of the River Scheldt. A diet at Liège in 1071 confirmed a settlement intended to secure the status of Hainaut as a fief of the empire. Richilda and Baldwin surrendered the fiefs of Hainaut and Valenciennes to the emperor, who granted them to the bishop of Liège; the bishop then granted them to Godfrey III as duke, who in turn granted them to Richilda and her son Baldwin II of Hainaut.[127] These events must have made it clear that a vassal of the French king such as the count of Boulogne would not have been acceptable as heir to substantial fiefs in the western frontier zone of the empire. The presence of Baldwin of Boulogne at the various acts discussed so far, and the absence of Eustace III of Boulogne from all but one of them, suggests that by 1096 at the latest, Baldwin was recognised as Godfrey's heir in Lotharingia.

Ida's dowry rather than possessions of Godfrey. However, the fact that Godfrey and Baldwin gave their consent is revealing of Baldwin's status.

[127] Hansay, 'L'inféodation du comté de Hainaut à l'église de Liège en 1071', pp. 45-58; Mohr, *Geschichte des Herzogtums Lothringen,* 2: 48-50.

This right of inheritance seems to have been actually put into effect in one case, which is all the more remarkable as it was recognised even by one of Godfrey's opponents. For most of the eleventh century the county of Verdun was normally held by the lords of Bouillon from the bishop of Verdun, and although the bishops had probably been given the right to nominate the count, the counts themselves had an expectation of hereditary succession to the office. Before departing on crusade, Godfrey surrendered the county to Bishop Richer, who then conferred it on Baldwin, who, however, after a short time (*mox post modicum*) decided to accompany his brother to the East and relinquished the county to the bishop.[128] Baldwin's decision must have been a consequence of what was happening to the rest of Godfrey's lands in Lotharingia. In an effort to raise funds and goodwill for the crusade, the duke sold, mortgaged or gave away all of his lands. For Baldwin, the lack of a territorial base outside the diocese of Verdun meant that the position of episcopal count offered little prospect of independence of action.[129]

The evidence discussed above demonstrates one important point. The inclusion of Baldwin's name in the charters of Godfrey and Ida and the consent that this implies, as well as his installation as count of Verdun, suggest that in the period immediately before the crusade he was already recognised as Godfrey's heir in Lotharingia. It is also probable that this position was recognised among key members of Godfrey's crusading army, despite its somewhat diverse composition. This becomes clear especially in the charter for the abbey of Nivelles. Among the witnesses were several lords and knights from the Ardennes region who subsequently accompanied Godfrey and Baldwin to the East.[130] Men such as these must have been quite clear about the status of Baldwin, and it is likely that they transmitted these views to others who took service with Godfrey during the course of the crusade.

The discussion of the role of Baldwin before the crusade yields two important insights. Firstly, while the Boulogne and Ardennes-Bouillon inheritances had been kept as separate blocs, Baldwin formed an

---

[128] LL p. 498.

[129] For the disposal of the Ardennes-Bouillon lands, see Chapter II.

[130] MGH DD H.IV, no. 459, p. 620: *Godefridus dux et frater eius Balduinus ... Cuno de Montacut, Warnerus de Greiz ... Henricus de Ase, frater eius Godefridus ... Henbrandus et Walterus de Bulon.*

important link between the two; to put it another way, he personified a joint Bouillon-Boulogne tradition, a role which continued throughout the crusade. He and his wife Godehilde travelled east in the army of Godfrey, but it is likely that he was personally acquainted with many of the men in the armies of Robert II of Flanders and Robert of Normandy. Secondly, Baldwin's move to Lotharingia and the status accorded him by Godfrey indicates that he was already recognised as his brother's heir before the departure of the crusade. This recognised status would prove to be crucial importance in the fortunes of the kingdom of Jerusalem on the death of Godfrey.

Chapter II

The Course of the First Crusade
(1095-99)

The Dissolution of the Ardennes-Bouillon Inheritance

On 27 November 1095, during the closing stages of the Council of Clermont in Auvergne, Pope Urban II preached to an assembled multitude, proclaiming a penitential expedition to Jerusalem with the objective of liberating the eastern Christian church from the Turks.[1] The following Feast of the Assumption, 15 August 1096, was fixed as the date for departure. Between these two dates Godfrey of Bouillon resolved to leave Lotharingia and go to the Holy Land. It is unclear at what precise point his decision was arrived at, or even at what time he first heard of the expedition. The Pope had evidently hoped that Lotharingians would come to Clermont, as can be discerned from a letter sent by him to Rainald, archbishop of Rheims, who in turn urged his suffragan, Lambert of Arras, to urge the notables of his diocese to attend, mentioning explicitly Count Baldwin of Mons. The bishopric of Cambrai was in dispute with Arras, and was itself disputed by two claimants. This meant that Cambrai sent a large contingent of clergy to the council, including the two rival bishops-elect, Walter and Manasses.[2] These, however, were special circumstances relating to ecclesiastical matters quite separate from the crusade; by and large the bishops and abbots of Lotharingia and western Germany, most of whom were imperialist in sentiment, stayed away from the council, although Richer, bishop of Verdun, sent representatives.[3] Even prelates belonging to the Gregorian party may have had

[1] There can now be little doubt that Jerusalem figured as the principal goal of the expedition as it had been conceived by Urban. On this question see especially H. E. J. Cowdrey, 'Pope Urban II and the Idea of Crusade', *Studi Medievali*, ser.3, 36 (1995), 721-42, and J. Flori, *Pierre l'Ermite et la Première Croisade* (Paris, 1999), pp. 161-77.

[2] R. Somerville, 'The Council of Clermont (1095) and Latin Christian Society', *Archivum Historiae Pontificiae* 12 (1974), 55-90.

[3] LL p. 497; *Annales s. Vitoni Virdunenses*, MGH SS 10: 526. Evidence for the presence of the bishops Poppo of Metz and Pibo of Toul cannot be traced further than undocumented secondary accounts. See Somerville, 'The Council of Clermont (1095) and Latin Christian Society', p. 70.

doubts about attending; with the conflict between empire and papacy still unresolved in Germany, they may well have considered it imprudent for them to leave their charges at such a critical time. The first news of the crusade to reach the western parts of Germany may have been brought by those groups of crusaders who left their homes before the official departure date, such as Peter the Hermit and his followers.

It is even more difficult to speculate on Godfrey's motivation for going on crusade. The desire to go on pilgrimage to Jerusalem was by no means unusual among the western nobility of the eleventh century, and Albert of Aachen states that Godfrey had often expressed such a wish to members of his household.[4] The opportunity to go at last to the Holy Land in the company of friends and kinsmen may have seemed particularly welcome after the years of relentless struggle to defend his inheritance. The abbey chronicle of Saint-Hubert implies that Godfrey's decision was only taken after he learned that many other princes planned to go.[5]

Godfrey's decision must have been made well in advance of the summer of 1096 since the journey would require careful preparation, above all in the matter of finance. Paradoxically, some funds for his pious undertaking were secured by the despoliation of religious houses. He attempted to dissolve the priory of St Peter at Bouillon, a house belonging to the abbey of Saint-Hubert, with the intention of confiscating its possessions. Only at the urging of his mother Ida, who travelled from Boulogne to Bouillon to intercede with him, did Godfrey make restitution; yet it is likely that he only agreed to this on condition that Ida agreed to help raise finance, since the subsequent sales of property included allods owned by her in Brabant and the Hesbaye.[6] The funds raised by such actions alone were unlikely to prove sufficient to support Godfrey and his retinue over the long journey to Palestine, and the surviving sources indicate that he decided to sell, mortgage or give away all of his properties: the crusade was thus the occasion for the dissolution of the entire Ardennes-Bouillon inheritance.

The duke took the opportunity offered by the dissolution to come to a general settlement of outstanding disputes with his enemies. The bishop of Verdun still claimed the right to dispose of the county of Verdun, and

---

[4] AA p. 481.

[5] *Cantatorium*, pp. 203-4.

[6] *Cantatorium*, pp. 203-6.

after the confiscation of the Countess Mathilda's German lands by the monarchy he also laid claim to Stenay and Mouzay.[7] For an unspecified sum, Bishop Richer bought out Godfrey's rights to the county of Verdun and to Stenay and Mouzay. The settlement obliged the duke to raze the fortifications of Montfaucon.[8] In Lower Lotharingia the allods of Baisy and Genappe were sold to the abbey of St Gertrude at Nivelles.[9] The smaller properties around Maastricht were either sold or given to the church as pious donations.[10] The crucial disposition, however, was the mortgage of the castle of Bouillon, along with its allodial territory and the fief of Rheims, to the bishopric of Liège. This transaction fitted into a long pattern of territorial expansion of the episcopal principality, and the acquisition of such an important fortress offered an unparalleled opportunity for Bishop Otbert (1091-1119) to consolidate the southern frontiers of his principality.[11] Godfrey and his brothers Eustace and Baldwin retained the right to redeem the mortgage. However, the disposal of every other property would seem to indicate that by the time he decided to alienate Bouillon, Godfrey had little intention of returning. As in the case of Verdun, the transactions in Lower Lotharingia seem to have incorporated the settlement of disputes. Three of the witnesses to the sale of Baisy and Genappe, named immediately after Godfrey and Baldwin, were *Gerardus lantgrave*, *Henricus frater eius* and *Gozuinus de Hinseberg*. The first two were also present at the donation of the church at Genappe to the abbey of Affligem, and can be identified as Gerard, count of Geldern, and Henry of Kriekenbeek, sons of the Theoderic *Flamens* who had claimed part of Godfrey's lands and died in the castle of Bouillon in 1082. The third, Gosuin of Heinsberg, was their uncle; it is significant that he received a share, namely 50 silver marks, of the sum paid by Bishop Otbert for Bouillon.[12] The decision to join the crusade and the financial preparations for it thus led directly to the dissolution of the landed

[7] MGH DD H.IV, no. 373.
[8] LL p. 498.
[9] MGH DD H.IV, no. 459 (1098).
[10] Ernst, *Histoire du Limbourg*, 6: 113-15; Miraeus, *Opera diplomatica et historica*, 1: 77.
[11] *Cantatorium*, 203-8; *Triumphus s. Lamberti de castro Bullonio*, MGH SS 20: 498-500; Renier of St Laurence, *Triumphale Bulonicum*, MGH SS 20: 584-85; Giselbert of Mons, p. 43.
[12] MGH DD H.IV, no. 459; Miraeus, *Opera diplomatica et historica*, 1: 77; Boeren, 'Overzicht', pp. 12-13.

possessions of the Ardennes-Bouillon dynasty. Godfrey seems to have remained duke of Lower Lotharingia; no successor was appointed until Henry IV conferred the duchy on Henry of Limburg in late 1101.[13] Nevertheless, the office of duke had no effective authority without the support of a landed power and military resources. Godfrey's departure and his eventual decision to remain in the East thus represented the wholesale transfer of the family tradition which had abandoned its Lotharingian roots.

The Financing of the Crusade

Godfrey of Bouillon had spent most of his adult life before the crusade in fighting to defend his inheritance. It was therefore unlikely that he had had much opportunity to accumulate significant financial reserves. Financial provision for the crusade up to the point where he and his fellow-crusaders left imperial territory derived from the despoliation of church property, the sale or mortgage of lands and rights, and – possibly – extortion from the Jewish communities of the Rhineland.

Religious houses and their treasuries were a tempting source of ready money and other valuables. As we have seen, Godfrey had attempted to seize the possessions of the priory of St Peter at Bouillon. Although his mother forced him to abandon the dissolution of the house, he may have been able to secure valuables from it. A chronicler of Saint-Trond also lists various depredations carried out against that abbey in 1095-96, and Godfrey's plundering of its possessions in Teisterbant and the Hesbaye may have occurred in the context of preparations for the crusade.[14]

Such gains were of course little compared with what could be realised by the sale of landed property. The exact price paid by Bishop Richer for the county of Verdun and the allodial properties of Stenay and Mouzay cannot be precisely ascertained. It was put at 'many pounds of gold and silver', and must have amounted to a substantial sum, since the bishop was obliged to collect contributions throughout the diocese.[15] The largest

---

[13] Mohr, *Geschichte des Herzogtums Lothringen,* 2: 74.

[14] Ralph of Saint-Trond, *Gesta abbatum Trudonensium*, MGH SS 10: 253: *Nam dux Godefridus, qui postea rex Iherosolimorum ibidem obiit, nostra sibi quaeque erant in Hasbania et in Testerbant ad libitum servire faciebat.*

[15] LL p. 498: *Unde episcopus auri et argenti pondera plurima, quae de episcopii ecclesiis collegerat, ei in sumptum sacrae expeditionis contulit.*

single amount was realised by the mortgage of the allodial territory of Bouillon along with the adjacent fief of the church of Rheims. The large numbers of crusaders trying to realise assets in the winter and spring of 1095-96 must have depressed land prices, but the strategic value of Bouillon was great. The obvious buyer was Bishop Otbert of Liège, not only because the acquisition of Bouillon would contribute to the security of the ecclesiastical principality, but also because the bishop was able to secure cash and its equivalents more readily than lay rulers. The sum that was paid over amounted to between 1300 and 1500 marks of silver.[16] It was raised by Bishop Otbert by the ransacking of churches and abbeys throughout the diocese for jewellery, plate, precious metals and other valuables.[17] Such efforts put great strain on the finances of the bishopric, since Otbert also acquired the castle of Couvin from Count Baldwin II of Hainaut at a price of 600 marks of silver, as well as the castle of Cler-

[16] Renier of St Laurence (p. 584) and Giles of Orval (p. 91) both give the sum of 1300 marks of silver and three marks of gold, which would equate with the sum of 1300 marks of silver and one pound of gold given by Laurence of Liège (p. 498). The Chronicle of St Hubert (*Cantatorium.* p. 206) gives 1500 pounds of silver, and Alberic of Troisfontaines (p. 804) 1500 marks of silver. The *Triumphus s. Lamberti de castro Bullonio* (p. 499) and the *Gesta abbatum Trudonensium continuatoris tertii auctorum*, MGH SS 10: 387, both give the smaller figure of 1300 silver marks. A rough idea of the relative value of the sum obtained by Godfrey of Bouillon can perhaps be gained by a comparison with the sum of 10,000 marks received by the crusader Robert Curthose for the mortgage of Normandy to his brother William II Rufus, king of England. The modern regions of Basse-Normandie and Haute-Normandie together amount to an area of *c.* 29,900 km^2. The medieval territory of Bouillon corresponds roughly to the present Belgian *arrondissement* of Neufchâteau (area approximately 1355 km^2) plus some adjacent parts of the French *département* of Ardennes. Even making a generous extra allowance for this by adding half as much again, and assuming a maximum of 2000 km^2 in total, it would seem that for a territory amounting to 6-7% of the area of that mortgaged by Robert, Godfrey received a sum amounting to 13-15% of that realised by Robert. Such a comparison of course assumes an equivalent value per km^2, but considering that the Bouillon territory was fairly heavily forested and sparsely inhabited, with only one urban centre, it commanded a high value relative to Normandy. Admittedly, the sum paid by William Rufus was for the usufruct of Normandy for a specified period of only three years. Yet as Godfrey and his brothers also had a right of redemption, they could have been expected to exercise this within a comparable time period.

[17] Giles of Orval, p. 91; *Cantatorium,* pp. 207-8, 249-50; *Gesta abbatum Lobbiensium*, MGH SS 21: 318.

mont-sur-Meuse from its owner, while individual abbeys were also purchasing property from crusaders.[18] In 1104 the bishop was accused of having debased the coinage of the bishopric, a circumstance that undoubtedly resulted from his policy of acquisition by purchase.[19]

It is questionable whether the amount realised by the other sales was greater than that brought by the strategically important territory of Bouillon. The total raised by all the alienations can only be conjectured, but clearly Godfrey must have had a considerable sum at his disposal on the eve of his departure. Much of the purchase price was probably transferred in the form of ingots, and a considerable proportion was probably taken on crusade in this form as they were easily transportable and their value easily ascertained.[20] However, provisioning on the march would present a major problem. Any food supplies taken with the army from its starting point would be used up after about forty days, long before the Byzantine frontier was reached.[21] Since food and other supplies would have to be purchased on the march, it would be useful to carry quantities of the standard low-denomination coins, i.e. deniers, and these may have been produced at one of the Liège episcopal mints, or at Bouillon itself. The dukes from the Ardennes-Bouillon dynasty had issued coins since the early eleventh century.[22] Two coins from separate finds in Russia may be examples of such currency. One was first identified by Bauer as a coin of Godfrey II, but it was argued by Tourneur as being similar to a second, which he identified as a denier of Godfrey bearing an inscription which he read as GODEFRIDUS IHEROSOLIMITANUS.[23]

---

[18] See Prosopographical Catalogue, nos. 21, 27, 81 and 133.

[19] J.-L. Kupper, 'Otbert de Liège: les manipulations monétaires d'un évêque d'Empire à l'aube du XIIe siècle', *Le Moyen Age* 86 (1980), 353-85.

[20] Kupper, 'Otbert de Liège', pp. 372-73.

[21] R. Hiestand, 'Der Erste Kreuzzug in der Welt des ausgehenden 11. Jahrhunderts', *Monatshefte für Evangelische Kirchengeschichte des Rheinlandes* 44 (1995), 1-36 (here 17-18).

[22] G. Albrecht, *Das Münzwesen im niederlothringischen und friesischen Raum vom 10. bis zum beginnenden 12. Jahrhundert* (Hamburg, 1959), pp. 66-67, 79-84. It is not correct, as claimed by J. Porteous, 'Crusader Coinage with Greek or Latin inscriptions', in *A History of the Crusades*, ed. Setton, 6: 354-420, that the dukes of Lower Lotharingia did not issue coins.

[23] N. Bauer, 'Der Fund von Spanko bei St Petersburg', *Zeitschrift für Numismatik* 36 (1926), 75-94; V. Tourneur, 'Un denier de Godefroid de Bouillon frappé en 1096', *Revue belge de numismatique* 83 (1931), 27-30.

During the spring and summer of 1096 various bands of crusaders had started to attack the Jewish communities of the Rhineland. These attacks also offered opportunities for plunder and extortion, and these crusaders attempted to despoil, forcibly convert or even massacre the Jews of Trier, Speyer, Worms, Mainz, and Cologne and environs, with persecutions extending as far as Regensburg and Prague. The result of this anti-Semitic frenzy was a great wave of Jewish martyrdom. Most of the massacres were carried out by groups of crusaders who had left their homes before the departure of the better organised princes' expeditions, and they were sometimes abetted by inhabitants of the communities they passed through.[24] There is no evidence of any violent persecutions or forced conversions by Godfrey and his army, but it is possible that they extorted money from German Jewry, although the precise circumstances are difficult to determine. The compiler known as Solomon bar Simson, writing in the 1140s, reports that a crusading leader who is usually identified as Duke Godfrey had sworn to avenge the blood of Christ with the blood of Israel by eradicating the Jews; fearing that a massacre would be carried out, the Rabbi Kalonymos of Mainz appealed to Henry IV, who issued a general mandate to the public authorities forbidding any such persecutions. In the Hebrew text the crusader is (twice) called דוכוס גוטברהט; this transliterates as *dwkws gwtbrht*, and has generally been taken as referring to Godfrey, although the ending *-brht* would seem to be relatively garbled for a name presumably deriving from Middle High German *Gotfrit*. Duke Godfrey – assuming that he was meant – was able to extort considerable sums of money from the Jewish communities of Cologne and Mainz. Solomon bar Simson gives the sum involved in each case as 500 *zekukim* of silver. Since the value of the *zakuk* is placed variously at either eight or twelve ounces of silver, the total must have been between 8000 and 12,000 ounces of silver, that is between 1000 and 1500 marks.[25]

---

[24] H. Möhring, 'Graf Emicho und die Judenverfolgungen von 1096', *Rheinische Vierteljahrsblätter* 56 (1992), 97-111; A. Grossman, 'The Cultural and Social Background of Jewish Martyrdom in Germany in 1096', in *Juden und Christen zur Zeit der Kreuzzüge*, ed. A. Haverkamp (Sigmaringen, 1999), pp. 73-86; F. Lotter, 'Tod oder Taufe. Das Problem der Zwangstaufen während des Ersten Kreuzzugs', in *Juden und Christen zur Zeit der Kreuzzüge*, pp. 107-52.

[25] E. Haverkamp, 'Hebräische Berichte über die Judenverfolgungen während des Ersten Kreuzzuges' (unpublished doctoral thesis, Univ. of Konstanz, 1999), pp. 310-

Yet, as Hiestand has pointed out, there are numerous contradictions in the detail of the account, particularly in the matter of chronology. The sums involved could only have been raised before the destruction of the communities of Mainz and Cologne, which occurred at the end of May 1096, long before Godfrey's army left Lotharingia. Solomon bar Simson implies that the Jews' attempts to buy off Godfrey were a reaction to the massacres in Worms and Speyer, which took place at the beginning of May. There was thus insufficient time for any message from Kalonymos of Mainz to reach Henry IV, at that time in Lombardy (not Apulia, as Solomon bar Simson states), and then for an imperial mandate to be sent back to Germany.[26] By contrast, the oldest Hebrew account of the persecutions, that of the Mainz Anonymous, composed soon after 1096, says that the Jews of northern France sent a warning about the dangers to be expected from crusaders moving east, to which the community in Mainz replied that they had nothing to fear, which raises the question why the German Jews would have made such substantial payments to Godfrey.[27] He had no authority over either Cologne or Mainz, cities which were under the lordship of their respective archbishops. If it is to be believed, Solomon bar Simson's account of Godfrey most probably derives either from an attempt by Godfrey to extort money in advance of his march, or from a pre-emptive move to buy his goodwill or co-operation, in the same way that had been done with Peter the Hermit. The massacre in Cologne at the end of May was carried out by an undisciplined army of Lotharingians, Flemings, French and English, most of whom must have previously travelled across Lower Lotharingia, and it is therefore possible that prior to this, the Rhineland Jews hoped that, as duke, Godfrey could

---

11; 'Chronicle of Solomon bar Simson', in S. Eidelberg, *The Jews and the Crusaders: The Hebrew Chronicles of the First and Second Crusades* (Madison, 1977), pp. 24-25. On the dating of the work of Solomon bar Simson, see A. S. Abulafia, 'The Interrelationship Between the Hebrew Chronicles on the First Crusade', *Journal of Semitic Studies* 27 (1982), 221-39, and Haverkamp, 'Hebräische Berichte über die Judenverfolgungen', pp. 148-66.

[26] R. Hiestand, 'Juden und Christen in der Kreuzzugspropaganda und bei den Kreuzzugspredigern', in *Juden und Christen zur Zeit der Kreuzzüge*, pp. 153-208 (here 177-78).

[27] Solomon bar Simson, trans, Eidelberg, p. 100; R. Chazan, *European Jewry and the First Crusade* (Berkeley, 1987), pp. 225-26.

be persuaded to keep them under control.[28] Yet given the feeble nature of ducal authority in Lower Lotharingia and its limited military resources, this would have been a fairly unrealistic hope.

There is no mention of any campaign of extortion by Godfrey by the Mainz Anonymous. In view of the problems of chronology and motivation, the possibility needs to be considered that the account of Godfrey given by Solomon bar Simson had a primarily representative function. The main purpose of the surviving accounts of the persecutions was to provide a commemoration of the martyrdom of the Jews and their steadfast refusal to convert in the face of overwhelming Christian hostility, and much of the detail in the narratives has been shown to be highly symbolic in character.[29] The main point about Solomon bar Simson's account is that the crusade leader was a sworn enemy of the Jewish people. A similar role is given to Godfrey in Jewish legends of the great sage and biblical commentator, Rabbi Solomon ben Isaac of Troyes (1040-1105), better known as Rashi. The first such surviving legends were recorded in the late sixteenth century from written and oral sources by the Rabbi Gedalya ibn Yahya in his compilation *Shalshelet ha-kabbalah*. The chapter concerning Rashi contains several interconnected episodes involving confrontations between the sage and the duke: Rashi prophesies how Godfrey will conquer Jerusalem but will ultimately be defeated, which comes to pass; he foretells how Godfrey will come to Troyes with two soldiers, a prophecy fulfilled when the duke arrives with three, one of whom is killed by divine intervention. These episodes, which are patently unhistorical, highlight the apparent might of a Christian leader and his ultimate humiliation by divine intervention.[30] As the first Latin ruler of Jerusalem, Godfrey was regarded by medieval posterity as the leader of the crusade, and it is possible that it was because of this prominence that he was given a place in the account of Solomon bar Simson as one of the prime movers of anti-Jewish actions, rather than as a true reflection of historical events.

---

[28] AA p. 291; D. Lohrmann, 'Albert von Aachen und die Judenpogrome des Jahres 1096', *Zeitschrift des Aachener Geschichtsvereins* 100 for 1995-96 (1996), 129-51 (here 137-38).

[29] J. Cohen, 'The Hebrew Crusade Chronicles in Their Christian Cultural Context', in *Juden und Christen zur Zeit der Kreuzzüge*, pp. 17-34.

[30] E. Yassif, 'Rashi Legends and Medieval Popular Culture', in *Rashi 1040-1990: Hommages à Ephraïm E. Urbach*, ed. G. Sed-Rajna (Paris, 1993), pp. 483-92.

The Crusading Army of Godfrey and Baldwin

COMPOSITION OF THE ARMY: FROM LOTHARINGIA TO ASIA MINOR

It is likely that the funds realised from the sales of property were employed primarily to cover the initial expenses of Godfrey and his own household and retinue of knights on crusade. They would have been spent on arms and armour, clothing, horses, harness, draft animals, and of course food supplies. Any unspent funds would have been taken on the journey. Household officers accompanying the duke included Baldric the Seneschal and Stabelo the Chamberlain.[31] There were also vassals from the territory of Bouillon, notably the castellan Heribrand and Walter of Bouillon.[32] By August 1096 the territory of Bouillon, where most of Godfrey's vassals held their fiefs, was in the possession of the bishop of Liège.[33] It is likely that those knights who wished to retain their fiefs were obliged to become vassals of the prince-bishop. Some may have been given a leave of absence by their new lord; one of these may have been Heribrand of Bouillon, who appears to have returned to Bouillon after the completion of the pilgrimage. Also among Godfrey's companions were Baldwin and his wife Godehilde. Their decision to go to the Holy Land in the company of Godfrey took them one further step away from Baldwin's interests in the Anglo-Norman realm. They were accompanied by their own household, which must have been considerably smaller than that of Godfrey.[34]

Other lords and knights and their followers from surrounding areas had also taken the cross, and for security and companionship it made sense for them to combine in a larger group for the journey east. It is likely that some of them met before their departure to discuss organisation and logistics, and opportunities for such meetings were provided by the various transactions which disposed of the Ardennes-Bouillon lands. One of these may well have been at the sale of Baisy and Genappe, the names of witnesses to which survive in a transumpt of February 1098:

> *Huic traditioni interfuerunt nobiles et liberi quam plurimi: Godefridus dux et frater eius Balduinus, Gerardus lantgrave, Heinricus frater eius, Gosuin de Hinseberg, Cuno de Montacut, Warnerus de Greiz, Henricus frater eius, Henricus de Ase, frater eius Godef-*

---

[31] Prosopographical Catalogue, nos. 17, 121.

[32] Prosopographical Catalogue, nos. 66, 128.

[33] Renier of St Laurence, *Triumphale Bulonicum*, p. 584.

[34] AA pp. 302, 358.

> *ridus, Godefridus de Sasfenberg, Walterus de Grimbergez, Henricus de Bierbas, Rainerus advocatus Leodiensis, Mainerus de Cortrec, Walderus de Bacunirnerz, Heribrandus et Walterus de Bulon, Godescalcus de Iace, Iohannes de Rosinel, Lambertus de Calmont.*[35]

Duke Godfrey and his brother Baldwin were of course present to give consent to the sale, while, as we have already seen, Gerard of Geldern (*Gerardus lantgrave*) and his brother Henry of Kriekenbeek, and their uncle Gosuin of Heinsberg were members of a family that had claims on the Bouillon lands, and were probably in the process of negotiating a settlement. The remainder of the witnesses appear to have been vassals of Liège, Brabant and Ardennes-Bouillon.

What is especially significant is that eight of the witnesses were also to be prominent members of the Lotharingian contingent on the crusade. From the Ardennes-Bouillon lands came Duke Godfrey, Baldwin, and Godfrey's vassals Heribrand and Walter of Bouillon. The other crusaders originated from surrounding parts of the Ardennes and Mosan regions of Lower Lotharingia. *Cuno de Montacut* was Cono, count of Montaigu and Huy, who belonged to one of the most prominent noble families of the church of Liège. He was the son of Gozelo, count of Behogne, and Ermentrude of Harzé, and it is likely that he was related to Godfrey of Bouillon through both of his parents. Cono sold land near Nassogne along with other property to the abbey of Saint-Hubert as a means of raising funds for the crusade, and he went east with two of his sons, Gozelo and Lambert.[36] *Warnerus de Greiz* was Warner, count of Grez, a small county between the lands of the bishop of Liège and the county of Louvain. Both Warner and his brother Henry held lands within the episcopal territory proper. They were also kinsmen of Godfrey and Baldwin, and Warner later became the most prominent of Godfrey's vassals in Jerusalem. He seems to have taken the cross fairly early: in late 1095 he and Henry divided the family property, and Warner sold the allod of Vaux to the abbey of Fosses, for which he received a gold chalice with a value of twenty and a quarter marks.[37] *Henricus de Ase* and *frater eius*

---

[35] MGH DD H.IV, no. 459.

[36] Prosopographical Catalogue, nos. 27, 60, 81.

[37] Documents extraits du cartulaire du chapitre de Fosses', *Analectes pour servir à l'histoire ecclésiastique de la Belgique* 4 (1867), no. 1, pp. 396-98. See also Prosopographical Catalogue, no. 133.

Godefridus were the brothers Henry and Godfrey of Esch-sur-Sûre in the eastern Ardennes. They were sons of a certain Fredelo, a relative of Duke Godfrey, who can be identified as sometime advocate of the abbeys of Malmédy and Echternach.[38]

These crusaders were either kinsmen or vassals of the Ardennes-Bouillon dynasty, but we can identify others from the region who joined them. They included the brothers Franco and Sigemar of Maasmechelen, relatives of Henry and Godfrey of Esch.[39] It is likely that the *Giselbertus de Monte Claro* who appears as a member of the *comitatus* formed by Baldwin of Boulogne in Cilicia was none other than the Giselbert, count of Clermont-sur-Meuse, who with his wife and brother donated the priory of St Symphorian to the abbey of Cluny in 1091. By 1095 the castle of Clermont had become such a menace to shipping on the River Meuse that Bishop Otbert assembled an army and besieged it from 29 June to 9 August 1095, but he was forced to abandon the siege because Godfrey of Bouillon and other nobles present refused to attack the castle on account of an unresolved dispute concerning the deposed abbot of Saint-Hubert. Later that year the bishop purchased the castle. The presence of a Giselbert of Clermont in the army of Godfrey can be explained by the fact that the count had decided to cut his losses and use the crusade as a way out of the relentless threat to his independence of action from the prince-bishop of Liège.[40]

From further afield, but still from within the duchy, came Baldwin II of Mons, count of Hainaut. Since he had claims on the county of Flanders, which his grandson Baldwin IV would try to make good in 1127-28, he probably preferred to avoid the company of Robert II of Flanders, who with Robert Curthose and Stephen of Blois was preparing to lead a large contingent of crusaders from Flanders, Artois, Normandy and northern France. In the summer of 1096 Baldwin of Mons, too, sold important territories to the bishop of Liège. As the ruler of a large county, he was probably accompanied by a substantial retinue.[41] Two of its members,

---

[38] Prosopographical Catalogue, nos. 58, 65.
[39] Prosopographical Catalogue, nos. 38, 119.
[40] AA p. 350; *Cantatorium*, pp. 194-97; Giles of Orval, p. 84; Murray, 'The Army of Godfrey of Bouillon', pp. 304-6.
[41] Prosopographical Catalogue, no. 21.

Gerard of Avesnes and Giselbert of Couvin, later appear among the following of Baldwin I as king of Jerusalem.[42]

The crusaders discussed so far all came from the duchy of Lower Lotharingia. They were joined by others from the neighbouring duchy of Upper Lotharingia and bordering areas of the kingdom of France. Understandably, these included kinsmen of Godfrey and Baldwin. Two of these were Peter of Dampierre, count of the district known as Astenois in Champagne, and his elder brother Rainald III, episcopal count of Toul.[43] Their father Frederick I, count of Astenois, was a relative of Godfrey of Bouillon, and also a *carus et fidelis* of both Godfrey and Theoderic, bishop of Verdun; it is likely that he and Peter as counts of Astenois held lands in the county of Verdun and were thus vassals of both count and bishop, although it is a significant indication of the relative strengths of the two institutions that Peter served as one of the commanders of the episcopal army during Theoderic's campaigns against Godfrey.[44] Documents from Toul issued after the crusade reveal the names of several laymen from the diocese who took part in the crusade: a nobleman, Rambert, son of Fraimerus of Lironville; Bencelin, a friend of Bishop Pibo; Aldo of Fontenoy and the family group of Lanfroi, his son Olri and brother Hugh. They may well have been encouraged in this undertaking by their bishop, who had himself made a pilgrimage to Jerusalem in 1086, along with Conrad, count of Luxembourg. It is likely that this group, as well as the archdeacon Louis of Toul, travelled east in the entourage of their count, Rainald.[45]

Another kinsman of Godfrey and Baldwin was Baldwin of Bourcq, the son of Count Hugh I of Rethel and Melisende of Montlhéry.[46] The county of Rethel, which had as its nucleus the territory of Omont, a fief of the church of Rheims, was situated in both the kingdom of France and the empire, and its counts were consequently involved in the politics of Lotharingia. Baldwin's grandfather Manasses had been an ally of Godfrey of Bouillon during the struggle over the Ardennes-Bouillon succession

---

42 Prosopographical Catalogue, nos. 47, 54.

43 Prosopographical Catalogue, nos. 93, 99.

44 Aimond, 'La nécrologe de la cathédrale de Verdun', p. 185; LL pp. 494-97; Giles of Orval, p. 88; Lambert of Hersfeld, p. 225; *Gesta Treverorum*, MGH SS 8: 126.

45 AA pp. 375-76; J. Choux, *Recherches sur le diocèse de Toul au temps de la réforme grégorienne. L'episcopat de Pibon (1069-1107)* (Nancy, 1952), pp. 102-5 and docs. 82, 124.

46 Prosopographical Catalogue, no. 20.

and invaded the bishopric of Verdun, although his castle of Sainte-Menehould was captured by episcopal forces.[47]

To these names can be added others who had no known ties to the Ardennes-Bouillon family: from Upper Lotharingia, Dudo, lord of Cons-la-Grandville in the Ardennes, and his wife Hadwida, daughter of Arnulf II of Chiny, and from north-eastern France, Roger of Rozoy.[48] Louis, son of Count Theoderic of Bar and Montbéliard, was a distant relative of Duke Godfrey, and he was evidently accompanied by another knight, Ralph of Mousson.[49] A number of Germans are subsequently found associated with Godfrey, but it is difficulty to establish whether they departed with him or joined his army at some later stage. In some cases, documents reveal an intention to travel east with Godfrey; a royal diploma of 26 July 1097 tells how a noblewoman called Cunihild had sold her estate of Obermeiser to the abbey of Helmarshausen, for which her son Reinhold received '36 marks to go to Jerusalem with Duke Godfrey', which implies that he joined the duke at an early stage.[50]

The other crusading armies included numbers of clerics, both secular and regular, many of whom later obtained ecclesiastical positions created by the crusaders in Syria and Palestine. We can identify very few named clerics in Godfrey's army: the aforementioned Louis of Toul, the career cleric Adalbero of Luxembourg, archdeacon of Metz,[51] and probably Baldwin, later archbishop of Caesarea.[52] Because of the struggles associated with the Investiture Contest it would have been risky for senior clerics to leave their charges. Yet there is evidence for the presence of numbers of monks in Godfrey's army. William of Tyre relates that the duke took with him a group of monks who celebrated the divine offices for him during the expedition. After the capture of Jerusalem he settled them at their own request in the abbey of St Mary in the valley of Josaphat.[53] William's account implies that the monks had come from Lotharingia. The religious house with which Godfrey was most closely

---

[47] LL p. 494; M. Bur, *La formation du comté de Champagne 950-1150* (Nancy, 1977), pp. 133-34, 412ff. Hugh of Bourcq was probably with Baldwin on crusade.

[48] Prosopographical Catalogue, nos. 30, 115.

[49] Prosopographical Catalogue, nos. 84, 104.

[50] MGH DD H.IV, no. 457.

[51] Prosopographical Catalogue, no. 2.

[52] Prosopographical Catalogue, no. 18.

[53] WT IX.9, p. 431.

associated before the crusade was the Benedictine abbey of Saint-Hubert, of which he was advocate. The abbey chronicle agrees that Godfrey took many regular clergy with him, without specifying which particular communities they came from.[54] The effects of the Investiture Contest in the diocese of Liège caused considerable disruption to monastic life, particularly as many of the leading personalities found themselves on opposite sides in the dispute. On the death of Henry of Verdun in 1091, the royal chaplain Otbert was appointed by Henry IV as bishop of Liège. Otbert proved to be one of the most passionate imperialists in the German episcopate, supporting the emperor right up to his death in 1106, a time when many of his other clerical supporters had deserted the fold.[55] It was in keeping with his imperialist policy that Otbert removed Berengar, the reformist abbot of St Laurence at Liège, who fled with his supporters to Saint-Hubert. Otbert then deposed Abbot Theoderic of Saint-Hubert for offering refuge to the reformers. The two reformist abbots and many of their monks fled outside the bishopric to the diocese of Rheims where they enjoyed the support of Godfrey of Bouillon and Dudo of Cons.[56] Since this dispute was not finally resolved until the autumn of 1096 there were probably significant numbers of displaced monks in central Lotharingia during the summer. At the Council of Clermont Pope Urban had declared that regular and secular clergy should only go on crusade with the permission of their abbots or bishops, and progressively tightened these restrictions in the succeeding months.[57] The situation of the displaced monks of St Laurence and Saint-Hubert was clearly exceptional, and the opportunity of a pilgrimage to Jerusalem may have appealed to them and their abbots during this time, particularly since those from Saint-Hubert would be able to enjoy the protection of their own advocate.

---

[54] *Cantatorium*, p. 208: *Nec multo post dux Hierosolimam vadens ... multos secum nobiles et religiosos abduxit.*

[55] Kupper, *Liège et l'église imperiale*, pp. 387-94.

[56] Ralph of Saint-Trond, 236ff; *Cantatorium*, pp. 53ff. It was because of Otbert's refusal to restore Theoderic as abbot that Godfrey abandoned the siege of Clermont-sous-Huy in 1095.

[57] A. Becker, *Papst Urban II. (1088-1099)*, 2 vols (Stuttgart, 1964-88), 2: 389-91.

HIERARCHIES

The majority of crusaders who accompanied Godfrey were not his vassals. However, it was clear that the army would need a military commander and an executive leader for negotiations with powers en route to Constantinople, even if it were expected that it would join up with other contingents there. The lords from Lower Lotharingia probably conceded to Godfrey the leadership of the army which was the traditional military function of the duke, and this was a decision that the French, Upper Lotharingians and others presumably accepted if they wished to march with the army. Nevertheless, it could be difficult to maintain military discipline; when they heard that a legation had been chosen to go and negotiate with the Byzantine emperor, two lords from Lower Lotharingia, Baldwin of Hainaut and Henry of Esch, simply absented themselves from the army and rushed on ahead of its chosen official representatives in the hope that they would receive better presents from the Emperor Alexios.[58]

From the time that the army under Godfrey's command left imperial German territory we can discern a clear hierarchy within it, which was reflected in the way that various military and diplomatic responsibilities were allocated. On reaching the Hungarian frontier at the River Leitha in September 1096 the army remained for three weeks on the German side of the border to assess the situation. Having heard reports of crusaders having been driven back or killed by the Hungarians, Godfrey and the other leaders decided to send a deputation to negotiate their passage with King Coloman of Hungary, but they were unwilling to risk sending 'any of the most renowned and chief men', for fear of what the king might do to them. The initial approach to Coloman was therefore made by members of Godfrey's own household, including Baldric the Seneschal and Stabelo the Chamberlain, and to Godfrey of Esch, who had previous experience of Hungary.[59] This was clearly an exceptional situation, and thereafter missions of this level of importance were not entrusted to household knights, but to those with a higher status in the army, particularly those of comital rank. Duke Godfrey went in person to the next series of negotiations with Coloman, at Sopron, taking with him Warner of Grez, the brothers Rainald of Toul and Peter of Dampierre,

[58] AA p. 305.
[59] AA p. 300.

and 300 troops.[60] Similar tentative approaches were made when the army first reached the environs of Constantinople in December 1096, as there had been problems in obtaining food supplies and Godfrey had heard rumours about maltreatment of crusaders by the Byzantine emperor, Alexios Komnenos. The first approach to the emperor was undertaken by Cono of Montaigu, Baldwin of Bourcq and Godfrey of Esch.[61] Eventually Alexios sent his son, John Komnenos, as a hostage to the crusaders as a sign of his good intentions, and he was placed in the care of Cono and Baldwin of Bourcq. After this Godfrey went in person to meet the emperor, taking with him many of the nobles, but Warner of Grez and Peter of Dampierre are mentioned specifically in this context.[62]

Godfrey's brother Baldwin of Boulogne was clearly his most trusted companion. Baldwin was left in charge of the army at Bruck an der Leitha on the German side of the border during the negotiations with King Coloman, and when the king demanded hostages in earnest of the crusaders' good behaviour it was Baldwin and his wife who were handed over. At Constantinople Baldwin commanded a detachment of 500 men and guarded the hostage John Komnenos.[63] However, he was not the only person to act as a divisional commander. Warner of Grez was placed in charge of a force sent to secure the port of St Simeon on the coast of northern Syria, and Rainald of Toul acted as commander of a reserve division at the Great Battle of Antioch.[64]

The examination of diplomatic and military missions reveals the existence of a select group of trusted individuals: Baldwin of Boulogne, Cono of Montaigu, Rainald of Toul, Peter of Dampierre, Warner of Grez, Godfrey of Esch and Baldwin of Bourcq. Men of this status probably had followers of their own on crusade, and it is probable that they and possibly some of Godfrey's own household officers functioned as a kind of council for the army while it was on the march, and even after it joined the other crusading armies after crossing over to Asia Minor. The bonds which held this group together were not of a vassalic nature. Baldwin of Bourcq, Peter of Dampierre and Rainald of Toul came from France and

---

[60] AA p. 301.

[61] AA p. 306.

[62] AA p. 310.

[63] AA pp. 301-2, 307-8.

[64] AA pp. 383, 424; BD p. 77; Orderic Vitalis, 5: 108-10.

Upper Lotharingia, areas where Godfrey had no ducal authority. The most significant ties within the core group seem to have been derived from kinship: each member was related in some way to Godfrey and Baldwin, a fact repeatedly reflected in the descriptions of them given by the chronicler Albert of Aachen.

Another important factor in the composition and hierarchies of Godfrey's army may have been the bonds of alliance forged during the wars fought by him to defend his inheritance in the period before the crusade. Cuno, Gozelo and Lambert of Montaigu, Warner of Grez and Baldwin of Hainaut were all vassals of his principal ally, the bishop of Liège. Baldwin of Bourcq's family had also fought on Godfrey's side against the bishop of Verdun. Admittedly Peter of Dampierre and Rainald of Toul had fought on the episcopal side in this conflict; but as far as the crusade was concerned this appears to have been outweighed by their particularly strong kinship ties to Godfrey and Baldwin. Conversely, the continued importance of kinship and alliance would explain the lack of prominence accorded to Dudo of Cons, a son-in-law of Godfrey's rival Arnulf II of Chiny, and to Louis of Mousson, cousin of Countess Mathilda of Tuscany, who was a rival claimant to the Ardennes-Bouillon inheritance.

Apart from those mentioned, Godfrey's army included relatively few of the major nobles of the area, especially those of comital rank. The nobles of Lower Lotharingia were not vassals of the duke and were consequently under no obligation to follow him. In many cases the phenomenon of non-participation was also influenced by the political constellations obtaining on the eve of the crusade. These resulted from two major conflicts, namely the Investiture Contest and the war of the Ardennes-Verdun succession, which reacted with each other and traditional local rivalries to produce oppositions and alliances which exerted influence and pressure either in favour of participation or against it. Among those who chose *not* to go on crusade were Albert III of Namur, Arnulf II of Chiny and Henry I of Limburg, as well as the three heirs of Theoderic *Flamens*: Gerard of Geldern, Henry of Kriekenbeek and Gosuin of Heinsberg. All of these dynasts belonged to lineages that had waged war on Godfrey or his main ally the ecclesiastical principality of Liège. A similar case was that of Godfrey of Louvain, traditionally a rival of the Ardennes-Bouillon family and an adversary of the church of Liège.[65] We know of no named crusaders at all from Lower Lotharingia north of Antwerp, although it is likely that Frisians were present.[66]

It has been suggested that Lotharingian participation in the crusade was low because most of the vassals of Henry IV were reluctant to become involved in what was perceived as a papal enterprise.[67] In fact it seems that precisely the opposite was the case. Under the bishops Henry of Verdun and Otbert the diocese of Liège was one of the areas which consistently offered the greatest support to the monarchy during the Investiture Contest.[68] Baldwin of Hainaut, Warner of Grez and Cono of Montaigu and his sons were all *fideles sancti Lamberti*. The point is often made that at the Council of Clermont Pope Urban had proclaimed that the property of crusaders should be placed under church protection until their return. The efficacy of this promise would of course depend on local conditions. It is doubtful whether the enthusiastic imperialist Otbert would have heeded the injunctions of a pope whom he would have considered schismatic, but the powerful ecclesiastical principality of Liège had both the incentive and the means to offer protection to its absent vassals. By contrast, other dynasts may have been disinclined to leave because of the unresolved conflicts connected with the Investiture Contest and the feuds which interacted with it. Thus Count Godfrey of Louvain, an old enemy of Liège, embarked on a new conflict with the bishop over the county of Brugeron in 1095-96.[69] Henry-Hezelin II, count of Grandpré, had been one of Godfrey's allies during his wars in the county of Verdun. Even after Godfrey reached a settlement with Bishop Richer, Henry-Hezelin continued to wage war on the bishopric until he took the cross sometime after 1099, although he died before he could leave.[70]

[65] *Vita Balderici episcopi Leodiensis*, MGH SS 4: 727-29, 733-34; *Gesta episcoporum Cameracensium*, pp. 467-69; *Annales Laubienses*, MGH SS 4: 18.

[66] H. Brassat, *Die Teilnahme der Friesen an den Kreuzzügen ultra mare vornehmlich im 12. Jahrhundert* (Berlin, 1970), pp. 17-32.

[67] C. D. J. Brandt, *Kruisvarders naar Jeruzalem. Geschiedenis van de eerste kruistocht* (Utrecht, 1950), p. 103.

[68] Kupper, *Liège et l'église imperiale*, pp. 387-94.

[69] Giles of Orval, pp. 91-92.

[70] LL p. 497.

COMPOSITION OF THE ARMY: FROM ASIA MINOR TO PALESTINE

From the time of its departure in August 1096 until its arrival at Constantinople in December of that year the army led by Godfrey consisted mainly of Lotharingians, with additional numbers of crusaders from north-eastern France and from the other German duchies. After arriving at the Byzantine capital it encountered the other contingents which had arrived by different routes: Normans, Bretons, English, Flemings, Artesians and northern French under Robert Curthose of Normandy, Robert II of Flanders and Stephen, count of Blois; more northern French under Hugh of Vermandois, southern French under Raymond of Saint-Gilles and Adhemar of Le Puy; and Normans of southern Italy under Bohemund. From this point the armies of the crusade were united, although they continued to form separate divisions on the march and in battle. After the crossing to Asia Minor in the spring of 1097 these contingents encountered the remnants of the so-called 'People's Crusades', that is, the expeditions led by Peter the Hermit, Walter Sans-Avoir and others, whose participants had mostly come from northern France, Lombardy and Germany. After being defeated by the forces of Kiliç Arslan I, the sultan of Nicaea, in September and October 1096, these crusaders had suffered privation through injury, hunger, loss of property and even captivity. They now attached themselves to the newly arrived contingents, seeking patrons who could provide them with protection and food, and often turned to those from their own home regions in the West. This human flotsam included a nun from the convent of St Mary at Trier who had been captured and forced into marriage with a Turk. She managed to escape to the crusaders' camp, and recognising Henry of Esch, appealed to him for assistance. Henry interceded on her behalf with Duke Godfrey, and eventually forgiveness for her sins was arranged at the highest level, via Adhemar of Le Puy. Albert of Aachen reveals that she was lured back to her Turkish lover by false promises or lust, and the purpose of his tale was probably a moralistic one, but the episode offers a glimpse of how patronage and connections operated within the army.[71] Fighting men would naturally wish to join up with patrons to whom they could at least offer their service. It was natural, therefore, for Germans to join the contingent of Duke Godfrey, the only major prince of the empire on crusade. They probably included Hartmann, count of Dillingen and

[71] AA pp. 327-28.

Kyburg, Wicher the Swabian, Gunter and Reinhard of Hemmersbach.[72] The increased presence of Germans in Godfrey's army is reflected in descriptions of it at the Great Battle of Antioch (February 1098) by Albert of Aachen, which mention natives of other German duchies as well as Lotharingians.[73] However, the number of Germans who joined Godfrey was in actual fact far smaller than has generally been assumed. Most modern histories of the crusade give the names of two dukes, and various bishops, counts and lords from Swabia, Bavaria and the Rhineland who are supposed to have been defeated by the Turks in October 1096, and whose survivors later joined Godfrey's army when it reached Asia Minor.[74] It has generally been assumed that these crusaders left Germany on one of the 'Peoples's Expeditions' that departed before August 1096. Their names derive from the account of the crusade in one very late source, the sixteenth-century Chronicle of Zimmern.[75] They are almost all anachronisms, inventions or creative constructions of its author, Froben Christoph, count of Zimmern (1519-66). The one name given in the Zimmern account of a crusader who joined Godfrey that be verified from

[72] Prosopographical Catalogue, nos. 64, 62, 134, 105.

[73] AA pp. 366: *Godefridus, dux .... cum innumeris milibus Lotharingiis, Saxonibus, Alemannis, Bawariis*; 422: *Godefridus cum Theutonicis, Alemannis, Bavariis, Saxonibus, Lotharingiis*; 425: *cum Alemannis, Bavariis, Saxonibus, Lotharingiis, Theutonicis et Romanis.* See also Orderic Vitalis, 5: 108-110.

[74] H. Hagenmeyer, *Peter der Eremite: Ein kritischer Beitrag zur Geschichte des ersten Kreuzzuges* (Leipzig, 1879), pp. 135-36, 200; Hagenmeyer, *Le Vrai et le faux sur Pierre l'Hermite* (Paris, 1883), pp. 158-61, 235-36; Hagenmeyer, 'Etude sur la Chronique de Zimmern: renseignements qu'elle fournit sur la première croisade', *Archives de l'Orient Latin* 2 (1884), 20-36 (here 72, 77-78); R. Röhricht, *Die Deutschen im Heiligen Lande* (Innsbruck, 1894), p. 19; Röhricht, *Geschichte des Ersten Kreuzzuges* (Innsbruck, 1901), pp. 36, 55, 56; F. Chalandon, *Histoire de la Première Croisade jusqu'à l'élection de Godefroi de Bouillon* (Paris, 1925), pp. 85, 86, 88-89; F. Cognasso, *La genesi delle crociate* (Torino, 1934), p. 117; A. Waas, *Geschichte der Kreuzzüge*, 2 vols (Freiburg, 1956), 1: 121; S. Runciman, *A History of the Crusades*, 3 vols (Cambridge, 1951-54), 1: 122, 131, 132; J. S. C. Riley-Smith, *The First Crusade and the Idea of Crusading* (London, 1986), p. 51; Riley-Smith, *The Crusades: A Short History* (London, 1987), p. 20; J. Flori, *La première croisade: l'Occident chrétien contre l'Islam* (Paris, 1992), pp. 49; J. Richard, *Histoire des croisades* (Paris, 1996), pp. 41.

[75] MSS. Stuttgart, Württembergische Landesbibliothek, Cod. Don. 580 and 581, edited as *Die Chronik der Grafen von Zimmern: Handschriften 580 und 581 der Fürstlich Fürstenbergischen Hofbibliothek Donaueschingen*, ed. H. Decker-Hauff et al., 7 vols (Konstanz, 1964-), 1: 74-85.

eleventh- or twelfth-century sources is that of Hartmann of Dillingen, which was probably derived from an early printed edition of the chronicle of William of Tyre.[76]

The duke was also joined by Frenchmen, such as Drogo of Nesle, who had been released from Byzantine captivity at his intervention. A more important addition to Godfrey's army was his older brother, Eustace of Boulogne, who had left Europe in the company of Robert II of Flanders, and Robert of Normandy, arriving with them at Constantinople some time after Godfrey.[77] From this point he seems to have associated more with his brothers than with the two Roberts. He and his men were included in Godfrey's division of the crusading army at the Great Battle of Antioch and again at the siege of Jerusalem where he fought in the same siege-tower as his brother.[78] The adhesion of Eustace was important as he had important vassals of his own, such as Hugh, count of Saint-Pol and his son Engelrand.[79] Others may have become more strongly bound to Godfrey when they lost their own lords, such as Gerard of Avesnes, in his service by 1099, whose lord Baldwin of Hainaut was killed while on an embassy to Alexios Komnenos.[80]

The march across the Anatolian plain and the siege of Antioch during the winter of 1097-98 witnessed a growth of ties of dependence between Godfrey and many of those in his army. During the march across Anatolia numerous horses and draught animals died of thirst. The loss of horses was especially telling for the knights in the army as it reduced their military effectiveness, and consequently, their status.[81] These losses were

---

[76] For detailed discussion of the evidence of the chronicle and its putative sources, see Murray, 'The Army of Godfrey of Bouillon', pp. 315-22; Murray, 'The Chronicle of Zimmern as a Source for the First Crusade: The Evidence of Ms. Stuttgart, Württembergische Landesbibliothek, Cod. Don. 580', in *The First Crusade: Origins and Impact*, ed. Jonathan P. Phillips (Manchester, 1997), pp. 78-106 (with English translation of the account of the crusade); Murray, 'Walther Duke of Teck: The Invention of a German Hero of the First Crusade', *Medieval Prosopography* 19 (1998), 35-54.

[77] AA p. 314; Andressohn, *Ancestry and Life of Godfrey of Bouillon*, p. 53.

[78] Orderic Vitalis, 5: 108-10, 168, 176; BD p. 102; AA pp. 472, 477, 495; GN p. 234.

[79] Prosopographical Catalogue, nos. 32, 76.

[80] AA pp. 499, 507, 516, 593.

[81] AA pp. 339-41. For conditions on the march, see France, *Victory in the East*, pp. 188-93, and K. Leyser, 'Money and Supplies on the First Crusade', in Leyser, *Communications and Power in Medieval Europe: The Gregorian Revolution and Beyond*, ed. T. Reuter (London, 1994), pp. 77-95 (here 85-94).

compounded by the privation suffered during the nine-month siege of Antioch. Hartmann, count of Dillingen, was one of the wealthiest men in southern Germany, and he could still afford to finance half of the construction costs of a siege machine at Nicaea, but by the time of the siege of Antioch he could only buy food by selling off his armour and weaponry and even his horse, and he was reduced to riding an ass and fighting with captured Turkish weapons. Godfrey took pity on Hartmann, giving him a daily allowance of bread and a piece of meat or fish.[82] The co-financier of the siege machine at Nicaea was Godfrey's kinsman Henry of Esch, who had been independent enough to leave the army in Thrace in his own interests, but whose reduced circumstances at Antioch now turned him into a dependent of the duke.[83] By the time of the siege of Antioch ever-increasing numbers of knights were penniless and had nothing to bargain with except their service.

Godfrey apparently possessed the means to support such men. Much of his accumulated funds must have been spent on equipment and supplies before the departure from Lotharingia and during the march across Germany, Hungary and the Balkans. Yet after his arrival on Byzantine territory, the duke, like other leaders, received from the Emperor Alexios gifts and money, delivered in cash every week from January to mid-May. Godfrey evidently distributed this money among his army according to the needs of each individual; most of it seems to have been immediately spent on food supplies by the recipients, and since the emperor imposed a monopoly on the sale of wine, grain and other foodstuffs, most of the disbursements actually found their way back to the imperial treasury.[84] This meant that the duke acquired a great degree of influence as the channel through which Byzantine financial assistance passed to the army.

When booty or forage were obtained by Godfrey's army fighting as a unit, it is likely that military discipline demanded that he and the inner core group had a major say in deciding how these were allocated. Most importantly, the duke had one important source of income that was not available to the other leaders. In the winter of 1097-98, with the aid of a

---

[82] AA pp. 322, 427.

[83] AA p. 427.

[84] AA pp. 310-11; WT II.12, pp. 175-77; Anne Comnène, *Alexiade*, ed. B. Leib, 4 vols (Paris, 1937-76), 2: 220-26.

military force he had put together, Baldwin established control over the city of Edessa and the surrounding areas. He was able to send to his brother 'many talents of gold and silver' (*plurima talenti auri et argenti*), a sum which was estimated at 50,000 bezants, as well as large quantities of corn, barley, wine and oil.[85] This massive support from Baldwin must have given Godfrey and Eustace a certain edge over the other leaders. Thus, at a time when many in his contingent were in serious financial difficulties, Godfrey had access to new sources of income in addition to whatever reserves had remained from earlier. These circumstances can only have tightened the bonds between Godfrey and those under his command. A further advantage was that after the capture of Antioch (2-3 June 1098) Godfrey and his troops were able to withdraw into areas held by Baldwin for rest and recuperation, where food and fodder must have been more plentiful than in the environs of Antioch, whose resources had been used up in the course of the long siege.

The long attrition of the siege of Antioch brought about numerous casualties to the crusaders through death in battle, capture, disease and starvation. Casualties among the more prominent members of Godfrey's army up to the time it left Syria included Gozelo of Montaigu, Henry of Esch, Folbert of Bouillon, Baldwin of Hainaut, Engelrand of Saint-Pol, Louis of Toul and Adalbero of Metz.[86] Nevertheless, although all contingents had suffered heavy casualties, Godfrey's army apparently remained strong relative to the others. During the famous conference in January 1099, when Raymond of Saint-Gilles tried in vain to persuade the other leaders to concede the leadership of the crusade to him, he offered Godfrey 10,000 *solidi,* a sum equalled only by that offered to Robert Curthose. This suggests that Godfrey had approximately as many troops prepared to accept his command as had the duke of Normandy, and more than either the count of Flanders or Tancred. This is all the more remarkable considering that a good number of those who had originally served with Godfrey were at this point with Baldwin in Edessa. Even between this time and the arrival of the crusade before the walls of Jerusalem, crusaders were evidently still prepared to leave the contingents with which they had hitherto been serving and join Godfrey and Eustace. They included the brothers Lethold and Engelbert of Tournai, who were

---

[85] AA pp. 395-96.

[86] Prosopographical Catalogue, nos. 60, 65, 37, 21, 32, 85, 2.

the first knights to mount the walls of Jerusalem on the day of its capture.[87] Even lords with retinues of their own were prepared to desert Raymond in favour of Godfrey, as in the case of Geldemar Carpenel, who remained in the duke's service after the capture of the Holy City.[88]

THE *COMITATUS BALDEWINI*

From the beginning of the crusade Baldwin and his wife Godehilde were accompanied by their household.[89] Baldwin broke away from the main army during the march across Cilicia, where he challenged Tancred for the possession of Tarsus. However, he eventually withdrew and moved north-east into the areas of Turbessel and Edessa, whose Armenian populations were in the process of driving out the Turkish occupying forces. For this campaign Baldwin was accompanied by a substantial military following described by Albert of Aachen as the *comitatus Baldewini*, a description which suggests a military force considerably greater in number than his household. At the beginning of 1098 Baldwin's following comprised 70 knights, but he had 200 when he moved to Edessa, even after having left small garrisons in towns that had already been captured.[90] They included several members of Godfrey's original contingent: Giselbert of Clermont, and Baldwin of Bourcq, Peter of Dampierre and Rainald of Toul serving on a temporary basis, as well as the Frenchman Drogo of Nesle, and two followers of Eustace of Boulogne, Udelrard and Pisellus of Wissant. Others seem to have joined Baldwin from other contingents. From the contingent of Stephen of Blois, who deserted from the army at Antioch, came Fulcher of Chartres, later lord of Sarūj, and his namesake the historian.[91] The number of men from Flanders and Artois who first appear in Baldwin's service in Jerusalem after his accession in 1100 suggests that he drew followers from Robert of Flanders and others of his vassals. Baldwin also had a secretary, Gerard, who had some responsibilities for financial affairs.[92] Once he had established control of Edessa Baldwin was in a position to reward his followers, since he was

[87] Prosopographical Catalogue, nos. 31, 82.
[88] Prosopographical Catalogue, no. 44.
[89] AA p. 302.
[90] AA pp. 350, 358, 366; RC p. 632.
[91] AA pp. 350, 357, 358, 366, 442, 446; FC pp. 163-64, 206-8.
[92] Prosopographical Catalogue, no. 46.

able to seize the treasure of Thoros, the previous ruler, and later confiscated moneys from some of the leading citizens of the town who conspired against him.[93] Albert of Aachen highlights how Baldwin used his newly acquired resources to reward those whose own funds had been used up in the course of the long march and the siege of Antioch.[94]

On the one hand, Baldwin's strike at Edessa can be considered as a piece of free enterprise, since it allowed him to set up a principality of his own. For the first time in his life, he ruled over substantial towns and lands, with both crusader and Armenian troops at his disposal. On the other hand, the campaign served wider strategic interests by depriving the Turks of much of the hinterland of Antioch and securing sorely needed sources of food and fodder, and was approved by the leaders of the crusade.[95] Certainly the successful outcome of the campaign depended on the co-operation of the Bouillon-Boulogne brothers, since Godfrey and Eustace permitted Baldwin to detach many of their followers, some of them on a temporary basis, while Baldwin supported his brothers with money and food from his newly won territories.

---

[93] AA pp. 354-55, 360-61, 443.

[94] AA pp. 441-442: *Erant enim summa necessitate gravati, et longa expeditione rebus exhausti necesariis. Affluebant et accrescebant singulis diebus in numero et virtute, dum fere tota civitas a Gallis obsessa, et eorum hospitalitate occupata est. Baldewinus singulis, de die in diem, in bisantiis auri, in talentis et vasis argenteis dona plurima conferebat.*

[95] France, *Victory in the East*, pp. 195-96.

Chapter III

Godfrey of Bouillon as Ruler of Jerusalem (1099-1100)

The Election and Title of Godfrey

It is unclear to what extent Urban II had made plans for the government of any lands that the crusade might recapture from Muslim powers. Certainly it was envisaged that any reconquest would be carried out in co-operation with the Byzantine empire, and agreements made by the leaders of the crusade with the Emperor Alexios at Constantinople recognised that they would restore to him those territories which had been subject to Byzantine rule up to the time of the Turkish conquests under the Seljuk rulers Alp Arslan (1063-72) and Malik Shāh (1072-92). This would apply to all of Asia Minor, Cilicia and most of Syria as far south as Antioch and its environs.[1] These were areas where there were substantial Greek-speaking populations, which could be expected to welcome and support the restoration of Byzantine rule. After the capture of Antioch, the refusal of Bohemund to surrender control of the city was to become a major bone of contention both within the crusading army and between the crusaders and Byzantium, and further tension arose as a result of attempts by some of the princes to conquer different parts of central and southern Syria.[2]

Palestine was a quite different case, as it had not been subject to Byzantine control since it was conquered by the Arabs under the Caliph ᶜUmar in the seventh century. It is doubtful whether the empire had the infrastructure or resources to absorb Palestine in addition to territories to its north; nevertheless, the emperor had in the past exercised a role as protector of the orthodox church, and might reasonably expect this to be

---

[1] France, *Victory in the East*, pp. 111-21, with the plausible suggestion that since Raymond of Saint-Gilles later controlled both Albara and Laodicea at a time when he was in alliance with the emperor, Antioch and its immediate region must have formed the southern limit of imperial possessions which Alexios expected to be restored to Byzantine rule.

[2] France, *Victory in the East*, pp. 297-323.

recognised by the crusaders. It is possible that the agreements with the emperor stipulated that any other lands conquered by the crusaders (i.e. to the south of those to be restored) were to be held from him in vassalic relationships, which would have presumably produced a series of Byzantine client states.[3] However, when Alexios failed to appear with military forces at Antioch the crusaders evidently regarded their agreements with him as null and void. After the departure of the crusade from southern Syria, the issue of the control of territories remained largely dormant, although some attempts were made to capture cities in the course of the march to Jerusalem. In early June the combined army of the crusade reached Ramla, whose inhabitants had fled, and discovered that the port of Jaffa had also been abandoned by its Fatimid garrison. While the army decided to press on inland into the Judaean highlands towards Jerusalem, it was thought essential to hold this coastal plain, since the port of Jaffa could be used to bring in supplies and reinforcements. The solution chosen by the crusaders was to leave the area of Lydda and Ramla under the control of a newly appointed bishop, a Norman called Robert, and a garrison. The erection of this ecclesiastical lordship was the first formal territorial disposition by the crusade in Palestine.[4]

When the Franks first reached the Middle East Jerusalem was held by Turks owing loyalty to the Seljuk sultanate, but in August 1098 the Fatimid vizier, al-Afdal, had been able to exploit Turkish weakness to recover the city. As the Franks advanced south, he attempted to negotiate a settlement that would keep Jerusalem under Fatimid control. Understandably, the crusade leaders were deaf to such overtures.[5] The army reached the outskirts of Jerusalem on 7 June 1099 and proceeded to invest the city. During the course of the siege, Bethlehem was seized by Tancred, who placed his banner on the church of the Nativity. This was a gesture which under western customs of warfare would normally be interpreted as the staking of a claim to possession after capture, and the fact that it was done at a site of such holiness aroused considerable opposition

---

[3] B. Hamilton, *The Latin Church in the Crusader States: The Secular Church* (London, 1980), p. 5.

[4] H. E. Mayer, 'The Origins of the Lordships of Ramla and Lydda in the Latin Kingdom of Jerusalem', *Speculum* 60 (1985), 537-52 (here 538-39).

[5] H. Dajani-Shakeel, 'Diplomatic Relations Between Muslim and Frankish Rulers 1097-1158 A.D.', in *Crusaders and Muslims in Twelfth-Century Syria*, ed. M. Shatzmiller (Leiden, 1993), pp. 190-215.

within the army, and seems to have provoked a debate that led on to the wider issue of the government of Jerusalem after it should be captured. Questions were raised about who the future ruler should be, whereupon many – especially the clerics – argued that it was not right to elect a king in the place where Christ had suffered and been crowned with thorns.[6] The outcome of this discussion seems to have been inconclusive, but it had aired an issue which must have become more acute between that point and the capture of the city on 15 July.[7]

One of the phrases reported by Raymond of Aguilers in connection with the debate was 'the kingdom of David', and it is likely that this expression was indeed a reflection of actual perceptions of the Holy Land in some sections of the army. According to Fulcher of Chartres, Urban II had described at Clermont how the Turks had 'devastated the kingdom of God',[8] while according to Baldric of Dol he cited Psalm 78:1 to illustrate how the gentile peoples had conquered the *haereditas* of God.[9] When the crusaders entered Palestine, they regarded it as constituting a *regnum*.[10] In some instances contemporary writers are more specific as to the nature of this *regnum*, referring variously to the kingdom of David, the kingdom of Judaea, the kingdom of God and the patrimony of Christ.[11] In the atmosphere of religious fervour generated in the course of the crusade and culminating in the arrival at the Holy City the crusaders evidently saw themselves as having entered a realm which was the kingdom of the ancient Jewish kings, whose true successor was Christ.[12] It was probably this messianic belief that was behind the feeling of many as reported by

---

[6] RA pp. 295-96.

[7] On the course of the siege, see France, *Victory in the East*, pp. 337-56.

[8] FC I.3, pp. 132-34.

[9] BD p. 14: *Deus, venerunt gentes in haereditatem tuam: polluerunt templum sanctuum tuum.*

[10] Riley-Smith, 'The Title of Godfrey of Bouillon', p. 83.

[11] *Regnum Judeae*: Lambert of Ardres, *Historia comitum Ghisnensium*, MGH SS 24: 577; Galbertus notarius Brugensis, *De multro, traditione, et occisione gloriosi Karoli comitis Flandriarum*, ed. J. Rider (Turnhout, 1994), p. 15; RA p. 302. *Regnum David*: Orderic Vitalis 5: 174, 342. *Regnum Dei*: H. Hagenmeyer, *Epistulae et chartae ad historiam primi belli sacrae spectantes: Die Kreuzzugsbriefe aus den Jahren 1088-1100* (Innsbruck, 1901), no. 18 (p. 171); *Regnum Christi*: Ekkehard of Aura, p. 154; FC I.2, p. 134. *Terra Dei*: *GF* p. 66. *Dei haereditas*: GN p. 137. *Christi hereditas*: Ekkehard of Aura, pp. 172, 174.

[12] PT p. 105; BD p. 15; GN pp. 138, 140; AA pp. 485E, 492E; Ekkehard of Aura, pp. 112, 114; RA, pp. 268, 285, 299.

Raymond of Aguilers that it would be wrong to elect a king in the place where Christ had been crowned with thorns.

On 17 July 1099, in the squalid splendour of a city still disfigured by the effects of a six-week siege and the ensuing massacre of its Muslim and Jewish inhabitants, the leaders of the crusade met at the *Templum Domini* (as the crusaders called the Dome of the Rock), and ordered that each man in the army should 'pray that God would choose for himself whomsoever he wished, to rule over the others and govern the city'. This seems like an attempt to take some of the heat out of the debate over the rulership; the actual election was postponed until the eighth day after the capture of the city, 22 July.[13] The interim ordinance also shows how the leaders regarded the problem of validation of a new ruler: it was believed that God would choose a ruler by means of an inspired election.[14] We have no information about the precise composition of the electoral college, although it is generally accepted that it was drawn from the princes and leading clerics, and possibly men of the second rank who had substantial followings of their own. The clerics among them demanded that the electors should choose a spiritual head (*vicarius spiritualis*) before any lay ruler.[15] It is unclear whether this demand simply related to the order of business, or whether it implied a primacy of authority for the spiritual head. Yet in the event, the princes simply ignored this demand and proceeded to the election of a secular ruler. This is not surprising, since the influence of the clergy had been declining within the leadership of the crusade. Two of the most influential bishops, Adhemar of Le Puy and William of Orange, were dead, while other capable clerics had been appointed to posts elsewhere.[16] The sole Latin bishop already appointed to a Palestinian diocese, Robert of Lydda, must have still been in his lordship at this time.

The election of the ruler was carried out on 22 July 1099.[17] The choice of potential candidates was fairly restricted. Two of the princes, Bohemund and Baldwin, were absent in principalities they had acquired for themselves in the north, which evidently excluded them as candidates. It

[13] *GF* p. 92: *Tunc nostri tenuerunt concilium, ut unusquisque faceret elemosinas cum orationibus, quatinus sibi Deus eligeret quem vellet regnare super alios et regere civitatem.*

[14] AA pp. 486A, 487D, 488, 489; PT p. 110; BD p. 105; *GF* p. 92; LL p. 498.

[15] RA p. 301.

[16] RA p. 301.

[17] *GF* p. 92; PT pp. 110-11.

is unlikely that those who intended to return home to the West were serious candidates, which excluded Robert of Flanders and probably Robert of Normandy. Of the others, Raymond of Saint-Gilles most obviously had hopes of becoming ruler, just as he had already made attempts to be recognised as leader of the crusade, but the latter actions especially, notably his offer at Rugia to purchase the service of the other princes, may well have set many of them against his candidature. He had also repeatedly attempted to secure territory for himself. He had disputed the possession of Antioch with Bohemund in the summer of 1098, and come off worse. Between September 1098 and January 1099 he tried to establish control of the Jabal al-Summāq, a plateau east of the River Orontes to the south-east of Antioch, containing the towns of Ma^carrat al-Nu^cmān, Kafartāb and Albara.[18] These campaigns may have antagonised those crusaders who wished only to press on to Jerusalem. Nevertheless, Raymond evidently tried to align himself with precisely this element when he led his contingent south from Ma^carrat on 13 January 1099, although his attempts to capture Arqah cost him much of the sympathy he had gained.[19] He had tended to associate himself with those in the army who set great store by visions, but he must have seemed compromised in the eyes of the other leaders when the visionary Peter Bartholomew, so often the mouthpiece of those who would brook no delays, did a volte-face to support Raymond's aims at Arqah.[20] Raymond's continuing faith in the Holy Lance, even when the relic had been discredited as a result of the ordeal of Peter Bartholomew, must have cost him support among the more rationale of the clerics, notably Arnulf of Chocques. Most importantly, he had often taken the part of the Byzantine emperor, whom many of the crusaders regarded as something of a traitor after his failure to come to the relief of the crusade at Antioch. By contrast, Godfrey of Bouillon had antagonised fewer of the other leaders in the course of the crusade; he had not laid himself open to charges of cupidity by attempting to seize cities and lands in the way that Bohemund

---

[18] J. Richard, 'Note sur l'archidiocèse d'Apamée et les conquêtes de Raymond de Saint-Gilles en Syrie du Nord', *Syria* 25 (1946-48), 102-8; T. Asbridge, 'The Principality of Antioch and the Jabal as-Summāq', in *The First Crusade: Origins and Impact,* ed. J. P. Phillips (Manchester, 1997), pp. 142-52.

[19] France, *Victory in the East*, pp. 315-24.

[20] France, *Victory in the East*, p. 322. On Raymond and the visionary element, see J. S. C. Riley-Smith, *The First Crusade and the Idea of Crusading* (London, 1986), pp. 101-7.

and Raymond had done, although he and his contingent had profited from Baldwin's conquest of Edessa; but the fact that his troops had made the first breakthrough into Jerusalem, and that he was the first of the princes to enter the city, must have been fresh in the minds of the electors and the army in general.

Chroniclers with such divergent standpoints as Raymond of Aguilers, Albert of Aachen, and Guibert of Nogent report that some sort of offer was made to Raymond of Saint-Gilles.[21] Most of the other sources merely state that Godfrey was made ruler.[22] These differences can best be reconciled if they are regarded as reflecting different parts of a fairly complex process. It is possible that the electors took preliminary soundings from the candidates to establish whether and on what terms they might accept the rulership. The idea of canvassing, which could have been construed as constituting a kind of offer, would also explain reports that the rulership was offered to Robert of Normandy, but that he declined, suggesting Godfrey as the most suitable choice.[23] Either Raymond of Saint-Gilles and the others were unable to come to mutually agreeable terms in advance, or a public offer was made which he then declined. Raymond of Aguilers states that the count was asked whether he would accept the *regnum*, but his reply, that the royal title in that city was unacceptable to him, indicates that he chose to associate himself with the sentiment that had manifested itself earlier, to the effect that the idea of an earthly king in Jerusalem was sacrilegious.[24] It could also be interpreted as a way of raising the stakes to prevent any rival being given royal powers. Raymond's refusal to hand over the Tower of David to Godfrey and his attempt to capture Ascalon in August 1099 demonstrate that he had ambitions of establishing a principality in Palestine.

Once Godfrey had been chosen as ruler, the questions arose as to what title he should be known by and what powers he should exercise. It was long accepted by historians that piety caused Godfrey to refuse a crown in

---

[21] RA p. 301; AA p. 485; GN p. 229.

[22] PT pp. 110-11; *GF* pp. 92-93; BD p. 104; Robert the Monk, p. 870.

[23] Tudebodus imitatus et continuatus, *Historia peregrinorum euntium Jerusolymam ad liberandum Sanctum Sepulcrum de potestate ethnicorum*, in RHC Occ. 3: 225; William of Malmesbury, *Gesta Regum Anglorum: The History of the English Kings*, ed. and trans. R. A. B. Mynors, R. M. Thomson and M. Winterbottom (Oxford, 1998), IV.389, p. 702.

[24] RA p. 301: *ille nomen regium se perhorrescere fatebatur in illa civitate.*

the city where Christ had worn a crown of thorns.[25] Even if true, this in itself reveals little about either title or powers of the incumbent. The *Lignages d'Outremer,* which represent a very late stage of tradition within the kingdom of Jerusalem, say that the barons and pilgrims elected Godfrey king, but that he refused to be crowned.[26] Quite bizarrely, Orderic Vitalis advances the idea of the crown of thorns as a *positive* reason for a coronation and royal title, stating that Godfrey was 'compelled by ecclesiastical election to wear a crown and be called king of Jerusalem to the honour of him who deigned to wear a crown of thorns'.[27] Guibert of Nogent, Baldric of Dol, Robert the Monk and other authors agree with Orderic Vitalis in referring to Godfrey as *rex.*[28] However, they and others dependent upon them had not been participants in the crusade themselves. They were writing in the West at a time when the royal title had been adopted by Godfrey's successor Baldwin I, and they probably rationalised Godfrey's title in line with subsequent developments.

The ideas encapsulated in the argument about the crown of thorns, which had been first raised during the siege of Jerusalem, obviously caught the popular imagination, but they were merely one element in a number of issues. The objection that it would be sacrilegious for the new ruler to be crowned could have been met by Godfrey in form if not in spirit by refusing a coronation; however, he could still have claimed the title of king and its attributes. He was certainly regarded as possessing a throne.[29] However, the stakes must have been raised by the terms in which Count Raymond refused the rulership, which took sentiments about sacrilege even further. If we accept the report of his chaplain, Raymond objected that even the royal title (*ille nomen regium*) was abhorrent in the Holy City, a development of the line of argument

---

[25] See the literature cited in Riley-Smith, 'The Title of Godfrey of Bouillon', p. 83.

[26] *Lignages d'Outremer*, in RHC Lois 2: 441: *Li baron et li pelerin esleurent à roy et à seigneur Godeffroy de Bouillon, duc de Lorraine, lequel ne se vost coroner, ne porter corone, car il dit que en la cité où nostre Sauveour porta corone d'espines le jour de la passion, ne porteroit corone d'or.*

[27] Orderic Vitalis: 5: 340: *ibi ad laudem eius qui spinea gestare serta pro salutae hominum dignatus est, diadema ferre et rex Ierusalem pro terrore gentilium cognominari aecclesiastica electione compulsus est.*

[28] GN pp. 229, 231; BD pp. 103-4; Robert the Monk, pp. 869-70; Orderic Vitalis, 5: 174, 178, 184; Tudebodus imitatus et continuatus, pp. 225-26.

[29] AA pp. 489, 524, 526.

concerned with sacrilege which must have made it more difficult for Godfrey to take the title of king.[30]

While writers who had not been on crusade tend to refer to Godfrey as *rex*, as we have already seen, a quite different title is given by Fulcher of Chartres, Peter Tudebode, and the anonymous author of the *Gesta Francorum*, all of whom took part in the crusade, as well as Albert of Aachen, who had good sources of information connected with the entourage of Godfrey. These authors all prefer the title *princeps*, sometimes qualified as *princeps regni* or *princeps civitati*.[31] This evidence is supported by the Annals of St James of Liège, which describe Godfrey's authority as a *principatus*, echoing a term used by Fulcher of Chartres.[32] The title *princeps*, then, seems to have been the solution arrived at by Godfrey and those advising him, and it was evidently chosen as a way of expressing the possession of monarchic authority while avoiding the objectionable title of king.[33] Godfrey may not have been king in name, but he was evidently regarded as the ruler of the *regnum Christi*, who had been chosen by God through the vehicle of an election by the leaders of the crusade. Thus Albert of Aachen describes him as the highest earthly authority in Jerusalem: *summus princeps Iherusalem* and *summus post Deum dominator Iherusalem*.[34]

The acceptance that Godfrey took the title of *princeps* would seem to contradict earlier scholarship, which held that his title was *advocatus Sancti Sepulchri*, defender of the Holy Sepulchre. The consensus of this view was that the title of *advocatus* reflected Godfrey's recognition of the suzerainty of the church; he was supposedly merely charged with the defence of the

---

[30] RA p. 301.

[31] FC I.30, p. 308, I.32, pp. 321-22 (*principatum*); PT pp. 110-11; *GF* p. 92; AA pp. 488-95. On the sources and reliability of Albert, see S. B. Edgington, 'The First Crusade: Reviewing the Evidence', in *The First Crusade: Origins and Impact*, pp. 57-77, and Edgington, 'Albert of Aachen Reappraised', in *From Clermont to Jerusalem: The Crusades and Crusader Societies, 1095-1500*, ed. A. V. Murray (Turnhout, 1998), pp. 55-67.

[32] FC I.32, pp. 321-22; *Annales s. Iacobi Leodiensis*, MGH SS 16: 639: *dux noster Godefridus sumit principatum.*

[33] Riley-Smith, 'The Title of Godfrey of Bouillon', pp. 83-86; Murray, 'The Title of Godfrey of Bouillon as Ruler of Jerusalem', pp. 163-78.

[34] AA pp. 490A, 494B, 495E, 520C.

Holy Places on its behalf.[35] Thus both the title of *advocatus* and its meaning as established by earlier scholarship are at variance with the title and significance of *princeps*, which, as Riley-Smith argues, 'suggests that he [Godfrey] was thought of as a ruler in a real sense rather than a church official'.[36]

The main evidence for the title of *advocatus* comes from a formulation in a letter sent by Archbishop Daibert of Pisa, Raymond of Saint-Gilles and Godfrey himself. It was written in Laodicea in September or October 1099 and was addressed to the successor to Urban II, who had himself died on 29 July.[37] Daibert had just arrived at Laodicea with a Pisan fleet; there he encountered Raymond of Saint-Gilles and other unnamed princes who were on their way back to the West.[38] However, Godfrey himself was still in Jerusalem at this time, and although the Laodicea letter included his name among its senders, it was by no means an official document which had his approval.[39] The status of the title *ecclesiae S. Sepulchri ... advocatus* is therefore unclear.

Nevertheless, supporting evidence for the use of a similar title by Godfrey can be found in the *Gesta episcoporum Virdunensium* of Laurence of Liège, writing in the 1140s. He gives a very detailed account of the preparations made by Godfrey and Baldwin for the crusade, and he may well

---

[35] Ch. Moeller, 'Godefroid de Bouillon et l'avouerie du Saint-Sépulcre', in *Mélanges Godefroid Kurth: Recueil de mémoires relatifs à l'histoire, à la philologie et à l'archéologie*, 2 vols (Liège, 1908), 1: 173-83; J. Hansen, *Das Problem eines Kirchenstaates in Jerusalem* (Luxembourg, 1928), pp. 11-20; A. Fliche, *La chrétienté médiévale* (Paris, 1929), p. xiv; J. L. La Monte, *Feudal Monarchy in the Latin Kingdom of Jerusalem* (Cambridge, Mass., 1932), pp. 4-5; R. Grousset, *Histoire des croisades et du royaume franc de Jérusalem*, 2 vols (Paris, 1934-36), 1: 166-71; Runciman, *History of the Crusades*, 1: 292-93; Waas, *Geschichte der Kreuzzüge*, 1: 157; P. E. Schramm, *Herrschaftszeichen und Staatsymbolik* (Stuttgart, 1956), 3: 917; Prawer, *Royaume latin*, 1: 237-38; Prawer, *Latin Kingdom*, p. 37; Zöllner, *Geschichte der Kreuzzüge*, p. 85; J. Richard, 'The Political and Ecclesiastical Organisation of the Crusader States', in Setton, *History of the Crusades*, 5: 197.

[36] Riley-Smith, 'The Title of Godfrey of Bouillon', p. 86.

[37] Hagenmeyer, *Epistulae*, no. 16: *ego Pisanus archiepiscopus et alii episcopi et Godefridus dux, gratia Dei ecclesiae S. Sepulchri nunc advocatus et Raimundus comes S. Aegidii et universus Dei exercitus qui est in terra Israel.*

[38] H. Hagenmeyer, 'Der Brief der Kreuzfahrer an den Pabst [*sic*] und die abendländische Kirche im Jahre 1099 nach der Schlacht bei Askalon', *Forschungen zur deutschen Geschichte* 13 (1873), 400-12.

[39] Riley-Smith, 'The Title of Godfrey of Bouillon', p. 83.

have had information from returning crusaders from Godfrey's contingent, many of whom originated in the diocese of Liège. He states that Godfrey was 'appointed by God to rule the kingdom of the Holy City', but that he was called not king, but *advocatus*.[40] This short account evidently displays an awareness of several key issues: the idea of a *regnum* in Palestine, the concept of divine direction, and the declining of the royal title.

The evidence in support of a *princeps*-title used by Godfrey does not necessarily exclude the possibility of *another* title being used in conjunction with it. It is striking that accounts of the election given by those sources which agree that he was called *princeps* often link two basic concepts: the government of the realm, expressed in terms such as *princeps, princeps regni, princeps Christianorum, princeps civitatis,* as well as verbal phrases such as *civitatem regere* and *super alios regnare*, and the defence of the Christian community against the pagans, expressed in terms such as *protegere, conservare, Christianos custodire, paganos debellare, paganos expoliare*, etc.[41] Albert of Aachen especially regularly links these two concepts elsewhere in his history, and applied them both to Godfrey and his successors. He describes Godfrey's authority as the *dominium urbis et custodia Dominici Sepulchri*.[42] He also relates that when Baldwin I was dying, he named his

---

40 LL p. 498: *Porro dux Godefridus ... pro Lothariorum ducata regnum Sanctae Urbis a Deo promeruit, quamvis ipse numquam se regem sed advocatum eius passus sit appellari.*

41 AA p. 486: ... *a Deo electum et constitutum ductorem ac principem atque praeceptorem christiani exercitus* ...; AA p. 489: *Godefridus quoque princeps Christianorum in throno Iherusalem exaltatus ad protegendam urbem ejusque habitores*; FC I.30, pp. 306-10: *Quem ob nobilitatis excellentiam, et militae probitatem ... in urbe sancta regni principem omnis populus dominici exercitus, ad illud conservandum atque regendum, eligit*; PT p. 110: *Alia autem die fecerunt concilium ante templum Domini, dicentes ni unusquisque faciat orationes et elemosynas atque jejunium, ut Deus eligeret sibi quempiam placuisset qui regnaret super alios, et civitatem regeret, et paganos exspoliaret*; PT pp. 110-11: *Octava vero die quod civitas fuit capta, celebraverunt festum ... in quo elegerunt ducem Godefredum principem civitatis, qui proeliaretur paganos et custodiret Christianos*; *GF* p. 92: *Octava autem die quo civitas fuit capta, elegerunt ducem Godefridum principem civitatis, qui proeliaretur paganos et custodiret Christianos.* There may be an echo of the concept of defence of the church in the dating for the year 1100 given by Ekkehard of Aura, p. 158: *Anno Domini MC. Sub Gotefrido duce Hierosolimitanam ecclesiam defensante.*

42 AA p. 485. In the Vatican codex (D) Albert's history begins with the following words: *Incipit liber primus Hierosolymitanae urbis, ubi clarissimi ducis Godefridi inclyta gesta narrantur, cuius labore et studio civitas sancta, ab infidelibus liberata, sanctae Ecclesiae filiis est*

brother Eustace as successor: in the event of Eustace refusing the crown the notables of the kingdom were to choose Baldwin, count of Edessa, 'or such a person as would rule the Christian people and defend the churches'.[43] When describing the situation of the kingdom after Baldwin I's death Albert twice uses the formulation *rex ac defensor*.[44] This terminology may reflect an actual royal usage; a privilege of Baldwin I for the Genoese in 1104 uses the titles *Balduinus rex Iudee et Iherusalem ac defensor sanctissimi Sepulchri domini nostri Ihesu Christi*.[45] The Antiochene official Walter the Chancellor also describes Baldwin II as *rex qui solus post Dominum dominus et defensor Christianitatis*.[46] Anselm, archbishop of Canterbury, who was a correspondent of Baldwin's mother, at one point also wrote to him with the admonition that he should behave towards the church as an *advocatus et defensor*.[47] A very late piece of evidence comes from William of Tyre, who refers to Amalric I as *rex Ierosolimorum, locorum venerabilium dominice passionis et resurrectionis defensor et advocatus*.[48] The protection of the eastern church had been one of Pope Urban's main themes at Clermont, included in every account of his speech.[49] Now that Jerusalem and the Holy Places had been liberated, the restoration of the eastern church could be regarded as having begun, and it would be understandable for the importance of the continuing defence of eastern Christendom to be reflected in the title of the ruler. This varied evidence for the use of such a title by Godfrey and three of his successors suggests that he originally adopted the title of *princeps*, which he used in con-

---

restituta. Thus the twin themes of the liberation of Jerusalem and the restitution of the eastern church are placed in a central position in the exposition of the work (AA p. 271).

[43] AA p. 709: *aut talis qui populum Christianum regat, ecclesias defendat.*

[44] AA p. 709: *clerus et populus tam rudis Ecclesiae, tanto Rege ac defensore viduatus, de Regis restitutione agere coeperunt, dicentes non esse utile consilium ut Rege ac defensoris solatio locus et gens diu careret, et locus et terra a nullo defensa periret.*

[45] RRH no. 43.

[46] Walter the Chancellor, *Galterii Cancelarii Bella Antiochena*, ed. H. Hagenmeyer (Innsbruck, 1896), p. 102.

[47] Anselm of Canterbury, *S. Anselmi Cantuarensis archiepiscopi opera*, ed. F. S. Schmitt (Edinburgh, 1949), 4: 143.

[48] WT XX.22, p. 942.

[49] D. C. Munro, 'The Speech of Pope Urban II at Clermont', *American Historical Review* 11 (1906), 236-37.

junction with another title with the vernacular meaning of 'defender', and which was variously rendered into Latin as *advocatus* or *defensor*.

In the past, scholars who held that Godfrey's title was *advocatus Sancti Sepulchri* tended to interpret its meaning as being analogous to the contemporary western institution of advocate. Especially in France and Germany, an *advocatus* was a layman, usually a nobleman, who represented an ecclesiastical institution in exercising certain public functions.[50] St Paul the Apostle had stated that it was against the dignity of clerics and the respect they were due for them to participate in wordly affairs.[51] Therefore dealings in temporal matters, especially those involving secular justice and the acquisition and disposal of property, were often entrusted to an *advocatus*.[52] The main problem in accepting that Godfrey of Bouillon could have used two titles in conjunction is that this interpretation of *advocatus* (or whatever vernacular word it may reflect), implying subordination to ecclesiastical authority, seems to be at variance with that of *princeps*.

Godfrey of course knew well what the duties, rights and opportunities of this kind of advocate were; like his uncle and grandfather, he had been advocate of the abbey of Saint-Hubert in the Ardennes. The advocacy of a monastery, especially if exercised on a hereditary basis, offered opportunities to exploit as well as to protect, and so such a title should not be automatically regarded as implying subservience to ecclesiastical authority. Yet it is questionable whether this kind of advocate is an appropriate

---

[50] Moeller, 'Godefroid de Bouillon et l'avouerie du Saint-Sépulcre', pp. 173-83; Hansen, *Das Problem eines Kirchenstaates in Jerusalem*, pp. 11-20; La Monte, *Feudal Monarchy in the Latin Kingdom of Jerusalem*, pp. 4-5; Grousset, *Histoire des croisades et du royaume franc de Jérusalem*, 1: 166-71; Runciman, *History of the Crusades*, 1: 292-93; Waas, *Geschichte der Kreuzzüge*, 1: 157; Prawer, *Latin Kingdom*, p. 37; Zöllner, *Geschichte der Kreuzzüge*, p. 85; Richard, 'The Political and Ecclesiastical Organisation of the Crusader States', p. 197. A notable exception was J. G. Rowe, 'Pascal II and the Relations Between the Spiritual and Temporal Powers in the Kingdom of Jerusalem', *Speculum* 32 (1959), 470-501 (here 475), who concluded that the institution of *advocatus Sancti Sepulchri* represented 'a full royal power shorn of its title by the piety of crusaders'.

[51] *Biblia Sacra iuxta Vulgatam versionem*, ed. R. Weber *et al.*, 3rd edn (Stuttgart, 1983), 2 Timothy 2: *nemo militans inplicat se negotiis saecularibus*.

[52] A. Waas, *Vogtei und Bede in der deutschen Kaiserzeit*, 2 vols (Berlin, 1919-23), 1: 28; N. Huyghebaert, 'Pourquoi l'église a-t-elle besoin d'avoués?', *PSIHGDL* 98 (1984), 33-42.

analogy for the ruler of the *regnum Iherusalem.* The patriarchate of Jerusalem may have been junior to those of Antioch, Alexandria and Constantinople, but in western eyes, it was second only to Rome itself in importance.[53] All Christian rulers were charged with the defence of the church, but the protection of the Roman Church, which could be regarded as embracing the whole of western Christendom, was a particular duty of the German emperors. As part of his coronation ritual the emperor promised to God and St Peter to be a defender and protector of the Roman Church.[54] This role was stressed in imperial ideology. For example, during the Investiture Contest the imperialist writer Benzo of Alba addressed Henry IV as *dominus noster ... sanctae Romanae aecclesia protector et amicus.*[55] The designations *defensor* and *advocatus* were frequently used in conjunction with the titles *imperator, rex* and also that of *princeps,* which had been taken over from Roman legal usage.[56]

From the eleventh century onwards theorists on the papal side saw a danger in such imperial titles being used to justify interference in church affairs, and attempted to develop a clerical interpretation of the defender not as the lord but as the servant of the church. At some point a new coronation ritual was introduced, changing the emperor's promise into an oath, and adding the name of the reigning pope to the formula. Despite these changes it is clear that the imperial perception of this role remained constant in the period leading up to the First Crusade. Henry III, a deposer of popes, and his like-minded son Henry IV, may have seen themselves as subordinate to God and St Peter, but not to the pope.[57] It

---

[53] A. Grabois, 'Charlemagne, Rome and Jerusalem', *RBPH* 59 (1981), 792-809.

[54] *Ordo Romanus ad benedicendam imperatore, quando coronam accepit,* in P. E. Schramm, 'Die Ordines der mittelalterlichen Kaiserkrönung', *Archiv für Urkundenforschung* 11 (1930), 371-72; *Die Ordines für die Weihe und Krönung des Kaisers und der Kaiserin,* ed. R. Elze, MGH Fontes iuris Germanici antiqui 9 (Hannover, 1960), pp. 2, 4-5, 19.

[55] Benzo of Alba, *Ad Heinricum IV imperatorem libri VII,* MGH SS 11: 651.

[56] J. Ficker, *Vom Reichsfürstenstande* 1 (Innsbruck, 1866), 24-33.

[57] Waas, *Vogtei und Bede,* 1: 144-50; P. E. Schramm, *Kaiser, Rom und Renovatio* (Bad Homburg, 1962), pp. 174-76; T. Struve, 'Kaisertum und Romgedanke in salischer Zeit', *Deutsches Archiv für Erforschung des Mittelalters* 44 (1988), 424-54; Struve, 'Die Stellung des Königtums in der politischen Theorie der Salierzeit', in *Die Salier und das Reich,* 3: *Gesellschaftlicher und ideengeschichtlicher Wandel im Reich der Salier,* ed. S. Weinfurter and H. Seibert (Sigmaringen, 1991), pp. 217-44. The term *defensor Romanae ecclesiae* had a direct equivalent in Middle High German, *voget von Rôme,* which had considerable currency in twelfth-and thirteenth-century vernacular

would be appropriate for the first ruler of the *regnum Iherusalem* to adopt a title reflecting the duty to protect the Christian community against the pagans in the same way that the emperor claimed to be the protector of the Roman Church.[58] The empire was an obvious constitutional model for the kingdom of Jerusalem, both in terms of the importance of Jerusalem and its church, and in terms of the experience of Godfrey of Bouillon himself and those who were likely to have been advising him. The election of the first ruler in Jerusalem is also reminiscent of German precedents, in that the king of Germany was elected by the German princes, even when this process simply consisted of the acclamation of the son of the ruling emperor in cases where he was strong enough to impose what was effectively a hereditary succession.[59] Godfrey had been duke of Lower Lotharingia and must have been familiar with imperial usages, as must many of those who had come with him from Lotharingia, particularly those who, as the previous chapter has shown, had all exercised important functions in Godfrey's army and who in July 1099 probably constituted his principal advisors.

In particular it is significant how men associated with Godfrey had close ties with the bishopric of Liège, which under the imperialist bishops Henry of Verdun (1075-91) and Otbert (1091-1119) constituted one of the main supports of the German monarchy during the Investiture Contest. The diocese was loyal to Henry IV for the entire duration of his dispute with the papacy.[60] Bishop Otbert even issued a coinage depicting

literature which assumed or asserted the emperor's pre-eminent position over the pope and other kings. See E. Nellman, *Die Reichsidee in deutschen Dichtungen der Salier- und frühen Stauferzeit* (Berlin, 1963), pp. 116-30, 176-80. For the dating of the coronation formula see Schramm, 'Ordines', pp. 281-390 and E. Eichmann, *Die Kaiserkrönung im Abendlande* (Würzburg, 1942), 1: 152-77.

[58] A further parallel may lie in the fact that imperial ideology also included the concept of fighting the pagans. One of the coronation *ordines*, the tenth-century Ottonian pontifical from Mainz, links this duty with the defence of the church: *Tribue ei, omnipotens Deus, ut sit fortissimus protector patriae et consolator ecclesiarum, atque coenobiorum sanctorum, maxima pietate regalis munificentiae; atque ut sit fortissimus regum, triumphat hostium ad opprimendas rebelles et paganos nationes. Ordines*, ed. Elze, pp. 4-5.

[59] Schramm, *Kaiser, Rom und Renovatio*, pp. 80ff.

[60] Even after the rebellion of his son Henry V in 1106 the emperor was welcomed rapturously at Liège by Otbert and the populace. After his death there his relics and coffin were venerated with *immoderatus favor*. *Cantatorium*, pp. 237-38; Sigebert of Gembloux, *Chronica*, pp. 371-72.

lay investiture, a practice which was a central target of the Reform Papacy.[61] Warner of Grez and Cono of Montaigu were vassals of the prince-bishops, and Cono and his son Lambert belonged to a family which was at the centre of the government of the principality. Cono's brother, the Archdeacon Henry, was known as a patron of imperialist polemic literature, having commissioned Sigebert of Gembloux to compose letters and tracts in reply to Gregorian literature which had attempted to justify the deposition of Henry IV.[62] Rainald of Toul and his brother Peter of Dampierre held lands in Upper Lotharingia and France, but they were nephews of a prince-bishop of Liège, Henry of Verdun. The political opinions and counsel of these men must have had a strong influence on the title adopted by Godfrey. Considering their origins and background, it would be most likely for them to incline towards a model of real monarchic power, even if for diplomatic reasons the potentially sacrilegious title of king was avoided. It seems likely that in disregarding the claims for an ecclesiastical state the electors established a secular monarchy to administer the *regnum Iherusalem* and defend the Christian community, and that both of the titles adopted by Godfrey, *princeps* and *advocatus*, implied a sovereignty derived directly from God.[63]

The Composition of the *Domus Godefridi*

Most of the crusaders who had come as far as Jerusalem remained in and around the Holy City well into August 1099. When a large Fatimid army

---

[61] J. Steen Jensen, 'A Maastricht Coin Representing the Investiture of Bishop Otbert of Liège by the Emperor Henry IV in 1091', *Spink Numismatic Circular* 98 (1990), 310-11.

[62] J. Beumann, *Sigebert von Gembloux und der Traktat de investitura episcoporum* (Sigmaringen, 1976), esp. pp. 25-38.

[63] Hansen, *Das Problem eines Kirchenstaates in Jerusalem*, p. 21 sees proof of Godfrey's acceptance of an ecclesiastical state in an oath to protect the Holy Sepulchre sworn after his election. Yet the principal source cited by him, a passage in the *Hierosolymitana* of Ekkehard of Aura (p. 126), refers not to Godfrey but to the accession of his brother Baldwin I a year later. Similarly the passage of Albert of Aachen (AA pp. 485-86) also cited him relates to the election of Godfrey, described as *ductor, princeps atque praeceptor christiani exercitus*, but has no reference to an oath or even to the Holy Sepulchre. We cannot exclude the possibility that Godfrey did swear an oath of some kind, but we can be certain that it was not an oath of homage to the patriarch, who was not elected until 1 August 1099.

entered Palestine under the command of the vizier al-Afdal, the crusaders were able to meet it with most of the effective military forces available to the princes, gaining a major victory at Ascalon on 12 August.[64] Soon after this Robert of Flanders and Robert of Normandy left for Syria, from where they intended to journey on back to the West, and Raymond of Saint-Gilles went with them, still hoping to win a territory for himself in an area not yet seized by other crusaders. These three princes seem to have been accompanied by the majority of the crusaders who had come to Jerusalem, who now regarded their pilgrimages as having been completed.

In the summer of 1099 Muslim powers still controlled most of Palestine, including the ports of Tyre, Acre, Ascalon, Caesarea, Sidon and Beirut. The actual territory under Godfrey's control was small, consisting of two blocs: Judaea, with Jerusalem, Bethlehem, Jericho and Hebron, and a coastal strip around Jaffa, Lydda and Ramla. Jaffa was the key bridgehead and only point of approach for ships coming from the West, but its fortifications had been destroyed by the Muslim garrison before it abandoned the town, and Albert of Aachen implies that ships did not put in to the port in significant numbers until Godfrey had it refortified with Genoese and Pisan help in early 1100.[65] Communications between Jaffa and Jerusalem were liable to be threatened by Fatimid forces based at Ascalon. Galilee was under the control of Tancred, who was by no means amenable to Godfrey's direction, but was attempting to establish an independent principality and to extend his domains to the coast, with particular designs on Haifa.[66]

Godfrey needed not only to defend his two small blocs of territory, but also to extend his rule if the new state was to have any hope of survival. However, the departure of the majority of crusaders had greatly reduced the military resources available to him. By this stage the original Lotharingian element of the army had been considerably depleted as a result of death in battle, capture and disease. Some of those who had fought alongside him were now with his brother Baldwin in Edessa. Other Lotharingians and Germans returned home to the West. They included

[64] Röhricht, *Geschichte des Ersten Kreuzzuges*, pp. 199-204.

[65] AA pp. 514-15.

[66] M. Rheinheimer, *Das Kreuzfahrerfürstentum Galiläa* (Frankfurt am Main, 1990), pp. 64-66.

Peter of Dampierre, Rainald of Toul, Dudo of Cons, Cono and Lambert of Montaigu, Louis of Mousson and Hartmann of Dillingen.[67]

To a certain extent the losses from Godfrey's own contingent were made up by men from other contingents deciding to remain in Palestine. Yet he was left with a much reduced force, which a later source put at 300 knights and 2000 foot-soldiers.[68] On several occasions Albert of Aachen describes a group known as the *domus Godefridi, clientela Godefridi* or *domus ducis.* This term may have referred to Godfrey's immediate retinue rather than the entirety of the Frankish forces. It seems to have included aulic officials and other members of the household in the narrow sense, field commanders, governors of towns and other officials. The members of this group constituted the key personnel through which Godfrey's rule functioned from the summer of 1099 through to the accession of his brother in November 1100, an event in which they were instrumental. Prawer described the household as an 'anonymous group of knights called the *domus Godefridi*', concluding that 'it is likely that had there been any among them of prominence our sources would have pointed out the fact and mentioned their names'.[69] This is something of an exaggeration. Many of the *domus Godefridi* may have been obscure in origin, but it is possible to establish the identities of a significant number of them. On two occasions Albert of Aachen gives information on the composition of the group, and we can flesh out this detail by collecting the names of those charged with military activities or other responsibilities during the reign.[70]

Those originating from Lotharingia (or probably so) included Baldric the Seneschal, Franco of Maasmechelen, Gerard of Avesnes, Milo of Clermont, Ralph of Mousson, Stabelo the Chamberlain and Warner of Grez.[71] Gunter and Wicher were Germans who had probably joined Godfrey at Constantinople or Nicaea.[72] There were also three Normans, Ralph of Montpinçon, Robert of Apulia and Robert FitzGerard of Buonalbergo,[73] a Fleming, Wirich the Butler,[74] and a southern Frenchman,

---

[67] Prosopographical Catalogue, nos. 93, 99, 30, 27, 81, 84, 64.

[68] WT IX.19, p. 445.

[69] J. Prawer, 'Social Classes in the Latin Kingdom: The Franks', in *A History of the Crusades*, ed. Setton, 5: 128.

[70] AA pp. 526, 531-32. See also pp. 358, 447.

[71] Prosopographical Catalogue, nos. 17, 38, 47, 89, 104, 121, 133.

[72] Prosopographical Catalogue, nos. 62, 134.

[73] Prosopographical Catalogue, nos. 103, 110, 111.

Geldemar Carpinel, who had originally served with Raymond of Saint-Gilles.[75] Peter *Longobardus* probably came from the Norman dominions in southern Italy.[76] The origins of Adelolf, Geoffrey the Chamberlain, Lambert, Matthew the Seneschal and Rothold are uncertain.[77] If we consider the higher clergy at this stage, there are even fewer names, since there were as yet few bishoprics for them to occupy. Two are prominent: the Norman Robert, bishop of Lydda, and Arnulf of Chocques, a Fleming who had travelled with Robert of Normandy and who had been elected as patriarch of Jerusalem on 1 August 1099.[78] Another important cleric was the Lotharingian priest Robert, who became a key official of the chancery of Baldwin I, and who probably came to Palestine with Godfrey.[79] Those whose names have survived probably did not constitute the entire *domus Godefridi*, but it is likely that they were its most prominent members and representative of the group as a whole. Only about half of them were Lotharingians.

Since the territory controlled by Godfrey was small, he evidently did not wish to support his followers by the allocation of lordships, other than Hebron, which was granted to Gerard of Avesnes in March 1100, and Haifa, which he intended to give to Geldemar Carpinel, probably as a means of keeping it out of the control of Tancred.[80] Most of Godfrey's revenues seem to have come from two main sources: plunder, as for example the rich pickings after the battle of Ascalon;[81] and in the form of tribute paid by the Muslim cities of the coast, although this does not seem to have been forthcoming in significant quantities until early 1100.[82]

[74] Prosopographical Catalogue, no. 140.

[75] Prosopographical Catalogue, no. 44.

[76] AA p. 509.

[77] AA pp. 509-10. Prosopographical Catalogue, nos. 4, 44, 80, 88, 118. These men are known only from the evidence of Albert of Aachen. Since Albert is normally fairly well-informed about the places of origin of Lotharingians and Germans, the lack of detail in these cases may be an indication that these men had joined Godfrey from other contingents.

[78] Prosopographical Catalogue, nos. 113, 12.

[79] H. E. Mayer, *Die Kanzlei der lateinischen Könige von Jerusalem*, 2 vols (Hannover, 1996), 1:373-421. Prosopographical Catalogue, no.108.

[80] H. E. Mayer, 'Die Herrschaftsbildung in Hebron', *Zeitschrift des Deutschen Palästinavereins* 101 (1985), 64-82 (here 66).

[81] *GF* pp. 96-97.

[82] Röhricht, *Geschichte des Ersten Kreuzzuges*, p. 210.

Tribute was sometimes collected by Franks installed as overseers, as was done by Gerard of Avesnes in respect of Arsuf in late 1099. We later hear of the revenues from Arsuf being assigned to the Norman knight Robert of Apulia.[83] This case of hypothecated revenues may be the origin of the money-fief, which developed into one of the most lasting institutions of the kingdom. The fact that this kind of fief seems to have been the norm under Godfrey is confirmed by the information given to Baldwin I after his arrival by Godfrey's vassals, who described the fiefs as they had been assigned to each of them from the revenues of the towns.[84]

The analysis of the *domus Godefridi* suggests that although when Godfrey's army departed from the West it was almost entirely Lotharingian in composition, during his reign as *princeps* of Jerusalem, the Lotharingian element amounted to only approximately half of his following. By the end of the summer of 1099, a significant number of Lotharingians, including most of the prominent lords closest to Godfrey, had returned to Europe. Men from other contingents were now in his service or that of Baldwin, soon to come to Jerusalem bringing most of his vassals with him. It would thus be wrong to assume too great a continuity of membership between Godfrey's army as it existed on its departure from Europe and the nobility of the early Latin kingdom.

The Dispute between Monarchy and Patriarchate

The political climate of the nascent kingdom changed dramatically on the arrival in the Holy Land of Daibert, archbishop of Pisa. Daibert had long been known as a supporter of the Reform Papacy, and was an ally and associate of Urban II.[85] He arrived at Laodicea with a fleet of 120 ships from Pisa in September 1099, and then proceeded to Jerusalem in the company of Bohemund and Baldwin of Edessa, who wished to fulfil their crusading vows. They arrived in the Holy City on 21 December.

---

[83] AA pp. 514-15.

[84] AA p. 532: ...*requisivit de suppellectili fratris sui Godefridi, de armatura et pecunia ejus, de beneficiis cujusque militis ac praepotentis. Qui nichil se de rebus fratris ejus habere attestati sunt, sed eas in elemosinas pauperum et solvendis debitis esse dispersas; beneficia vero, prout cuique statuta errant de reditibus civitatum, protulerunt..*

[85] On Daibert's early career and especially the correct form of his name, see M. Matzke, *Daibert von Pisa. Zwischen Pisa, Papst und erstem Kreuzzug* (Sigmaringen, 1998), pp. 1-101.

Daibert and the Pisan fleet had been sent by the pope from Italy in the autumn of 1098; they were intended as reinforcements for the crusade, which had become bogged down in Antioch, and whose legate, Adhemar of Le Puy, had died the previous year. It is possible that Daibert had been appointed as legate by Urban to replace Adhemar, although the evidence for this is scant. Formulations used by Bernold of St Blasien and Guibert of Nogent seem to suggest a legatine status.[86] Yet in the Laodicea letter sent by him and leaders of the crusade to the new pope in September 1099 he is referred to merely as *Pisanus archiepiscopus* although, unlike Godfrey, he was undoubtedly present when this letter was written and thus had every opportunity as well as motive to insist on the correct use of his titles.[87] Matzke rationalises this discrepancy with the explanation that news of the death of Urban II (29 July 1099) had reached Syria by the time of Daibert's arrival. This would have meant that Daibert's legatine powers had expired, and Matzke concludes that he consciously refrained from exercising these powers.[88] Certainly the situation he found on his arrival no longer corresponded to what he had evidently been prepared for by Urban. He may have been sent to direct a leaderless crusading army in northern Syria, but he now found Jerusalem under Frankish control and three new Latin states established in the East under the government of secular rulers.

---

[86] Bernold of St Blasien, *Chronicon*, MGH SS 5: 466; GN p. 233. On these sources, see Matzke, *Daibert von Pisa*, pp. 135-39. A *notitium* of a donation of Tancred for the church of Mount Thabor, advanced as evidence of legatine status by Hamilton, *Latin Church*, pp. 15-16, and Matzke, *Daibert von Pisa*, p. 137 gives the formulation *presidente in Jerosolymis donno Dei gratia Patriarcha Dalberto, qui a Deo per apostolicam sedem in orientales regiones directus Latinorum primus sanctam eandem rexit ecclesiam*, yet this merely implies that he was sent to the East by the papacy: 'Cartulaire de Mont Thabor', no. 1, in *C. Hosp.* 2: 897-98 (= RRH no. 36).

[87] Hagenmeyer, *Epistulae*, no. 18. Two Pisan sources make reference to the fleet *quorum rector et ductor Daibertus Pisane urbis archiepiscopo excitito*, which merely reveals that he was commander of the fleet: Bernard Maragone, *Annales Pisani*, MGH SS 19: 239; *Gesta triumphalia per Pisanos facta*, in Rerum Italiarum Scriptores, ed. L. A. Muratori, 6/2: 89.

[88] Matzke, *Daibert von Pisa*, pp. 139-41. The text of the Laodicea letter (September 1099), addressed only to an unnamed *Domino papae Romanae ecclesiae*, indicates that by this time Urban's death was known to the crusaders, but that they were still unaware of who his successor was (Hagenmeyer, *Epistulae*, no. 18). Becker, *Papst Urban II.*, 2: 429 doubts Daibert's legatine status.

At Christmas 1099, only six days after Daibert's arrival in Jerusalem, the Patriarch Arnulf was deposed and Daibert elected in his place. This event is not immediately easy to understand. One explanation which has been advanced is that Arnulf was of illegitimate birth, being the son of a priest, which would have barred him from holding episcopal office.[89] Yet since he later was able to obtain a dispensation from Pope Paschal II there is no reason why he could not have applied for this in 1099 if his illegitmacy was regarded as a canonical impediment. A more serious objection is that Arnulf's election was regarded as requiring ratification by the pope or his representative.[90] It is difficult to judge this, since the election of a Latin Christian to an eastern patriarchate was a novel event without obvious precedent. However, if Daibert's legatine powers had lapsed by this stage then presumably he would not have had the authority to confirm Arnulf's election or not. Daibert's own election was carried out by clergy and people, but the obvious influence of Godfrey, Bohemund of Antioch and Baldwin of Edessa in it was hardly in the spirit of the Gregorian Reform, and neither was the fact that Daibert would thereby be a pluralist on a grand scale, holding the patriarchate in addition to his Italian archbishopric.[91] The fact that Arnulf did not contest the decision, but was compensated with the office of archdeacon of Jerusalem, suggests that the whole hurried procedure was something of a political fix reflecting the temporary coincidence of the interests of Daibert, Godfrey and Bohemund, in which agreement was reached through Arnulf being prevailed upon to give up the patriarchate. Whether or not Daibert was personally ambitious, as is often assumed, is difficult to say, but if he was to carry out the mission of building up the Latin church in the East, then the position of patriarch offered the best basis for this. Bohemund, who was occupying territories which the Byzantine emperor regarded as having been illegally kept from him by the crusaders, required some sort of legitimation as prince of Antioch, and he was more likely to receive this from Daibert than from the Greek patriarch of Antioch, John of Oxeia. Godfrey did not require legitimation in the same way that Bohemund did, since there were no Byzantine claims on his territories, but he did have a more practical need, namely the assistance of the Pisan fleet, which could

[89] GN p. 233; Hamilton, *The Latin Church*, p. 13; Matzke, *Daibert von Pisa*, p. 157.
[90] Hamilton, *The Latin Church*, p. 14; Matzke, *Daibert von Pisa*, p. 158.
[91] The cathedral chapter of Pisa did not elect a successor until after Daibert's death.

only be enlisted by way of an accommodation with the Pisan archbishop. The election of Daibert therefore needs to be seen in connection with other constitutional acts that took place at Christmas 1099.

Shortly after the election of the new patriarch, Godfrey and Bohemund took part in a ceremony in which Daibert gave some sort of confirmation of their rule. According to Fulcher of Chartres, at Christmas 1099 both Godfrey and Bohemond received their lands from the new patriarch 'for the love of God'.[92] However, Fulcher's account is not placed by him in the context of the events of 1100, but in a passage dealing with a dispute between the Latin patriarchs of Jerusalem and Antioch in 1124 concerning supremacy over the archbishopric of Tyre. William of Tyre relates that Godfrey and Bohemund received the 'investiture' (*investitura*) of kingdom and principality respectively.[93] One can quickly grasp why Bohemund was keen on having his possession of Antioch confirmed by a Latin church authority, but Daibert's motivation and jurisdiction in doing so must have been questionable, since his authority as patriarch of Jerusalem did not extend to Antioch; he seems to have had no qualms about infringing the rights of John of Oxeia, whom both papacy and crusaders alike had recognised as the legitimate patriarch of Antioch.[94] This act in itself suggests that Daibert was going further in his ambit than anything Urban II had envisaged.

The interpretation of the investiture of Godfrey is more problematic. Older scholarship, especially the influential work of Joseph Hansen, regarded it as an acceptance of Daibert's theocratic ideas, namely that the Holy Land was regarded as an ecclesiastical state.[95] However, this view

---

[92] FC III.34, pp. 741-42: *In Hierusalem quoque dux Godefridus et dominus Boamundus acceperunt terram suam a patriarcha Daiberto propter amore Dei.*

[93] WT IX.15, pp. 440-41: *Predicto ergo viro dei in sede collocato, tam dominus dux Godefridus quam princeps Boamundus, hic regni, ille principatus, humiliter ab eo susceperunt investituram.*

[94] Hamilton, *The Latin Church*, pp. 7, 53.

[95] Hansen, *Das Problem eines Kirchenstaates in Jerusalem,* pp. 42-49. In earlier scholarship Hansen's book is one of the most frequently cited works on the relationship between Godfrey and Daibert. Hansen argues that there were three possible models for the government of Jerusalem. The first of these, a strong centralised monarchy, is immediately dismissed on the grounds that it was too advanced for the time: 'Die Gemüter am Ende des 11. Jahrhunderts waren jedoch auf ein zentralisches Regiment noch nicht vorbereitet' (p. 13). This effectively leaves two possible models: either a monarchy with a loose feudal structure, or an ecclesiastical state with the patriarch at its head, along the pattern of the Papal States in Italy or the

fails to take the element of expediency into account. Godfrey clearly had to make some concessions to Daibert in order to gain the assistance of the Pisan fleet. Like many political agreements and public acts in medieval and modern life, the investiture could be interpreted and explained by each party in different ways. Godfrey and his supporters could have regarded it as merely similar to ceremonies in which western monarchs were given consecration or inauguration by the senior ecclesiastics of their realms, or possibly even, bearing Godfrey's own background in mind, analogous to the constitutional situation by which an elected king of Germany was not regarded as possessing full imperial authority until he had been crowned by the pope.

What is much more important is the matter of temporal power in Frankish Palestine. After his installation as patriarch, Daibert proceeded with a campaign to change the relationship between the ecclesiastical and the secular powers in the Latin state. It is generally held that in the second

---

episcopal principalities in Germany (pp. 13-18). Hansen claims that the idea of a theocratic state was approved by the papacy and originally propounded in Palestine by the *first* Latin patriarch, Arnulf of Chocques, a view which can hardly be upheld in light of Arnulf's loyal and co-operative attitude towards Godfrey and Baldwin I. Hansen describes Godfrey acting as a 'military advocate of the Holy Sepulchre' and loyal vassal of Armulf during the first six months of his rule; only after the advent of Daibert did he supposedly wish to rule as an independent prince (p. 40). This interpretation completely ignores the changing relative strengths of Godfrey and the patriarchate, and Hansen fails to explain convincingly why Godfrey should suddenly wish to increase his authority relative to that of the patriarch at a time when his position was considerably weaker than it had been in the summer of 1099, advancing only an unmotivated change of heart: 'Gottfried war anfangs dem Verlangen Daimberts total abgeneigt. Die Zeit war vorüber, wo er sich mit der Rolle eines militärischen Vogts von Jerusalem begnügte. Er wollte in dem neuen Reich als selbständiger Fürst das Regiment führen' (p. 48). One of the great weaknesses of Hansen's work is his tendency to interpret events in the light of the presumed character of the personages concerned, rather than the other way around. At times these presumptions border on self-contradiction, as in the judgement of Godfrey's character: 'Überwiegend Choleriker, war er stets einer Sache entweder mit Leib und Seele ergeben oder abgeneigt. War jedoch das erste Feuer der Begeisterung vorüber so verstand er es ebenfalls, den Umständen entsprechend nachzugeben'. Similarly, having just argued for Godfrey's determination to increase his power, Hansen is forced to explain his sudden acceptance of Daibert's claims as the triumph of religious feeling ('das religiöse Gefühl') over Godfrey's chivalric nature ('Ritternatur').

half of his short reign Godfrey was obliged to make three separate concessions of territory to Daibert: at Christmas 1099, a quarter of the city of Jerusalem; at Candlemas 1100, a quarter of the city of Jaffa; and at Easter 1100, the remainder of Jerusalem including the Tower of David, as well as the remainder of Jaffa.[96] Taken together, these concessions represent a considerable proportion of the territory under Godfrey's control at this stage. Leaving aside for the moment the question of the evidence, each of the three concessions needs to be looked at separately. The first can best be explained as relating to the north-western quadrant of Jerusalem, centred on the church of the Holy Sepulchre and the patriarchal palace, which had been in the possession of the patriarchate during Muslim rule.[97] Since the Patriarch's Quarter, as it came to be known, continued to be held by the church as a temporal lordship long after Godfrey's death, there is no reason to doubt that Godfrey actually made this grant, or – to put it more precisely – confirmed the patriarchate's possession.[98] By contrast, there is no evident precedent for the second concession, that is the acquisition of a quarter of Jaffa by the patriarch. Nevertheless, it can be seen as an understandable demand by Daibert in his dual role of patriarch and representative of the maritime interests of Pisa. At that moment Jaffa was the only port in Palestine under Christian control, and it was the usual place of disembarkation for pilgrims going to Jerusalem. While Jaffa would remain vital for pilgrim traffic, it might be desirable, though hardly necessary, for the patriarchate to have a foothold in this city, but it is much more likely that the demand for a quarter of Jaffa derived from the commercial interests of the city of Pisa, whose ships could be expected to convey much of the commercial trade and pilgrim traffic of the kingdom in the future. The concession of a section of a city to a naval power assisting in its capture was in line with later privileges offered or made by kings of Jerusalem to the republics of Venice and Genoa, and should not be regarded as unusual. The third reported concession – three-quarters each of Jerusalem and Jaffa, in effect both cities in their entirety – is the most problematic. It would have meant that Godfrey was handing over both his capital and the only port of the Frankish settlements, while retaining only minimal territory for

[96] WT IX.16-18, pp. 441-42, X.4, pp. 456-58.

[97] J. Prawer, *Crusader Institutions* (Oxford, 1980), pp. 296-301.

[98] H. E. Mayer, *Bistümer, Klöster und Stifte im Königreich Jerusalem* (Stuttgart, 1977), pp. 7-9.

himself. It is therefore most important that a rider to the third concession stipulated that Godfrey was to remain in possession of Jerusalem and Jaffa until he was able to conquer other comparable cities, although if he should die without an heir before achieving this, they were to pass immediately to the patriarch.[99]

Nothing about the second and third concessions is mentioned in any contemporary source; the sole authority for them is William of Tyre, writing over seventy years after the events. Moreover, all of the relevant details given by him can be seen to derive from a section of his chronicle, entitled *Epistola domini Daiberti ad principem Antiochenum*, which supposedly represents the text of a letter sent by Daimbert to Bohemund I of Antioch after the death of Godfrey on 18 July 1099.[100] This text sets out

---

[99] WT IX.16-18, pp. 441-42, X.4, pp. 456-58.

[100] WT X.4, pp. 456-58: *Scis, fili karissime, quoniam me ignorantem et invitum, bone tamen ac sancte intentionis affectu, in eam, que omnium ecclesiarum singularis est mater et gentium domina, rectorem et patriarcham elegeris electumque communi tam cleri ac plebis quam principum assensu in huius summe dignitatis sedem, licet indignum, dei preeunte gratia locaveris. In quo ego culmine constitutus quanta pericula, quot labores, quot persecutiones sustineam, iniuriis offensus mille, meus cognoscit animus, cognoscit et ipse omnium inspector Christus. Vix enim Dux Godefridus, dum adhuc viveret, non tam proprie voluntatis arbitrio quam malorum persuasione seductus, ea reliquit ecclesie tenenda, que Turcorum temporibus qui tunc fuerat patriarcha tenuerat et sancta ecclesia, cum amplius honorari et exaltari debuit, tunc maiora desolationis atque confusionis sue obprobria sustinuit. Resipuit ille tamen per misericordiam dei et ab impietatis desistens proposito, in die Purificationis beate Marie de Ioppe quartam partem ecclesie Sancti Sepulchri dedit et post in die Paschalis sollempnitatis, iam ultra superbe sapere aut in seculari pompa confidere respuens, divino nutu compunctus cuncta que iuris erant ecclesie libera reddidit et homo Sancti Sepulchri ac noster effectus fideliter deo et nobis se amodo militaturum spopondit. Reddidit itaque nostre potestati turrim David cum tota Ierosolimitana urbe eiusque pertinentiis et quod in Ioppe ipse tenebat, sic tamen, ut ob rerum temporalium insufficientiam nostra concessione ipse hec tam diu teneret, donec illum deus in captione Babilonis aut aliarum urbium amplificasset; si autem absque herede masculo ille moreretur, hec omnia cum in presentia totius cleri ac populi in die sollempni Pasche ante sacrosanctum Sepulchrum confirmasset, etiam in lecto egritudinis, de qua mortuus est, coram multis et probatis testibus ipse constituit. Quo defuncto comes Garnerius, ut hostis contra ecclesiam dei insurgens, fidem pactumque iusticie nichili pendens turrim David contra nos munivit et legatis suis ad Balduinum directis mandat, uti ecclesiam dei drepturus resque eius violenter occupaturus quantocius veniat. Unde iudicio dei percussus quarto post obitum ducis die obiit. Hoc ipso autem mortuo viri ignobiles ac de plebe adhuc eandem turrim cum tota urbe occupantes tenent, adventum Balduini ad ruinam ecclesie et totius Christianitatis interitum prestolantes. Ast ego, qui solius dei clementie tueque dilectioni, fili karissime, sum relictus, miseriis omnibus calumpniisque insidiantium michi malignorum circumventus, tibi soli, quia in te solo post deum confido et spei mee*

details of the concessions of Christmas, Candlemas and Easter, adding that they were confirmed by Godfrey on his death-bed. It also claims that after Godfrey's death, Warner of Grez and his men had seized the Tower of David and summoned Godfrey's brother Baldwin to come to Jerusalem. The implication of these statements is that the men of the *domus Godefridi* had urged Baldwin to seize the kingdom, and in doing so were acting in defiance of existing agreements and of Godfrey's testament. The evident purpose of the letter was to encourage Daibert's ally Bohemund to prevent Baldwin coming to Jerusalem, a move which it claims would lead to the 'ruin of the church'.

This text cannot be regarded as faithfully reproducing an original letter composed by Daibert; most authorities accept that its phraseology shows at least editorial intervention by William of Tyre. Edbury and Rowe think it possible that 'William himself composed it on the basis of a report of such a letter having been sent', which he found in sources which have not survived.[101] There is no reason to doubt that some message was sent by Daibert to Bohemund, since Albert of Aachen reports that a letter carried by his secretary Morellus was intercepted at Laodicea by followers of

---

anchoram in tue dilectionis soliditate figo, tibi, inquam, soli quas patior erumpnas, immo quas ecclesia patitur, voce flebili et anxia cogitatio ne refero. Tu autem, si quid pietatis habes et nisi paterne glorie vis esse degener filius, qui tyrannica crudelitate clausum ab impia manu domnum apostolicum G(regorium) de urbe Roma eripuit, unde memorabile seculis omnibus nomen emeruit, omni occasione remota festina venire et, terre regnique tui cura in militibus tuis prudentioribuis sapienter disposita, sancte ecclesie miserabiliter laboranti misericorditer succure. Et certe scis ipse quoniam auxilium tuum consiliumque promiseris et debitorem te sancte ecclesie ac michi sponte tua feceris. Scribe igitur ad Balduinum litteras, interdicens ei ne sine licentia nostra et legatione, cum ille tecum in patriarcham et rectorem ecclesie Ierosolimitane me elegerit, sanctam ecclesiam devastaturus et res eius occupaturus ullo modo veniat, monstrans ei quoniam inrationabile est tot pro eadem ecclesia labores sustinuisse totque pericula ut illa libera fieret, si nunc vilis et abiecta servire cogatur illis, quibus dominari et preesse materno iure debet. Quod si ille, iusticie resistens, rationabilibus acquiescere noluerit, per eam quam beato Petro obedientiam debes te contestor, ut quibuscumque modis vales aut etiam, si necesse sit, vi adventum eius impedias. Quicquid autem super his que mando tu facturus sis, galea tua ad me sub festinatione missa per hunc eundem, quem ad te mitto, nuntium, michi karissime, manifesta

[101] P. W. Edbury and J. G. Rowe, *William of Tyre, Historian of the Latin East* (Cambridge, 1988), pp. 49-50. Edbury and Rowe suggest that the letter or its source material may have been originally composed in connection with a *later* dispute between church and monarchy, possibly that involving the Patriarch Stephen and Baldwin II.

Raymond of Saint-Gilles.[102] Even William himself took an ambivalent attitude to the evidence of the text he incorporated in his chronicle. He was certainly able to satisfy himself that it was right for the church to hold the Patriarch's Quarter, whose origins he elucidates, but he found it difficult to accept the validity of some of the other claims set out in the letter. He admits that he was hard put to reconcile Daibert's claims with the constitutional status of the state as he had understood it to have been established by the leaders of the crusade.[103] In particular, he was unable to explain with what justification Daibert was able to claim all of Jaffa and Jerusalem.

Even if the terms of the purported letter are to be regarded as genuine, and consented to by Godfrey, its conditions could still be interpreted as an attempt by him to buy time by making concessions which would only take effect at a later date. Godfrey was not required to surrender Jaffa and the greater part of Jerusalem until such time as he could be compensated with comparable newly conquered cities, and since one of these is identified as *Babylon* (i.e. Cairo), this was a condition which could hardly be met quickly. At this time most of the coast of Palestine was still under Egyptian control, and up to 1105 at least, it was the Fatimids who were able to mount major invasions of Frankish territory, rather than the other way round. Thus, until Godfrey gained comparable territories, the patriarch could not claim Jerusalem and Jaffa in their entirety unless Godfrey died without heirs.

It has been argued that the agreements gave Godfrey a huge incentive to marry and produce an heir, since this would negate the consequences of the final concession.[104] However, neither the purported letter of Daibert nor William's own exegesis of its reported concessions actually stipulated that Godfrey had to be succeeded by an heir *of his own body* for the third concession to become invalid. Rather, they specify a 'legitimate

---

[102] AA p. 524.

[103] *Hec omnia, etsi aliorum relatione comperta et etiam quorundam opera scripto mandata, presenti interseruimus narrationi, miramur tamen quibus rationibus motus dominus patriarcha hanc adversus ducem suscitaverit questionem, cum nec uspiam legerimus aut a viris fide dignis audierimus, ea conditione domino duci regnum a victoribus principibus fuisse traditum, ut alicui persone alicuius prestationis annue vel perpetue vinculo se sciret obligatum.* WT IX.16-17, pp. 441-42.

[104] Mayer, *Bistümer, Klöster und Stifte*, pp. 36-37; M-L. Favreau-Lilie, *Die Italiener im Heiligen Land vom ersten Kreuzzug bis zum Tode Heinrichs von Champagne (1098-1197)* (Amsterdam, 1989), pp. 57-59, 75-79.

heir' (*legitimo ... herede*) and a 'male heir' (*herede masculo*).[105] Godfrey was unmarried and had no legitimate children, but of course he had two heirs who were both male and legitimate: his brothers Eustace, count of Boulogne, and Baldwin I, count of Edessa.[106] If the agreements *had* specified that the heir needed to be a child of Godfrey's, then he did indeed have an incentive to marry, but this was not easily done in the circumstances. Any marriage partner would need to belong to a branch of Christianity that was in communion with the Latin church, and be of suitable social standing. It is questionable how many unmarried aristocratic women of appropriate rank were available in the Latin settlements in the spring of 1100. In Palestine there was no social group among the native Christians that the Franks would have accepted as noble, in contrast to the situation in Syria and Cilicia where there was an Armenian population with a native aristocracy, many of whom belonged to the orthodox rather than the monophysite faith; Godfrey's brother Baldwin married into this class.[107] In the second half of the twelfth century two kings of Jerusalem (Baldwin III and Amalric) found wives from the Byzantine imperial family. In 1099, however, given the fraught relationship between Alexios Komnenos and the Frankish states it is questionable whether he would have been willing to provide a Byzantine princess for a ruler of such short standing as Godfrey. Therefore, if it were politically necessary for Godfrey to have an heir of his own body, this would have entailed possibly protracted negotiations with a suitable dynasty in the West, and a lengthy journey of a marriage partner to Jerusalem. Given these difficulties it is hard to see Godfrey and his advisors agreeing to such a condition. But if the agreements with Daibert recognised that Godfrey could be succeeded by *any* legitimate male heir, then such practical considerations could hardly have been regarded as problematic for Godfrey and his advisors.

A further problem with the evidence provided by William of Tyre is that it is contradicted by two other sources which give a different interpretation of Godfrey's testamentary dispositions. Albert of Aachen relates

[105] WT IX.16, p. 441, X.4, p. 456.

[106] Claims that Godfrey had a son in England are erroneous. See Appendix A, 'The Descendants of Eustace II of Boulogne'.

[107] B. Hamilton, 'Women in the Crusader States: The Queens of Jerusalem, 1100-1190', in *Medieval Women*, ed. Derek Baker (Oxford, 1978), pp. 143-74; J. H. Forse, 'Armenians and the First Crusade', *Journal of Medieval History* 17 (1991), 13-22.

that Daibert's approach to Bohemund was in contravention of the oath both Daibert and Tancred had sworn to Godfrey that no-one but *one of his brothers or another of his blood* should be allowed to succeed to the kingdom of Jerusalem.[108] Radulph of Caen portrays a death-bed scene in which Daibert, the Archdeacon Arnulf and others unanimously agreed by oath to Godfrey's designation of Baldwin as his successor. Although we cannot regard the speeches quoted as verbatim reproductions, the import of Radulph's account essentially agrees with that of Albert.[109] The purported letter of Daibert also contains at least one internal contradiction, in that it recognises the possibility of Godfrey being succeeded by an heir, which is difficult to reconcile with what it says about Daibert's attempts to prevent that heir taking up the inheritance. This suggests that whatever evidence lay behind William of Tyre's reconstruction of the letter, it is more likely to represent Daibert's unilateral and tendencious interpretation of the constitutional position rather than something to which Godfrey had agreed.

The earlier discussion of Baldwin before the crusade has shown that he was already recognised as Godfrey's heir in Lotharingia in 1095-96. It is also probable that this position was accepted among the *domus Godefridi.* The role of one man especially was crucial. The Lotharingian nobleman Warner, count of Grez, was a kinsman of Godfrey; he had witnessed at least one of the acts of Godfrey and his mother Ida at which Baldwin's

---

[108] AA p. 524: *Legatio denique haec Patriarchae et Tancredi sine mora directa est. Verum ejusdem legationis portitor, Morellus nomine, secretarius Patriarchae, quia in dolo missus est et contra jusjurandum quod idem Patriarcha Duci fecerat cum Tancredo, si forte obiret, nulli regnum Iherusalem se reddituros, nisi fratribus suis aut uni de sanguine ejus, ira Dei adversante, Laodicae in manus Reimundi comitis irruit.*

[109] Radulph of Caen, *Gesta Tancredi in expeditione Hierosolymitana*, RHC Occ. 3: 705: *Nam Gottifredus, rex optimus et timens Deum, capto mox Boamundo, ex hac luce migravit. Erat enim jam annus evolutus ex quo regnare coeperat, quum ad obitum pervenisset. Qui tamen antequam praesenti luce caruisset, dum corporis infirmate teneretur, ad se patriarcham Daybertum atque Arnulfum, ceterosque accersiri jubet, quibus ille: 'Ecce', inquit 'viam universae terrae ingredior. Modo ergo, adhuc me vivente, consilium inter vos habeatur; et quis vice mei in Jerusalem regnare debeat praevidentur'. At illi respondentes: 'Nos', inquiunt, 'magis hoc in tua providentia ponimus, et quem nobis ad hoc ipsum elegeris, ei procul dubio subdemur'. At ille: 'Si, inquit, in mea dispositione statuitur, Balduinum fratrem meum ad hoc culmen suscipiendum idoneum judico'. At illi Balduinum audientes, continuo unanimiter consentiunt, laudant, eique jurejurando fidelitate firmata subduntur: quoniam illum virum liberalem pecuniae, studiosum militiae, affata humilem, magnanimitate sublimem cognoverant.*

status as Godfrey's heir was implicitly recognised; he had served in a prominent capacity in Godfrey's army on crusade, and he now acted as leader of the *domus Godefridi* in its attempt to do justice to Baldwin's status. When they defied the Patriarch Daibert after the death of Godfrey of Bouillon, the men of the *domus Godefridi* were actually attempting to put into effect a designated dynastic succession.

Daibert's demands for temporal power in Jerusalem and Jaffa can well be interpreted as being an attempt to secure the *libertas ecclesiae* in the spirit of the Gregorian Reform.[110] Yet it is questionable whether the extent of his demands were in accordance with the aims of either Urban II, who had determined his mission, or of Urban's successor Paschal II. The political situation Daibert found in existence in the East was quite different from what his mission from Urban had envisaged, and he was attempting to change a political settlement in Palestine that had been established by the leaders of the crusade and accepted by the local representatives of the Latin church. Matzke argues that Daibert's demands were an inducement to Godfrey to expand the Christian territory, and therefore contributed to the military security of the Holy Sepulchre, yet all indications are that Godfrey and the rest of the Frankish population were quite aware of the need for expansion, and were doing everything in their power to bring this about before Daibert's arrival.[111]

The balance of power turned back in Godfrey's favour with the departure of the Pisan fleet in the spring of 1100, and the arrival of a Venetian fleet in June allowed the campaigns against the coastal cities to be continued. However, the siege of Acre by land and sea, which would have secured an excellent harbour if it had proved successful, was interrupted by news that Godfrey had died on 18 July. Daibert's attempt to prevent Baldwin succeeding to the kingdom was an action which went beyond any agreements he had reached with Godfrey, and threatened civil war in Frankish Palestine between the supporters of Daibert and Tancred, who controlled Galilee, and Godfrey's forces (and probably most of the rest of the Frankish population), which controlled Judaea and the coast. On Godfrey's death Warner of Grez and his followers seized the Tower of David, as the Franks called the citadel of Jerusalem. Godfrey's

---

110 Matzke, *Daibert von Pisa*, pp. 166-67.
111 Matzke, *Daibert von Pisa*, p. 167.

supporters also had control of Jaffa.[112] These actions were made easier by the fact that Daibert and Tancred had moved north from the siege of Acre in an attempt to take the port of Haifa. The resulting situation was something of a stalemate that continued into the autumn. Warner of Grez died on 22 July, only four days after the demise of his lord. Yet Godfrey's retinue continued to act with the same determination that Warner had demonstrated. Leadership was now provided by Geldemar Carpinel, Arnulf of Chocques and Robert, bishop of Lydda, the involvement of the last two being an indication that the Latin church in Jerusalem was anything but unanimous in support of the patriarch. In the name of Godfrey's followers, Robert and two knights set off for Edessa, to bring Baldwin the message that he should come to Jerusalem to secure the succession to his brother's kingdom.[113]

---

[112] In October Tancred was refused admittance by the garrison of Jaffa, and besieged the city for a short time: AA p. 531.
[113] AA p. 526.

Chapter IV

Baldwin I as King of Jerusalem
(1100-18)

The Accession of Baldwin I

The question of the succession hung in the balance in the period between news reaching Baldwin of his brother's death, and his own arrival in Palestine in November 1100. Baldwin was determined to contest the issue; he handed over the county of Edessa to his kinsman Baldwin of Bourcq, and took with him a substantial number of his Edessan followers, including the historian Fulcher of Chartres, and Hugh of Fauquembergues, who was sent with Robert of Lydda ahead of the main party to establish contact with the garrison of the Tower of David in Jerusalem. Baldwin's supporters thus had warning of his arrival, which occurred on or around 9 November, and probably were instrumental in staging a welcoming ceremony in which he was met by Franks, Greeks, and Syrians and conducted to the church of the Holy Sepulchre.[1] According to Ekkehard of Aura, Baldwin then pledged himself to serve the Sepulchre.[2] It would seem that these events were intended to be a public demonstration of support from the different ethnic groups various making up the urban population as well as an official inauguration or consecration of Baldwin's rule. The Patriarch Daibert was not present at the Holy Sepulchre, since he remained at the abbey of Mount Zion, a religious house which had probably been founded by him.[3] It lay just beyond the southern wall of the city, and therefore was one of the few places near Jerusalem to which the patriarch could gain access, since Godfrey's knights were refusing entry to all but Baldwin's supporters.

---

[1] FC II.3, p. 368; For the date, see T. Vogtherr, 'Die Regierungsdaten der lateinischen Könige von Jerusalem', *Zeitschrift des Deutschen Palästinavereins* 110 (1994), 51-81 (here 53-54).

[2] Ekkehard of Aura, p. 162: *nec multo post inclinans caput suum super dominici sepulchri tumbam ipsius se servituti perpetualiter subiugavit.*

[3] FC II.3, p. 368; Mayer, *Bistümer, Klöster und Stifte*, pp. 230-35; Matzke, *Daibert von Pisa*, p. 181.

Baldwin's initial oath of office, if it can be called that, was made 'to the Sepulchre', and thus by implication to God directly, rather than to the absent patriarch. This ceremony may have been carried out in conscious imitation of a precedent set by Godfrey, who, it will be remembered, was inaugurated as ruler before the election of Arnulf of Chocques as patriarch. Nevertheless, from Baldwin's point of view this was a far from ideal solution as long as he lacked recognition from the highest ecclesiastical authority in the kingdom. There is some evidence that at first Baldwin continued to use those titles adopted by Godfrey. For Albert of Aachen, Baldwin had come to assume the *regnum Iherusalem*, the *regnum Godefridi ducis* or the *thronum regni eius*.[4] During the period between his arrival in Jerusalem and his coronation at Christmas, Albert tends to refer to Baldwin as *princeps*.[5] At one point a hybrid title of *rex Christianorum et princeps Iherusalem* is mentioned, but after the coronation Baldwin is generally called *rex*, sometimes with the addition *et defensor*.[6]

Daibert was a cleric who had been in the forefront of the Gregorian Reform movement during the pontificate of Urban II. Baldwin was undoubtedly aware of the issues in the great struggle between *regnum* and *sacerdotium*, both from his own early clerical training and his brother Godfrey's experiences in Lotharingia, which had been one of the principal battlegrounds of the Investiture Contest. During November and December Baldwin and his advisers must have rapidly became convinced of the unambiguous political advantages of a royal title and the attributes that went with it. In this respect the rite of unction was particularly important, as it gave a king a mystical, quasi-divine power and was a formal and tangible demonstration of the idea that royal authority derived from God.[7] Another practical imperative was the need to counter any claims from Tancred that implied he was an independent ruler of part of Palestine. The acquisition of Haifa in defiance of Godfrey, who had assigned it to his follower Geldemar Carpinel, extended Tancred's domains from Galilee to the coast, making the establishment of an independent princi-

[4] AA pp. 524, 531.

[5] AA pp. 527, 529, 534, 536.

[6] AA p. 526.

[7] F. Kern, *Gottesgnadentum und Widerstandsrecht im früheren Mittelalter: Zur Entwicklungsgeschichte der Monarchie* (Münster, 1954), pp. 68-95; Hamilton, *The Latin Church*, p. 55. Up to 1109/1110 Baldwin's documents emphasise the legitimacy of his succession to Godfrey: Mayer, *Die Kanzlei der lateinischen Könige*, 1: 31.

pality a practical possibility. Haifa was recovered from Tancred in November, but this was by no means final. Tancred and his forces remained the major support for Daibert and were thus a potential focus of Frankish opposition to the new monarch until Tancred left Palestine to assume the regency of Antioch in March 1101.[8] The adoption of a royal title by Baldwin would not only express his position as a ruler independent of the church, but also stress his overlordship over Tancred and Galilee.

By Christmas, Daimbert seems to have recognised that his position was no longer tenable, and came to an arrangement with Baldwin. Fulcher of Chartres reports that an objection was raised to a royal coronation in Jerusalem, the city where Christ had worn a crown of thorns.[9] This statement may be an echo of arguments used by Daibert and his supporters in the period before the coronation. It is less likely that the religious fervour and messianic feeling, evident at the election of Godfrey, were anything like as strong a year later. The majority of the pilgrims, their crusading vows fulfilled, had returned to the West. Most of those who remained were of necessity practical people who had to buckle down to the task of ensuring the survival of the Frankish community in the Holy Land. The decision by Baldwin and his advisors to hold the coronation ceremony in Bethlehem got round possible accusations of sacrilege, but there were no serious objections to Baldwin being crowned king, and Daibert's participation amounted to a public abandonment of his theocratic claims. The balance of power had changed. Since Daibert and his ally Tancred were no longer able to challenge Baldwin's possession of Jerusalem and Judaea, the longer the patriarch refused an accommodation, the greater the likelihood that Baldwin might seek a coronation from another ecclesiastical authority, which would have created a precedent damaging to the standing of the patriarchate. Thus it was that Daibert came to crown and anoint Baldwin in the church of the Nativity in Bethlehem on Christmas Day 1100.[10] The auspicious place and date indicate that the avoidance of Jerusalem was not really a major concession to Daibert and his party; the coronation at Christmas in the second most important place

---

[8] FC II.7, pp. 390-93; AA pp. 537-38; Rheinheimer, *Das Kreuzfahrerfürstentum Galiläa*, pp. 102-7.

[9] FC II.6, pp. 384-90.

[10] AA pp. 536-37; FC II.6, pp. 384-85.

of pilgrimage in the Holy Land clearly associated Baldwin I with Christ and the succession of the Jewish kings. In fact, a comparison with Judas Maccabaeus was evidently one that Baldwin approved of and encouraged. In 1118 he was himself buried in the church of the Holy Sepulchre. Although his tomb did not survive the Muslim occupation it is likely that it bore the inscription:

> REX BALDWINUS, IUDAS ALTER MACHABAEUS,
> SPES PATRIAE, VIGOR ECCLESIAE, VIRTUS UTRIUSQUE.[11]

This evidence indicates that the monarchy's adoption of the royal title and its appropriation of the royal Jewish tradition were no longer regarded as sacrilegious but on the contrary, had received the highest ecclesiastical sanction.

The Composition of the Ruling Class

The Frankish lords, knights and higher clergy who remained in or came to the Holy land after the summer of 1099 were the main instruments through which Baldwin I governed and defended the kingdom of Jerusalem. They constituted a very small group. After the conquest of Palestine the Franks remained a minority among the native population, which consisted mainly of Muslims and Christians of various rites, most of whom spoke Arabic or Syriac. There were small groups of Jews and Samaritans. Most of the Frankish population were burgesses, living in towns and some rural settlements. Because of this legal distinction it seems appropriate to regard the nobility as constituting one group, from the lords of important cities down to simple knights with no vassals of their own.[12] Nevertheless, there were considerable differences of status within the noble class. The sources usually distinguish a higher nobility, called *principes*, *proceres* or *optimates*, from the majority of the knights (*milites*). On the death of Godfrey, his brother Baldwin was summoned to assume the throne by the *milites et principes regni Iherusalem*.[13] On his arrival in Jerusalem he was welcomed by the *universi milites et principes de domo ducis*

---

[11] Sabino de Sandoli, *Corpus inscriptionum crucesignatorum terrae sanctae 1099-1291* (Jerusalem, 1974), pp. 57-58.
[12] Prawer, 'Social Classes in the Latin Kingdom: The Franks', 5: 117-92.
[13] AA p. 526F.

Godefridi.[14] The *optimates nostri et equites cuncti* at the First Battle of Ramla would appear to be a parallel formulation.[15]

In the period 1100-18 the kingdom was far smaller in extent compared to the second half of the twelfth century. The reign of Baldwin I saw a gradual conquest of the Muslim coastal cities and of inland border areas such as the Transjordan. However, on his death the major ports of Tyre and Ascalon still remained under Muslim control. Even allowing for tribute and booty as additional (and sometimes irregular) income, the amount of land and revenues that could be used to support military service was much smaller than in subsequent reigns. There were as yet no military orders, which made an increasingly significant contribution to the forces of the kingdom after the foundation of the Order of the Temple and the militarisation of the Order of the Hospital.

An idea of the number of knights in the following years can be obtained from accounts of the military campaigns fought by the army of the kingdom. In cases of major invasions from Egypt or Damascus, garrisons were reduced to an absolute minimum in order to raise as large a field army as possible.[16] The First Battle of Ramla (7-8 September 1101) was fought *cum omni virtute peditum et equitum.* The number of knights was put at either 260,[17] or 300.[18] The army at the Second Battle of Ramla (17 May 1102) had 200 knights, but many of these were probably westerners who had arrived with the crusade of 1101. This army was defeated by the Egyptians in an initial engagement, but before joining battle again it was subsequently reinforced by 80 more knights from Galilee under Hugh of Fauquembergues and 90 sergeants from Jerusalem.[19] This would indicate a total figure of at least 280 knights available in the kingdom in May 1102, but it also raises the question whether under normal circumstances the forces of the lord of Tiberias would be sent to meet an invasion from Egypt, or whether they would remain to defend the eastern frontier which was vulnerable to attack from Damascus. At the Third Battle of Ramla (27

[14] AA p. 532E.
[15] AA p. 552.
[16] R. C. Smail, *Crusading Warfare* (Cambridge, 1956), pp. 95-109.
[17] FC II.11, p. 409.
[18] AA p. 549.
[19] FC II.18-21, pp. 436-55.

August 1105) the Franks managed to put 500 knights into the field.[20] The expedition to Edessa in 1110 included 600 knights.[21] The army defeated by the combined Turkish forces of Mawdūd of Mosul and Tughtikin of Damascus in 1113 had 700.[22] The expedition to northern Syria in 1115 had 500.[23]

For Baldwin's expedition into Idumaea and Sinai in 1116, Fulcher gives a figure of 'nearly 200 knights', [24] and Albert one of 200.[25] For the expedition against Egypt undertaken by Baldwin in the final year of his reign (spring 1118), Albert gives an exact figure of 216 knights.[26] The figures for these two expeditions are relatively small compared to those for the campaigns of the years immediately before, and it is therefore likely that fewer forces were regarded as being necessary for this type of enterprise which had the character of a reconnaissance in strength rather than an expedition intended to meet a full-scale enemy invasion.

These figures can be compared with information given by Fulcher for the first years of the next reign. Baldwin II's relief expedition to Antioch after the battle of the *Ager Sanguinis* in 1119 comprised 250 knights, a figure which seems to have included a contingent from the county of Tripoli.[27] The expedition to Antioch in 1122 took 300 knights.[28]

It would be unlikely for the Franks of Jerusalem to weaken the defences of the kingdom by committing the bulk of their forces beyond its frontiers for lengthy periods. Therefore expeditions to northern Syria must have involved a smaller proportion of the total forces available than had the armies that fought defensive battles within the frontiers of the kingdom, so that Fulcher's figures of 250-300 for 1119-22 probably represent a smaller proportion of the total available than those of 500-700 given by Fulcher and Albert for 1105-10. The figures for 1101-5 relate to defensive campaigns that met invasions from Egypt; we should therefore

[20] FC II.32, p. 496; WT XI.3, pp. 498-500: *Quod audiens rex, Ioppen cum universis regni viribus celer pervenit, lege edictali precipiens ut omnes illuc de singulis urbibus sine mora conveniant.*

[21] AA p. 672.

[22] AA p. 695.

[23] AA p. 701.

[24] FC II.56, p. 594.

[25] AA pp. 702-3.

[26] AA p. 705.

[27] FC III.4, p. 626.

[28] FC III.11, p. 649.

probably allow in addition a fairly substantial figure for the lordship of Tiberias, if we assume that it kept a greater proportion of its troops under normal circumstances. As lord of Tiberias, Hugh of Fauquembergues took 80 knights to assist the king after the Second Battle of Ramla, which represented a major emergency; yet even then he may have left some sort of skeleton force to defend the frontier. In 1119 his successor Joscelin of Courtenay was able to take 160 knights plus footsoldiers on an invasion of the *Terre de Suete*, so this may represent something like the total strength available to the lord of Tiberias.[29] The Turkish invasion of 1113 was directed into the Galilee and would have been met by troops from Tiberias as well as the rest of the kingdom. Therefore Albert's highest figure of 700 knights compares roughly with an aggregate of Fulcher's highest of 500 plus some 80-160 for Tiberias, which suggests that by the second half of the reign, some 500-700 knights were available to Baldwin I.

The basic stock of the ruling classes of the kingdom under Baldwin I consisted of nobles and clerics who had taken the decision to remain in Palestine after the conquest of Jerusalem, rather than return to the West with the majority of crusaders. These were joined in the summer of 1100 by a substantial number of nobles, knights (and presumably clerics) who decided to leave Edessa with Baldwin and settle in the kingdom. Over the course of the next eighteen years, they were reinforced by others arriving from the West. The crusade of 1101 suffered heavy casualties on its march across Asia Minor, but a significant number of participants reached Jerusalem and joined Baldwin I's expedition to meet a Fatimid invasion, which resulted in defeat at the Second Battle of Ramla in 1102. The crusaders of 1101 were allies of the king rather than members of his ruling class, but it seems that some of them took service with him.

In addition to the participants of major crusading expeditions, the sudden accessibility of the Holy Places brought a constant stream of pilgrims coming individually or in groups throughout the eighteen years of Baldwin's reign. Many of these people assisted the king in his campaigns on a temporary basis, particularly in his attempts to reduce the Muslim cities of the coast, and some of them probably stayed on in the kingdom in his service. Others came by more circuitous routes. Joscelin of Courtenay left the west around 1101 to make for the county of Edessa, then

[29] AA pp. 710-12.

held by his cousin Baldwin (II) of Bourcq, who gave him important fiefs west of the River Euphrates. As a result of a dispute with Baldwin II, Joscelin came south to Palestine, where King Baldwin I gave him the fief of Tiberias. William of Normandy, an illegitimate son of Duke Robert Curthose, appears to have come to Palestine more as a refugee than as a settler after the defeat of his father at the battle of Tinchebray by Henry I of England in 1106, but gained preferential treatment from Baldwin.

The identification of actual places of origin in the West is dependent on a rather limited corpus of sources. Very few documents survive for the reign of Baldwin I, and most of these relate to major ecclesiastical institutions such as the order of the Hospital and the abbey of Josaphat in Jerusalem. The documents provide a restricted number of names in their witness-lists and to a lesser extent, their dispositive clauses, and even then not all names can be identified in terms of western origins. Although patronymics or nicknames can sometimes assist in identifying individuals, it is primarily locative surnames that give clues to origins, although many placename forms are relatively common, especially in France, and thus in many cases can only be the subject of speculation, however informed. Many nobles appear under their forenames only, and bishops under their forename plus the name of their diocese, which tells us nothing about their places of origin. A significant number of names are also provided by the main narrative sources for the period, notably Albert of Aachen, Fulcher of Chartres, Guibert of Nogent, Orderic Vitalis and William of Malmesbury. Often such writers give circumstantial detail about western origins that allows a precise identification, but equally, as with the documents, many names are difficult to identify.[30]

This means that the place of origin of the individuals whose names have come down to us cannot be identified in all cases. Nevertheless, considering the relatively small numbers of the ruling classes, a survey of the proportion whose origins *can* be identified should give some indication about the overall character of the group. The phenomenon of groups of relatives, especially brothers, going on crusade has been pointed out by

[30] For a detailed discussion of the source materials, see A. V. Murray, 'The Prosopography and Onomastics of the Franks in the Kingdom of Jerusalem, 1099-1187', in *Onomastique et parenté dans l'Occident médiévale*, ed. K. S. B. Keats-Rohan and Ch. Settipani (Oxford, 2000), forthcoming.

Riley-Smith.[31] Some crusaders brought wives and families with them from the West. Others were joined by members of their families or more distant relatives some time after the initial settlement. Shared origins were not limited to kinsmen. Geldemar Carpinel was accompanied on the crusade by a retinue that remained with him in Palestine. The origins of the most prominent members of the nobility will therefore probably tell us about the origins of others who rarely or never appear on documents.

The analysis of the *domus Godefridi* suggests that about half of his household and followers were Lotharingians or Germans, and this group was instrumental in securing Baldwin's succession. However, several of them died or were killed before Baldwin arrived in the kingdom, notably Warner of Grez. In the period 1100-18 there is very little evidence for any nobles who had been vassals of Godfrey before the crusade, which is probable only in the cases of Philip of Bouillon, Stabelo the Chamberlain, Theobald of Nivelles and Walter of Bouillon.[32] A greater number of Lotharingians had no known vassalic or kinship ties with the Ardennes-Bouillon dynasty: from Lower Lotharingia, Gotmann of Brussels, Lithard of Cambrai, Milo of Clermont and the two Hennuyers Gerard of Avesnes and Giselbert of Couvin;[33] from Upper Lotharingia, Ralph of Mousson and Reinard of Verdun.[34] Lotharingia was even more poorly represented among the bishops, with only the case of Baldwin, archbishop of Caesarea, as a probable native of this region.[35] This circumstance must have resulted from the low participation of senior Lotharingian clerics in the crusade, in addition to effects of casualties during it. It is interesting to speculate whether someone such as the well-connected Adalbero, archdeacon of Metz, could have looked forward to a church career in the Holy Land if he had survived.[36] With the prominent exception of Gotmann of Brussels and (possibly) the Viscount Pisellus, no known Lotharingians apparently were left among the nobility or bishops after 1115, although they were to appear again in the reign of Baldwin II.[37] Godfrey's abandonment of his inheritance severed the dynasty's connections with Lothar-

[31] Riley-Smith, *The First Crusade and the Idea of Crusading*, pp. 44-45.

[32] Prosopographical Catalogue, nos. 96, 121, 123, 128.

[33] Prosopographical Catalogue, nos. 59, 83, 89, 47, 54.

[34] Prosopographical Catalogue, nos. 104, 106.

[35] Prosopographical Catalogue, no. 18.

[36] Prosopographical Catalogue, no. 2.

[37] Prosopographical Catalogue, nos. 59, 97.

ingia, which evidently had a negative effect on further immigration from that area.

A more important element was that from Flanders, Artois and Picardy. Nobles who definitely or probably originated from the county of Flanders included Azo of Drouvin, Arnulf of Oudenaarde, Baldwin of Ramla, Eustace and Hugh of Cassel, the brothers Gerard and Hugh of Fauquembergues, Gerbod of Scheldewindeke, Hugh of Rebecques, Ralph of Aalst and William of Tincques.[38] Those from the satellite counties which bordered on Flanders to the west and south, that is, the counties of Boulogne, Lens, Ardres, Hesdin, Guînes and Saint-Pol, included Berwold, Eustace Granarius, Fulk of Guînes, Peter of Lens, and possibly Anselm *de Parenti*.[39] Most of these men must have been on crusade with Robert II of Flanders, Eustace III of Boulogne and Hugh of Saint-Pol, although some may have come on the crusade of 1101. Picardy, to the south of Flanders and Artois, also provided a significant number of nobles: Ado of Quierzy and his son Warmund, Drogo of Nesle, Gervase of Bazoches, Guy of Milly and Roger of Rozoy.[40] However, it is striking that this group had the greatest weight among the higher clergy and the holders of lordships. Two patriarchs, Arnulf and Evremar, came from the same village of Chocques in the Ternois.[41] Achard, first prior of the *Templum Domini*, came from Arrouaise.[42] Fulk of Guînes was the first lord of Beirut, whose first bishop, Baldwin, came from Boulogne.[43] Hugh of Fauquembergues held the great fief of Tiberias.[44] Hebron was held by Hugh of Rebecques.[45] Eustace Granarius was easily the most prominent of the men from Flanders and Artois, holding two important lordships, Sidon and Caesarea.[46]

Normans in the kingdom could have originated either in the Anglo-Norman world or the Italian duchies of Apulia and Calabria. Men from southern Italy who had originally come on crusade with Bohemund and

---

[38] Prosopographical Catalogue, nos. 16, 15, 22, 34, 71, 49, 73, 50, 75, 101, 138.
[39] Prosopographical Catalogue, nos. 26, 35, 42, 96, 8.
[40] Prosopographical Catalogue, nos. 5, 132, 29, 51, 63, 115.
[41] Prosopographical Catalogue, nos. 12, 36.
[42] *Versus ... Tarvanensis*, pp. 191-92.
[43] Prosopographical Catalogue, nos. 42, 19.
[44] Prosopographical Catalogue, no. 73.
[45] Prosopographical Catalogue, no. 75.
[46] Prosopographical Catalogue, no. 35.

Tancred included Robert of Apulia, Robert FitzGerard of Buonalbergo and Robert Giffard.[47] Anschetin, the first bishop of Bethlehem, may have also come with this contingent.[48] Presumably most of the followers of Tancred during his tenure of Galilee originated from southern Italy, but many of them may have accompanied him to Antioch when he left the kingdom to take up the regency there. We have less precise knowledge about Rainer Brus, Ralph of Montpinçon and Walter Bigod, some or all of whom may have come on crusade with Duke Robert Curthose.[49] To these we can add the companion of Edgar the Ætheling, Robert *Anglus*, who if not a Norman by blood, came from a land ruled by a Norman king.[50] A later arrival from Normandy was William of Normandy, a bastard son of Robert Curthose.[51] The favouring of Normans in the kingdom of Jerusalem can be partly explained by Baldwin I's connections with Normandy and England before the crusade.

The fourth major element in the ruling class originated in Francia in its narrower sense, that is the lands of the French royal domain, which extended over the Ile-de-France, the Orléanais and the Gâtinais, and the surrounding territories of the counts of Champagne, Brie and Chartres and their vassals. On the crusade these men had been predominantly in the armies of Hugh of Vermandois, brother of the king of France, and Stephen of Blois, although Baldwin of Bourcq, from the periphery of Champagne, had chosen to accompany Godfrey and Baldwin. Stephen of Blois deserted from the crusading army during the siege of Antioch, a time when many crusaders were in financial difficulties, it is likely that many of his followers attached themselves to other leaders, as was the case with the historian Fulcher of Chartres.[52] A sizeable contingent from Francia can be found among the nobles of Baldwin I: Andrew of Baudement, Drogo of Brie, Frederick of Corbeil, Hugh of Le Puiset, Hugh of Bourcq, Ralph of La Fontanelle, Joscelin of Courtenay, and the brothers Godfrey and William of Bures.[53] As far as can be ascertained, the *Franciens* did not provide any bishops, but Joscelin held the major fief of

[47] Prosopographical Catalogue, nos. 110, 111, 112.
[48] Prosopographical Catalogue, no. 7.
[49] Prosopographical Catalogue, nos. 100, 103, 127.
[50] Prosopographical Catalogue, no. 109.
[51] Prosopographical Catalogue, no. 137.
[52] Prosopographical Catalogue, no. 40.
[53] Prosopographical Catalogue, nos. 6, 28, 39, 74, 69, 102, 79, 57, 135.

Tiberias, evidently with William and Godfrey of Bures as his most important vassals.

These four groups constituted the largest number of nobles and bishops whose origins can be established. Those who can be identified as coming from other regions are relatively few. From France south of the Loire came two nobles: Geldemar Carpinel and Roman of Le Puy.[54] Geldemar had originally accompanied Raymond of Saint-Gilles, but transferred his service to Godfrey. It would seem that when Raymond failed to be elected *princeps* in the summer of 1099 the knights of his army, with a few exceptions, either returned to southern France or eventually settled with him in the county of Tripoli whose nobility retained a predominantly southern French character up to the reign of Count Raymond III.[55] Italians, other than the Normans of Apulia and Calabria, were equally few. The Lombard Otto Altaspata came to the Holy Land with the Crusade of 1101, but died in 1104.[56] Barisan (Balian), who founded what proved to be the most famous dynasty in Outremer, the Ibelins, was probably originally a follower of Daibert of Pisa.[57] Nevertheless it is often overlooked that the early fortune of the Ibelins owed a great deal to the acquisition of the lordship of Ramla through the marriage of Balian and Helvis, daughter of Baldwin of Ramla. There are strong indications that Baldwin was a Fleming, which is further evidence of the importance of the Flemish element.[58] The only German nobleman to be found after the arrival of Baldwin was the famous Wicher, a ministerial of Fulda, although Gerard, abbot of Schaffhausen, became prior of the Holy Sepulchre in the time of Godfrey and Daibert.[59] The paucity of Germans was a general trend. Years after the death of Wicher, the sight of his purported tomb prompted the German pilgrim John of Würzburg to reflect on how few

---

[54] Prosopographical Catalogue, nos. 44, 116.

[55] J. Richard, *Le comté de Tripoli sous la dynastie toulousaine*, 1102-1187 (Paris, 1945), pp. 78-91.

[56] Prosopographical Catalogue, no. 90.

[57] Prosopographical Catalogue, no. 24.

[58] Prosopographical Catalogue, no. 22. The name Baldwin, which evidently derived from the lord of Ramla, was used by the family well into the thirteenth century: Charles du Fresne Du Cange, *Les Familles d'Outremer*, ed. Emmanuel-Guillaume Rey (Paris, 1869), pp. 360-79.

[59] Bernold of St Blasien, p. 467; Matzke, *Daibert von Pisa*, p. 184-86; Prosopographical Catalogue, no. 134.

Germans appeared to have settled in the Holy Land, and consoled himself with the reflection that if it had been populated by Germans rather than French, they would surely have conquered much more land than he found under Christian control.[60] Finally, there is at least one case of non-Frankish origin: Walter Mahomet, an important nobleman who held the lordship of Hebron, but whose name indicates he was a converted Muslim.[61] The Franks had a need for expertise about Palestine and the neighbouring countries. In some cases this was provided by Franks with experience of the East, such as Hugh Bunell, a Norman who had murdered Mabel of Bellême in 1077 and fled to Apulia, then Byzantium and ultimately to Muslim territory. For twenty years he studied the customs and languages of the Muslims and turned up at the siege of Jerusalem to offer his services to a no doubt surprised Robert of Normandy 'as his natural lord', and proved invaluable as a source of information about the tactics of the Turks.[62] Such exotic specimens, however, must have been rare. Fulcher's description of the preparations for Baldwin I's expedition into Arabia in November-December 1100 gives us a picture of the Franks collecting information about the geography of Palestine from natives, especially from ex-Muslims who had converted to Christianity after the conquest.[63] The Franks seem to have made extended use of individual Muslim converts who they retained in their service in various capacities. One of these was sponsored at baptism by King Baldwin, whose name he took, and whom he served as *familiaris* and *quasi cubicularius*.[64] The urgent need for local expertise would explain the case of Walter Mahomet as a particularly useful and trusted individual who had demonstrated his loyalty by undergoing conversion.

Thus, apart from a small number of knights of southern French, German, Italian and non-Frankish origin the vast majority of the ruling classes of Jerusalem in the reign of Baldwin I can be shown to have origi-

---

[60] John of Würzburg, in *Peregrinationes Tres: Saewulf, John of Würzburg, Theodericus*, ed. R. B. C. Huygens (Turnhout, 1994), p. 125.
[61] Prosopographical Catalogue, no. 130.
[62] Orderic Vitalis, 5: 156-59.
[63] FC II.3, pp. 374-75: *Et cum cuncta ... et nihil nobis utile amplius invenire possemus, inito consilio cum quibusdam patriae alumnis, prius Saracenis, sed nuper Christianis, qui loca culta et inculta longe lateque sciebant, in Arabiam secedere dispositum est.*
[64] WT XI.11, p. 518.

nated from four principal areas: Flanders, Artois and Picardy; Norman Italy and the Anglo-Norman world, Lotharingia, and the Ile-de-France.

The ruling classes were by no means static in composition, even during this relatively short reign. Many individuals are documented only for very short periods, or even single instances. This phenomenon reflects to a certain extent the restricted source material. The presence of one knight or baron, Walter of Bouillon, is known solely from a casale (village) to which he gave his name.[65] However, restricted documentation provides only a partial explanation. If we look at the better documented lordships and castellanies, we find a lack of continuity. The lordship or castellany of Hebron, or St Abraham as the Franks called it, was held in turn by Geldemar Carpinel, Gerard of Avesnes, Hugh of Rebecques, Walter Mahomet and Baldwin of St Abraham, none of whom are known to have been related to each other. The deaths of only the first two are explicitly recorded, and so the precise reasons for the rapid succession of the next three are necessarily speculative. The great fief of Tiberias was held in turn by Tancred, Hugh of Fauquembergues, Gervase of Bazoches and Joscelin of Courtenay. Tancred relinquished the lordship when he accepted the regency of Antioch in 1101. Hugh and Gervase were killed in fighting against the Turks of Damascus. These instances leave open the question to what extent lordships were heritable, but they do demonstrate the significance of death in battle as a major contributory factor to the lack of continuity.

The kingdom was involved in offensive or defensive warfare for most of the reign. Some impression of the effects of this can be gained by looking at some of the important engagements. The first major defeat to be suffered by the Franks was the Second Battle of Ramla, 17 May 1102. In the first, disastrous engagement only the king and a handful of knights managed to escape alive.[66] Thus a great number of both the king's forces and the crusaders of 1101 must have been killed. On 28 June 1113 the Franks of Jerusalem, supported by contingents from Tripoli and Antioch, suffered another major defeat at al-Sinnābrah in Galilee at the hands of Mawdūd of Mosul and Tughtikin of Damascus. Although it is likely that most of the losses were sustained by the foot-soldiers Fulcher gives the low but believable figure of thirty casualties among the knights, a

[65] Prosopographical Catalogue, no. 128.
[66] FC II.18-19, pp. 436-44.

significant proportion of the whole.[67] These major defeats were exceptions to the general trend. In large, set-piece battles the Franks normally had the upper hand. Nevertheless the losses sustained in victories or indecisive engagements must have had a significant cumulative effect. In small numbers the Franks were especially vulnerable to ambush or surprise attack, particularly in the early years when the Muslims still controlled several of the coastal cities from which they could mount attacks when the Frankish forces were split up. Roger of Rozoy lost forty of his men and was almost killed himself in an ambush mounted by the Fatimid garrison of Ascalon in 1107.[68] The Fatimid troops followed up this victory with a surprise attack on Chastel Hernaut, killing the entire garrison except for the commander, Gunfrid of the Tower of David, who was taken prisoner.[69] Hugh of Fauquembergues, lord of Tiberias, was killed in an ambush by Turks from Damascus after returning from a raid in the Hauran.[70] A similar fate struck the force led by his successor, Gervase of Bazoches, all of whose men were either killed or captured.[71] The Franks were also vulnerable when they were left in Muslim-held cities to act as residents, as in the case of Gerard of Avesnes, or those sent to garrison Ascalon, massacred in July 1110 by the populace and the Egyptian soldiers it had admitted to the city.[72] It is therefore likely that the known cases of death in combat among the nobles surveyed merely represent the tip of the iceberg.[73]

In many cases the Frankish knights, who of course had warhorses and heavy armour, must have been in greater danger of being captured than

---

[67] FC II.49, pp. 565-73; Ibn al-Qalānisī, *The Damascus Chronicle of the Crusades*, trans. H. A. R. Gibb (London, 1932), pp. 134-36; Ibn al-Athīr, *Extraits de la chronique intitulée Kamel-Altevarykh*, RHC Or. 1: 288-89; Bar Hebraeus, *Chronography*, ed. E. A. W. Budge (Oxford, 1932), p. 245.

[68] AA pp. 635-36.

[69] AA pp. 625-38.

[70] AA pp. 633-35.

[71] Prosopographical Catalogue, no. 51.

[72] AA pp. 680-81.

[73] Arnulf of Oudenaarde (Prosopographical Catalogue, no. 15), Gerard of Avesnes (no. 47), Gerbod of Scheldewindeke (no. 50), Gervase of Bazoches (no. 51), Giselbert of Couvin (no. 53), Godfrey the *nepos* of Baldwin I (no. 56), Gerard of Fauquembergues (no. 49), Godfrey of Bures (no. 57), Hugh of Fauquembergues (no. 73), Otto Altaspata (no. 90), Rainier Brus (no. 100), Reinold (no. 107), Reinard of Verdun (no. 106), Robert *Anglus* (no. 109), Stabelo the Chamberlain (no. 121).

being killed, especially after their enemies began to realise the value of their more prominent prisoners. In the second half of the twelfth century we find detailed cases of lords and knights raising money to pay ransoms, suggesting that this was a common practice by that time.[74] By contrast, apart from the special cases of rulers of the Frankish states, ransom of captives does not seem to have been common up to about 1130. In known cases of capture the Franks seem to have been reluctant to come to terms in order to secure the release of prisoners. Godfrey of Bouillon refused to negotiate for the release of Gerard of Avesnes, held prisoner by the Muslims of Arsuf in 1100, declaring that even if his own brother Eustace were held captive he would not desist from his attack on the city.[75] Baldwin I refused to pay the price demanded for the release of Gervase of Bazoches, which resulted in Gervase's execution.[76] A quite startling example is the fate of Gunfrid of the Tower of David, who languished in Egyptian, or as the crusaders would have described it, Babylonian captivity for over thirty years, and whose release resulted from the initiative of native Christians rather than of his fellow Franks.[77] Thus while capture may have led to financial difficulties in the second half of the twelfth century it could have far more serious consequences in the first. It is no coincidence that captivity forms one of the principal literary themes in the epic poetry inspired by the First Crusade and the deeds of the Franks in the East, notably in the poem known as *Les Chétifs*, which was probably composed at Antioch sometime before 1147 and which along with the *Chanson d'Antioche* and the *Chanson de Jérusalem* represents the oldest portions of the Old French Crusading Cycle.[78]

---

[74] John Gotmann sold 5 casalia in 1161 to pay his ransom, raising the sum of 1400 bezants (RRH nos. 368, 369). Hugh of Ibelin was captured sometime before 1155; RRH no. 335 reveals how his vassals were obliged to sell property to raise his ransom. Walter of Beirut and his brothers Guy and Bernard were captured by Nūr al-Dīn in 1164; to secure his release he was forced to surrender his lordship of Beirut, receiving in exchange money for his ransom and the less important fief of Blanchegarde: M. E. Nickerson, 'The Seigneurie of Beirut in the 12th Century and Brisebarre Family of Beirut-Blanchegarde', *Byzantion* 19 (1949), 166-68.

[75] AA pp. 507-8.

[76] Prosopographical Catalogue, no. 51.

[77] Prosopographical Catalogue, no. 61.

[78] U. T. Holmes and W. M. Macleod, 'Source Problems of the *Chétifs*, a Crusade Chanson de Geste', *Romanic Review* 28 (1937), 99-108.

Known cases of mortality as a result of illness are fewer than those of violent death.[79] Nevertheless, the life expectancy of the Franks must have been shortened by the combined effects of inadequate hygiene, war injuries, diseases and an unfamiliar climate. The gaps caused by death and captivity, especially among holders of lordships and castellanies had to be filled by in most cases by less prominent men. Gervase of Bazoches, who obtained the lordship of Tiberias on the death of Hugh of Fauquembergues, had been seneschal to Baldwin I.[80] William of Bures, originally a rear-vassal in Galilee, eventually became lord of Tiberias in succession to Joscelin of Courtenay.[81]

By contrast to the high casualty rates among the nobility, there was a greater permanence among the bishops. This can be partly explained by lifestyle, but bishops could not avoid warfare and its dangers. The bishopric of Lydda was primarily set up to control a strategic site close to Jaffa, and the bishop could expect attacks and raids from nearby Ascalon. The patriarch and other bishops also often accompanied the king on campaign. Baldwin I died in the arms of Roger, bishop of Lydda, during his ill-fated final campaign against Egypt in March-April 1118.[82] Paradoxically, it was the most senior figure in the hierarchy who was the most exposed to battle. The patriarch (or a substitute) was expected to carry the relic of the True Cross into battle, and this was done several times in the reign of Baldwin, by Arnulf of Chocques, Evremar of Chocques and Gibelin of Arles.[83] The patriarchate enjoyed less stability than the episcopate, having four incumbents during the reign, two of whom, Daibert of Pisa and Evremar, were deposed by Baldwin. This was a reflection of the reality that the patriarch needed to be both an able administrator and enjoy the full confidence of the king, which mattered rather less in the case of bishops, since Baldwin was happy for Evremar to be translated to the see of Caesarea.[84]

---

[79] Prosopographical Catalogue, nos. 117, 133, 134.

[80] Prosopographical Catalogue, no. 51.

[81] Prosopographical Catalogue, no. 135.

[82] RHC Occ. 4: 543.

[83] A. V. Murray, 'Mighty Against the Enemies of Christ: The Relic of the True Cross in the Armies of the Kingdom of Jerusalem', in *The Crusades and Their Sources: Essays Presented to Bernard Hamilton*, ed. J. France and W. G. Zajac (Aldershot, 1998), pp. 217-38.

[84] Hamilton, *The Latin Church*, pp. 53-64.

Proximity to Power

The most important members of the nobility were those men who held lordships over major towns or territories. They were a small and select band. Godfrey granted two cities to members of his nobility, Haifa and St Abraham. The lordship of Tiberias had been established independently by Tancred. Baldwin continued to grant out these three lordships. However, he was sparing in the creation of more. This was undoubtedly a result of the situation that the territorial expansion of the kingdom, particularly the capture of towns, was a slow and gradual process; while some lordships, especially those at a distance from Jerusalem such as Beirut and Sidon, were granted out, the king clearly wished to retain direct control over key areas. Thus important new conquests such as Arsuf (1101) and Acre (1104) were retained in the royal domain. Little is known of the origins of the lords of Haifa except for Geldemar Carpinel, a southern Frenchman who also held St Abraham.[85] Among the other holders of lordships in the reign of Baldwin I we find one Lotharingian, Gerard of Avesnes and one native Palestinian, Walter Mahomet, both in St Abraham;[86] one Francian, Joscelin of Courtenay, and a Norman, Tancred, during two tenures over Tiberias.[87] Tancred, however, was not the choice of either Godfrey or Baldwin; his nominal restoration in 1109 was part of a general settlement in the Frankish East.

When Tancred left the kingdom to take up the regency of Antioch, Baldwin was evidently determined to keep the great fief of Tiberias in the hands of men he could trust. In the first instance, he gave it to Hugh of Fauquembergues, who was not only a Fleming, but particularly close to the king, since he had been a follower of Baldwin in Edessa. On his death, Hugh was succeeded by the Picard Gervase of Bazoches, who had been one of the king's aulic officers.[88] St Abraham was held by Hugh of Rebecques.[89] Baldwin, the first lord of Ramla, was probably also a Fleming.[90] The Flemish-Picard group also received three of the important

---

[85] Prosopographical Catalogue, no. 44.
[86] Prosopographical Catalogue, nos. 47, 130.
[87] Prosopographical Catalogue, nos. 79, 122.
[88] Prosopographical Catalogue, nos. 51, 73.
[89] Prosopographical Catalogue, no. 75.
[90] Prosopographical Catalogue, no. 22.

coastal cities acquired in the course of the reign: Fulk of Guînes, who received Beirut, and Eustace I Granarius, who as lord of both Sidon and Caesarea acquired a concentration of power unequalled in this reign.[91] Thus among the holders of lordships it was above all men from Flanders, Artois and Picardy who enjoyed the royal favour in the period up to 1118.

An additional perspective on proximity to the king can be obtained from an investigation into those members of the ruling class who witnessed royal charters. In her study of the group she termed royal *familiares*, Corliss Slack analysed the frequency of attestations, producing statistics for the number of appearances overall as well as for the rate of attestation per year.[92] Certainly the frequency of attestation gives a clear indication of the identity of those individuals who were regularly in attendance at the royal court; this shows that those present most frequently were the senior secular clergy (patriarchs, archbishops and bishops), heads of religious houses, household officers, holders of lordships and some tenants of the royal demesne lands in Judaea and Galilee. However, the simple analysis of frequency of attestation says little about the *relative* status of the individuals concerned. For this reason it is also illuminating to consider the relative placing of individuals within witness-lists, on the grounds that their names would have been recorded according to their importance.[93] There is a correlation between status (as derived from dignity) in the case of clerical witnesses, where there is a clear ranking of patriarchs, archbishops, bishops and priors. Within each of these ranks, status seems to have derived from seniority, so that, for example, Bernard, bishop of Nazareth, twice appears before Roger, bishop of Lydda. Among the lay witnesses, status is less clear-cut, but three categories are significant in the ranking. As we might expect, officials of the royal household (constable and chamberlain) and the administration of the capital (viscount of Jerusalem and castellan of the Tower of David) are well represented. Holders of lordships are represented by only two lay witnesses with two or more attestations: Eustace Granarius (lord of Sidon and Caesarea) and Walter Mahomet (lord of St Abraham). The third category consists of those who are not known to

---

[91] Prosopographical Catalogue, nos. 42, 35.

[92] C. K. Slack, 'Royal *Familiares* in the Latin Kingdom of Jerusalem, 1100-1187', *Viator* 22 (1991), 15-67

[93] See Appendix B, 'Principal Witnesses to Documents of Baldwin I'.

have held household offices or lordships, but who seem to have held substantial lands: Ralph of La Fontanelle, Guy of Milly, Roman of Le Puy, Gotmann of Brussels and Anselm *de Parenti*. The relatively few appearances of holders of lordship is perhaps surprising at first sight, but it can probably be explained by the fact that lords of frontier areas, particular those at some distance from Jerusalem such as Tiberias or Beirut, would necessarily have to spend considerable time in their lordships. This would also explain why most of the members of the third group seem to have been men with lands close to Jerusalem, since they would normally have resided in the capital. The factor of distance of course somewhat limits the value of frequency analysis as a guide to status. Nevertheless, it is striking that the analysis of witness lists confirms the pre-eminent position of Eustace Granarius, who was clearly in first position according to placing (although not by frequency), despite the fact that one of his lordships, Sidon, was almost 200 kilometres distant from the city of Jerusalem.

The majority of knights seem to have held smaller properties, often single casalia or parts of casalia, as well as urban property. However, a significant number of knights held money-fiefs, presumably in addition to property in most cases. The money-fief seems to have consisted of hypothecated revenues, which could derive from various sources. The first pattern was where knights were assigned part of the revenues of cities retained by the king. Thus in 1107 one of the king's household officers, Gerard the Chamberlain, is recorded as having been awarded income drawn on the revenues of Jaffa, which at the time was administered by a royal castellan, in return for military service.[94] A second source was tribute paid by Muslim cities, as in the cases of Robert of Apulia, and Gerard of Avesnes, who acted as resident and overseer in Arsuf.[95] The important point about the tenure of money-fiefs was that they were essentially a continuation of the relationship that had evolved in the course of the crusade itself, and kept the holder dependent on the monarch.

The revenues of Frankish lords and knights were supplemented from other, irregular sources. One was a kind of protection-money extorted

---

[94] AA pp. 636-37: *Ad haec Gerhardus quidam eques de domo regis Baldewini, qui partem reditus civitatis Japhet pro militari obsequio obtinebat,* ...; Mayer, 'The Origins of the Lordships of Ramla and Lydda', pp. 537-52.

[95] Prosopographical Catalogue, nos. 110, 47.

when the Franks invested Muslim cities but then abandoned their siege in return for cash payments. Given that the Frankish forces were limited in number, this kind of campaign was often far more profitable in the short term than lengthy sieges. In 1106 Baldwin preferred to break off the siege of Sidon in return for a payment of 15,000 bezants, dismissing many of the pilgrims from the West who had joined his army. The following year he extracted another large sum from Tyre.[96] A related irregular source of income was booty. This was obtained in large quantities after some of the major Frankish victories of the reign, particularly against large Fatimid armies. However, numerous expeditions were organised with the express purpose of capturing cash and trade goods, or moveables in the form of cattle, sheep, mules and camels. After the capture of a caravan going from Tyre to Damascus in 1111, Baldwin I distributed money to his vassals who, it was reported, had long been in financial difficulties.[97] In the spring of 1112, after the Easter festival, the king led an expedition into the Wadi Mūsa in the hope of plundering the Bedouin tribes of the region, and more profitably, caravans moving between Egypt and Syria. It was undertaken with the aim of obtaining booty for distribution to his vassals, and comprised a force of 200 knights and 100 infantry, a quite substantial force compared to the usual numbers assembled for defensive campaigns.[98] Referring to another occasion, Albert of Aachen criticised the Franks for thinking more of booty than of the pursuit of the enemy.[99] In such cases the division of the spoils seems to have been a third to the king and two-thirds to his vassals.[100]

---

[96] AA pp. 633-34, 680-81; Ibn al-Qalānisī, p. 82.

[97] AA p. 690: *Thesauri miri et inauditi illic capti sunt, quos Rex liberali manu militibus, longa usque nunc indigentia oppressis, benigne largitus est.*

[98] AA p. 693: *Rex vero vix partes Arabiae intraverat, et ecce Idumaei, quos moderni vocant Biduinos, viri mercatores cum immensis copiis diversarum mercium, in mulis et camelis, inter manus Regis et suorum affuerunt, qui nullatenus effugere valentes, omnibus rebus divitiarum suarum tam in auro quam in argento, gemmis pretiosis, ostro diversi generis et operis, pariterque pigmentis exspoliati sunt; plures pariter capti, Iherusalem abducti, in custodiam mancipati sunt, praeda vero et spolia eorum inter milites divisa sunt.*

[99] AA pp. 647.

[100] AA pp. 645: *ubi praeda inter Regem et milites divisa est ... Rex cum praeda sua, quae illi in tertiam partem juxta divisionem contigerat ... .*

The Succession as a Source of Conflict

It is easy to gain a (mistaken) impression of Baldwin I as a kind of absolute ruler, who could remove lords and castellans as he wished, and even replace patriarchs of Jerusalem with the right amount of pressure on the Curia. His preference for using revenues rather than lands as a means of supporting barons and knights gave him a greater hold over the nobility than many of his successors. After the defeat of the claims of Daibert in 1100, and the departure of Tancred for Antioch in 1101, Baldwin was undisputed master in his kingdom. He was to face no baronial revolts, unlike his successors Baldwin II and Fulk of Anjou.[101] The survival of a Christian kingdom administered and defended by a minority Frankish population depended on close co-operation between its various institutions and interest groups, particularly given the security problems of Baldwin's reign, in which much of the coast remained in Muslim hands. It would seem that rebellion was a luxury that came with increased security. Yet medieval kings by and large depended on the co-operation of the great men who served them, and one event towards the end of Baldwin's reign demonstrated how the king could be forced to back down in the face of determined opposition. At some point after his accession Baldwin I repudiated his second, Armenian wife. In 1112-13 he negotiated a new marriage with Adelaide, widow of Roger I, count of Sicily. Up to that time she had acted as regent for her son Roger II who had just attained his majority, and since her role in government had been an active one, it is likely that she was personally involved in the negotiations.[102] The marriage offered the prospect of a considerable cash dowry, which was welcome to the financially hard-pressed king, but the Sicilian negotiators imposed the condition that if Baldwin and his new queen had

---

[101] H. E. Mayer, 'Jérusalem et Antioche au temps de Baudouin II', in *Comptes rendus des séances de l'Académie des Inscriptions et Belles-Lettres*, 1980, pp. 717-36; Mayer, 'Angevins versus Normans: The New Men of King Fulk of Jerusalem', *Proceedings of the American Philosophical Society* 133 (1989), 1-25; A. V. Murray, 'Baldwin II and his Nobles: Baronial Factionalism and Dissent in the Kingdom of Jerusalem, 1118-1134', *Nottingham Medieval Studies* 38 (1994), 60-85.

[102] S. Hamm, 'Regentinnen und minderjährige Herrscher im normannischen Italien', in *Roma, magistra mundi: Itineraria culturae medievalis – parvi flores*, ed. J. Hamesse (Louvain-la-Neuve, 1998), pp. 123-39.

no heirs, the throne of Jerusalem should revert on his death to Roger II.[103] This condition would have been particularly attractive to Adelaide and her son. The acquisition of a royal title by the count of Sicily would have enhanced his prestige relative to his cousin William, duke of Apulia, and kingship specifically linked with Jerusalem would possibly also have impressed the hierarchy of the Greek church, to which a significant proportion of Roger's subjects belonged.

Baldwin had no known children from his two previous marriages, and it is therefore likely that prior to the Sicilian marriage, his heir presumptive was his elder brother Eustace III of Boulogne, whose rights would have been set aside by the new marriage agreement. It is unclear whether there was any protest at this constitutional novelty at the time of Baldwin's marriage, but the matter came to a head during the winter of 1116-17, when the king's illness meant there was a real possibility that he might die.[104] In that case, since he and Adelaide had no children, the throne of Jerusalem would pass to Roger of Sicily, a prospect which was evidently regarded with little enthusiasm among the ruling classes. Many of them had fought alongside Eustace of Boulogne on the crusade; some, such as Eustace Granarius, lord of Sidon and Caesarea, had probably been vassals or rear-vassals of the counts of Boulogne. By contrast, there was no significant sentiment in favour of Roger; as count of Sicily, he was likely to be an absentee monarch for much of the time. The nobility and the patriarch, Arnulf of Chocques, were strongly opposed to this prospect and exploited the circumstances of Baldwin's ill-health to pressurise him into an agreement to repudiate Adelaide. In the event this was easily done, as it could be argued that the marriage had been invalid, since the king's second wife was still alive. At a council of nobles and clergy presided over by the patriarch the marriage was annulled and in April 1117 Adelaide left the kingdom for Sicily.[105]

The dismissal of Adelaide and the removal of Roger of Sicily as heir to the kingdom made the question of the succession more acute than ever before. The supporters of Eustace of Boulogne could now assume that he

---

[103] AA pp. 696-98; FC II.51, pp. 574-78; WT XI.21, pp. 525-27. It is uncertain when Baldwin repudiated his second wife. See Hamilton, 'Women in the Crusader States', pp. 143-46.

[104] FC II.59, pp. 600-1: *exitu siquidem anni appropinquante, molestia corporis ingruente, quia rex mori tunc timuit, dimist uxorem suam superius memoratam.*

[105] AA p. 704; FC II.59, p. 601; Mayer, *Mélanges*, pp. 59-72.

was once again the obvious successor. He was the only close male, legitimate relative of the king left alive.[106] Yet Baldwin himself may have already had reservations as to whether his elder brother's advanced age would make him suitable for the kingship of Jerusalem and the rigours it entailed. Shortly before his death the king was to voice the fear that Eustace would decline the offer of the throne,[107] and even if he were to accept it, he might well still be incapable (or so Baldwin may have feared) of playing the active, military role required by a king of Jerusalem. Indeed it may have been such considerations that had already prompted Baldwin to agree to a right of succession for Roger of Sicily. As Mayer has argued, there is some evidence that in the last year of his life the king was actively considering designating his distant kinsman Baldwin of Bourcq, count of Edessa, as his new successor; the initiative in this matter may well have been played by the count's cousin, Joscelin of Tiberias, who was later to play a key role in securing the throne for him. The arrival of Baldwin of Edessa in Jerusalem at Easter 1118, shortly after Baldwin I's death, has always seemed more than fortuitous, and the visit may have actually been planned so that the two Baldwins could negotiate the terms of succession.[108]

Before this meeting could take place, however, the king launched what was to be his last military campaign. In March 1118 he left Jerusalem at the head of an expedition across the Sinai peninsula towards the borders of Fatimid Egypt.[109] Baldwin could hope to conciliate his nobles with the opportunity to seize caravans and plunder frontier settlements, but the campaign may also have been intended to weaken the exposed Fatimid exclave of Ascalon by destroying the fortifications of some of the settlements that served as staging posts for Fatimid armies moving from Egypt to Palestine. After a march of eleven days the Frankish army reached one of the eastern arms of the Nile, and on 22 March it occupied the port of al-Farāma (*Pelusium*), whose inhabitants had fled. There the Franks found

---

[106] Godfrey, a member of the Bouillon-Boulogne dynasty by illegitimate descent, had been killed in the Holy Land in 1113. See Prosopographical Catalogue, no. 56. For the relationship between Baldwin I and Baldwin II, see Appendix C, 'The Claim of Baldwin II to the Throne of Jerusalem'.

[107] AA p. 707.

[108] Mayer, *Mélanges*, pp. 84-88.

[109] AA pp. 705-7 (with the most detailed chronology); FC II.64, pp. 609-13; WT XI.31, pp. 543-44.

abundant stores of food and wine, but after a day or two spent in enjoyment of their spoils, Baldwin's vassals demanded to be allowed to proceed towards Cairo. Admittedly, Cairo was only three days' march away, but the Frankish force of just over 200 knights and 400 foot-soldiers was considerably less than the full military strength of the kingdom and certainly too small for an attack on the Fatimid capital. This, and the demands of the vassals suggest that the king's intention had been to proceed not much further than al-Farāma; the demand for an attack on Cairo, which had minimal chances of success, may simply have been intended to delay a return to Jerusalem in time for Easter and thus disrupt the king's prospective negotiations with Baldwin of Edessa.[110] If this interpretation is correct, then it would seem that the partisans of Eustace had the upper hand among those nobles and clerics accompanying the expedition. Baldwin ordered the destruction of the fortifications of al-Farāma, but during this action, on 25 March, the king suddenly became so ill that he could no longer ride. Clearly any advance further into Fatimid territory was now completely out of the question, and the army began a slow return along the edge of the Sinai Desert. Although it might have seemed that the king's sudden indisposition was merely a diplomatic illness intended to frustrate the designs of his vassals, it was in fact the gravest ever threat to his health. He had already been weakened by illness in 1116-17. Now the rigours of the Sinai campaign caused an old wound to open.[111] It had been originally sustained in 1103, causing serious damage to the internal organs, and required a long convalescence as well as repeated treatment over the subsequent years.[112] On 2 April 1118, at the little frontier village of al-ᶜArish, the king died. At the end he was most concerned to secure burial alongside his brother Godfrey in the church of the Holy Sepulchre, and gave instructions to his cook, Addo, for the care of his corpse. His intestines were removed and his body embalmed, and the army made haste to Jerusalem, arriving on Palm Sunday. On his death-bed, Baldwin had been pressed for his wishes concerning the succession. He designated his brother Eustace as successor, but added that if Eustace declined to accept the kingdom on account of his age, the magnates should elect Baldwin of Bourcq or someone else 'who would

[110] Mayer, *Mélanges*, p. 89.
[111] FC II.64, p. 610; AA p. 706; WT XI.31, p. 544.
[112] GN pp. 230-31; Hiestand, 'König Balduin und sein Tanzbär', pp. 343-60.

rule the Christian people and defend the churches'.[113] The dying king was evidently less than confident that his brother would come to the Holy Land to take up his inheritance. Eustace and his supporters would prove him wrong.

---

[113] AA p. 707: *Qui fratri Eustachio regnum destinat, si forte venerit; si vero aetate nequiverit, Baldewinus de Burg eligatur, aut talis qui populum Christianum regat, Ecclesias defendat, qui stabilis in fide maneat, quem nulla adversariorum virtus terreat, aut merces leviter corrumpat.*

Chapter V

The End of the Bouillon-Boulogne Ascendancy
(1118-25)

The Disputed Succession of 1118

The burial of Baldwin I was followed by a period of intensive debate in which the ruling classes of the kingdom lined up behind the two possible candidates for the throne. Legitimist opinion, which had been dominant since the repudiation of Queen Adelaide, demanded that hereditary principles should be maintained and that the throne should pass to Baldwin I's elder brother, Eustace of Boulogne. The opposing party, led by the Patriarch Arnulf and Joscelin, lord of Tiberias, favoured the late king's more distant kinsman Baldwin of Bourcq, count of Edessa. This faction took an essentially pragmatic (if not opportunistic) view, arguing that since Baldwin was already in the East, and at that very moment present in Jerusalem, he could be inaugurated immediately, thus avoiding an interregnum.[1] Those who defended hereditary principles could claim that their candidate was not only the better qualified, but had the additional advantage of designation by the late king. According to Albert of Aachen, Baldwin I had expressly designated Eustace as his successor, with Baldwin of Edessa only as second choice if Eustace should decline the throne.[2] It would seem, therefore, that the legitimist faction had the initial advantage, and sent a legation to summon Eustace to take up his inheritance. This mission was entrusted to 'certain nobles and great men' (*quidam nobiles et*

---

[1] WT XII.2-3, pp. 547-50. Eustace's supporters argued that his succession would be in keeping with the *hereditarie successionis antiquissimam legem*, a phrase which William uses twice. The adjective *antiquissima* could hardly apply to a specific law or assize governing the succession in the kingdom of Jerusalem, which had only been in existence for eighteen years; it is more probable that the legitimists were appealing to more general and long-established principles of hereditary succession to secular territories. For the most detailed and considered account of the succession debate, see Mayer, *Mélanges*, pp. 73-91.

[2] AA pp. 708-9.

magni viri).[3] These people very probably included leaders of the legitimist faction since, if Eustace was to be persuaded to leave Boulogne and travel several hundred miles to the Holy Land, he would need to be convinced that he had the support of the Frankish ruling class, which would be achieved more convincingly if an approach were entrusted to some of the leaders of those who supported his succession rather than simply being conveyed by messengers.

Certainly events moved very quickly. Baldwin I had died on Tuesday, 2 April. The Frankish army carrying his body arrived in Jerusalem on Palm Sunday (7 April), although it is possible that news of the king's death had been brought to the capital by messengers riding in advance of the main army. The debate must have therefore taken place in a very short time, between Palm Sunday and Easter Sunday (14 April), when Baldwin II was anointed.[4] The departure of the legation to Eustace should be dated to this time. It is difficult to say whether the legitimists were acting by general consent, or whether they were simply trying to seize the advantage. What is probable is that the departure of some of the legitimist leaders altered the balance of opinion among the nobility and higher clergy at a crucial time, enabling the pragmatic faction to gain the upper hand. This group's case was most forcefully put by the head of the church, the Patriarch Arnulf, and Joscelin, lord of Tiberias, the major lay vassal. Joscelin praised Baldwin of Bourcq's personal qualities, suggesting quite disingenuously that he had no reason to favour Baldwin, who had deprived him of his fiefs in the county of Edessa.[5] More tellingly, Joscelin argued that since Baldwin was actually present, having come to Jerusalem for the Easter celebrations, he could be inaugurated immediately; he was also known to be a *consanguineus* of the late king, a point made to deflect the argument that hereditary principles should be maintained. These argu-

---

[3] WT XII.3, p. 550.

[4] Mayer, *Mélanges*, pp. 77-78.

[5] The famous quarrel that led to the confiscation of Joscelin's Edessan fiefs by Baldwin is something of an exception in the relationship between the two men. After ransoming himself from Turkish imprisonment in 1107 Joscelin raised funds for the release of Baldwin, actually surrendering himself as surety for the outstanding ransom. Their common interest is most evident in the events of 1113, and it was Joscelin who escorted Baldwin's wife, Morphia, and their children to Jerusalem from Edessa a year later: R. L. Nicholson, *Joscelyn I, Prince of Edessa* (Urbana, 1954), pp. 13-16.

ments convinced many of those involved, and Arnulf, Joscelin and their supporters were strong enough to carry the vote against a legitimist faction now weakened by the absence of some its key members.[6] The sequence of events may explain the rather unsatisfactory treatment of the succession by Fulcher of Chartres. The one short chapter (a mere three sentences) he devotes to Baldwin's accession is but a fraction of the corresponding accounts by William of Tyre and Albert of Aachen, although Fulcher, writing in Jerusalem only a few years after the events he was describing, was clearly far better placed than either to ascertain what had transpired. He merely states that on the death of Baldwin I the people of Jerusalem unanimously chose as successor his kinsman (*cognatus*) Baldwin of Edessa.[7] A simple explanation would be that Fulcher was reflecting not the course, but the final outcome of deliberations. Medieval electoral processes preferred the idea of unanimity, and it is possible that once they realised they could no longer prevail, the members of the legitimist party conceded defeat, thus allowing at least a semblance of unanimity to be maintained.

Against the evident expectations of his late brother, Count Eustace actually decided – possibly only after some persuasion – to take up his inheritance. He left Boulogne on receiving word of his brother's death, but when he reached Apulia, he received word that Baldwin of Edessa had been consecrated king in the meantime. Allowing time for the legation to reach Boulogne, and for Eustace to reach Italy, this must have been well into the summer of 1118.[8] Nevertheless, the nobles accompanying Eustace urged him to press his claims on the grounds that the consecration of Baldwin II was 'against natural and divine law and against the ancient right of hereditary succession' (*contra ius et fas et contra hereditarie successionis legem antiquissimam*), although by this time the pragmatists' position was stronger than ever before. As Baldwin and his supporters were now hardly likely to give up the advantage they held, it would seem that at this point at least some of the prominent legitimists

---

[6] WT XII.3, p. 549: *Ioscelinus, qui maximae erat in regno auctoritatis, illorum iuvans partem qui dicebat regem statim esse ordinandum, diremit, dicens presentem esse dominum comitem Edessanum, virum iustum et timoratum, domini regis consanguineum, industrium et in armis strenuum, per omnia commendabilem, quo meliorem nulla nobis regio, nulla provincia posset ministrare: commodius esse ipsum in regem assumere quam casus periculosios expectare.*

[7] FC III.1, pp. 615-16.

[8] Mayer, *Mélanges*, p. 81.

were prepared to risk civil war in order to place their candidate on the throne. Only Eustace's refusal to contest the issue any further meant that his party, now deprived of a cause, had no choice but to accept Baldwin II as king.[9]

Baldwin II's position thus seemed to be secure after his coronation on Christmas Day 1119. Yet the division of opinion over the succession to Baldwin I had important implications for the coming reign. Joscelin had argued that the choice of the count of Edessa would avoid an interregnum, but also stressed his acceptability as a *consanguineus* of the late king. Yet this point in itself had little significance; Baldwin of Edessa was a fairly distant relative of his predecessor, unlike his rival.[10] Eustace had the advantages in law: designation by the previous king and a close blood relationship with him, and he clearly enjoyed substantial support among the ruling classes. Given his age, Eustace was unlikely to press his claims a second time, and his daughter Mathilda, as yet unmarried, would hardly be an adequate substitute candidate. Yet whenever Mathilda *did* marry, legitimist sentiment might well reassert itself. Therefore even in 1118 it was by no means certain that if the opportunity arose in the future, Eustace's family might not once again claim the throne, possibly with the backing of nobles and clerics within the kingdom.

Whereas we can identify Joscelin of Courtenay and Arnulf of Chocques as leaders of the pragmatist party we do not know the names of any of the legitimists. Nevertheless, it is likely that these men were drawn from the ranks of the older nobles (and clerics) who either possessed ties to the Bouillon-Boulogne brothers stemming from the period before 1096, or had developed them in the course of the First Crusade. Most of these men came from Lotharingia, Normandy, Flanders, Artois and Picardy. If the legitimist nobles and prelates were a potential source of discontent the circumstances of his accession must have made the new king dependent on the support of the pragmatists, who could expect to be rewarded for their promotion of his candidature. The new king had every incentive to promote kinsmen, friends and allies in church and nobility in order to create a source of future support.

---

[9] WT XII.3, p. 550.

[10] See Appendix C, 'The Claim of Baldwin II to the Throne of Jerusalem'.

The Dynastic Connections of Baldwin II

As far as kinsmen were concerned, the new king had an ample supply, both in Outremer and in the West. Baldwin II was a son of Hugh, count of Rethel, who had lands in the north-east of the kingdom of France which were held from the archbishop of Rheims and the count of Champagne.[11] Baldwin's mother was Melisende, daughter of Guy the Great, lord of Montlhéry, and Hodierna of Gometz. Through this single connection, the family of Hugh of Rethel was closely related to a great number of the noble families of the Ile-de-France, Champagne, Blois and Chartres. In particular, Baldwin II was closely related to the counts of Rochefort, the lords of Montlhéry-Bray, the lords of Courtenay and the lords of Le Puiset.[12] However, the connections of the Rethel family went far beyond this group, and it is striking how some of them contrasted with the kinship ties of the Boulogne-Bouillon dynasty. There was some kind of blood relationship with Calixtus II, a son of Count William of Burgundy and pope since 1119, who himself alluded to the kinship in a letter to Baldwin.[13] Godfrey of Bouillon had of course been in the imperialist party before the crusade, and he and Baldwin I had little in the way of ties to the Reform Papacy. In the case of the correspondence between Baldwin II and Calixtus II, one should perhaps not overemphasise the significance of what was primarily a diplomatic formulation, but it cannot be denied that Calixtus was a pope who took a keen interest in the security of the Holy Land, and that the allusion to kinship came from the initiative of the Curia rather than Baldwin.[14]

Another striking contrast between the two kings is provided by the case of the counts of Namur, long-standing rivals of the Ardennes-Bouillon dynasty in Lotharingia. In 1076 Albert III of Namur joined forces with the bishop of Verdun and Mathilda of Tuscany to dispute Godfrey IV's

---

[11] Bur, *La formation du comté de Champagne*, pp. 133-40; P. Feuchère, 'Essai sur l'évolution territoriale des principautés français (Xe-XIIIe siècles)', *Le Moyen Age* 58 (1952), 85-117 (here 117).

[12] A. V. Murray, 'Dynastic Continuity or Dynastic Change? The Accession of Baldwin II and the Nobility of the Kingdom of Jerusalem', *Medieval Prosopography* 13 (1992), 1-28; Riley-Smith, *The First Crusaders,* pp. 169-75.

[13] Calixtus II, *Epistolae et privilegia*, PL 158, no. 148: *illustri quoque atque charissimo filio et consanguineo Balduino regi.*

[14] Riley-Smith, *The First Crusaders,* pp. 176-77.

inheritance in a struggle that raged intermittently until the eve of the First Crusade. A quite different relationship existed between Namur and Rethel around the time of the First Crusade. Albert III's son Godfrey, who succeeded as count around 1102, had around 1088 married Sibylla, heiress to the small county of Château-Porcien, which was held from the count of Rethel.[15] Their daughter Isabella married Baldwin II's brother Gervase (originally a cleric), who succeeded to the county of Rethel on the death of their father, Hugh I. Another daughter, Beatrix, eventually married Gervase's successor Ither, the son of Baldwin II's sister Mathilda.[16]

The Montlhéry and Le Puiset families had strong traditions of independence that regularly set them against the Capetian monarchy, which under Philip I and Louis VI was attempting to establish effective royal control over the Ile-de-France and its neighbouring areas. The Capetians employed various strategies to assert royal authority over the turbulent baronage, including offers of marriage alliances, enlistment of church support, the purchase of properties and rights and, if all else failed, the use of force. Le Puiset was – at least in theory – a royal castellany, whose lords were also vassals of the count of Chartres for their *vicomté* in that city.[17] The Le Puiset family had a long history of resistance to the Capetians and despoliation of church property. When William, duke of Normandy, attempted to destabilise Capetian authority in 1079 he did this by paying subsidies to various lords of the Ile-de-France to get them to revolt against King Philip I. The king was obliged to seek support from Odo, count of Burgundy, William, count of Nevers, and Geoffrey, bishop of Auxerre, which is in itself an indication of the extent of the revolt among the nobility of the Ile-de-France. Philip's reaction was to lay siege to Le Puiset, an action that points to its lord, Hugh I Blavons, as one of the leaders of the uprising.[18] The family of Montlhéry-Bray was equally intractable. In his eulogistic biography of Louis VI, Abbot Suger of Saint-Denis said of the lords of Montlhéry that 'nothing evil was done in the

[15] *Cantatorium*, pp. 148-50; Rousseau, *Actes des comtes de Namur*, p. xcix. As count of Château-Porcien, Godfrey of Namur witnessed a charter of Hugh of Rethel in 1097: G. Saige and H. Lacaille, *Trésor des chartes du comté de Rethel*, 5 vols (Monaco, 1902-16), 1, no. 2.

[16] Rousseau, *Actes des comtes de Namur*, pp. c, cxii.

[17] A. de Dion, 'Le Puiset au XIe et XIIe siècle', *Mémoires de la Société Archéologique d'Eure et Loir* 9 (1889), 1-34, 71-85.

[18] A. Fliche, *Le règne de Philippe Ie, roi de France* (Paris, 1912), pp. 313-26.

entire kingdom without their consent or assistance'.[19] It is an indication of the importance of the lords and their castle that Philip I went to great lengths to neutralise them. In 1104 he arranged a marriage for his younger son Philip with Elisabeth, daughter of Guy II Troussel, lord of Montlhéry, and even agreed to a betrothal between his heir, Louis VI, and Lucienne, daughter of Guy's uncle Guy the Red, count of Rochefort. Louis evidently expected to gain control of Montlhéry, but when Guy Troussel died in 1108 the possession of the castle was disputed by his brother Milo II, who continued to resist royal authority until his death in 1118.[20]

The struggle between the Capetians and the lords of Le Puiset reached a climax in the first two decades of the twelfth century, when the repeated devastations of ecclesiastical property by Hugh III and his uncle and sometime guardian Hugh II gave Philip and Louis the opportunity to pose as defenders of the church.[21] In the period before 1111, Hugh III made war against his own lord, Theobald IV, count of Blois and Chartres, ravaging his lands. Such was Theobald's impotence that he was obliged to seek assistance from the king. The allies attacked Le Puiset from two sides, and took it by assault. The fortifications were demolished and Hugh taken prisoner by the king.[22] Nevertheless the temporary coalition between the Capetian monarchy and the count of Chartres soon collapsed, and Hugh was set free by Louis, promising never to fortify Le Puiset without the king's consent. In 1112 Hugh raised a final major baronial revolt in the Ile-de-France, centred yet again on an interrelated group: Hugh III of Le Puiset, Milo II of Bray, Hugh of Crécy, and Guy II of Rochefort, along with Hugh of Troyes and Ralph of Beaugency, with

---

[19] Suger, *Vie de Louis le Gros*, ed. and trans. Henri Waquet (Paris, 1964), p. 38. Translation taken from Suger, *The Deeds of Louis the Fat*, trans. Richard Cusimano and John Moorhead (Washington, 1992), pp. 40-41.

[20] Suger, *Vie de Louis le Gros*, pp. 34-43; A. Luchaire, *Louis le Gros. Annales de sa vie et de son règne (1081-1137)* (Paris, 1890), nos. 53, 246.

[21] Ivo of Chartres, *Epistolae*, PL 162, nos. 75, 111, 112; Luchaire, *Louis le Gros*, nos. 118, 119, 200, 237. Hugh I's third son Guy was originally a canon of Chartres, but later married the daughter of Mark of Etampes and succeeded to his *vicomté*. From 1106 to 1109 Guy was guardian and administrator for his nephew Hugh III and was excommunicated by Ivo of Chartres for the spoliation of the estates of the cathedral he had once served.

[22] Suger, *Vie de Louis le Gros*, pp. 128-49; Luchaire, *Louis le Gros*, no. 128; Fliche, *Philippe Ier*, p. 142.

support from Normandy, and – astonishingly – Theobald of Chartres. King Louis gradually prevailed, and again captured Le Puiset, razing the fortifications. This defeat of Hugh III was a real turning point. In 1118 he rebelled again, but after being defeated for a third and final time, Hugh announced his intention to go to Palestine.[23]

The Montlhéry-Courtenay-Le Puiset connection meant that Baldwin II was closely related to a considerable group of the French nobility which possessed established traditions of independence and resistance to royal authority, but whose freedom of action was being increasingly restricted by the Capetian monarchy in the first quarter of the twelfth century. The year of Baldwin II's accession, 1118, also marked the final triumph of Louis VI over the lords of Le Puiset and Montlhéry. It would be understandable if the new-found fortune in Outremer of a dynasty which most of its relatives probably regarded as their equals should have been perceived as an opportunity and an outlet which could compensate for diminishing prospects in the West. In fact this had already begun to happen during Baldwin's rule in Edessa. Only a few years after he became count, his first cousin Joscelin of Courtenay had arrived from the Gâtinais, and was given a fief centred on Turbessel (now Tilbeshar, Turkey), which comprised most of the county of Edessa west of the Euphrates.[24] Another first cousin, Waleran of Le Puiset, also came to Edessa, where he was given the fiefs of Sarūj and Bira.[25] It must have also been during Baldwin's tenure of Edessa that his sister Cecilia married Roger, prince-regent of Antioch.[26]

---

[23] Suger, *Vie de Louis le Gros*, pp. 150-71; Luchaire, *Louis le Gros*, nos. 134, 236, 237; Dion, 'Le Puiset au XIe et XIIe siècle', p. 29.

[24] WT X.23, pp. 482-83.

[25] Matthew of Edessa, *Chronicle*, trans. A. E. Dostourian, 2 vols (Ann Arbor, 1972), pp. 399-400.

[26] Roger was killed in battle in June 1119. Walter the Chancellor, p. 105, reveals that Baldwin II's sister was the *principissa* of Antioch in 1119, while William of Tyre refers to Roger as *domini Regis sororius* (WT XII.9, p. 556). She can be identified as the *Cecilia domina Tharsensis scilicet soror regis Ierosolimorum* who gave lands in the area of Mamistra to the abbey of Josaphat in Jerusalem in 1126. She had evidently received Tarsus as her dower lands: Mayer, *Die Kanzlei der lateinischen Könige*, 2: 889-90 (= RRH no. 114c).

The Policies of Baldwin II

BALDWIN II AND THE NOBILITY

Given the division of opinion on the death of his predecessor, and the possibility that a member of the Boulogne dynasty might still assert a claim to the throne, Baldwin II needed to bolster his support among the nobility and clergy. In the first instance, the king would clearly need men he could trust around him on a day-to-day basis, and the appearance of new aulic officers indicates that the royal household was reorganised soon after Baldwin's accession: there was a new constable, Hugh Caulis,[27] a butler, Pagan,[28] and a chamberlain, John.[29] By 1120 a new viscount of Jerusalem had been appointed, Anschetin.[30] Another newcomer who seems to have had a trusted role was Bernard *Vaccarius*.[31] It was the allocation of lordships and other fiefs that give the king the greatest scope to ensure loyalty by conferring benefits on men who would owe their preferment to him. During the first year of his reign, Baldwin carried out a major distribution of fiefs, granting out some lordships but retaining other towns and territories as domain lands.[32] The redistribution was made

---

[27] *Hugo Caulis constabularius*. RRH nos. 91.

[28] *Paganus pincerna*. RRH nos. 91, 121, 164 (1120-36). Pagan was clearly a favourite of the new regime, since he rose to become lord of the strategically important fief of Transjordan around 1126 (RRH nos. 115, 142).

[29] *Johannes camerarius (regis)*. RRH nos. 87, 90a, 91, 121 (1119-28). RRH no. 137a cannot be dated with certainty.

[30] RRH nos. 91, 101, 111, 110, 115, 120, 130, 137, 141, 158, 183, 257, 273. He was in office until 1132/1134: Mayer, *Die Kanzlei der lateinischen Könige*, 1: 518. His name indicates that Anschetin was a Norman.

[31] Attested in Palestine between 1122 and 1146. In the reign of Fulk Bernard was described as a *familiaris domini regis* and royal standard-bearer, and held lands in the royal domain south of Nablus (RRH nos. 100a, 104a, 115, 121, 137a, 153, 164, 174, 181, 240, 983; WT XV.6, p. 683). Mayer, 'Angevins versus Normans', pp. 13-14, points out that Bernard was one of few nobles of the kingdom prepared to accompany the king to Antioch in 1122. He also identifies him with one *Bernardus Vacca* documented at the court of Flanders in 1122/23: F. Vercauteren, *Actes des comtes de Flandre 1071-1128* (Brussels, 1938), nos. 108, 112. However, there is a significant difference in the meaning of the surname *Vaccarius* and its vernacular forms *Vachir* or *Vacers* ('cowherd') and the more pointed nickname *Vacca* ('cow') which make this identification problematic.

[32] AA pp. 709-10: *Die vero statuta, sicut justum est et reges decet, universis primoribus regni in palatium Solomonis regis convocatis, singulis beneficia contulit, fidem et sacramentum ab eis*

easier by the king's need to find a successor for Edessa. The obvious solution was to reward his principal partisan among the nobility by conferring the county on Joscelin of Courtenay, who had the double advantage of having spent considerable time in northern Syria, and being married to a member of the Armenian nobility. This move immediately freed up the fief of Tiberias, a lordship which had in the past been held by men from the extreme north of the French kingdom such as the Fleming Hugh of Fauquembergues and the Picard Gervase of Bazoches. It was now granted to William of Bures. Originally a vassal of the Montlhéry-Gometz family from the Ile-de-France, and a rear-vassal in Galilee during the reign of Baldwin I, he owed his new-found fortune completely to the king's favour.[33]

The only member of the Le Puiset family known among the nobility under Baldwin I was Hugh II, sometime guardian to his nephew Hugh III. He arrived in the kingdom after 1106, and seems to held property in Jaffa, which was then part of the royal domain lands. After the accession of Baldwin II, Jaffa was made into a lordship for Hugh. Jaffa was the second most important port of the kingdom and the usual point of arrival for pilgrims going to Jerusalem. Hugh evidently died soon after being made lord, and his son Hugh (II of Jaffa) was still under age. Jaffa was kept within the circle of the king's immediate kinsmen by being bestowed on Albert of Namur, who for good measure was married to Hugh's widow, Mabel of Roucy.[34] The accession of Baldwin II marked the beginning of new opportunities for the Le Puiset family, which must have been particularly welcome after its recent defeats at the hands of Louis VI of France. The acquisition of Jaffa was soon accompanied by major prize in the church. Gilduin of Le Puiset was the fourth son of Hugh I Blavons and Alice of Montlhéry; he entered the abbey of Saint-Martin-des-Champs, and between 1108 and 1119 became prior of the Cluniac house of Lurcy-le-Bourg. By the end of January 1120 Gilduin appeared as abbot-elect of the monastery of St Mary of the Valley of Josaphat. Among the

---

suscipiens, et honorifice quemque in sua remisit. Civitates vero, Neapolin, Sarzanam, Joppen, Cayphas, castellum Sancti Abrahae, Ptolomaidam, Sagittam, tabariam, et ceteras civitates et loca quae erant de regno Iherusalem, suo subjecit imperio, quoslibet reditus earum suis constituens primatibus, quoslibet vero suae mensae attitulavit.

[33] Prosopographical Catalogue, no. 79.

[34] Prosopographical Catalogue, no. 74.

religious sites of Jerusalem this shrine was regarded by the Franks as second only to the Holy Sepulchre in importance, a status reflected in the numerous charitable donations it received, particularly after Gilduin became abbot.[35] Among the known benefactors of the abbey during this time were of several members of the Le Puiset, Montlhéry, Courtenay and Rethel families from both Outremer and France: Hugh II of Jaffa, Joscelin I of Edessa, Waleran of Bira, Alice of Corbeil (widow of Everard III of Le Puiset and wife of Guy the Red, count of Rochefort), Cecilia of Tarsus, and of course Baldwin II himself, one of whose documents expressly alludes to his blood relationship with Gilduin.[36] Apart from the key figures of Joscelin of Courtenay, Gilduin, Hugh II of Le Puiset and his son Hugh II of Jaffa, several other French kinsmen of Baldwin II, particular members of the Le Puiset clan, spent time in the Holy Land, although it is at times difficult to establish whether they were permanent settlers or temporary visitors.[37] The presence of this inter-related group in Outremer constituted another significant difference from the previous reign. Apart from his *nepos* Godfrey, who died in 1115, Baldwin I had two distantly related kinsmen in the East, Fulk of Guînes, lord of Beirut, and Baldwin II, then count of Edessa. After the latter succeeded to the throne, there was a growing number of influential nobles and clerics who were first or second cousins of the king. These men were now acquiring power

[35] *Tractatus de reliquiis S. Stephani*, RHC Occ. 5: 317; Mayer, *Bistümer, Klöster und Stifte*, pp. 259-65; Riley-Smith, *First Crusaders*, pp. 169-70.

[36] RRH nos. 90, 91, 100a, 102a, 113a, 114b, 114c, 134, 137a.

[37] An unnamed nephew of the king was with him when they were captured by the Artukid emir Balak in September 1123; he died in captivity: Murray, 'Dynastic Continuity or Dynastic Change?', pp. 20-21. A charter issued in 1127 by Barisan, constable of Jaffa, and confirmed by Count Hugh of Jaffa gives as its first two witnesses *Wido scilicet de Puteolo* and *Wido de Domnapetra*: Delaborde, *Chartes de Terre Sainte provenant de l'abbaye de N.-D. de Josaphat,* no. 15 (= RRH no. 120). The first can be identified as Guy of Le Puiset, lord of Méréville (Essonne, arr. Etampes) and uncle to Hugh II of Jaffa: E. Mabille, *Cartulaire de Marmoutier pour le Dunois* (Châteaudun, 1874), no. 144; Dion, 'Le Puiset au XIe et XIIe siècle', pp. 22-23. The second was Guy, son of Theobald of Dampierre-en-Yvelines (Yvelines, arr. Rambouillet) and Isabella, daughter of Milo I of Montlhéry and Bray: *Cartulaire du prieuré de Nôtre-Dame de Longpont* (Lyon, 1879), nos. 46, 84. The *Guitterius sororius regis* who witnessed a charter of Baldwin II in 1128 (RRH no. 121) was undoubtedly Ither, son of the king's sister Mathilda; he later became count of Rethel on the death of Baldwin's brother Gervase.

and prestige on a far greater scale than Baldwin I had ever permitted. One striking expression of baronial self-assertion was the adoption of seals for use in authenticating documents, the first two lords to do so being cousins of the king: Joscelin of Courtenay for Tiberias and Hugh of Le Puiset for Jaffa.[38]

The king's cousin Hugh, who was in possession of the fief of Jaffa by 1123, was in many ways the most favoured member of this privileged circle. One expression of this was his title. His seal bore the inscription COMES HUGO, while his documents described him as *comes* and even *princeps*.[39] This sudden appearance of a comital title was a novelty among the nobility of the kingdom, even more so considering that the lords of Le Puiset had not held this rank in France. Two of his documents reveal that Hugh's ambitions extended beyond his county of Jaffa. In 1123 he made a donation of properties to St Mary of Josaphat where his uncle Gilduin was abbot. The lands he gave comprised a third of the casale of Machoz, situated about 5 km north-east of Ascalon, as well as a mosque and an orchard inside Ascalon.[40] The interesting thing about this donation is that Ascalon was at that time still in Muslim hands, although of course it was one of the most obvious targets for Frankish expansion. Three years later Hugh made a similar donation in favour of the order of the Hospital, promising it three casalia 'in the territory and lordship of the city of Ascalon' *(in territorio et dominio eiusdem civitatis Ascalonis)* whenever it fell to the Christians and the lands specified were in his possession.[41] The rights that Hugh was exercising in this territory in advance of its capture suggest that he had been promised the lordship (*dominium*) of Ascalon by Baldwin II, a concession which must have been made in 1123 or earlier.

The privileging of a new, favoured circle men such as Hugh of Jaffa could only proceed without repercussions as long as they could be accommodated with fiefs, offices and revenues without overly depriving and antagonising those who had enjoyed such benefits during the

---

[38] H. E. Mayer, *Das Siegelwesen in den Kreuzfahrerstaaten* (Munich, 1978), pp. 33-53.

[39] *Comes*: Ch. Kohler, 'Chartes de l'abbaye de Notre-Dame de la Vallée de Josaphat (1108-1291)', *ROL* 7 (1900), 108-222, no. 9 (= RRH no. 102a); Delaborde, *Chartes de Terre Sainte provenant de l'abbaye de N.-D. de Josaphat*, no. 15 (= RRH no. 120). *Princeps*: *C. Hosp.* 1, no. 77 (= RRH no. 113); G. Bresc-Bautier, *Le Cartulaire du chapitre du Saint-Sépulcre de Jérusalem* (Paris, 1984), no. 94 (= RRH no. 104).

[40] Kohler, 'Chartes de l'abbaye de Notre-Dame de la Vallée de Josaphat', no. 9.

[41] *C. Hosp.* 1, no. 77.

previous reign. Baldwin I had inherited few cities and little territory from his brother, but put great efforts into defending and then expanding the realm. His eighteen-year reign saw the capture of Arsuf (1101), Caesarea (1101), Acre (1104), Sidon (1110) and Beirut (1110), as well as the extension of Frankish power over much of the Transjordan. Yet the important coastal cities of Tyre and Ascalon remained in Muslim hands, and the Franks had done little to penetrate the *Terre de Suète*, the fertile area which lay between between the River Jordan and Damascus. Soon after his accession, Baldwin II led an invasion of this region and captured the town of Der'a, and in 1121 returned and destroyed a fortification at Jerash which had been constructed by the Damascenes.[42] This aggressive policy offered the prospect of territorial gain and increased revenues, but it was soon ended by political developments in the Frankish north.

THE REGENCY OF ANTIOCH

On 27 June 1119, the army of the principality of Antioch sustained a major defeat by the forces of Najm al-Dīn Ilghāzī ibn Artuk, one of the Turkish emirs of northern Syria. Roger, the prince-regent, died and the majority of his troops were killed or captured; so great were the casualties among the Antiochenes that the battle was afterwards known to the Franks simply as the Field of Blood (*Ager Sanguinis* or *Campus Sanguinis*). The security strategy employed by the Franks of Outremer over the previous two decades demanded that in circumstances such as these, the kingdom of Jerusalem was expected to provide military assistance to defend the weakened principality. In August 1119 Baldwin II marched to the relief of Antioch, winning the victory of Zerdana, and remained in the north for most of the rest of the year to deal with pressing business, only returning to Jerusalem for his coronation on Christmas Day. Roger's heir, Bohemund II, was still a minor, and Antioch required an active governor. The solution arrived at was for Baldwin II to take over the regency of the principality, a decision which was probably assisted by the fact that Roger had been married to his sister Cecilia. Baldwin acted as regent from 1119 to 1126, when Bohemund II arrived from Sicily. At this point the Rethel-Hauteville family ties were further strengthened by a marriage between

---

[42] Ibn al-Athīr, 315-16, 784; Sibt Ibn al-Jawzi, *Extraits du Mirat Ez-Zeman*, RHC Or. 3: 560; FC III.10, pp. 643-54; WT XII.16, pp. 565-66.

Bohemund and Baldwin's daughter Alice.[43] The responsibilities of the regency of Antioch meant that the king and the army of Jerusalem were obliged to spend long periods in the north defending the principality from the Turkish powers of northern Syria. A fresh invasion by Ilghāzī in 1120 required another northern campaign which lasted from June to October.[44] In June 1122 yet another invasion was launched by Ilghāzī, this time in conjunction with his nephew, Nūr al-Dawla Balak of Aleppo. Most of that summer was spent on campaign, after which Baldwin sent most of the Jerusalem army home, while himself remained in the north.[45]

These long northern campaigns were crucial to the continuing security of the Latin states as a whole, but they were nevertheless unpopular among certain sections of the nobility and clergy of Jerusalem. After the appeal for assistance from Antioch in 1120 Baldwin asked the new patriarch, Warmund of Picquigny, to allow the True Cross to accompany the army. This relic played a significant role in the military strategy of the kingdom. It was a fragment believed to have been part of the Cross of Christ, which had been discovered in Jerusalem shortly after the capture of the city, and was normally kept in the church of the Holy Sepulchre. The fragment was set in a larger metal cross decorated with gold and silver.[46] It was often taken into battle by the armies of the kingdom, as it was thought to have the power to bring victory. In such cases it was usually carried by the patriarch, and often displayed to the troops in the context of an inspiring sermon before battle.[47]

In military terms, then, the True Cross had a practical, morale-building quality. It might be expected that when Antioch was threatened in 1120, there would be every reason for the relic to accompany the army. On this occasion, however, the Patriarch Warmund and some of the nobility tried to prevent its departure from the kingdom, but the underlying reason was opposition to the campaigns in the north. Fulcher's description of differences between those going to war and those remaining in Jerusalem (*inter euntes ad bellum et remanentes in Jerusalem*) indicates the existence of two

---

[43] FC III.3-7, pp. 620-35; WT XII.9-10, pp. 556-59, XIII.20-21, pp. 612-14; Walter the Chancellor, pp. 79-87, 96-107.

[44] FC III.9, pp. 638-42; WT XII.11-12, pp. 559-62.

[45] FC III.11-12, pp. 646-53, III.16-17, pp. 658-61.

[46] AA pp. 488-89; FC I.30, pp. 306-10; WT IX.4, pp. 424-25.

[47] On the military use of the relic, see Murray, 'Mighty Against the Enemies of Christ', pp. 217-38.

factions. The dissidents, who were opposed to participation in the expedition, had allied themselves with the patriarch in order to keep the Cross in Jerusalem, in the hope that the army would be reluctant to set off without the precious relic, thus sabotaging the entire campaign. However, precedent was on the king's side. Baldwin could argue that the Cross had gone outside the kingdom only the previous year, in 1119. Warmund's opposition can be seen in the fact that he released the relic but refused to accompany it himself. As in 1119, the greater part of the army returned home at the earliest possible opportunity while the king remained in the north.[48] Mayer has pointed out the importance of an insertion in a royal charter of 1120 stressing the precedent of the victories of that year 'gained by the sign of the cross'. Yet as the document was issued on 30 December 1120 its purpose could hardly have been to support the king's case *before* the campaign of that year; it seems rather to anticipate further trouble in the future. We know that in 1122 Count Pons of Tripoli renounced his allegiance to Baldwin. It is unlikely that this defiance was an unmotivated step; it may have been timed to take advantage of continuing domestic difficulties in Jerusalem.[49]

There were several reasons why the campaigns in the north may have been unpopular. The absence of a king from his realm necessarily slowed down the process of government. Justice could not function properly, since the king's court was the highest legal authority in the kingdom, and his absences meant delays. Repeated campaigns far outside the kingdom called on its military resources, which from the barons' point of view might have been more profitably deployed in a way that would benefit them and the kingdom directly. From a period starting around fifteen months after his accession Baldwin II had been repeatedly campaigning beyond the borders of his kingdom. Campaigns in the north may have offered some prospect of plunder, but any such gains needed to be offset against the expenses involved in long marches to the north. If the army had been used in attacking Muslim-held territories bordering Palestine, there would have been additional incentives of lands, tribute or booty to be gained. In defensive campaigns for the benefit of Antioch, there was little prospect of compensations to such an extent. Although many of the

---

[48] FC III.9, pp. 638-42; Mayer, *Jérusalem et Antioche au temps de Baudouin II*, pp. 719-30.

[49] FC III.11, pp. 646-48; WT XII.17, pp. 566-68.

Antiochene fief-holders had been killed at the Field of Blood, Baldwin II could not simply hand out fiefs to barons from Jerusalem, since the terms of his regency obliged him to re-grant fiefs to relatives of their former lords even if they had to be summoned from Europe.[50] This deprivation would have been felt especially keenly by the older nobility established under Baldwin I as they saw more fiefs within the kingdom pass into the hands of *novi homines*.

THE CAPTIVITY OF BALDWIN II

In September 1122 Count Joscelin of Edessa, Waleran of Bira and several other Edessan vassals were captured by Balak near the town of Sarūj, and imprisoned in the fortress of Khartpert. In the following year Baldwin once more led an army north, but on 18 April he was himself surprised by Artukid forces, and sent to join the Edessan captives.[51] In the middle of August the Frankish prisoners at Khartpert managed to seize control of the fortress with the help of some of Joscelin's Armenian subjects who had infiltrated the Turkish defences. Joscelin was chosen to attempt an escape past the Turks who had surrounded the walls, and succeeded in reaching Turbessel, while the other Franks and Armenians tried to defend the castle. When news of this upturn in fortunes reached Jerusalem, the army departed for the north, hoping to join contingents from Tripoli and Antioch in order to rescue the king. However, on reaching Turbessel the combined forces discovered that Balak had recaptured Khartpert and ordered Baldwin to be moved to the town of Harran.[52] Having assembled considerable forces, the Franks decided to make best use of the opportunity with a strike against Aleppo, but although they devastated the areas outside the town walls they were unable to achieve more and dispersed after four days.

When Balak died, his Frankish captives were taken over by another Artukid, Husām al-Dīn Timurtash, the son of Ilghāzī, who eventually came to terms for the king's release. In August 1124 Baldwin handed over hostages and paid the first instalment of a ransom, and was then set free.

---

[50] Walter the Chancellor, pp. 98-100; WT XII.12, p. 562; Mayer, *Jérusalem et Antioche*, pp. 732-35.

[51] FC III.12, pp. 651-52, III.16, pp. 658-61; Ibn al-Qalānisī, pp. 167-69; Ibn al-Athīr, pp. 352-53; Matthew of Edessa, trans. Dostourian, pp. 416-18.

[52] FC III.25-26, pp. 687-93; Matthew of Edessa, trans. Dostourian, pp. 418-19.

However, the problems posed by the defence and government of Antioch required him to remain in the north for another eight months, and it was not until April 1125 that he finally returned to his capital.

The Attempt to Depose Baldwin II

Baldwin II was a captive for a period of sixteen months, from 18 April 1123 to 29 August 1124, but he was absent from his kingdom for a total of two years. The summer of 1123 was a particular time of danger for Outremer. As king of Jerusalem, Baldwin had been appointed regent of Antioch for the principality's under-age heir. When the king was taken prisoner, joining Joscelin of Edessa in captivity, three of the four Latin states in the East (Jerusalem, Antioch and Edessa) were without their appointed governors, a potentially dangerous circumstance that was certain to be rapidly exploited by the enemies of the Franks. In the middle of May 1123, Fatimid land and naval forces arrived from Egypt at their forward base of Ascalon, and launched an attack on the port of Jaffa. The Jerusalem army marched out, taking the True Cross with it, and won a major victory on 29 May. The defeated Fatimid forces were pursued back as far as al-ᶜArish by a Venetian fleet which had arrived at about the middle of the month.[53]

The defeat of the immediate Fatimid threat left the ruling classes of Jerusalem free to direct the affairs of the kingdom without the constraints of the absentee king and his policies. One of the first acts of the nobles and prelates in council on the capture of Baldwin had been the election of a regent. The regent was evidently meant to act as executive leader, and to this end the position was bolstered by being combined with tenure of office of constable. However, the regent was obliged to share government with the patriarch and other *regni principes* in council. The man elected was Eustace Granarius, lord of Sidon and Caesarea. This choice may have simply been a matter of seniority. Eustace had been a major fief-holder since the first decade of the kingdom's existence, and therefore was probably regarded as more entitled to exercise the regency than lords of other important fiefs such as William of Bures, whose tenure of Tiberias dated from only 1119. Yet other factors may have been involved. Eustace was a Fleming from the diocese of Thérouanne, and was the most

[53] FC III.16-20, pp. 658-72.

prominent surviving member of the older nobility, which came predominantly from Flanders, Artois, Picardy, Lotharingia and Normandy.[54] No other member of the Jerusalem nobility alive in 1123 had been so favoured during the previous reign as Eustace Granarius had been. In view of his origins it is quite possible he may have been a representative of the legitimist party during the succession disputes of 1116-18, which was precisely that section of the ruling classes with most reason to resent the growth of power of the newcomers favoured in the present reign. It is thus likely that discontented members of the nobility and clergy took advantage of the captivity of Baldwin II to express their opposition to his policies by electing as regent a leading representative of the old order.

The real energies of the Franks went into the expansion of the kingdom. The two obvious targets were Ascalon, the Egyptian-held exclave on the south-west frontier of the kingdom, and Tyre, the best harbour on the coast north of Acre. Predictably, opinion in the council was divided along geographical lines as to which of the two cities should be besieged. The decision was therefore taken by casting lots, which fell in favour of a campaign against Tyre. Although short of ready money, the nobles and higher clergy made great efforts to raise funds to pay mercenary troops, and also enlisted the help of a Venetian fleet. Despite diversionary attacks from Ascalon, Tyre fell after a siege of five months, on 7 July 1124.[55]

Something of the climate of political opinion in the kingdom during Baldwin's captivity may be discerned in the account of this period given in the *Historia Hierosolymitana* of Fulcher of Chartres, which is the principal narrative source for the history of the kingdom in the period 1119 to 1127. Although Fulcher had left France with Stephen of Blois, in 1097 he had joined Baldwin I, whom he then served as chaplain.[56] Baldwin I was very much the hero of his work, but Fulcher was far less laudatory in the case of Baldwin II. This becomes clear in a section devoted to the king's captivity, which follows a description of how the Franks of Jerusalem had defeated the Fatimid invasion. Fulcher stresses how, although their king

[54] FC III.16, pp. 658-61; A. V. Murray, 'A Note on the Origin of Eustace Grenier', *Bulletin of the Society for the Study of the Crusades and the Latin East* 6 (1986), 28-30.

[55] FC III.27-36, pp. 693-46; WT XII.24, pp. 575-603.

[56] V. Epp, *Fulcher von Chartres: Studien zur Geschichtsschreibung des ersten Kreuzzuges* (Düsseldorf, 1990), pp. 24-35.

was a captive and they were threatened by the Egyptians, the people of Jerusalem had not been abandoned by God. After describing how the Fatimids were defeated, Fulcher gives a short exegesis of a passage from Psalm 32.12, *Beata gens cuius est Dominus Deus eius*. In this he contrasts the nature of earthly kingship with that of divine kingship. He offers the reflection that *forsitan non erat rex, quem forte fortuitu perdideramus, sed hic, qui nuper vicit, non solum est rex in Hierusalem sed in omni terra.*[57] He continues with more specific comments:

> *Quomodo ergo rex erit qui semper vitiis vincitur? numquid promeretur dici rex, si semper habeatur exlex? quia legem Dei nec tenet, nec tuetur; et quia non timet Deum, timebit quidem hominem inimicum suum. adulter est vel periurus sive sacrilegus; hic talis nomen perdit. mendax et fraudulentus, qui confidet in eo? aequus et impiis, quomodo exaudiet illum Deus? Si ecclesiarum est dissipator, si pauperum oppressor, tunc non regit sed confundit?*[58]

It is possible that Fulcher's reflections on kingship were of a general, philosophical nature, but then one wonders why they should be linked specifically to the case of Baldwin II. In particular, the thought that perhaps Baldwin *was not a king* is significant. To someone who saw God's hand in the direction of major events, as Fulcher did, the fact that Baldwin II had been allowed by divine power to fall into captivity might have been an indication that the people of Jerusalem had made the wrong choice of king during the debate over the succession in 1118. If these beliefs were shared by others, they could only have been strengthened by the fact that the kingdom's leaders had been able to ward off external

---

[57] FC III.21, p. 673: 'Perhaps he was no king whom we had lost by accident, but he who recently won the victory is not only King in Jerusalem but over all the Earth'. Translation taken from Fulcher of Chartres, *A History of the Expedition to Jerusalem, 1095-1127*, trans. F. R. Ryan (Knoxville, 1969), p. 245.

[58] FC III.21, pp. 673-74: 'How indeed shall he be called a king who is always conquered by his vices? How does one deserve to be called king if he is always outside the law? Because he does not keep the law of God, he is not obeyed; and because he does not fear God, he shall fear the man who is his enemy. Whoever is an adulterer, a perjurer, or a sacrilegious man, such a one has lost the name of king. A deceiver and a cheat, who will trust in him? If he is favorable to the impious how will God listen to him? If he is a robber of churches, if he is an oppressor of the poor, then he does not reign but confounds'. Translation from Fulcher of Chartres, *A History of the Expedition to Jerusalem,* trans. Ryan, pp. 245-46.

threats and also capture a major enemy-held city without Baldwin's leadership.

The king's captivity acted as a catalyst to the latent opposition to Baldwin II and his policies, so much so, in fact, that the opponents of the king were prepared to take extreme action. For over a century historians of the Latin East have been aware of a statement by the Flemish chronicler, Galbert of Bruges, to the effect that during the captivity of Baldwin the throne of Jerusalem was offered to Charles of Denmark, count of Flanders (1119-27). However, while Galbert's evidence has often been alluded to, little attempt has been made to evaluate it and set it in context.[59] The relevant passage occurs early on in the work, and was probably written in the summer of 1127:

> *Ejus quoque vitae tempore contigit regem Hierosolimorum in captivitatem Saracenorum incurrisse, et desolata sedebat civitas Hierusalem absque rege suo quem, sicut didicimus, christiani nominis milites qui militiae christianae ibidem studuerant odio habebant eo quod tenax et parcus fuisset rex ille captus, nec bene rexisset populum Dei. Inierunt ergo consilium et communi consensu litteras direxerunt comiti Karolo ut ascendens Hierosolimam, regnum Judeae assumeret et in loco et sancta civitate imperii catholici coronam dignitatemque regiam possideret. Noluit igitur, super hoc fidelium suorum accepto consilio, deserere patriam Flandriarum, quam vita comite bene recturus foret et satis melius quam adhuc rexisset, nisi traditores illi pessimi, pleni demonio, dominum et patrem plenum spiritu pietatis et consilii et fortitudinis enecassent. Proh dolor! Quod tantum virum ab ecclesia Dei tollerent, de quo regem ecclesiae et populus orientalis imperii et Hierosolimorum civitas sancta simul cum populo christianorum peroptaverat et disposuerat simulque expostulaverat constituere.*[60]

---

[59] See G. Dodu, *Histoire des institutions monarchiques dans le royaume latin de Jérusalem* (Paris, 1894), pp. 141-42; R. Grousset, *Histoire des croisades et du royaume franc de Jérusalem*, 3 vols (Paris, 1934-36), 1: 588 n. 1; Richard, *Latin Kingdom*, p. 70; Riley-Smith, *The First Crusaders*, p. 176; Y. Friedman, 'The Ransom of Captives in the Latin Kingdom of Jerusalem', in *Autour de la Première Croisade: Actes du Colloque de la Society for the Study of the Crusades and the Latin East (Clermont-Ferrand, 22-25 juin 1995)*, ed. M. Balard (Paris, 1996), pp. 177-89 (here 186). J. P. Phillips, *Defenders of the Holy Land: Relations Between the Latin East and the West, 1119-1187* (Oxford, 1996), pp. 20-21, gives some discussion.

[60] Galbertus notarius Brugensis, p. 15: 'During his [Charles'] lifetime it happened that the King of Jerusalem was taken captive by the Saracens, and the city of Jerusalem sat desolate without her king. As we have learned, the crusaders who were pursuing the course of Christian knighthood there hated that captive king because he was grasping and penurious, and had not governed the people of God

One of Galbert's main purposes was to glorify his hero, Charles, who was murdered on 2 March 1127 as a result of a conspiracy centred around a powerful family called the Erembalds – the *traditores* of Galbert's account. As far as Galbert is concerned, the important point in the passage cited is that Charles was not seduced by the offer of a crown, preferring to remain in Flanders and govern that country well.

We need to consider whether Galbert simply fabricated the offer of the crown of Jerusalem in order to place his martyred hero in as favourable a light as possible. Galbert gives a similar account of an offer of the German crown, made to Charles in 1125 on the death of Henry V, the last ruler from the Salian dynasty. Although this episode relates to a time *after* the captivity of Baldwin II of Jerusalem, Galbert transposes the order of events in his narrative. His description of them is therefore not chronological, but hierarchical, reflecting the relative importance of the crowns of Germany and Jerusalem. Galbert relates that the leading men of Germany deliberated on a suitable candidate to be their next ruler, and eventually decided to offer the throne to Charles:

> *Igitur, circumspectis terrarum et regnorum principibus, considerate inierunt consilium, quatenus illi sapientiores et potentiores in regno legatos idoneos, scilicet cancellarium archiepiscopi Coloniensis civitatis, et cum eo comitem Godefridum sollempniter transmitterent ad consulem Flandriarum Karolum Pium, ex parte totius cleri et ex parte totius populi regni et imperii Teutonicorum, expostulantes et obsecrantes potentiam et pietatem ipsius, ut imperii honores et dignitates regias cum suis facultatibus pro sola caritate assumeret.*[61]

---

well. Therefore they took counsel and by general consent sent a letter to Count Charles asking him to come to Jerusalem and receive the kingdom of Judaea, and in that place and in the holy city take possession of the crown of the Catholic realm and the royal dignity. But he was unwilling, after consulting his vassals, to desert the fatherland of Flanders, which in his lifetime he was to govern well, and would have ruled even better if these evil traitors, full of the demon, had not slain their lord and father who was imbued with the spirit of piety and wisdom and courage. Alas, what sorrow, that they should rob the Church of God of such a great man whom the church and the people of the Eastern Empire, and the Holy City of Jerusalem and its Christian population had preferred and chosen, and even demanded as its king'. Translation taken from J. B. Ross, *The Murder of Charles the Good, Count of Flanders by Galbert of Bruges*, 2nd edn (New York, 1967), pp. 92-93.

[61] Galbertus notarius Brugensis, pp. 8-9: 'After weighing the merits of rulers of various lands and kingdoms, those wise and powerful men of the realm decided, after due consideration, that they would formally send suitable delegates, namely, the chancellor of the archbishop of Cologne and with him Count Godfrey, to the

The purpose of this passage was evidently similar to that dealing with the kingdom of Jerusalem: that Charles could have been a king had he so wished, but preferred to devote himself to Flanders. While Galbert gives the impression of a unanimous approach to Charles made by the leading men of Germany, the actual situation was more complicated. Otto of Freising, who with his Hohenstaufen connections had no interest in glorifying Charles, confirms that he was one of four candidates in the election of the new king of Germany, along with Frederick II, duke of Swabia, Leopold III, margrave of Austria, and Lothar of Supplinburg, duke of Saxony. The candidature of Charles was advanced by a Rhineland party led by Frederick I, archbishop of Cologne, who wished to prevent his suffragan bishops in Saxony coming under the influence of Lothar, and who therefore proposed Charles as an alternative.[62] Thus, in the case of the candidature for the German throne Galbert's account can be shown to be accurate in its essence, although he made a rather selective use of facts in order to create the impression that Charles was offered the throne unanimously rather than being one of four contenders.

The analysis of the parallel case of a proposed candidature for the German throne indicates that there is no good reason to regard Galbert's account of the offer of the throne of Jerusalem as a fabrication. He belonged to the central comital administration of Flanders based at Bruges, he had access to official records, and he was writing only four years after Baldwin II was captured. There is nothing in Galbert's account to suggest that the ruling classes of Jerusalem were merely looking for a regent for the duration of their king's captivity. Nor could they have been offering only the *succession* to the throne in conjunction with a marriage to Baldwin's eldest daughter and heir, Melisende, since Charles was already married to Margaret, daughter of Renaud, count of Clermont.[63] What was

---

count of Flanders, Charles the Pious, on behalf of the whole clergy and people of the kingdom and empire of the Germans, to beg and entreat him by virtue of his power and piety to assume the honors of empire and regal dignities with their appurtenances, if only for the sake of charity'. Translation from Ross, *The Murder of Charles the Good*, p. 90.

[62] Otto von Freising, *Chronica sive historia de duabus civitatibus*, ed. W. Lammers (Darmstadt, 1960), p. 521; H. Sproemberg, 'Eine rheinische Königskandidatur im Jahre 1125', in *Aus Geschichte und Landeskunde*, ed. M. Braubach et al. (Bonn, 1960), pp. 50-70.

[63] Vercauteren, *Actes des comtes de Flandre 1071-1128*, nos. 100, 103, 116.

under discussion implied nothing less than the deposition of the king, and Baldwin's captivity was merely the occasion, rather than the cause of this attempted coup.

What comes over clearly in Galbert's account is the hostility of the barons of Jerusalem towards the king and his policies (*quem ... christiani nominis milites qui militiae Christianae ibidem studuerant odio habebant*); the reasons for this hostility are specificied as bad government in the kingdom (*nec bene rexisset populum Dei*) and the grasping and penurious nature of the king (*quod tenax et parcus fuisset rex*). This last point is echoed by the Armenian chronicler Matthew of Edessa, who complains of his 'ingenious avariciousness in seizing and accumulating the wealth of others, his insatiable love for money, and his deep lack of generosity', criticisms which are placed, interestingly, in the context of Baldwin's reign as king of Jerusalem rather than that as count of Edessa.[64] To the medieval mind, complaints of bad government could cover a multitude of ills, but the obvious grievances in 1123 would probably have had to do with the disruption to government caused by the king's repeated absences in the north. Justice could not function properly if the king was not present to hold court. Even the day-to-day business of government was severely hampered by the fact that for at least part of the period between 1119 and 1123 the chancery had decamped to Antioch along with the king.[65] The complaint about Baldwin's grasping and penurious nature could relate to his failure to provide patronage in the form of fiefs, which were tending instead to go to a favoured circle of newcomers.[66]

While it is easy to accept that there was considerable hostility to Baldwin II and his policies, Galbert's evidence raises one important question: why did those elements hostile to Baldwin choose to approach the count of Flanders rather than Eustace of Boulogne, who had been a contender for the throne in 1118? On that occasion Eustace disappointed his supporters by declining to press his claims, even though he had been assured of support, and this experience may have made them wary of promoting him subsequently. The simple answer, however, was probably that Eustace was no longer available. He was clearly an old man by this time; both of his brothers, who were younger than he was, were dead by

---

[64] Matthew of Edessa, trans. Dostourian, p. 402.

[65] Mayer, *Die Kanzlei der lateinischen Könige*, 1: 66-67.

[66] Galbertus notarius Brugensis, p. 15.

1118. Even if he survived the rigours of a journey to Palestine and a possible struggle for the throne, it would be questionable how long he might live after gaining the throne. Towards the end of his life his thoughts evidently turned to entry into a religious order. He was still count in 1122, but certainly by 1125 and possibly as early as 1123 he had entered a Cluniac priory. His daughter and heir Mathilda was still unmarried in 1123, and therefore would not have been acceptable to the kingdom of Jerusalem, which required a man on the throne, who could lead the army in the field.[67]

Charles of Flanders was thus a choice of opportunism rather than purely legitimist sentiment, but he did possess advantages from the point of view of Baldwin's opponents. He had impressive dynastic and crusading connections. He was of royal blood, being the son of Cnut the Holy, king of Denmark, and Adela, daughter of Robert I of Flanders.[68] His uncle Robert II of Flanders ('the Jerusalemite') had been one of the leaders of the first crusade.[69] Charles was born in Denmark around 1082/1086; when his father was assassinated at Odense in 1086, his mother took him to Flanders for safety. She later married Roger Borsa (†1111), the brother of Bohemund I of Antioch; Charles was thus related to the Norman rulers of southern Italy, being a half-brother of William, duke of Apulia and Calabria in 1123. In 1119 Charles succeeded his cousin, Robert II's son Baldwin VII. As count of Flanders, Charles was considered as the head of the lineage from which the counts of Boulogne had originally sprung. It would therefore be understandable if he were to be considered as an alternative candidate in the absence of a suitable member of the Boulogne dynasty.

In this respect it is even possible that Charles's partisans saw themselves as acting in accordance with the dispositions made by Baldwin I just before his death. Concerning the succession, the king had told his nobles

---

[67] D. Haigneré, *Les chartes de St Bertin* (Saint-Omer, 1886) 1, no. 146; Wauters, 2, 132; Mayer, *Die Kanzlei der lateinischen Könige*, 2: 926. The first reigning queen of Jerusalem was Baldwin II's daughter Melisende; she was married when she came to the throne.

[68] Charles' royal descent is mentioned in several of his charters (Vercauteren, *Actes des comtes de Flandre*, nos. 106, 117, 123) and also in the inscription on his seal: KAROLUS COMES FLANDRIE ET FILIUS REGIS DATIAE (p. cvii).

[69] M. M. Knappen, 'Robert II of Flanders in the First Crusade', in *The Crusades and Other Historical Essays presented to Dana C. Munro by his Former Students*, ed. L. J. Paetow (New York, 1928), pp. 79-100.

and prelates that Eustace of Boulogne should be made king, but if he were to decline on account of his age, they should choose Baldwin of Bourcq or someone else 'who would rule the Christian people and defend the churches, someone who was strong in faith, but who would not be intimidated by the strength of his enemies, nor easily corrupted by riches'.[70] If Baldwin of Bourcq was considered to have failed in his royal duties, his opponents could claim they were fulfilling his predecessor's will by replacing him with a more suitable candidate.

Many of the Flemings and Artesians in Jerusalem may well have been sympathetic towards the count of Flanders. It is probable that he was known personally to some of the older members of the ruling classes. Both Galbert and another Flemish chronicler, Walter of Thérouanne, relate that before he became count, Charles made a pilgrimage to Palestine. Since Walter says Galbert had already been knighted at the time, the *terminus a quo* for the pilgrimage would be the earliest date at which he could have come of age, i.e. *c.* 1097, but it is unlikely that he could have taken part in the First Crusade, since his presence is not mentioned by any of the numerous sources. The *terminus ad quem* is 1111, when Charles was received in Flanders by Robert II, who died in that year.[71] The most likely date would be 1107, when a large number of English, Danish and Flemish pilgrims arrived by sea in the Holy Land. Many of them fought alongside Baldwin I in the unsuccessful siege of Sidon.[72]

---

[70] AA p. 707: *Qui fratri Eustachio regnum destinat, si forte venerit; si vero aetate nequiverit, Baldewinus de Burg eligatur, aut talis qui populum Christianum regat, Ecclesias defendat, qui stabilis in fide maneat, quem nulla adversariorum virtus terreat, aut merces leviter corrumpat.*

[71] Galbertus notarius Brugensis, p. 31: *Cumque ante comitatum multa insignia et egregia fecisset, arripuit sanctae peregrinationis viam Hierosolimitanorum, atque maris profunda trans-navigando, tandem post multa pericula et vulnera pro amore Christi saepe perpessa, voto peroptato et laetissimo in Hierusalem ascendit, ubi et contra hostes christianae fidei strenue dimicavit*; Walter of Thérouanne, *Vita Karoli comitis Flandriae*, MGH SS 12: 540.

[72] According to Albert of Aachen (AA pp. 631-34), this fleet arrived in the seventh year of the reign of Baldwin I. While Ross's translation of Galbert (p. 113) depicts Charles as a simple pilgrim rather than as an armed crusader, Galbert's words *contra hostes christianae fidei strenue dimicavit* do imply participation in military activity. Since Eustace Granarius was later given the fief of Sidon, it is possible that he had been earmarked as its lord during the earlier siege, and that Charles got to know him at that time.

Why did nothing come of the approach to Charles? According to Galbert, Charles refused the offer put to him, on the grounds that he wished to maintain good government in Flanders. Since Charles had no children of his own, his departure would have caused difficulties for the governance of the county. It is also difficult to know how he assessed the situation in Jerusalem. When Eustace Granarius died on 15 June 1123 he was succeeded as regent by William of Bures, who was very much one of the *novi homines*, and unlikely to countenance action against the king. Eustace's two sons were minors, and their inheritance was rapidly brought under the influence of another of the king's allies. By April 1124 Eustace's widow, Emma, had married Hugh, count of Jaffa, who was a cousin of the king.[73] It is difficult to know whether Emma made a free choice of husband, whether she was pressurised into the new marriage, or simply whether she saw it as the best way to protect the rights of her sons, but these developments undoubtedly represented a major swing in the balance of power among the nobility.

As William of Bures so obviously remained in the royal favour after Baldwin's release, the offer of the crown to Charles is more understandable as a relatively early reaction to the king's captivity, taking place during the regency of Eustace Granarius. The events of 1123 mark a potential crisis of the Jerusalem monarchy, averted only by Charles' refusal to accept the offer of the crown. If he *had* accepted it is likely that civil war would have been the result, bearing in mind the helpless position of the king at that time. Yet this was the second time that opponents of Baldwin of Bourcq had been disappointed by their chosen candidate. The events of 1123 were storm clouds that failed to break.

The main reason why the evidence of Galbert of Bruges has been neglected is that it has been regarded as isolated. Yet there is another important piece of evidence which emanates from the Holy Land and also testifies to a threat to the position of the king. The decision to attack Tyre was made at a meeting of the *regni principes* and the doge of Venice at Christmas 1123. Those present included the Patriarch Warmund, the regent William of Bures (*regni constabularius et procurator*) and the chancellor Pagan, as well as bishops and a large number of barons of the kingdom.[74] The terms of the partnership between Franks and Venetians, which set

[73] RRH no. 104.

[74] WT XII.24, pp. 575-77.

out the privileges to be enjoyed by the Venetians in Tyre after its capture as well as elsewhere in the kingdom, were recorded in a document known as the *Pactum Warmundi*, whose text was preserved in the history of William of Tyre.[75] Before they concluded an agreement, the Venetians needed to be certain that it would not be repudiated by the king when he was eventually released from captivity, and so the patriarch promised that in that case he would make Baldwin confirm the treaty by swearing on the gospels.[76] Yet the *Pactum Warmundi* immediately goes on to raise the possibility that *another person* might be made king of Jerusalem, in which case he would be obliged to confirm the treaty before becoming king.[77] This condition would suggest that while they were in Palestine, the Venetian leaders had learned about a possible attempt to replace Baldwin, and were shrewd enough to insist on a clause in the treaty for the eventuality of something similar happening in the future.[78]

Epilogue: Baldwin of Bourcq Secure

Baldwin II was released from captivity in August 1124, and finally returned to his kingdom in April 1125. As there had been some sort of attempt to depose him, as in 1118, he had every incentive to weaken the opposition and build up his own support. The constableship was safe in the hands of William of Bures, but the office of marshal seems to have been given to a new incumbent, Sado.[79] Other changes affected the lordships. One of the king's first actions on his return was to confirm the

---

[75] WT XII.25, pp. 577-81.

[76] WT XII.25, p. 580: *Universaliter igitur supradictas conventiones ipsum regem, deo auxiliante si aliquando egressurus de captivitate est, nos Warmundus Ierusalem patriarcha confirmare per evangelium faciemus.*

[77] WT XII.25, p. 580: *Si vero alter ad Ierosolimitanum regnum in regem promovendus advenerit, aut superius ordinatas promissiones, antequam promoveatur, sicut ante dictum est ipsum firmare faciemus, alioquin ipsum nullo modo ad regnum provehi assentiemus.*

[78] The clause specifies someone who will become *rex*, and therefore could not apply to Baldwin's heir Melisende, who would be described as *regina*.

[79] *Sado marescallus* is attested for the period 1125 to 1154 (RRH nos. 109, 113, 121, 164, 174, 179, 226, 227, 240, 291). He thus served as household officer to three kings: Baldwin II, Fulk and Baldwin III. Little else is known about him. The office of marshal had considerably less status than that of constable.

Pactum Warmundi, which was done on 2 May 1125.[80] One of the witnesses to this document was Walter Brisebarre, a man previously unknown, who was described as *Berritti dominus*. This means that by May 1125 at the latest, the important northern lordship of Beirut, formerly held by the Fleming Fulk of Guînes, was in the hands of Walter Brisebarre. In January of the next year Walter and his brother Guy witnessed two more documents, both appearing in prominent positions in the witness lists.[81] The origins of the Brisebarres are obscure, but the fact that Walter's brother Guy was soon entrusted with an important diplomatic mission to the West indicates that the brothers were obviously trusted supporters of the king.[82] This suggests that the Brisebarres owed their rise to prominence to dispositions made by the king after his return from captivity. Even though changes of personnel in key positions would have bolstered the king's position, the lack of enthusiasm for campaigns in the north persisted despite the continuing dangers to the security of Antioch. In the spring of 1125 the Turkish atabeg of Mosul, Aksunkur al-Bursuki, invaded Antiochene territory, capturing the town of Kafartāb and threatening ᶜAzāz. In response, Baldwin went north in order to meet this threat by joining forces with troops from Tripoli, Edessa and Antioch itself. Yet he was able to take relatively few fighting men from Jerusalem, a circumstance that Fulcher of Chartres attributed to war-weariness caused by the constant campaigning of that and the previous year.[83] The chronicler proceeded to explain this poor response with an eloquent statement of how the men of Jerusalem had endured constant labours, having to go on campaign laden with provisions and equipment, wondering whether they would ever return to their homes.[84] Once again it would

[80] G. L. Tafel and G. M. Thomas, *Urkunden zur älteren Handels- und Staatsgeschichte der Republik Venedig mit besonderer Berücksichtigung auf Byzanz und die Levante*, 3 vols (Vienna, 1856-57), 1, no. 41 (= RRH no. 105).

[81] *C. Hosp.*, 1, nos. 74, 77 (= RRH nos. 112, 113).

[82] WT XIV.2, p. 633.

[83] FC III.42, p. 763: *de Hierosolymitanis autem paucis habebat, quoniam in presenti et in praeterito anno valde fatigati fuerant.*

[84] FC III.42, p. 763: *Nam quomodo tot labores adsidue tolerare poterant, quibus vix uno mense in domibus suis quiescere licebat? Certe crudelis corde est qui eis, qui circa Hierusalem inhabitabant, pie non compatitur, qui die ac nocte in Domini servitio gravissime tribulantur, qui etiam, cum de hospitio suo exeunt, ne reverti postea possint timidi ambigunt. Si longe tendunt, necessario alimentis suis et utensilibus onerati incedunt.*

seem that Fulcher of Chartres was acting as an apologetic mouthpiece for dissident opinion. The king's continuing support for the principality of Antioch was still resented among his vassals.

The events of 1123-25 had shown how fragile the kingship of Baldwin II had been, and it is likely that the realisation of his continuing vulnerability prompted him to take two crucial initiatives. While he was count of Edessa, Baldwin had married an Armenian princess, Morphia, a match that made sense in terms of the dynastic politics of northern Syria and Cilicia, but counted for far less in the international orbit of the kingdom of Jerusalem and the western powers which constituted its major sources of military assistance. Morphia had borne only daughters, all of them still unmarried in 1125, and Baldwin's period of captivity must have made clear to him how precarious his family's grip on the throne was as long as this situation continued, particularly in respect of the heir, Melisende.[85] Even though the candidature of Charles of Flanders ultimately failed to materialise, the potential threat to Baldwin and his family was probably actually greater *after* his return to Jerusalem. Mathilda, the heiress to Eustace of Boulogne, was still unmarried in 1123, but in 1124 or 1125 she married Stephen of Blois. This Stephen was the third son of Adela, sister of Henry I of England, and Stephen, count of Blois and Chartres, who had served with dishonour on the First Crusade but in some measure redeemed himself by his death in battle after his returning to the Holy Land with the crusade of 1101. The younger Stephen was very much a favourite nephew of Henry I of England, who had favoured him with numerous grants. By 1113 he held the county of Mortain in Normandy, and the Honour of Eye (in Suffolk) and the lordship of Lancaster in England. The marriage to Mathilda of Boulogne was an exceptionally good match for Stephen. Mathilda was not only descended from Charlemagne through her Boulogne ancestry; her mother Mary was a daughter of Malcolm III *Ceann Mór*, king of Scotland, and a sister of Henry I's own wife Mathilda, and was also descended from the old Anglo-Saxon royal family through Malcolm's wife St Margaret, the sister of Edgar the Ætheling. Thus Stephen and Mathilda had prestigious ties, and were major landholders on both sides of the English Channel.[86] The potential claims

---

[85] Phillips, *Defenders of the Holy Land*, pp. 20-21.

[86] J. T. Appleby, *The Troubled Reign of King Stephen* (London, 1969), pp. 1-10 (dating the marriage to 1124); R. H. C. Davis, *King Stephen 1135-1154,* 3rd edn (London,

of this exceptionally well-connected couple and their prospective descendants, possibly backed by political interests and resources of the Anglo-Norman realm, must have seemed like a frightening prospect to a first-generation *parvenu* like Baldwin of Bourcq, who had been on the throne of Jerusalem for only eight years, and whom a body of opinion in the kingdom believed had been a bad ruler. The political and military situation of the Frankish states made it quite possible that the king might be captured once again or even killed in battle, leaving an unmarried woman as successor.[87]

Baldwin's solution was to seek a husband from the west for Melisende. During 1127, after consultation with his leading clerics and barons, the king decided to approach Fulk V, count of Anjou, who had become a widower in 1126. The mission to Fulk was placed in the hands of two noblemen: one of Baldwin's most trusted associates, William of Bures, and a member of a family which had recently come to prominence, Guy Brisebarre. Negotiations between Fulk and Baldwin's representatives were complicated, mainly because the count proposed to turn the government of Anjou over to his son, Geoffrey, and wanted to make sure that, as Melisende's husband, he would eventually become king of Jerusalem.[88]

In the meantime a second initiative was under way. Probably as a conciliatory policy toward his nobles, the king embarked on a new, aggressive policy aimed at expansion of the kingdom, beginning with an invasion of the *Terre de Suète* in 1126. In contrast to the feeble efforts of previous years, this expedition attracted the entire available military strength of the kingdom.[89] The climax of the king's aggressive policy came in 1129, when he mounted a major, albeit unsuccessful attempt to capture Damascus itself. He not only succeeded in assembling troops from all four Frankish states, but he had put considerable effort into recruiting crusaders from the West by means of a mission under Hugh of Payns, the master of the Templars, which was an indication of the influence the military orders

---

1990), pp. 1-11 (to 1125); D. Crouch, *The Reign of King Stephen, 1135-1154* (Harlow, 2000), pp. 20-23 (to 1125).

87 Phillips, *Defenders of the Holy Land,* p. 20.

88 H. E. Mayer, 'The Succession to Baldwin II of Jerusalem: English Impact on the East', *Dumbarton Oaks Papers* 39 (1985), 139-47; Phillips, *Defenders of the Holy Land,* pp. 24-35.

89 FC III.50, pp. 784-93; WT XIII.18, pp. 620-22; Ibn al-Athīr, pp. 352-53, 372; Ibn al-Qalānisī, pp. 174-77.

were beginning to develop in the affairs of the kingdom.[90] In the years that followed their marriage there is no evidence of any inclination of Stephen and Mathilda to press their claims, and the opportunities for doing so diminished as Baldwin II spent more of his time and energies in attempting to expand his own kingdom. On his death on 21 August 1131, he was succeeded by joint rulers: Melisende, Fulk, and their son Baldwin III, born in 1130.[91] It was now certain that the kingdom of Jerusalem would be ruled by descendants of Baldwin of Bourcq.[92]

---

[90] WT XIII.28; Ibn al-Athīr, pp. 385-86; Ibn al-Qalānisī, pp. 195-208; J. P. Phillips, 'Hugh of Payns and the 1129 Damascus Crusade', in *The Military Orders: Fighting for the Faith and Caring for the Sick*, ed. Malcolm Barber (Aldershot, 1994), pp. 142-47.

[91] Vogtherr, 'Die Regierungsdaten der lateinischen Könige von Jerusalem', pp. 56-61.

[92] The use of the name Baldwin, given to eldest sons in the royal family of Jerusalem up to the birth of Baldwin V (1177 or 1178), should be considered as deriving from Baldwin II rather than from his predecessor. It is perhaps also significant that the name Godfrey was never used by the descendants of Baldwin II, despite the exalted reputation of the first ruler.

Conclusion

The first ruling house of the Latin kingdom of Jerusalem had two distinct dynastic traditions: a Lotharingian tradition based on the house of Ardennes-Bouillon, and its possessions in the Empire; and a Flemish-Artesian tradition based on the counts of Boulogne, vassals of the king of France. The first was represented primarily by Godfrey of Bouillon, the second by Eustace of Boulogne, while the third brother, Baldwin, acted both in the West and on the course of the crusade as a link between the two. These two component traditions were quite different in terms of power and influence. The Boulogne tradition was in an ascendant on the eve of the crusade. The counts had expanded their possessions on the continent and augmented these by profiting from the Norman Conquest of England, which had brought Boulogne a new political and economic importance. The Lotharingian tradition, on the other hand, was in an eclipse; the power of the Ardennes-Bouillon dynasty had entered a rapid decline in the mid-eleventh century. As lord of Bouillon and count of Verdun, Godfrey was merely one of many competing dynasts, forced to fight to maintain possession of his hereditary domains for most of his adult life prior to the crusade; as duke of Lower Lotharingia from 1087, he was a removable imperial official, unable to assert an enfeebled ducal authority which had been progressively diminished by the German monarchy to the benefit of the ecclesiastical principalities. His decision to leave for the East was coupled with the abandonment of his inheritance; only the sale or mortgage of his lands enabled Godfrey to raise sufficient funds for the journey. What is most significant for the early history of the kingdom of Jerusalem, the abandonment of the Lotharingian lands of its ruling house meant that only Boulogne remained as a western point of contact for the ruling dynasty of Jerusalem.

Lotharingian lords and knights were under no obligation to accompany the duke to the Holy Land; indeed, participation in the crusade was relatively low in his duchy. Nevertheless, Godfrey and his brother Baldwin were successful in asserting and maintaining leadership over a considerable number of crusaders from Lotharingia, Germany and the north-east of France, and from the time of the passage to Asia Minor, they were also able to gain the service of crusaders from other contingents. The financial and alimentary resources secured by the conquest of Edessa played a crucial role in helping to attract and retain service, particularly during the privations of the siege of Antioch. The relative support enjoyed by each of the princes would become an important factor in determining who was to rule the new Frankish state in Palestine, a decision which could no longer be postponed after the capture of the Holy City in July 1099. The territory conquered from the pagans, the *regnum Iherusalem*, was regarded by the crusaders as constituting the patrimony of Christ, and when their leaders met to decide on its government, they ignored demands for the establishment of an ecclesiastical polity, and proceeded to set up a secular monarchy to rule the kingdom and defend the church of the East. The duties and powers of the new ruler were reflected in his titles: *princeps regni* and defender of the Holy Sepulchre, whose authority was regarded as deriving directly from God. It was Godfrey who was preferred by the electors to Raymond of Saint-Gilles, who had antagonised a large number of crusaders in the course of the expedition.

During the reigns of Godfrey and his brother Baldwin I, the territory of the *regnum Iherusalem* was expanded from fragmented blocs in Judaea, Galilee and the south-western coast to control of the greater part of the Holy Land apart from the ports of Tyre and Ascalon. This was achieved with the help of various groups and institutions: the new Frankish population of the Holy Land, the Italian maritime republics, and fresh waves of crusaders, pilgrims and settlers. A key role in the expansion and security of the kingdom was played by the nobles, knights and clerics who formed the military and adminstrative support of the monarchy. The most trusted and influential of these men were predominantly Lotharingians, Normans, Flemings, Picards and Artesians. In a few cases, they had ties of vassalage or service to the Bouillon-Boulogne dynasty dating to before 1096, but in many more cases they only acquired such ties in the course of the crusade and the first years of the Frankish settlement in the kingdom of Jerusalem and the county of Edessa. After about 1110 the Lotharingians became fewer in number and influence; the decision by Godfrey and Baldwin to dispose of their lands had severed the monarchy's connection with Lotharingia. The nobility of Jerusalem had at most been only partly Lotharingian in character, and became considerably less so after 1110.

The character of the ruling classes as well as the nature of their relationship to the monarchy began to change significantly after the claims of

Eustace III of Boulogne were defeated by Baldwin of Bourcq and his supporters. From 1118 onwards, influence in both nobility and clergy began to pass into the hands of new men who had arrived in the kingdom after, rather than on the First Crusade, whose geographical origins lay in the Ile-de-France and surrounding regions, and who had ties of kinship and vassalage with each other and with the family of Baldwin II. The preferment of this new group and the problems caused by repeated military campaigns in the north after 1119 created increasing resentment among the ruling classes for a faction to exploit the absence of Baldwin II in Turkish captivity, by attempting to put Charles of Flanders on the throne in his place. This action can be regarded as a bold attempt to remove an unpopular monarch by reversing the outcome of the disputed succession of 1118, with Charles as a substitute for Eustace of Boulogne. Although it marked a crisis for the kingship of Baldwin of Bourcq, the revolt failed to run its full course, and the return of Baldwin to Jerusalem in 1125 and the marriage of his daughter to Fulk of Anjou saw the dynasty of Rethel-Anjou, if we can call it that, secure on the throne until the kingdom was overrun by Saladin in 1187.

Baldwin of Bourcq was a survivor not only in political terms; he seems to have outlived almost all of those who had come to the Holy Land on the First Crusade. His accession to the throne of Jerusalem not only marked the advent of a new dynastic element. More importantly for the history of Outremer, however, his reign witnessed some key developments which would determine the political characteristics of the kingdom for the best part of the century. The distribution of much of the kingdom's territory in the form of lordships to be held by hereditary tenure established a small, privileged and powerful group within the kingdom's nobility. The foundation of a new military monastic order, the Temple, and the militarisation of an existing charitable order, the Hospital, established institutions of a new kind which not only took on part of the burden of the defence of the kingdom, but which would increasingly play a major role in its politics, although this role was complicated by the fact that the orders were accountable only to the papacy. It could even be argued that the concentration of monarchs of Jerusalem on the security and expansion of their own kingdom from 1126 onwards ultimately proceeded to the detriment of the Frankish states in northern Outremer.

The end of the ascendancy of the house of Bouillon-Boulogne was the precursor of not only dynastic, but far-reaching political change.

Appendix A

The Descendants of Eustace II of Boulogne

The details of the marriages and descendants of Eustace II of Boulogne have been sources of considerable confusion in scholarship. The purpose of this appendix is to give an overview of Eustace's descendants over the following two generations, several of whom were of significance in the early history of the kingdom of Jerusalem.

It is generally accepted that Eustace was married twice. His first wife was Godgifu (Goda), a daughter of the English king Æthelred II Unræd (†1016) and his second consort, Emma (known in England as Ælfgifu), daughter of Richard I of Normandy. Godgifu's date of birth is uncertain; it must have been after 1002, and Barlow conjectures a date between 1003 and 1014.[1] During the reign of Cnut, while she and her brother Edward (the Confessor) were exiles in Normandy, Godgifu was married to Drogo, count of Amiens and the Vexin. They had two sons: Walter III, count of Mantes and Ralph 'the Timid', earl of Hereford. Only Ralph (†1057) is known to have had any issue: Harold of Ewias, later lord of Sudeley in Gloucestershire. Drogo himself died in 1035 while on pilgrimage to Jerusalem.[2]

Godgifu's marriage to Eustace II must have occurred sometime after 1035, but indications are extremely sketchy. In September 1051 Eustace paid a diplomatic visit to Edward the Confessor, who had been king of

---

[1] F. Barlow, *Edward the Confessor* (London, 1970), pp. 28-31.

[2] Round, *Studies in Peerage and Family History*, pp. 147-50; A. E. Ellis, 'On the Landholders of Gloucestershire named in Domesday Book', *Transactions of the Bristol and Gloucestershire Archaeological Society* 4 (1879-80), 86-98; Barlow, *Edward the Confessor*, pp. 39, 41, 307-8; D. Bates, 'Lord Sudely's Ancestors: The Family of the Counts of Amiens, Valois, and the Vexin in France and England During the Eleventh Century', in *The Sudelys, Lords of Toddington*, ed. R. Smith (London, 1987), pp. 36-38; A. Williams, 'The King's Nephew: The Family and Career of Ralph, Earl of Hereford', in *Studies in Medieval History Presented to R. Allen Brown*, ed. C. Harper-Bill, C. J. Holdsworth and J. L. Nelson (Woodbridge, 1989), pp. 327-43; K. S. B. Keats-Rohan, *Domesday People. A Prosopography of Persons Occurring in English Documents, 1066-1166, 1: Domesday Book* (Woodbridge, 1998), p. 245.

England since 1043. During this Eustace's men were involved in an affray with the citizens of Dover, and Eustace complained to the king, who ordered retribution against Dover, an action which was greatly resented by Earl Godwin of Wessex and his supporters.[3] The obvious influence that Eustace had with the king is an indication that they were already related by marriage, although it is of course unclear how long previous to this date the marriage had taken place.[4] There is no direct evidence of any offspring of Eustace and Godgifu, and even the date of Godgifu's death is uncertain.

It is equally difficult to date Eustace II's marriage to Ida of Bouillon (†1113), daughter of Godfrey II ('the Bearded'), duke of Upper and Lower Lotharingia (†1069), and his first wife, Doda/Uota, a lady of noble lineage whose precise family affiliations remain unclear. Since her brother Godfrey III had no direct heirs, it was through Ida that the succession to the Ardennes-Bouillon lands was transmitted to her second son, Godfrey (IV). If we accept that Godfrey must have been aged at least fifteen or sixteen when he was allowed to take up his Lotharingian inheritance in 1076, then his elder brother Eustace III must have been born in 1060 or earlier, and most historians have dated the marriage of his parents to 1057.[5] The question is complicated by a record of the Council of Rheims (1049), at which Pope Leo IX excommunicated for incest a Count Eustace and a Count Engelrand; they have been identified as the count of Boulogne and the count of Ponthieu, although there are no indications as to the identity of their wives.[6] As for Eustace, Barlow argued that 'this can hardly be an indication of when he married Godgifu, who would have been about forty at the time: the sentence marks either the end of that union or the beginning of his marriage to Ida'.[7] Tanner assumes that the

---

[3] Barlow, *Edward the Confessor*, pp. 109-11.

[4] Andressohn, *Ancestry and Life of Godfrey of Bouillon,* p. 20 assumes 1050 or 1051 for the marriage; Mayer, *Mélanges*, p. 15, assumes 1050.

[5] Mayer, *Mélanges*, p. 16 and literature cited there. Andressohn, *Ancestry and Life of Godfrey of Bouillon,* p. 21 n. 60, gives 1057, citing H. Ellis, *A General Introduction to Domesday Book*, 2 vols (London, 1833), 1: 384, but it is not made clear on what original sources this assumption is based.

[6] *Concilium Remense*, in Recueil des Historiens des Gaules et de France 11: 527: *Excommunicavit etiam Comites Angelrai et Eustacium propter incestum, et Hugonem de Braina, quia legitimam uxorem dimiserat, et aliam sibi in matrimonio sociaverat.*

[7] Barlow, *Edward the Confessor*, pp. 307-8.

marriage which was condemned in 1049 was that of Eustace and Ida, although she admits that there is no surviving evidence to indicate that they were related within the seven degrees prohibited by the church.[8] It also seems inconceivable that they should have remained married for several decades and that Ida should have been ultimately beatified if the marriage was regarded as sufficiently incestuous to warrant papal excommunication.[9]

Barlow argues that Eustace and Godgifu must have been married 'in, or shortly after, 1036'.[10] This chronology, however, is based an assumption relating to Eustace's involvement in English politics after the Norman Conquest. William of Poitiers relates that in 1067, Eustace II invaded Kent and attempted to capture Dover. During this attack Eustace's *nepos*, a young knight of noble birth (*nobilissimus tiro*), was killed.[11] Barlow interprets the word *nepos* to mean 'grandson', and argues that he was the son of a daughter of Eustace and Godgifu; since he was a potential heir to the throne of England, Eustace was attempting to assert or safeguard his rights. This construction is problematic in several respects. Not only is the putative daughter of Eustace and Godgifu entirely undocumented; Barlow concedes that to fit the chronology, she would need to have been born in 1037 and married in 1049 at twelve, to produce a son of military age in 1067 (fifteen) born in 1052. This is itself unlikely, and even more so considering that Harold of Ewias, grandson of Godgifu and her *first* husband, was still a minor in 1067.[12] Furthermore, the theory of a grandson of Godgifu gives an implausible motivation for Eustace's invasion of Kent. There was no tradition in England of the kingship passing via

---

[8] Tanner, 'The Expansion of the Power and Influence of the Counts of Boulogne', p. 263.

[9] Ida had a great reputation for personal piety and charity, founding monastic houses at St Wulmer of Boulogne, Le Wast, and Vasconvillers near Calais. She was also a friend and valued correspondent of Anselm, archbishop of Canterbury: N. Huyghebaert, 'La mère de Godefroid de Bouillon: La comtesse Ide de Boulogne', *PSHIGDL* 95 (1981), 43-63; S. N. Vaughn, 'St. Anselm and Women', *Haskins Society Journal* 2 (1990), 83-93.

[10] Barlow, *Edward the Confessor*, pp. 307-8.

[11] William of Poitiers, *The Gesta Guillelmi of William of Poitiers*, ed. and trans. R. H. C. Davis and M. Chibnall (Oxford, 1998), p. 184.

[12] Ellis, 'On the Landholders of Gloucestershire'; Williams, 'The King's Nephew', p. 329.

females, and since William the Conqueror had just made himself king of England by force of arms, it is quite far-fetched to imagine that Eustace could have cherished *any* expectation of forcing him to recognise claims based on descent from the Anglo-Saxon dynasty in the female line.[13]

Eustace II and Ida of Bouillon are known to have had three sons. According to William of Tyre, writing in late twelfth-century Jerusalem, Godfrey was the eldest, Baldwin the second, and Eustace the youngest son.[14] This order, however, appears to be a subsequent rationalisation based on the brothers' respective importance in the history of the kingdom of Jerusalem, and is contradicted by earlier sources connected with the Boulogne family. The true order of birth of the three brothers is given in all variants of the *Genealogia comitum Boloniensium*, whose earliest versions date from the late eleventh century, in the life of Ida composed in 1130/1136 by a monk of Le Wast, a Cluniac priory founded by her, and by William of Malmesbury, who seems to have had personal knowledge of Eustace II's descendants.[15]

Eustace III, count of Boulogne (†1125), was the eldest son, named for his father and paternal grandfather. He married Mary, daughter of Malcolm III *Ceann Mór*, king of Scotland (†1093), and Margaret of Hungary, sister of Edgar the Ætheling. **Godfrey of Bouillon,** duke of Lower Lotharingia and later ruler of Jerusalem (†1100), was the second son, named for his maternal uncle and grandfather. He was unmarried. **Baldwin I, king of Jerusalem** (†1118), was married three times: first, to Godehilde of Tosny (†1097); second, to an Armenian princess whose name has not survived; and third, to Adelaide del Vasto (†1118), widow of Roger I, count of Sicily.[16]

---

[13] The identity of the *nepos* mentioned by William of Poitiers remains problematic. It is conceivable that he was an otherwise unknown son of Eustace's brother Lambert of Lens.

[14] WT IX.5, pp. 425-26.

[15] *Genealogia comitum Buloniensium*, MGH SS 9: 300-1; L. Genicot, *Etudes sur les principautés lotharingiennes* (Louvain, 1975), pp. 217-306; *Vita Beatae Idae*, PL 155: 439; William of Malmesbury, ed. Mynors *et al.*, II.199, p. 356. For the dating of the *Vita Beatae Idae*, see Huyghebaert, 'La mère de Godefroid de Bouillon', pp. 43-63.

[16] There is no evidence for the statement of Runciman, *A History of the Crusades*, 1: 147, 200-1, that Baldwin and Godehilde had young children who died in 1097. See Prosopographical Catalogue, no. 55.

Of the three sons of Eustace II and Ida, only Eustace III had any issue. His heiress by Mary of Scotland was **Mathilda of Boulogne** (†1152), who in 1124/1125 married Stephen of Blois, count of Mortain and later king of England (†1154). Subsequent counts and countesses of Boulogne descended from this marriage.[17] Eustace III had at least two illegitimate sons, **Ralph** and **Eustace**. A charter issued by him in 1106 in favour of the cathedral of St Paul's, London, lists among its witnesses *Radulfus filius comitis* and *Eustachius frater eius.*[18] This information is confirmed by two other charters. A confirmation by Eustace III in favour of Roger *de Sumerio* and William *camerarius*, dated to 1120/1125 and preserved in the Hospitaller cartulary for Essex, was witnessed by *Radulpho filio comiti et Eustaceo fratre suo.*[19] An undated charter of Eustace III for the monastery of St John in Colchester gives the information *testibus ejusdem comitis Eustachii filiis Radulfo scilicet et Eustachio.*[20] Since the brothers appear in the same order in all three documents, it is likely that Ralph was the elder and Eustace the younger of the two.

There is considerable evidence that Eustace II had offspring outwith his marriage to Ida of Bouillon. The best documented case is a son, **Geoffrey, son of Count Eustace**. He was the *Gaufridus filius comitis Eustachii* mentioned in a writ of William I, dated to 1066/1071.[21] In a document dated to between 1076 and 1084/1085 the same king confirmed a donation of three hides made by *Gaufridus filius comitis Eustachii pro Beatrice uxore sua*, which had been done with the consent of Geoffrey of Mandeville.[22] A final piece of information on Geoffrey comes from Domesday Book, which records that a certain Wesman held from *Goisfrido filio Eustachii comit'* six hides in Wallington Hundred (Surrey),

---

[17] Round, *Studies in Peerage and Family History*, pp. 163-80.

[18] M. Gibbs, *Early Charters of the Cathedral Church of St. Paul, London*, Camden Third Series, 58 (London, 1939), no. 198, pp. 157-58; *Regesta Regum Anglo-Normannorum, 1066-1154, 2: Regesta Henrici Primi, 1100-1135*, ed. C. Johnson and H. A. Cronne (Oxford, 1956), no. 749, pp. 52-53 (with dating to 18 April 1106).

[19] *The Cartulary of the Knights of St John of Jerusalem in England: Secunda Camera*, ed. Gervers (Oxford, 1982), no. 212, p. 133.

[20] *Cartularium Monasterii Sancti Johannis Baptiste de Colecestria*, ed. S. A. More, 2 vols (London, 1897), 1: 47.

[21] *Regesta Regum Anglo-Normannorum: The Acta of William I (1066-1083)*, ed. D. Bates (Oxford, 1998), no. 290.

[22] *Regesta Regum Anglo-Normannorum: The Acta of William I*, nos. 314, 324.

which Geoffrey had been given by Geoffrey de Mandeville 'along with his daughter'.[23] Thus Eustace II had a son called Geoffrey, who by 1085 had married Beatrice, the daughter of Geoffrey I de Mandeville, a Norman originating from Manneville (dép. Seine-Maritime, arr. Dieppe), who after the conquest of England had risen from relative obscurity to become a major landholder in England and castellan of the Tower of London.[24] A charter of Faramus, lord of Tingry (*Faramus filius Willelmi Bolonie*), probably issued after 1159, confirms a grant of land at Balham near Clapham given to the abbey of Bec-Hellouin in Normandy by his ancestors, named as *Gaufridus filius comitis Eustacii de Bolonia avus meus et Willelmus de Bolonia filius ipsius, pater meus.* Among the witnesses are *fratres mei Eustacius et Simon.*[25] This shows that Geoffrey and Beatrice of Mandeville had a son, **William of Boulogne**, who was the father of Faramus, Eustace and Simon. It is likely that this William was the same *Willelmus nepos comitis* who witnessed the charter of Eustace III of Boulogne for St Paul's in 1106, along with his cousins Ralph and Eustace.[26]

The *Gaufridus* or *Goisfridus* who appears in England as son of Count Eustace and father of William was identified by Davis and Whitwell with Eustace's better-known son, Godfrey of Bouillon.[27] This identification must be declined for several reasons. Firstly, there is the different form of the name. Documents of the later eleventh and twelfth centuries regularly distinguish between the names rendered in modern English as Geoffrey and Godfrey: one, usually trisyllabic in Latin and written *Gaufridus*, *Galfridus*, *Goi(s)fridus* or *Joi(s)fridus* (sometimes with variant endings in *-edus*); the other usually tetrasyllabic and written *Godefridus* or *Gotefridus.* Scribes could undoubtedly distinguish between the underlying vernacular names,

---

[23] *Domesday Book, 3: Surrey*, ed. John Morris and Sara Wood (Chichester, 1975), ch. 25.

[24] K. S. B. Keats-Rohan, 'The Prosopography of Post-Conquest England: Four Case Studies', *Medieval Prosopography* 14 (1993), 1-52 (here 8-12); Keats-Rohan, *Domesday People,* 1: 229.

[25] MS. Cambridge, Kings College, Dd. 34; M. Chibnall, *Select Documents of the English Lands of the Abbey of Bec*, Camden Third Series 73 (London, 1951), no. 59, pp. 25-26.

[26] Gibb, *Early Charters*, no. 198, pp. 157-58; *Regesta Regum Anglo-Normannorum, 1066-1154, 2: Regesta Henrici Primi,* no. 749.

[27] *Regesta Regum Anglo-Normannorum, 1066-1154, 1: Regesta Willelmi Conquestoris et Willelmi Rufi, 1066-1100*, ed. H. W. C. Davis and R. J. Whitwell (Oxford, 1913), 1, no. 202.

and render them distinctly in Latin. This can be seen quite clearly in Domesday Book,[28] as well as in documents produced in the kingdom of Jerusalem in the twelfth century.[29] Secondly, there is the issue of motivation. Godfrey had been groomed to succeed to the Ardennes-Bouillon lands in Lotharingia; as heir to the territory of Bouillon and county of Verdun, it would have been strange for him to seek a wife among middling members of the Anglo-Norman nobility. Furthermore, the presence of Godfrey in England during a period when he is known to have been defending his inheritance in Lotharingia would be difficult to explain. Thirdly, there is the question of transmission of information. A wife and son are unknown to the Lotharingian pre-crusade sources, and to the numerous narratives of the crusade itself. By contrast, we know about the identity of the first wife of Godfrey's brother Baldwin, although *his* life before the crusade is considerably less well documented than Godfrey's. Most importantly, if the William of Boulogne who was the father of Faramus was indeed the (legitimate) son of Godfrey of Bouillon, then he must have been born between the marriage of his mother, which was 1085 at the latest, and the death of Godfrey in 1100, and he must have lived long enough to produce a son of his own. In this case that son would have been Godfrey's heir, with better rights to the succession of Jerusalem than either Baldwin I or Eustace III.[30] The claims of this heir and his descendants would therefore have had an enormous significance in the question of the succession to Jerusalem, not only on Godfrey's death in 1100, but during the illness of Baldwin I in 1116-17 and the

---

[28] K. S. B. Keats-Rohan and D. E. Thornton, *Domesday Names: An Index of Latin Personal Names in Domesday Book* (Woodbridge, 1997), pp. 85-86, 90-91, 98-100. Geoffrey of Mandeville, for example, appears as both *Gaufridus* and *Goisfridus*.

[29] A charter of William, patriarch of Jerusalem, of 1135/1136, ed. Geneviève Bresc-Bautier, *Le Cartulaire du chapitre du Saint-Sépulcre de Jérusalem* (Paris, 1984), no. 22, lists among its witnesses *Gaufridus Constantinopolitanus* and one *Godefridus*. Other examples can be found in the same cartulary. A document of 1135 distinguishes the onomastic forms *dux Godefridus* (Godfrey of Bouillon) and *Gaufridus abbas ecclesie Templi Domini* (Bresc-Bautier, *Cartulaire*, no. 23), and one of 1145 mentions the latter name alongside that of *Godefridus thesaurarius* (Bresc-Bautier, *Cartulaire*, no. 23). A long list of names of burgesses of Magna Mahomeria (al-Bira) recorded in 1156 distinguishes between one *Godefridus Lombardus* and five men called *Gaufridus* with various surnames (Bresc-Bautier, *Cartulaire*, no. 117),

[30] Mayer, *Mélanges*, pp. 19-20.

dispute over the succession in 1118. There is no indication in any source of any such claim being considered.

Since the Geoffrey of Domesday Book cannot be identified with the later ruler of Jerusalem, his parentage needs to be considered. There is no reason to doubt that he was a son of Eustace II. The obvious inference would be simply that he was a bastard, i.e. born of an extra-marital liaison. However, he was able to marry a daughter of Geoffrey of Mandeville, who, even if she did not belong to the uppermost rank of the Anglo-Norman nobility, nevertheless would have represented a relatively high-status marriage partner for a bastard. There are two onomastic features which are indicative of the status of Geoffrey and his descendants. Firstly, he had been given a name which had been used in the Boulogne dynasty. Eustace II had a brother who was bishop of Paris and chancellor to Philip I of France, and whose name is given in some modern works as Godfrey.[31] However, he is mentioned in numerous royal documents issued between 1065 and 1092, and the actual forms are *Gau(s)fridus*, *Goi(s)fridus* and variants.[32] The bishop's name was Geoffrey, and the same name was given to Eustace's son. Secondly, the descent alluded to by Faramus of Tingry shows that his father was known as William *de Bolonia*,

---

[31] For example, in the tables given in Tanner, 'The Expansion of the Power and Influence of the Counts of Boulogne Under Eustace II'.

[32] M. Prou, *Recueil des actes de Philippe Ier, roi de France (1059-1100)* (Paris, 1908). Only instances where Geoffrey is explcitly identified as bishop of Paris are counted. Taking nominative and oblique forms together, the variants are: *Gaufridus* (nos. 30, 39, 42, 66, 77, 96, 118), *Gauffridus* (nos. 60, 80), *Gaufredus* (nos. 18, 29, 32), *Gausfridus* (nos. 37, 61, 81), *Gausfredus* (nos. 57, 58, 106), *Goifridus* (no. 124), *Goiffridus* (nos. 78, 79, 82, 108), *Gosfridus* (nos. 48, 49, 86, 87, 102, 116), *Gosfredus* (no. 109), *Goisfridus* (nos. 63, 75, 107, 110, 114, 117, 123), *Guisfridus* (no. 72), *Jozfridus* (no. 120). The only unexpected variant is *Godfredus* (no. 76), which may simply result from a scribal error in transmission, and in fact one MS has *Goafridus*. Narrative sources with particular knowledge give similar information. Lambert of Ardres, *Historia comitum Ghisnensium*, MGH SS 24: 574, which details the bishop's relationship to Count Eustace, gives the form *Guiffridi*. The extract from a chronicle of the abbey of St Bertin given in *Ex chronico Sithiensi*, in Recueil des Historiens des Gaules et de la France 11: 384, gives the names *Eustachium Boloniae comitem, et fratrem ejus Goffridum Parisiensem episcopum*. The abbey chronicle of Saint-Hubert, which was entirely familiar with the name *Godefridus*, which was borne by several of its hereditary advocates, refers to the bishop as *Josfridus* (*Cantatorium*, p. 36).

which may indicate that Geoffrey's family continued to bear the name of, and be associated with the legitimate branch of the Boulogne family.

If Eustace had contracted a marriage which was subsequently dissolved (for whatever reason), then any child would have been regarded as illegitimate. In this respect the excommunication of Count Eustace for incest by Pope Leo IX in 1049 may be significant. For most of the early eleventh century the papacy had been mired in the particularist interests of the Roman nobility, and its influence over western Christendom had declined. In 1046 the Emperor Henry III intervened, deposing the three rival popes (Benedict IX, Gregory IX and Sylvester III), and imposing his own candidate, Suidger, bishop of Bamberg. However, Clement II, as he was known, died after a pontificate of little more than nine moths, and his successor, Damasus II, after only twenty-four days. It was only the third German pope installed by Henry, the Lotharingian Leo IX (enthroned February 1049), who was able to embark on a sustained and wide-ranging programme of reform, and travelled throughout western Europe to implement it.[33] An early manifestation of this activity was the council of Rheims, which among other reforming decrees pronounced several excommunications on the grounds of consanguinity. It is possible that under the new reforming zeal of Leo IX the papacy was turning its attention to, and condemning marriages within the prohibited degrees which had not previously been regarded as problematic. In this respect it may be significant that Eustace II and Godgifu were both descended from Alfred the Great: Godgifu via the Anglo-Saxon male royal line (Æthelred II – Edgar – Edmund – Edward the Elder – Alfred), and Eustace from Alfred's daughter Ælfthryth (Elstrude) who had married Baldwin II of Flanders; their son was Adelolf, count of Boulogne, great-great-great-grandfather of Eustace II.[34]

If, as is likely, the marriage of Eustace II and Godgifu was one of those condemned at Rheims and presumably dissolved thereafter, it is possible that Geoffrey was the product of this union; branded as illegitimate, he

[33] U.-R. Blumenthal, *The Investiture Controversy: Church and Monarchy from the Ninth to the Twelfth Century* (Philadelphia, 1988), pp. 64-79; G. Frech, 'Die deutschen Päpste – Kontinuität und Wandel', in *Die Salier und das Reich*, 2: *Die Reichskirche in der Salierzeit*, ed. Stefan Weinfurter and Frank Martin Siefarth (Sigmaringen, 1991), pp. 303-32.

[34] See genealogical tables in Tanner, 'The Expansion of the Power and Influence of the Counts of Boulogne'. I am grateful to Dr Ann Williams for bringing this connection to my attention.

was unable to succeed to Boulogne but he may well have retained sufficient status – more so than a son of a casual liaison – to have been an attractive marriage partner for the Mandevilles. This construction could accommodate the known chronology of Geoffrey and his son: a man born before 1049 could easily have been married before 1086, and produced a son old enough to have witnessed a charter by 1106.

There remain at least two children or grandchildren of Eustace II whose parentage cannot be precisely determined. William of Tyre relates that Godfrey of Bouillon had a *third* brother called **William**; he says that while the other three brothers took part in the expedition to Jerusalem, William remained at home.[35] There is some support for this information in a fourteenth-century manuscript of the *Genealogia comitum Boloniensium* (MS. Paris, Bibliothèque nationale, lat.4998), which says that Eustace and Ida had four sons *Guillermum, Godefridum qui est nunc dux Lotharingie, Balduinum et Eustachium*.[36] It is possible that this William derived from a confused memory of William of Boulogne, son of Geoffrey.[37] Yet although it is inconceivable that he was a son of Eustace and Ida, it is also possible that he could have been a *half-brother* of their three sons; in this case William could have been a full brother of Geoffrey. Finally, there is the case of **Godfrey**, a *nepos* or *abnepos* of Baldwin I of Jerusalem, documented in 1112 and killed in 1113. He could have been a legitimate son of Geoffrey (and thus a brother of William of Boulogne) or of another illegitimate son of Eustace II of Boulogne, or indeed an illegitimate son of Eustace III.[38] The existence of Eustace III's bastard son Eustace shows that the counts of Boulogne did not restrict traditional family names to legitimate offspring. The name Godfrey passed into the Boulogne family through Ida of Bouillon, and was first given to her second son, Godfrey of Bouillon. It is more likely that this name would have been given by Godfrey's full brother (Eustace III) to one of his sons after Godfrey had reached adulthood, than for a half-brother of Godfrey by an earlier union of Eustace II to have given it to his own son.

---

[35] WT IX.5, p. 426.

[36] Genicot, *Etudes sur les principautés lotharingiennes*, pp. 260-61.

[37] This is suggested by Mayer, *Mélanges*, p. 20 n. 28.

[38] See Prosopographical Catalogue, no. 56.

The identities and probable order of birth of the children and grandchildren of Eustace II, both legitimate and illegitimate, can be summarised as follows:

(a) Geoffrey, son of Eustace II either by an extra-marital union or by a marriage (to Godgifu?), dissolved on grounds of consanguinity. Documented between 1066/1071 and 1086.

(b) Eustace III, count of Boulogne, eldest son of Eustace II and Ida of Bouillon. Died 1125.

(c) Godfrey of Bouillon, duke of Lower Lotharingia and ruler of Jerusalem, second son of Eustace II and Ida. Died 1100.

(d) Baldwin I, king of Jerusalem, third son of Eustace II and Ida. Died 1118.

(e) William of Boulogne, son of Geoffrey (a) by Beatrice of Mandeville. Documented 1106.

(f) Ralph, illegitimate son of Eustace III (b). Documented between 1106 and1120/1125.

(g) Eustace, illegitimate son of Eustace III (b). Documented between 1106 and 1120/1125.

(h) Godfrey, probably an illegitimate son of Eustace III (b). Documented 1112.

(i) Mathilda, countess of Boulogne, daughter of Eustace III (b) and Mary of Scotland.

At least one undocumented descendant can also be conjectured:

(j)* William, illegitimate son of Eustace II, and possibly a full brother of Geoffrey (a).

Appendix B

Principal Witnesses to Documents of Baldwin I

This section presents information on the main witnesses to the charters of the reign of Baldwin I (1100-18), particularly concerning the frequency and ranking of the witnesses. The documents evaluated are all royal charters of the reign which include names of witnesses.[1] To these have been added a charter of Bernard, bishop of Nazareth (RRH no. 56a), and one of Roger, bishop of Lydda (RRH no. 76b), which were both clearly issued in the presence of Baldwin I and were witnessed by several of the king's lay followers. Table 1 lists all clerical witnesses of the rank of patriarch, archbishop, bishop, abbot and prior, as well as any other clerics appearing at least twice; excluded are those who were clearly not members of the hierarchy of the kingdom at the time of issue (e.g. Gibelin, archbishop of Arles, on RRH no. 56a). Table 2 lists all lay witnesses appearing at least twice.

The first two columns give name and office (where applicable) of those appearing as witnesses. The third column lists those documents in which the individuals appear. The fourth column gives the *frequency*, that is, the total number of attestations. The fifth column gives the relative *ranking*, which is the average placing (first, second etc.) within the group of witnesses. Since the names of clerical witnesses normally appear in a group before those of lay witnesses, each group is treated separately for the purposes of ranking: thus the first lay witness in a given document is ranked as being first, even though his name may appears only after all those of clerical witnesses. In cases where two individuals have the same average ranking, the one with the greater frequency of appearances has been placed higher.

[1] RRH nos. 45, 51, 74 have no witnesses named.

Documentary Table 1: Clerical Witnesses

Name	Office	RRH nos	frq	rnk
Arnulf of Chocques	patriarch of Jerusalem[2]	59, 68a, 76b, 80	4	**1**
Baldwin	archbishop of Caesarea	52	1	**1**
Evremar of Chocques	archbishop of Caesarea	56a, 76b, 80	3	**2**
Bernard	bishop of Nazareth	68a, 76b, 80	3	**2.66**
Roger	bishop of Lydda	52, 68a, 80	3	**3**
Pagan	chancellor	76b, 79	2	**3**
Anschetin	bishop of Bethlehem	56a, 76a	2	**3.5**
Achard of Arrouaise	prior of Templum Domini	68a, 80	2	**4.5**
Arnold	prior of Mount Zion	68a	1	**5**
Peter	abbot (unspecified)	56a	1	**7**
Rainer	prior of Hebron	68a	1	**10**

Documentary Table 2: Lay Witnesses

Name	Office	RRH nos	frq	rnk
Eustace Granarius	lord of Sidon, Caesarea	52, 57, 59, 76b, 80	5	**1.8**
Simon	constable	52, 59, 68a, 76b, 79	5	**2.2**
Anselm	castellan of T. of David	57, 76a, 76b, 79, 80	5	**2.3**
Ralph of La Fontanelle		52, 56a, 59, 76b, 80	5	**3.6**
Guy of Milly		57, 76a, 76b, 79, 80	5	**4**
Roman of Le Puy		68a, 79	2	**5**
Gotmann of Brussels		43, 52, 56a, 57, 76a, 76b, 80	7	**6.1**
Pisellus	viscount of Jerusalem	43, 52, 56a, 57, 59, 76b, 79, 80	8	**6.25**
Walter Mahomet	lord of Hebron	43, 52, 57, 76b, 79, 80	6	**6.8**
Anselm *de Parenti*		52, 76b, 80	3	**8.7**
Gerard	chamberlain	52, 59, 68a, 76b, 80	5	**10.4**
Andrew of Baudement		52, 80	2	**11**
Eustace of Cassel		52, 80	2	**12**
Ardo		52, 80	2	**15.5**

[2] Witnesses RRH no. 59 as archdeacon.

Concordance of Documents

RRH no. 43 (1104) = C. Imperiale di Sant'Angelo, *Codice Diplomatico della Repubblica di Genova*, 1, no. 15.
Baldwin I grants to the church of S. Laurence in Genoa squares in Jerusalem and Jaffa, a third of Arsuf, a third of Caesarea and Acre, with the promise of a third of all cities and lands that he conquers with the help of the Genoese.
Witnesses: (1) *Ugo de Tabaria*, (2) *Ugo de Sancto Habraam*, (3) *Gervasius dapifer*, (4) *Galterius Mahomet*, (5) *Fredericus de Corbolio*, (6) *Peselus vicecomes*, (7) *Gaufridus de Turre David*, (8) *Gotman*.

RRH no. 52 (1108) = Ch. Kohler, 'Chartes de l'abbaye de Notre-Dame de la Vallée de Josaphat (1108-1291)', *ROL* 7 (1900), 108-222, no. 1, pp. 112-13.
Baldwin I gives to the abbey of Josaphat the casale of Aschar, and the land called *Dorsum Asini*.
Witnesses: (1) *B[alduinus] Caesariensis archiepiscopus*, (2) *R. Ramathensis episcopus*, (3) *R. Monachus*, (4) *P... M...* (5) *Galterius Bigotus*, (6) *Fulcherius clericus*, (1) *W. Filius Comitis*, (2) *Symon constabilis*, (3) *Rogerius de Rosarum*, (4) *E. Granarius*, (5) *R. de Fontei*, (6) *Guido de Miliaco*, (7) *Gothman*, (8) *G. Mahumet*, (9) *Anselinus de Parenti*, (10) *Pisel*, (11) *Andreas de Valdemunt*, (12) *Eustachius de Cassel*, (13) *Hubertus de Paci*, (14) *Gerardus camerarius*, (15) *Ardo*.

RRH no. 56a (1109) = Kohler, 'Chartes de l'abbaye de Notre-Dame de la Vallée de Josaphat', no. 2, pp. 113-14.
Bernard, bishop of Nazareth, in the presence of Baldwin I, gives to the abbey of Josaphat the church of St George in Tiberias.
Witnesses: (1) *domnus Gibelinus archiepiscopus*, (2) *Evremarus archiepiscopus*, (3) *Anschetinus episcopus*, (4) *A... diaconus*, (5) *Acardus decanus*, (6) *Ansellus praecentor*, (7) *Petrus abbas*, (1) *Radulfus de Funteneio*, (2) *Pisellus vicecomes*, (3) *Ado de Chirisiaco*, (4) *Arnulfus Loteringus*, (5) *Gomagnus*.

RRH no. 57 (1110 September 28) = *C. Hosp.* 1, no. 20, pp. 21-22.
Baldwin I confirms various donations to the Hospital.
Witnesses: (1) *Hugo de Puzath*, (2) *Eusthacius Graner sive* (3) *vicecomes de Jerusalem*[3] (4) *Anselmus de Turre David*, (5) *Gauterius Baffumeth*, (6) *Guido de Miliaco*, (7) *Gotman*.

---

[3] i.e Pisellus, viscount of Jerusalem.

RRH no. 59 (1109/1110) = WT XI.12, pp. 513-15.
Baldwin I establishes a new bishopric at Bethlehem.
Witnesses: (1) *Arnulfus archidiaconus*, (2) *Aicardus decanus*, (1) *Eustachius Granerius*, (2) *Anselmus turris David custos*, (3) *Radulfus de Fontaneto*, (4) *Pisellus vicecomes*, (5) *Symon ducis filius*, (3) *Anfredus vir religiosus*, (6) *Girardus camerarius.*

RRH no. 68a (1112 June 20) = *C. Hosp.* 1, no. 28, pp. 27-28.
Baldwin I confirms various possessions of the Hospital.
Witnesses: (1) *Arnulfe patriarche*, (2) *Bernarde episcopi Nazare* (3) *Rogerii Ramulensis episcopi* (4) *Aicardi prioris templi Domini*, (5) *Arnaldi prioris Montis Sion*, (6) *Aselli cantor*, (7) *Girardi, thesaurii*, (8) *Aremandi,* (9) *Fulco Willelmus subcentor*, (10) *Rainerii prioris de S. Habraham*, (1) *Simonis ducis, chonestabuli* (2) *Ugonis Chostard dapiferi*, (3) *Gotafredi nepotis regis*, (4) *Romani de Podio*, (5) *Johannis interpres*, (6) *Ottonis Egidii* (7) *Alberti*, (8) *Garini de Verno* (9) *Girardi cubicularii regis*, (11) *Roberti sacerdotis* (scribe)

RRH no. 76a (1114) = Kohler, 'Chartes de l'abbaye de Notre-Dame de la Vallée de Josaphat', no. 5, p. 116.
Baldwin I confirms for the abbey of Josaphat the possession of casalia given by Pisellus the Viscount and his wife and brother.
Witnesses: (1) *Anselmus de Turre Davit*, (2) *Gotman*, (3) *Wido de Miliaco*, (4) *Asquittinus*, (5) *Drogo de Nigella*, (6) *Georgius filius Megor*, (7) *Fattis notarius*, (8) *Samuel interpres.*

RRH no. 76b (1115) = Mayer, *Die Kanzlei der lateinischen Könige*, 2 : 887-88.
Roger, bishop of (Lydda-)Ramla with the consent of Baldwin I gives to the abbey of Josaphat the casale of Sephoria and other properties.
Witnesses: [4] (1) *Arnulfi patriarchae* (*) *gloriossimi regis Balduini,*[5] (2) *Euuremari Caesareae archiepiscopi*, (3) *Bernardi Nazareni episcopi* (4) *Ansketini Bethlemitae episcopi* (1) *Eustachii Granarii*, (2) *Symonis constabularii*, (3) *Radulfi de Fontenei*, (4) *Guidonis de Mili.* (5) *Gotman,* (6) *Gauterii Mahumet*, (7) *Anselmi de Parenti*, (8) *Piselli*, (5) *Pagani cancellarii regis*, (9) *Giraldi camerarii.*

RRH no. 79 (25 December 1114/31 August 1115) = H.-F. Delaborde, *Chartes de Terre Sainte provenant de l'abbaye de N.-D. de Josaphat* (Paris, 1880), no. 5, pp. 27-28.[6]

---

[4] Three members of the cathedral chapter of Lydda are not counted in the ranking.
[5] King Baldwin is not counted in the ranking.
[6] For the dating, see Mayer, *Die Kreuzfahrerherrschaft Montréal (Šōbak)*, pp. 263-64.

Baldwin I confirms to the abbey of Josaphat donations made by William of Bures.

Witnesses: (1) *Paganus cancellarius*, (1) *Symon constabularius*, (2) *Pisellus vicecomes*, (3) *Guido de Milli*, (4) *Robertus Giffarz*, (5) *Galterius Mahumet*, (6) *Romanus de Podio.* [7]

RRH no. 80 (1115) = Delaborde, *Chartes de Terre Sainte provenant de l'abbaye de N.-D. de Josaphat*, no. 6, pp. 29-32.

Baldwin I confirms all the possessions of the abbey of Josaphat.

Witnesses: (1) *patriarcha Jherusalem Arnulfus*, (2) *E[bremarus] Caesariensis archiepiscopus*, (3) *B[ernardus] episcopus Nazarenus*, (4) *Rogerius Ramathensis episcopus*, (5) *Achardus prior Templi Domini*, (1) *Eustachius Granerius*, (2) *Willelmus de Buris*, (3) *Balduinus de Ramis*, (4) *Wido de Miliaco*, (5) *Manasses de Caiphas*, (6) *Rodulfus de Fontanei*, (7) *Ulricus vicecomes Neapolis*, (8) *Balduinus de Sancto Abraham*, (9) *Gothman*, (10) *Anselmus de Parentei*, (11) *Andreas de Baldement*, (12) *Eustachius de Cassel*, (13) *Galterius Mahumet*, (14) *Girardus camerarius* (15) *Pisel*, (16) *Ardo*.

[7] Individuals described as *testes Jocelini* are not counted in the ranking.

Appendix C

The Claim of Baldwin II to the Throne of Jerusalem

Narrative sources concerning the First Crusade agree that Baldwin of Bourcq was a blood relative of the Bouillon-Boulogne brothers, but they do not elaborate on the precise nature of the relationship.[1] The fullest information on the family connections of Baldwin II is provided by William of Tyre.[2] He gives precise details on his parents Hugh and Melisende, his brothers Manasses and Gervase, and his sisters Mathilda and Hodierna as well as their respective marriages and descendants. William had considerable advantages for the study of the royal family of Jerusalem. As chancellor of the kingdom he had had access to the royal archives, and as tutor to the young Baldwin IV, he had spent considerable time in the company of the royal family, descendants of Baldwin II. He had also studied at Paris, not far from the home of the counts of Rethel. Yet William can give no details of the precise relationship between the

---

[1] AA pp. 527, 707-8; FC III.1, pp. 615-16.

[2] WT XII.12, pp. 511-12: *Hic fuit natione Francus, de episcopatu Remensi, filius domini Hugonis comitis de Retest et Milissendis preclare comitisse, que tot dicitur sorores habuisse, unde tanta multitudo filiorum et filiarum dicitur procreata, quantam hii noverunt qui principum genealogias sollicita investigant diligentia. Hic, vivente adhuc patre, cum aliis nobilibus qui iter Ierosolimitanum arripuerant, in comitatu domini ducis Godefridi, cuius erat consanguineus, eandem viam ea devotione qua alii ingressus est, reliquens domi apud patrem iam grandvum fratres duos et sorores totidem, quorum ipse omnium primogenitus erat. Nomen alterius fratrum Gervasius, qui postea fuit electus ad ecclesiam Remensem, alterius Manasses; sororum autem alteram habuit castellanus de Vitriaco, nomine Mahaldem, alteram dominus Herbrandus de Herges, vir nobilis et potens, nomine Hodiernam, ex qua natus est Manasses de Herges, quem nos postmodum, tempore domine Milissendis regine, regium vidimus constabularium. Porro patre huius domini Balduini regis defuncto, Manasses, filius eius, quia dominum Balduinum, qui primogenitus erat, regni occupatio detinebat, successit; quo etiam sine liberis decedente, Gervasius, frater eorum, dimisso Remensi archiepiscopatu uxorem contra instituta ecclesiastica ducens, eundem comitatum iure possedit hereditario, Susceptam autem ex uxore unicam filiam cuidam nobili viro in Normannia matrimonio copulavit; quo defuncto, sororis illorum filius Mahaldis videlicet que casteliano Vitriacensi nupserat, Iterius nomine, in eodem comitatu successit.* An unexplained omission by William is that of Baldwin's sister Cecilia who married Roger, prince of Antioch (RRH no. 114c).

two Baldwins. As this is the crux of the issue he is discussing it is inconceivable that he would not have used the information had he possessed it. There is thus a dichotomy between the detailed account of Baldwin's immediate origins and a near silence on his relationship to his predecessor, an omission that William apparently attempts to compensate for by repetition of the word *consanguineus*.

There is little agreement among modern historians on this issue. Most have been content to describe Baldwin II as a cousin of his predecessor, although of course the medieval term *consanguineus* could be applied to a much wider range of relationships than the modern equivalent.[3] A more precise assumption has been that Baldwin of Bourcq's father or grandfather married a female member of the family of the counts of Boulogne. According to Comte Riant, Baldwin's father Hugh I of Rethel was the son of a Count Manasses of Rethel and an aunt of the Bouillon-Boulogne brothers, and therefore must have been a daughter of Eustace I of Boulogne.[4] Runciman makes the similar claim that 'Baldwin's father, Count Hugh I of Rethel, was the son of a princess of Boulogne, aunt to Godfrey of Lorraine and King Baldwin'.[5] Riley-Smith claims that 'Baldwin was also related to the families of the counts of Burgundy and of Boulogne, one of his paternal grandmothers, Ida of Boulogne, being the aunt of Godfrey of Bouillon and Baldwin of Boulogne'.[6] Richard sees Melisende, wife of Hugh I of Rethel, as a sister of Eustace II of Boulogne.[7] Yet none of these authors offer any evidence for such marriage connections, or even for the existence of an aunt of the Bouillon-Boulogne brothers. The only known daughter of Eustace I of Boulogne was named Gerberga, who married Frederick of Luxembourg, duke of Lower Lotharingia (†1065); she predeceased her husband and was buried at the abbey of Stavelot.[8]

---

[3] Prawer, *Crusaders' Kingdom*, p. 118; Richard, *Latin Kingdom*, p. 3.

[4] Riant in RHC Occ. 5: 631. Röhricht, *Königreich Jerusalem*, p. 125 calls Baldwin II a nephew of Godfrey and Baldwin I, which is quite inaccurate.

[5] Runciman, *History of the Crusades*, 2: 36. The genealogical table in the same volume gives her name as Ida.

[6] Riley-Smith, *The First Crusaders*, p. 171.

[7] Richard, *Histoire des Croisades*, p. 504.

[8] Renn, *Luxemburger Grafenhaus*, pp. 121-23; Parisse, 'Généalogie de la Maison d'Ardenne', p. 32.

It is certain that the parents of Baldwin's father Hugh of Rethel were called Manasses and Judith. All three are named in a document of 1081 for the church of Braux.[9] The genealogies of Foigny and Alberic of Trois-fontaines agree that the wife of Manasses and mother of Hugh was called Yvette or Jutta, and that she was a sister of Ebalus I, count of Roucy.[10] Ebalus is known to have been married to Beatrix of Hainaut before becoming archbishop of Rheims in 1021. Mathieu has raised a fundamental objection to this construction on the grounds that Ebalus, who died in 1033, could not have had a sister who was still alive in 1081.[11] He goes on to suggest that Judith (Yvette) must have belonged to a quite different family from that of Roucy, and in view of William of Tyre's remarks on Baldwin of Bourcq's consanguinity with Godfrey and Baldwin I, that she was probably a daughter of Eustace I of Boulogne. He argues that the name Judith was transmitted from Judith, daughter of Charles the Bald and wife of Baldwin I of Flanders. Mathieu's hypothesis is very much along the same lines as those of Riant, Runciman and Riley-Smith, although it offers a more detailed case. One objection to it would be that there is no allusion to Judith or any other connection between the Rethel and Boulogne families in the *Genealogia comitum Boloniensium*, which was being copied and extended in the mid-twelfth century when descendants of Manasses of Rethel were ruling the kingdom of Jerusalem.[12]

A quite different possibility would be that the connection of the Rethel family was not with the counts of Boulogne, but with the Ardennes-Bouillon dynasty. Certainly Hugh's father Manasses had fought on the side of Godfrey of Bouillon during the war of the Bouillon succession, an alliance which may reflect ties of friendship which may have included a marriage connection.[13] The first known count of Rethel named as such is another Manasses who appears with his wife, *domna Dada comitissa uxor*

---

[9] Saige, Lacaille and Labande, *Trésor des chartes du comté de Rethel*, 1, no 1.

[10] *Genealogiae Fusniacensis*, MGH SS 13: 251-56; Alberic of Troisfontaines, p. 823.

[11] Jean-Noël Mathieu, 'Sur les comtesses de Rethel au XIe siècle. Contribution à l'histoire des comtes de Rethel et des comtes de Porcien', *Revue historique ardennaise* 32 (1997), 3-19.

[12] *Genealogia comitum Buloniensium*, pp. 300-1. On manuscripts and dating, see Genicot, *Etudes sur les principautés lotharingiennes*, pp. 217-306.

[13] LL p. 494.

Manasse comitis de Reitest, in 1026.[14] This name is similar to at least one form of the name of the first wife of Godfrey II, who was the mother of Ida, wife of Eustace II of Boulogne. The life of Ida by a monk of Le Wast describes her parentage: *Pater eius supra potentes atque fama maiores, coram imperatore Alemannorum; gradum altiorem et quasi privilegium dignitatis obtinens fuit, nomine Godefridus. Mater vero eius, non minus egregia, Doda vocabatur.*[15] Unfortunately there are only two other references to her. A diploma of Henry III of 16 June 1040 confirms a donation to the church of St Mary Magdalene of Verdun by 'Guota, wife of Duke Godfrey'.[16] A charter of Ida herself for the abbey of Munsterbilzen refers to it as the resting place of her mother Uoda.[17] If we can accept Doda/Dada as the correct form of the name it is possible that the Manasses of Rethel and Dada documented in 1026 had a daughter who received her mother's name and married Godfrey II.[18] This putative relationship would make Baldwin II a second cousin of Baldwin I and place both in the same generation. It must of course remain a hypothesis. However, the general imprecision of the First Crusade narratives on the relationship suggests a not particularly close link between the two families; the connection may have been even more remote than in this model. On crusade Baldwin of Bourcq was merely one of a group of several *consanguinei* of Godfrey of Bouillon, and was by no means the most prominent one of them. It is unlikely that we can assume a principle to the effect that Baldwin of Bourcq was offered the throne on the grounds that he was Baldwin I's closest relative in Outremer, which would have been an innovation in an age which had a strong aversion to innovations in matters of inheritance. In fact, he may

---

[14] Bloch, 'Die älteren Urkunden des Klosters S. Vanne zu Verdun', pp. 338-449, no. 32; Bur, *La formation du comté de Champagne*, p. 123.

[15] *Vita Beatae Idae*, PL 155, p. 438

[16] MGH DD H.III, no. 53: *alodium de Resengis cum familia pratis campis silvis et duobus molendinis quod dedit eidem aecclesiae Guota per manus mariti sui Gotefridi ducis.*

[17] Ernst, *Histoire du Limbourg*, 1: 113-15: *piae animae matris meae Vodae et avi mei marchionis Godizonis.*

[18] The origins of Manasses's wife are unclear. Mathieu, 'Sur les comtesses de Rethel', pp. 4-6, argues that if Hugh I could not have been married to a sister of Ebalus of Roucy, then it is possible that the sister of Ebalus was actually Dada, a suggestion which would fit the chronology of the Roucy family better since it would place their connection with the Rethel family one generation earlier than that given by the genealogies of Foigny.

have been the king's only blood relative in the East by 1118, but by either of the two principal hypotheses, his claim was far worse than that of Eustace III of Boulogne. If we are to believe Albert of Aachen, Baldwin I had designated Eustace as his preferred successor, with Baldwin of Bourcq as the next choice if Eustace should decline the throne.[19] It may simply have been the case that this designation offered an opportunity for Joscelin of Tiberias and others to promote him as being someone amenable to their own interests, whose presence in Jerusalem would avoid an interregnum, and that the qualification of consanguinity was merely advanced as a sop to those who felt strongly that the kingdom should be passed on by hereditary succession.

---

[19] AA pp. 708-9.

Prosopographical Catalogue

The Personal Basis of Bouillon-Boulogne Power, 1095-1118

Introduction

The following repertory provides prosopographical documentation on 140 individuals who were companions of Godfrey of Bouillon and Baldwin I during the course of the First Crusade or who constituted the main military and administrative support of the Bouillon-Boulogne dynasty in the kingdom of Jerusalem. The chronological limits for inclusion are the departure of Godfrey's army from Lotharingia (August 1096) and the end of the reign of Baldwin I (April 1118).

The following categories are included: (1) Relatives (by birth or marriage) of the Bouillon-Boulogne dynasty who were involved in the crusade and the government of the kingdom. (2) Companions of Godfrey and Baldwin on crusade, that is, crusaders who left Lotharingia with the brothers in 1096, or took service with either of them between that time and the capture of Jerusalem in 1099. These include members of the *comitatus Baldewini*, the separate force put together by Baldwin in Cilicia and Edessa in 1097-98. (3) The top rank of the nobility in the kingdom of Jerusalem, that is holders of lordships, castellans and crown vassals from the royal domain. (4) Higher clergy in the kingdom: patriarchs, archbishops, and bishops.[1] (5) Aulic officers, military commanders, viscounts and household knights. (6) Finally, some rear-vassals in the kingdom of Jerusalem have been included in cases where their European origins can be established. Since several individuals can be assigned to more than one category, all are given in one alphabetical listing according to forenames (in their modern English form), and are numbered for reference in the main text of the book.

The documentation (both primary and secondary sources) on which each entry is based is listed immediately after the text under 'Sources'; works referred to only in passing are given in footnotes. An asterisk (*)

---

[1] The patriarch Daibert of Pisa I is not included, on the grounds that he was forced on Godfrey of Bouillon by external pressure.

before a name serves as a cross-reference, indicating a separate entry under that name. Entries are not conceived as exhaustive listings of primary sources; they are primarily intended to document western origins as well as the nature of ties of individuals to the Bouillon-Boulogne dynasty, and thus concentrate on the period up to 1118. In the cases of particularly well-known figures (e.g. patriarchs) references are mostly given to secondary literature. The identification of crusaders as companions of Godfrey and Baldwin cannot be achieved with absolute certainty in all cases. Some crusaders changed the leaders they served under more than once, and in any case the degree of dependence between crusader and leader varied in individual cases. Similarly, it is sometimes difficult to distinguish between knights who had actually taken service with the rulers of Jerusalem and individuals who had merely come to the Holy Land on pilgrimage or expeditions such as the crusade of 1101.

For reasons of space it is not possible to give a complete listing of different forms of personal names as they appear in the sources, desirable though this may have been. However, in the majority of cases each entry contains either a form of name which is representative of those most commonly found in the sources, or one which has sufficient detail to enable a geographical identification. Where a western European place of origin can be identified with a reasonable degree of certainty this is given in its modern official form, along with a location in parentheses according to present-day administrative units: in Belgium (B) by province and *arrondissement*; in France (F) by *département* and *arrondissement*, in Germany (Ger), by federal state (*Land*) and *Kreis*; and in Italy (I) by region and province. Places in the Grand-Duchy of Luxembourg (Lux) are not located in any further detail. Where locative surnames are problematic or impossible to identify these have been left in their original form (*italics*) in the headings. Placenames in the kingdom of Jerusalem are given in the form in which they appear on the map 'Palestine Under the Crusaders', ed. J. Prawer and M. Benevisti, in *Atlas of Israel* (Jerusalem, 1970), IX/10, except where common English forms exist.

1. A[...] of Beaurain

The name of a witness to a charter of 1116 issued by *Eustace I Granarius and his wife Emma is given in printed editions as *Aaluns de Belram*. The first element could possibly reflect an original scribal form meant to represent *Alardus* or *Aleran(n)us*. The Breton forename *Alanus* is unlikely in light of the known circumstances of this individual. There is an obvious connection with one *Johannes de Belram* who witnessed a charter of Emma in 1124 and who appears again as *Johannes de Bellorano* in 1131 on a charter of Eustace's son *Walter of Caesarea. Both of these men seem to have been vassals or followers of the Granarius family. Considering the known origins of Eustace in the diocese of Thérouanne the surname *Belram* probably derives from Beaurain-Château (F, Pas-de-Calais, arr. Montreuil-sur-Mer) or the nearby Beaurainville.

SOURCES: RRH nos. 82, 104, 139.

2. Adalbero of Luxembourg, archdeacon of Metz

Albert of Aachen describes one *filium comitis Cunradi de Luezelenburch, Adelberonem nomine, clericum et archidiaconum Metensis Ecclesie*, who was of royal blood, and a relative of the Emperor Henry IV (*juvenem nobilissimim de regio sanguine, et proximum Henrici tertii R. Augusti*). He is known on crusade only from an incident in 1097 during the siege of Antioch in which he was playing dice with a lady (*matrona*) of great nobility and beauty in a garden outside the city, and was captured and killed during a sortie by the Turkish garrison. He was a son of Conrad I, count of Luxembourg (1059-86), whose family had strong connections with Metz (F, Moselle, arr. Metz), and who died during a penitential pilgrimage to the Holy Land. The name Adalbero was relatively rare among laymen but from the time of Bishop Adalbero of Augsburg (†909) it was considered to be an auspicious one for bishops, so much so that in the period 887-1148, 26 members of the higher clergy in France and Germany bore the name,[2] and it was especially popular in the related lineages of Ardennes-Bouillon, Bar and Luxembourg for younger sons destined for ecclesiastical office, for example, the archdeacon's uncle Adalbero III, bishop of Metz 1047-72. Albert of Aachen's rather salacious account of the incident in which he met his death suggests that Adalbero was a fairly worldly career cleric for whom the crusade may have offered a welcome diversion during the wait to secure a higher ecclesiastical office. He was evidently known personally to Duke Godfrey, who grieved at his death and made arrangements for his burial.

[2] K. F. Werner, 'Liens de parenté et noms de personne', in *Famille et parenté dans l'occident médiéval*, ed. G. Duby and J. Le Goff (Rome, 1977), pp. 13-34 (here 31-32).

SOURCES: AA pp. 370-71; H. Renn, *Das erste Luxemburger Grafenhaus* (Berlin, 1941), pp. 9, 146-48; M. Twellenkamp, 'Das Haus der Luxemburger', in *Die Salier und das Reich*, 1: *Salier, Adel und Reichsverfassung*, ed. S. Weinfurter and H. Kluger (Sigmaringen, 1991), pp. 475-502.

3. Adelaide del Vasto, queen of Jerusalem

The third wife of Baldwin I of Jerusalem belonged to the Aleramid dynasty of northern Italy. She was a daughter of Manfred del Vasto (†1079), a younger brother of the marquis Boniface, who was one of the wealthiest and most powerful noblemen in Liguria. Adelaide married Roger I, count of Sicily, after the death of his second wife, Eremburga of Mortain. The marriage took place in 1089/1090 and it is likely that Adelaide was born around the year 1075. From the time of death of Roger (June 1101), she acted as regent for their eldest son, Simon, and after his death (1105) for the second son, Roger II, who attained his majority in December 1111. Shortly after this, Baldwin I negotiated a marriage with Adelaide, despite the fact that his second wife (*Arda) was still alive. The Sicilian monarchy promised a large cash dowry, but agreed to the marriage only under the condition that if the couple had no heirs, the succession to the throne of Jerusalem would revert to Roger. The marriage took place in Jerusalem in September 1113, but produced no heir. The illness of Baldwin during the winter of 1116-17 opened up the real possibility of a Sicilian succession to the kingdom, and a significant section among the ruling classes of Jerusalem led by *Arnulf of Chocques persuaded the king to repudiate Adelaide, a move which was confirmed at a synod held at Acre, after she returned to Sicily (April 1117). She died on 16 April 1118 and was buried in the abbey of St Salvator in Patti.

SOURCES: E. Pontieri, 'La madre di Re Ruggiero, Adelaide del Vasto, contessa di Sicilia, regina di Gerusalemme', in *Atti del Convegno internazionale di studi ruggeriani*, 2 vols (Palermo, 1955), 2: 322-432; Mayer, *Melanges*, pp. 59-72; H. Houben, 'Adelaide "del Vasto" nella storia del Regno di Sicilia', in *Bianca Lancia D'Agliano: Fra il Piemonte e il Regno di Sicilia,* ed. R. Bordone (Alessandria, 1992), pp. 121-45; Houben, *Roger II. von Sizilien: Herrscher zwischen Orient und Okzident* (Darmstadt, 1997), pp. 26-31; Hamm, 'Regentinnen und minderjährige Herrscher im normannischen Italien', pp. 123-39.

4. Adelolf

Adelolfus is mentioned along with *Baldric the Seneschal and *Stabelo as a member of Godfrey's household on crusade at the time of the siege of Jerusalem.

SOURCES: AA p. 481.

5. Ado of Quierzy

Ado de Cheresio, *Chirisiaco* or *Cirisy* is attested in Palestine from 1102 until 1115. He was probably originally a relative or vassal of Gerard, lord of Quierzy (F, Aisne, arr. Laon) who took part in the crusade but subsequently returned to France and was assassinated in the cathedral of Laon on 7 January 1110.[3] Ado fought at the Second Battle of Ramla in 1102. He appears to have been a rear-vassal in Tiberias, appearing as a witness for *Joscelin of Courtenay and for *Bernard, bishop of Nazareth. Before 1115 he and his wife Richoldis and their son *Warmund gave to the abbey of Josaphat the casale of Lichorat (Khirbet el-Kura), situated to the south of Toron.

SOURCES: AA p. 593; RRH nos. 56a, 79, 80, 81a.

6. Andrew of Baudement

Andreas de Valdemunt or *Baldemunt*, witness to royal charters of 1108 and 1115 was probably a relative of the Andrew of Baudement (F, Marne, arr. Epernay) who was related to the counts of Corbeil and served from 1111 to 1133 as seneschal to Theobald IV, count of Chartres, Blois and Champagne (†1152).

SOURCES: RRH nos. 52, 80; Bur, *La formation du comté de Champagne,* p. 431; Suger, p. 66.

7. Anschetin, bishop of Bethlehem

The name of this cleric appears mostly as variants of the basic forms *Anschetinus* or *Aschetinus*, which are derivatives of the Old Norse name *Asketill.* As Mayer argues, these forms were found predominantly among the Normans of southern Italy rather than of Normandy itself, where the usual form is *A(n)schetillus*.[4] It is therefore most likely that Anschetin had come from southern Italy, possibly with the contingent led on the crusade by Bohemund. Before 1108 he functioned successively as cantor of the Holy Sepulchre and prior of Bethlehem, and while serving as prior was named as bishop of Ascalon, although the latter city was still in Fatimid possession. In 1108 Anschetin was chosen as first bishop of the newly-erected see of Bethlehem, into which Ascalon was incorporated. He must have died before 1128, when one Anselm appears as bishop of Bethlehem.

---

[3] *Gerardus de Keresi castello*: AA pp. 315, 331, 332, 467, 468, 494; *Chanson d'Antioche*, lines 1606, 8799. For his later career see *Self and Society in Medieval France: The Memoirs of Abbot Guibert of Nogent (1064?-1125)*, ed. J. F. Benton (New York, 1970), pp. 156-60.

[4] Mayer, 'Angevins versus Normans', p. 21. In one instance (RRH no. 83) the form *Asquetillus* occurs for the bishop.

SOURCES: RRH nos. 56a, 59, 76b, 83, 89, 91, 102, 105, 121; WT XI.12, pp. 513-15, XII.13, p. 563, XII.25, p. 581; Mayer, *Bistümer, Klöster und Stifte*, pp. 44-80.

8. Anselm *de Parenti*

Anselm appears as a witness to royal documents and as holder of lands in the royal domain between 1110 and 1126. Mayer suggests that he was the son of one Geoffrey Parented of Segré, one of several Angevins who took part in the First Crusade.[5] Yet there is a problem with this identification, in that *Parented* appears to be a (hereditary?) surname, whereas the usual onomastic forms of *Anselmus de Parenti* and his brother *Gaufridus de Parenti*, who is documented between 1125 and 1133,[6] clearly indicate that *Parenti* is a locative. Corresponding modern placenames are relatively rare; one possible identification is Parenty (F, Pas-de-Calais, arr. Montreuil-sur-Mer), a village situated on the Course, a tributary of the River Canche, in the *pagus Bononiensis* about 20 km south-east of Boulogne.[7] Anselm's land-holdings are known only from later sources. In 1179 Pope Alexander III confirmed his donation of Dersophath, north of Jerusalem, to the abbey of Mount Zion, while a bull of Gregory IX of 1227 mentions his lands between Bethlehem, Artasium and Bethbezan. This fief, which included Solomon's Pools, was thus close to other lands in the royal domain held by his brother Geoffrey and Geoffrey's father-in-law *Ralph of La Fontanelle. This family group seems to have been the main landholders around Bethlehem in the 1120s.

SOURCES: RRH nos. 52 (*de Parenti*), 76b (*de Parenti*), 80 (*de Parentei*), 115 (*de Parentea*), 576, 983.

9. Anselm of the Tower of David

Anselmus de Turre David is attested in Palestine between 1110 and 1116. This chronology and Anselm's surname indicate that he held the office of castellan of the Tower of David (*custos Turris David*) in Jerusalem in succession to *Gunfrid, who had been captured by the Fatimids in 1106. Anselm held lands in the *terra de Azoto*, i.e. Ashdod, north of Ascalon.

---

[5] Orderic Vitalis, 5: 90; Mayer, 'Angevins versus Normans', p. 10. See also Riley-Smith, *The First Crusaders*, pp. 101-2.

[6] RRH nos. 111, 112, 133, 115, 130, 133, 134, 147. Geoffrey also witnessed a charter of King Fulk which can only be dated only approximately to 1131/34, printed in R. Hiestand, 'Zwei unbekannte Diplome der lateinischen Könige von Jerusalem aus Lucca', *Quellen und Forschungen aus italienischen Archiven und Bibliotheken* 50 (1971), 1-57 (here 54-55).

[7] A. Longnon, *Etudes sur les pagi de la Gaule*, 2 vols (Paris 1869-72), 1: 35.

SOURCES: RRH nos. 57, 59, 76a, 82, 293.

10. [Arda], queen of Jerusalem

In 1098, after Baldwin I attained sole rule in Edessa, he married the daughter of one of the Armenian chieftains of the region. Her name is not given in any medieval sources, but the name Arda has come to be applied to her in modern scholarship. Her father's name is given variously in Latin sources as *Taphnuz* or *Tafroc*. He has been generally identified with Thathoul, lord of Marash. Thathoul ruled Marash as an independent prince, but had been awarded the titles of *πρωτονωβελισσιμος* and *αρχων των αρχοντων* by the Byzantine emperor Alexios Komnenos. The marriage should be a seen as part of an attempt by Baldwin to ally himself with the Armenian rulers of Cilicia after the coup d'etat which removed his adoptive father *Thoros from power. Baldwin's wife was promised a dowry of 60,000 bezants, of which only 7,000 were paid over. She joined him in Jerusalem after his accession as king, but between 1102 and 1108 Baldwin repudiated her, and attempted to force her into the convent of St Anne in Jerusalem, but she went to Constantinople, to where her father had retired in 1104. There is no evidence that the marriage was ever dissolved; in fact, its continuing validity was apparently used to justify the king's separation from his third wife, *Adelaide del Vasto.

SOURCES: AA p. 361; GN p. 259; WT X.1, pp. 453-54; Mayer, *Mélanges*, pp. 51-72; J-C. Cheynet, 'Thathoul, archonte des archontes', *Revue des études byzantines* 48 (1990), 233-42.

11. Ardo

Ardo appears as witness on royal documents of 1108 and 1115, in a relatively lowly position in each case.

SOURCES: RRH nos. 52, 80.

12. Arnulf of Chocques, patriarch of Jerusalem

Arnulf came from the village of Chocques (F, Pas-de-Calais, arr. Béthune) in Flanders, but pursued his early clerical career in Normandy. He became tutor to Cecilia, daughter of William the Conqueror, while she was a nun at Holy Trinity in Caen, and later served as chancellor to Robert Curthose, duke of Normandy, with whom he came on crusade as chaplain. Arnulf was of illegimate birth, being the son of a cleric. By the time of the capture of Jerusalem Arnulf was one of the best qualified of the clerics remaining with the crusade army, and the fact that he was chosen along with Peter the Hermit to give a sermon to the army before the walls of Jerusalem is evidence of his reputation and preaching ability.[8] There was undoubtedly a hostile attitude to him in some sections of the crusade, as exemplified by Raymond of Aguilers, but this may derive from Arnulf's sceptical attitude towards the authenticity of the Holy Lance. He was chosen by the leaders of the crusade as patriarch of Jerusalem on 1 August 1099, but this appointment was nullified by the papal representative Daibert of Pisa, and Arnulf was compensated with the post of archdeacon of Jerusalem. He clearly retained the confidence of Baldwin I throughout this period, and it was largely through the king's influence that he was eventually appointed as patriarch on the death of Gibelin of Arles (1112). His niece, Emma, was married to *Eustace Granarius, lord of Sidon and Caesarea. After the king's death (1118) Arnulf was instrumental in forcing through the succession of Baldwin II, but died soon after his accession.

SOURCES: AA pp. 489, 470-71, 489-93, 510, 526, 545, 599, 653, 658-59, 704, 708-9; GN pp. 232-37; BD pp. 105-7; RRH nos. 59, 64, 67, 68, 68a, 69, 74, 75, 76b, 80, 82; *Versus de viris illustribus dioecesis Tarvanensis qui in sacra fuere expeditione*, in Ch. Moeller, 'Les flamands du Ternois au royaume latin de Jérusalem', *Mélanges Paul Fredericq* (Brussels, 1903), pp. 189-202 (here 191); *Regesta Regum Anglo-Normannorum, 1066-1154, 1: Regesta Willelmi Conquestoris et Willelmi Rufi*, no. 384; D. Douglas, 'The Domesday Tenant of Hawling', *Transactions of the Bristol and Gloucestershire Archaeological Society* 84 (1965), 28-30; Hamilton, *The Latin Church*, pp. 12-16, 56-58, 61-64; Mayer, *Die Kanzlei der lateinischen Könige*, 1: 47-48.

13. Arnulf, viscount of Jericho

Arnulfus vicecomes de Jhericho appears as witness to donations to the church of Quarantene (north-west of Jericho) issued by *Eustace I Granarius in 1116 and by Eustace's widow Emma in 1124. The town of Jericho had been originally a property of the Holy Sepulchre, but was alienated by Emma's uncle, the Patriarch *Arnulf of Chocques, to provide her with a dowry on her marriage to Eustace. The Viscount Arnulf's appearances provide confirmation of this alienation, which is otherwise known only from William of Tyre.

SOURCES: RRH nos. 82, 104; WT XI.15, p. 519.

---

[8] J. Richard, 'Quelques textes sur les premiers temps de l'église latin de Jérusalem', in *Recueil Clovis Brunel*, 2 (Paris, 1955), pp. 420-30 (here 420-23), highlighted the evidence of the Chronicle of Saint-Pierre-le-Vif that Arnulf was given the *licentia ligandi et solvendi* by Urban II, which, he suggested, implies legatine powers, which Arnulf exercised after the death of Adhemar of Le Puy.

14. Arnulf Loteringus

Arnulfus Loferencus or *Loteringus* is attested only for the period 1109-10. He evidently held lands in Galilee; before 1110 he granted to the Hospital the casale of Capharmazre (Kafr Misr) south of Mount Thabor. His surname indicates a Lotharingian origin.

SOURCES: RRH nos. 56a, 57, 293

15. Arnulf of Oudenaarde

Arnulf, the *probus eques ac princeps de castello Aldenardis* can be identified as Arnulf II, lord of Oudenaarde (B, Oost-Vlaanderen, arr. Oudenaarde), who was probably a son of Arnulf I of Oudenaarde (1034/1058-65). Arnulf II is documented in Flanders from 1095/1096, with the descriptors *princeps* and *optimas*. He was killed in an ambush by Muslims near Ascalon in 1106 and buried in the abbey of Josaphat. Albert of Aachen reveals that Arnulf had come to the East with the wife of *Baldwin II of Hainaut (Ida of Brabant), and presumably taken care of the countess after her husband's death. Thus, despite Arnulf's relatively late first appearance in Palestine, it would seem that he had belonged to the Hainaut contingent on the First Crusade.

SOURCES: AA pp. 625-26; Warlop, *Flemish Nobility*, pp. 1035-36.

16. Azo of Drouvin

Azo de Drouino is known only from a charter of 1116, issued by *Eustace I Granarius and his wife Emma for the abbey of Quarantene. If we can thus assume that Azo was a vassal or follower of Eustace, a possible place of origin would be Drouvin-le-Marais (F, Pas-de-Calais, arr. Béthune).

SOURCES: RRH no. 82.

17. Baldric the Seneschal

Baldric is described as *dapifer* of Godfrey (*ex familia ipsius ducis*), and mentioned from such an early stage that it is likely that he was in the duke's service prior to the crusade. He was one of the members of the duke's household sent to negotiate with King Coloman during the march across Hungary in 1096. At the siege of Antioch he was evidently responsible for organising food supplies for the duke's table at a time of great scarcity. He is last mentioned at the time of the capture of Jerusalem (July 1099).

SOURCES: AA pp. 300, 412, 481.

18. Baldwin, archbishop of Caesarea

When Caesarea was captured by the Franks in May 1101, the first archbishop chosen was one Baldwin, who according to William of Tyre had come to

Palestine with Godfrey of Bouillon (*electo ibi archiepiscopo quodam Balduino, qui cum domino duce Godefrido in expeditione venerat*). It is therefore probable that he was a Lotharingian by origin. Guibert of Nogent tells of a certain abbot who had cut the sign of a cross on his forehead as a means of fraudulently securing pious donations to finance his pilgrimage, but adds that his conduct later improved so that he proved useful to the crusading army, becoming in turn abbot of St Mary of Josaphat and then archbishop of Caesarea, so it is possible that this individual was Baldwin. Certainly the archbishop took part in the church council which deposed the patriarch Daibert of Pisa in 1102, and celebrated Lent with King Baldwin at Jerusalem in 1107. He must have died before 1108, when *Evremar of Chocques was translated to Caesarea from the patriarchate.

SOURCES: RRH no. 52; AA pp. 509, 644; WT X.14-15, pp. 469-72; FC II.10, pp. 404-5; GN pp. 182-83.

19. Baldwin of Boulogne, bishop of Beirut

The coastal town of Beirut was captured by Baldwin I's army and a Genoese fleet in May 1101. At some time after this a certain Baldwin was installed as its bishop: a *Balduinus electus Baruti* appears as witness to a document of 1111/1112. His consecration was probably delayed because of a dispute between the patriarchates of Jerusalem and Antioch concerning authority over the ecclesiastical province of Tyre, which was only resolved by Pope Paschal II in 1113. The *Versus de viris illustribus dioecesis Tarvanensis qui in sacra fuere expeditione* identifies Baldwin as a native of the diocese of Thérouanne, with the specific place of origin given as Boulogne (F, Pas-de-Calais, arr. Boulogne-sur-Mer), which suggests a close connection with the family of Baldwin I (*Baruth, in qua Antistes sedit Balduinus boloniensis*). He appears to have had a particularly long tenure, since a Baldwin still appears as bishop in 1139.

SOURCES: *Versus ... Tarvanensis*, pp. 191-92; RRH nos. 69, 144; WT XIV.13, p. 648, XV.16, p. 696; Hamilton, *The Latin Church*, pp. 27-28.

20. Baldwin of Bourcq

The successor to Baldwin I as king of Jerusalem is generally referred to in the sources as *Baldewinus de Burch* or *de Burgo*. He was a son of Hugh I, count of Rethel and Melisende, daughter of Guy I of Montlhéry and Hodierna of Gometz. Another son of Hugh, called Manasses, appears with his parents on a charter of 1097, and since Manasses was the traditional leading-name of the counts of Rethel (and their predecessors the counts of Omont) it is likely that he, and not Baldwin, was the eldest son. Baldwin's surname has often been given as 'Le Bourg' in modern works, but it undoubtedly relates to Bourcq (F,

Ardennes, arr. Vouziers) in the valley of the Aisne.[9] Most narratives of the crusade agree that Baldwin was a kinsman of the Bouillon-Boulogne brothers, but the precise relationship is unclear. He joined the *comitatus Baldewini* in Cilicia in 1097, and after completing his pilgrimage he returned to join Baldwin I in the county of Edessa, and succeeded him as count in the summer of 1100. He soon married Morfia, daughter of Gabriel, lord of Melitene, an Armenian who belonged to the Melkite church. They had four daughters: Melisende, queen of Jerusalem and wife of Fulk of Anjou; Alice, wife of Bohemund II of Antioch; Hodierna, wife of Raymond II of Tripoli, and Yvette, abbess of Bethany.

SOURCES: AA pp. 299, 306, 310, 315, 332, 343, 350, 422, 464, 468, 527; GN p. 254; Saige, Lacaille and Labande, *Trésor des chartes du comté de Rethel* 1, no. 2; WT X.23, pp. 482-83; Riley-Smith, *The First Crusaders*, pp. 169-173, 200; Appendix C, 'The Claim of Baldwin II to the Throne of Jerusalem'.

21. Baldwin II of Mons, count of Hainaut

Baldewinus de Monte castello, Hainaucorum comes et princeps was the second son of Baldwin VI, count of Flanders (†1070) and Richilda, countess of Hainaut. His elder brother Arnulf III was meant to succeed to both counties, but was deposed and killed in 1070 by their uncle Robert I 'the Frisian', who gained control of Flanders. With the support of Henry IV and Theoduin, bishop of Liège, Baldwin was able to maintain himself in Hainaut, a settlement that was guaranteed by an imperial diet held at Liège in 1071. He was married to Ida, daughter of Henry II of Louvain. Baldwin and his successors continued to assert their claims to Flanders well into the second half of the next century, and this enmity was probably the reason why Baldwin travelled east in the company of Godfrey of Bouillon rather than the army of Robert II of Flanders and Robert of Normandy. In June 1096 he sold the castle of Couvin and its dependencies to Otbert, bishop of Liège, in what was evidently a fund-raising measure for the crusade. He was accompanied by a number of vassals of his own, including *Arnulf of Oudenaarde, *Gerard of Avesnes and *Giselbert of Couvin. In 1098 he and Hugh of Vermandois were sent in charge of an embassy to the emperor Alexios Komnenos, but Baldwin was killed in a Turkish ambush near Nicaea.

SOURCES: AA pp. 315, 434-35; BD p. 17; GN pp. 147, 208; *GF* p. 2; Sigebert of Gembloux, p. 367; Giselbert of Mons, p. 43; *Cantatorium*, pp. 175-76; *Chanson d'Antioche*, lines 1163, 8986 (*Bauduïns de Mons*); Bormans, Schoolmeesters and Poncelet, *Cartulaire de l'église de Saint-Lambert*, 1, no. 29; Hansay,

[9] Richard, *Le royaume latin de Jérusalem*, p. 19.

'L'inféodation du comté de Hainaut à l'église de Liège en 1071', pp. 45-58; Mohr, *Geschichte des Herzogtums Lothringen*, 2: 49.

22. Baldwin of Ramla

A certain Baldwin was in charge of the defence of the castle at Ramla by 1106 and also held property in the town and territory of Ramla. He seems to have been first a royal castellan, later becoming (by 1126) a vassal of Hugh, count of Jaffa. After the revolt and dispossession of Hugh, Baldwin held Ramla directly from the crown. His lordship eventually passed to his daughter Helvis, wife of *Barisan of Ibelin. Nothing is known directly of Baldwin's origins, although it is possible that he could be identified with *Baldwinus de Hestrut* or *Hastrut castellis Flandriae*, who first appears in 1102, but is last mentioned under this surname at the Third Battle of Ramla in August 1105. If he had been given lands at Ramla then it is possible that from 1105/1107 the new designation 'of Ramla' was commonly applied to him. The toponymic form *Hestrud* was a Walloon variant of the placename Heestert in Flanders (B, West-Vlaanderen, arr. Kortrijk).[10]

SOURCES: AA pp. 591-93, 621, 636; RRH nos. 57, 80, 87, 90, 129a, 164, 181; Mayer, 'Carving up Crusaders: The Early Ibelins and Ramlas', in *Outremer: Studies in the History of the Crusading Kingdom of Jerusalem presented to Joshua Prawer*, ed. B. Z. Kedar, H. E. Mayer and R. C. Smail (Jerusalem, 1982), pp. 101-18; Mayer, 'The Origins of the Lordships of Ramla and Lydda', 537-52.

23. Baldwin of St Abraham

Baldwin is attested between 1115 and 1136, and seems to have succeeded *Walter Mahomet as castellan of St Abraham (Hebron). His daughter Gilia married Anselm of Brie.

SOURCES: RRH nos. 80, 90, 91, 115, 120, 121, 133, 164; J. Delaville Le Roulx, 'Chartes de Terre-Sainte', *ROL* 11 (1905-8), 181-91 (here 185-86); Mayer, 'Die Herrschaftsbildung in Hebron', pp. 68-70.

24. Barisan

Barisanus (a name given in Old French sources as *Balian*) was in the kingdom of Jerusalem by 1115, when a confirmation of grants to the abbey of Josaphat records his gift of a property with vineyards *in territorio Jherosolimitano*. In the reign of Fulk he became lord of Ibelin, and by his marriage with Elisabeth (Helvis), daughter of *Baldwin of Ramla he became the founder of what was

---

[10] M. Gysseling, *Toponymisch woordenboek van België, Nederland, Luxemburg, Noord-Frankrijk en West-Duitsland (vóór 1226)*, 2 vols (Brussels, 1960), 1: 463. Baldwin of Heestert may have been related to the *Ansel de Hestrut et Balduinus frater eius* who appear on a charter for the abbey of St Bertin in 1119: Haigneré, *Chartes de St Bertin*, 1, no. 134.

to become the most enduring and important dynasties of the Latin East. His origins are obscure. The *Lignages d'Outremer*, a genealogical work originally composed by an author close to the Ibelin family, claim him as *Balian le François*, who was supposedly a brother of one Count Guilin of Chartres, and who arrived in the Holy Land around 1140. Since the chronology and descent from a non-existent count of Chartres are impossible, the reference to Chartres has been explained as a case of *Ansippung* or appropriation of the genealogy of the Le Puiset family, who had been viscounts of Chartres.[11] Riley-Smith has made the ingenious suggestion that in fact the name Guilin refers to Gilduin of Le Puiset, abbot of Josaphat, and that Barisan was probably the brother of Gilduin and Hugh II of Le Puiset, and uncle to Count Hugh of Jaffa.[12] The most convincing explanation of Barisan's origins is probably still that given by Richard, who showed that the name *Barisanus*, originally meaning 'inhabitant of Bari', was common in eleventh-century Sardinia and other parts of Italy and that Barisan was originally a Pisan who came to the East in the entourage of Daibert, archbishop of Pisa.

SOURCES: RRH nos. 80, 87, 89, 91, 101, 104, 112, 113, 120, 127; 135, 137a, 147, 164, 174, 181; J. Richard, 'Guy d'Ibelin OP, évêque de Limassol et l'inventaire de ses biens', *Bulletin de correspondance héllenique* 74 (1950), 98-100; Mayer, 'Carving Up Crusaders: The Early Ibelins and Ramlas', in *Outremer*, pp. 101-18.

25. Bernard, bishop of Nazareth

Bernard appears as the first Latin bishop of Nazareth in 1109, when the bishopric was established, and is documented until 1125. He must have died before March 1128, when William I appears as bishop. Bernard's origins are unknown.

SOURCES: RRH nos. 56a, 68a, 69, 76b, 80, 81a, 89, 90, 91, 92, 93, 97, 102, 105, 106, 121; WT XII.3, p. 563, XII.25, p. 581.

---

[11] Du Cange, *Les Familles d'Outre-Mer*, pp. 360-61; J. L. La Monte, 'The Lords of Le Puiset on the Crusades', *Speculum* 17 (1942), 100-18 (here 113-18).

[12] Riley-Smith, *The First Crusaders*, pp. 172-73. However, no documents of Barisan or the Le Puisets allude to any such relationship. For example, in RRH no. 120 Barisan refers to Hugh of Jaffa only as *dominus meus Hugo, comes Jope*, where one might have expected an allusion to a kinship. It is also noticeable that when Hugh of Jaffa revolted against Fulk in 1134 in defence of the rights of his cousin Queen Melisende, his constable Barisan refused to support him, and deserted to the king's side, which is not so likely of a close kinsman when other vassals remained loyal: WT XIV.16, p. 653.

26. Berwold

Bervoldus miles nobilissimus is known from his presence at the First Battle of Ramla (September 1101) and the donation of lands he held *in monte* to the abbey of Josaphat before 1112. Despite the paucity of references he was evidently of some importance. At Ramla he commanded one of five divisions of the Frankish army, the other commanders being *Geldemar Carpinel, *Hugh of Fauquembergues and Baldwin I who retained two divisions. A donation of Ida of Bouillon, countess of Boulogne, to the abbey of St Bertin in 1098 'for the preservation of her sons Godfrey and Baldwin who have gone to Jerusalem to fight the pagans' renounces rights over a *terra quam Ongyz et Berwoldus Deo et S. Bertino ad eleemosynam pauperum tradiderunt*. It is therefore possible that Berwold was originally a vassal of the count of Boulogne who remained in the east in Baldwin's service. He may have given his name to the *Castellum Beroart*, a fortification on the road between Ramla and Ascalon.

SOURCES: AA p. 549; RRH no. 67; Miraeus, *Opera diplomatica et historica*, 1: 79; A. J. G. Le Glay, *Revue des opera diplomatica de Miraeus* (Brussels, 1856), p. 15.

27. Cono, count of Montaigu

Cuno de Monte Acuto or *Cono comes de Monteacuto Leodiensis dyocesis* was the eldest son of Gozelo, count of Behogne (†1064), and Ermentrude of Harzé, a noblewoman who held lands in the Hesbaye. The castle of Montaigu (B, Luxembourg, arr. Marche-en-Famenne) was situated on the left bank of the River Ourthe near Marcourt in the Ardennes. The family of the counts of Montaigu was prominent in both temporal and ecclesiastical affairs within the principality of Liège. Before 1028 Gozelo was enfeoffed with the county of Huy, which had been granted to the bishop of Liège by the Emperor Otto III in 985; this was an important position of trust, as the town of Huy lay at the centre of the bishop's domains and its fortress was his principal place of refuge in times of danger. A younger son of this Gozelo, the Archdeacon Henry the Elder (†1124) was dean of the church of St Lambert, as well as an associate of the writer Sigebert of Gembloux, whom he encouraged to produce imperialist tracts as part of the polemic against the papal party in the Investiture Contest. One of Cono's own sons, Henry the Younger (†1125), was also an archdeacon and provost of the church of Fosses. Cono succeeded his father as count of Huy, and also became advocate of Dinant, and it is an indication of his high status that between 1064 and his death, Cono was present at most of the important transactions of the bishops Theoduin, Henry of Verdun and Otbert. Cono has sometimes been mistakenly referred to as brother-in-law to Duke

Godfrey.[13] This information derives from Orderic Vitalis, who states that Cono was married to a sister of Godfrey of Bouillon, but this claim is not confirmed by any sources with knowledge local to Lotharingia or Boulogne, and Orderic's information may simply be a result of confusion over the name Ida. Eustace II of Boulogne and Ida of Bouillon are not known to have had any daughters, while the chronicle of the abbey of Saint-Hubert states that Cono's only known wife, also called Ida, was a daughter of Lambert 'the Old', a nobleman of the territory of Liège, who was buried at the abbey of Saint-Hubert. Nevertheless a kinship is indicated by the name Gozelo, borne by Cono's father as well as his eldest son, as well as in several generations of the Ardennes-Bouillon dynasty, although not, significantly, by the Luxembourg and Bar branches of the Ardennes lineage. A further link may have been via Ermentrude, who was a blood relative (*proximus in sanguine*) of Henry of Verdun, himself known to have been related to the Ardennes-Bouillon family.[14] Cono was present at the sale of Baisy and Genappe by Ida and Godfrey of Bouillon in 1095, and in 1096 he sold the allod of *Felc* near Nassogne along with other property to the abbey of Saint-Hubert as means of raising funds for the crusade. He was accompanied on the expedition by his sons *Gozelo (the younger) and *Lambert, and played a prominent role within Godfrey's contingent, acting as envoy to the Emperor Alexios and later receiving the emperor's representative John Komnenos. Cono fought at the battle of Ascalon (12 August 1099), but then returned to the West; he was in Liège by 10 March 1100. He died at the castle of Dalhem on 30 April 1106 and was buried at Dinant.

SOURCES: AA pp. 306-7, 310, 317, 359, 366, 385, 422, 464, 495, 504; Alberic of Troisfontaines, *Chronicon*, pp. 804, 815; *Chanson d'Antioche*, line 1397; Kurth, *Chartes de l'abbaye de St Hubert* 1, nos. 48, 56, pp. 59-62, 69-72; Bormans, Schoolmeesters and Poncelet, *Cartulaire de l'église de Saint-Lambert*, 1, nos. 26, 29, pp. 38-43, 46-48; Orderic Vitalis, 5: 166; *Cantatorium*, pp. 181, 208, 253-54; MGH DD K.II, no. 116; DD H.IV, no. 459; C. G. Roland, 'Les seigneurs et comtes de Rochefort', *Annales de la Société archéologique de Namur* 20 (1893), 63-141; A. Joris, *La ville de Huy au Moyen Age* (Paris, 1959), pp. 140-44; Beumann, *Sigebert von Gembloux und der Traktat de investitura episcoporum*, pp. 25-26; Kupper, *Liège et l'église impériale*, pp. 396-403; Kupper, '*Mulier*

---

13 A. Le Prevost, in *Orderici Vitalis Anglicenae coenobii Uticensis monachi Historiae Ecclesiasticae*, 5 vols (Paris, 1838-55), 3: 477 n. 2; Röhricht, *Geschichte des Ersten Kreuzzuges*, p. 35 n. 5; Riley-Smith, *The First Crusade and the Idea of Crusading*, p. 45; Keats-Rohan, *Domesday People, 1*: 196-97.

14 Mathieu, 'Sur les comtesses de Rethel au XIe siècle', pp. 9-10 suggests that Ermentrude was a sister of Hermann-Hezelin II, count of Grandpré.

nobilissima Ermengardis nomine: Contribution à l'histoire de la seigneurie rurale en Basse-Lotharingie', *PSHIDL* 102 (1986), 69-74.

28. Drogo of Brie

Drogo de Bria appears on a royal confirmation of donations made by *Joscelin of Courtenay and *William of Bures to the abbey of Josaphat in 1115. The description *testis Jocelini* implies he was a vassal of Joscelin in Galilee; he may be the same Drogo who appears as witness for William in 1126. He probably came from the Brie, the district between the Ile-de-France and Champagne around Brie-Comte-Robert (F, Seine-et-Marne, arr. Melun). It is possible he was the father of the brothers Simon and Thomas, both described as *filius Drogonis de Braia*, who witnessed a charter of Bernard of Chevreuse for the priory of Longpont, a foundation of Joscelin's grandfather Guy I of Montlhéry.

SOURCES: RRH nos. 79, 115; *Cartulaire du prieuré de Nôtre-Dame de Longpont*, no. 282.

29. Drogo of Nesle

Drogo de Nahella or *Nigella* originally left the West on one of the so-called people's expeditions. At Constantinople he was held in captivity by the Emperor Alexios, but was later released and joined Godfrey's army. He was with Baldwin in Edessa, and in 1100 presumably accompanied him to Jerusalem where he is attested until 1126. A Drogo, son of Ralph, lord of Nesle (F, Somme, arr. Péronne) and brother of Ivo II, lord of Nesle and count of Soissons, is attested in France from 1115 to 1157, which means that he cannot be identified with the crusader. It is nevertheless likely that Drogo the crusader was a member of this family, probably belonging to Ralph's generation.

SOURCES: AA pp. 299, 304, 305, 315, 398, 442; *Chanson d'Antioche*, lines 1432, 1522 (*Droe de Noiele*), 1553, 1577, 1587, 1617, 1627, 8971; RRH nos 76a (1114) and 115 which should read *Niella* not *Maloe* (RRH Add.); W. M. Newman, *Les seigneurs de Nesle en Picardie* (Philadelphia, 1971), 2, nos. 2, 4, 6, 7, 10, 12, 15, 16, 18, 31.

30. Dudo, lord of Cons

Dudo de Cons has been often identified in scholarship as originating from Konz, south of Trier at the confluence of the Moselle and the Saar.[15] He was actually

---

[15] Editors of AA, in RHC Occ. 4: 299 note f; Runciman, *History of the Crusades*, 1: 147; Knoch, *Studien zu Albert von Aachen*, pp. 114, 157; Röhricht, *Die Deutschen im heiligen Lande*, p. 17; Röhricht, *Geschichte des Ersten Kreuzzuges*, p. 62; Andressohn,

lord of Cons-la-Grandville (F, Meurthe-et-Moselle, arr. Briey) on the River Chiers in the Ardennes. His father Adelo was castellan of Dun, a castle on the Meuse south of Stenay, which the Emperor Henry IV gave to the bishop of Verdun in 1065. Adelo's properties were divided between his two sons, Walter receiving Dun itself and Dudo receiving Cons. Dudo was married to *Hadwida, a daughter of Arnulf II, count of Chiny (1068-1106). The marriage must have taken place before 1091, when Dudo, Hadwida and Walter donated the priory of St Michael at Cons to the abbey of Saint-Hubert. Dudo was accompanied by Hadwida on crusade, and his relative insignificance within Godfrey's army can probably be explained by his dynastic connection with the counts of Chiny, who were long-standing enemies of the Ardennes-Bouillon family. The return of Dudo and Hadwida from Jerusalem was commemorated in a list of benefactors of the abbey of Saint-Hubert in the Ardennes: *commemoratio Hadwidis filiae comitis Arnulphi de Chisnei, quae cum viro suo Dudone Cunensi ab Hierosolimis reversa.*

SOURCES: AA pp. 299, 317; DD Heinrich IV, no. 162; Kurth, *Chartes de l'abbaye de St. Hubert*, 1, no. 63, pp. 80-82; *Cantatorium*, pp. 150, 164, 186; Parisse, *La Noblesse lorraine*, pp. 196-98; R. Pagny, 'Les seigneurs et la seigneurie de Cons-la-Grandville', *Bulletin de l'Association 'Les Amis du Vieux Longwy'* 5 (1962), 3-9, 74-78.

31. Engelbert of Tournai

Along with his brother *Letold, Engelbert distinguished himself in the successful crusader assault on Jerusalem on 15 July 1099. They are both described by Albert of Aachen as *ortos de civitate Tornacio*, i.e. the town of Tournai (B, Hainaut, arr. Tournai), which at the time of the crusade was a lordship of its bishop. It is likely that both brothers had left the West in the contingent of Robert of Flanders, but at some stage they evidently joined that of Godfrey of Bouillon, since by the time of the siege of Jerusalem they were fighting in a siege-tower commanded by Godfrey and his brother Eustace III of Boulogne.

SOURCES: AA pp. 472, 477; PT p. 108; Robert the Monk, p. 867.

32. Engelrand of Saint-Pol

Enjorrandus, comitis Sancti Pauli filius was Engelrand, son of *Hugh, count of Saint-Pol (F, Pas-de-Calais, arr. Saint-Pol-sur-Ternoise), whom he accompanied on crusade, probably with Count *Eustace III of Boulogne, whose vassals they were. He developed a reputation for valour during the siege of

---

Ancestry and Life of Godfrey of Bouillon, p. 52; Duparc-Quioc, in *Chanson d'Antioche*, p. 73 (in some cases given as 'Conz-Saarbrücken', presumably a mistake for Saarburg).

Antioch, but died of disease after the capture of Ma^carrat (late December 1098), and was buried in the church of St Andrew there.

SOURCES: AA pp. 315, 372, 373, 422, 463; BD pp. 47, 76; P. Feuchère, 'Les origines du comté de Saint-Pol', *Revue du Nord* 35 (1953), 125-49.

33. Eustace III, count of Boulogne

The elder brother of Godfrey of Bouillon and Baldwin I, Eustace succeeded to his father's county by 1088 at the latest. Although some sources imply that he left the West with his brother Godfrey, it is practically certain that he was originally with Robert of Flanders and Robert of Normandy. Albert of Aachen, the best informed source on Godfrey's contingent, never mentions Eustace's presence in it during its march to Constantinople. After the crossing to Asia Minor, however, he and his own followers seem to have joined Godfrey's contingent. He returned to Boulogne after the completion of the crusade. On the death of Baldwin I (1118) he was the preferred successor of a significant section of the ruling classes of Jerusalem, and although he travelled as far as Apulia, he declined to press his claims after hearing of the conecration of Baldwin II. Shortly before his death (1125) he had retired to the Cluniac monastery at Rumilly.

SOURCES: AA pp. 314, 315, 398, 424, 448, 451, 472, 477, 491, 495; BD pp. 20, 28, 34, 35, 100 n.13, 110 n.6; GN pp. 226, 234, 235; Henry of Huntingdon, *Historia Anglorum*, Rolls Series 74 (London, 1879), p. 219; Andressohn, *The Ancestry and Life of Godfrey of Bouillon,* pp. 21-26, 53; Mayer, *Mélanges*, pp. 15-18, 73-91; Tanner, 'The Expansion of the Power and Influence of the Counts of Boulogne Under Eustace II', pp. 251-86; Mayer, *Die Kanzlei der lateinischen Könige*, 2: 926-28.

34. Eustace of Cassel

Eustachius de Castel or *Cassel* appears as witness to documents of Baldwin I in 1108 and 1115. He may have came from Cassel (F, Nord, arr. Dunkerque) in Flanders.

SOURCES: RRH nos. 52, 80.

35. Eustace Granarius

Eustace *Granarius* or *Granerius* first appears at the Third Battle of Ramla (August 1105). Within only a few years he made a meteoric rise to become one of the most powerful nobles of the kingdom. In late 1110 he was enfeoffed with the newly captured city of Sidon. In 1111 he accompanied Baldwin I on the joint Frankish expedition against Shaizar, and was prominent at the siege of Tyre, building siege machines at his own expense. He was probably already lord of Caesarea, since he is recorded as previously having made donations of property in that lordship. He married Emma, niece of the Patriarch *Arnulf of Chocques, who gave her the town of Jericho, originally a property of the church. This accumulation of fiefs was exceptional in the reign of Baldwin I, and Eustace could rightly be described as *primus in domo et consilio regis*, a status which is reflected in his prominent position on witness lists. It has been claimed that 'the reasons for his wealth and status in the early days of the kingdom are lost along with his origins in Europe'.[16] However, his origins can be established with a high degree of certainty. The *Versus de viris illustribus dioecesis Tarvanensis qui in sacra fuere expeditione* identifies him as a Fleming from the diocese of Thérouanne: *Par belramensis, fit princeps Caesariensis / Eustachius notus miles, cognomine Gernirs*. The form *Gernirs* is also used by William of Tyre, and seems to be a vernacular equivalent of the Latin forms of Eustace's surname which would seem to indicate an official in charge of a *granarium* (store-house), although as this appears to have become a hereditary surname carried on by his descendants it does not necessarily reveal anything about Eustace himself. The phrase *par belramensis* can most satisfactorily be explained as the noun *par* in the sense of 'peer', a military office with an attached fief known in the county of Flanders from the mid-eleventh century, plus an adjective deriving from a toponym; since this must necessarily be sought in the diocese of Thérouanne it must refer to Beaurain-Château (F, Pas-de-Calais, arr. Montreuil-sur-Mer) on the River Canche, which is mentioned in 723 as *Belrinio super Quanchia sitas in pago Tarvaninse* and in the eleventh and twelfth centuries as *Belrem* and *castellum de Belrain*.[17] As Beaurain-Château was part of the county of Saint-Pol, held from the count of Boulogne,[18] it is likely that Eustace was originally on crusade with Count *Hugh of Saint-Pol and his son *Engelrand. Eustace remained prominent after the death of Baldwin I. When Baldwin II was captured (April 1123) Eustace was chosen by the chief nobles and clerics as regent and constable of the kingdom. He died while holding this office (15 June 1123) and was buried in the abbey of St Maria Latina in Jerusalem. His fiefs were divided between his two sons, Eustace II of Sidon and Walter of Caesarea, and his widow married Hugh, count of Jaffa.

---

[16] Slack, 'Royal *Familiares* in the Latin Kingdom of Jerusalem', p.18. Ch. Lauranson-Rosaz, 'Le Velay et la croisade', in *Le Concile de Clermont de 1095 et l'appel à la croisade* (Rome, 1997), 33-64 (here 52 n. 72) talks of 'Eustache d'Agrain, qui devint prince de Sidon et de Césarée', who is mistakenly identified as a native of the Velay.

[17] Maurits Gysseling and A. C. F. Koch, *Diplomata Belgica ante annum millesimum centesimum scripta*, 2 vols (Brussels, 1950), 1: 28; A. de Loisne, *Dictionnaire topographique du Pas-de-Calais* (Paris, 1907), p. 37.

[18] Feuchère, 'Les origines du Comté de Saint-Pol', 123-49; Warlop, *Flemish Nobility*, pp. 136-56.

SOURCES: AA pp. 621, 667, 683, 692; RRH nos. 59, 76b, 80, 82, 89, 90, 91, 101, 104, 139; FC III.16, pp. 658-61, III.22, 674-75; WT XI.14-15, pp. 518-19, XII.17, pp. 567-68, XII.21, pp. 571-73; *Versus … Tarvanensis*, pp. 189-203; J. L. La Monte, 'The Lords of Sidon in the Twelfth and Thirteenth Centuries', *Byzantion* 17 (1944-45), 183-211; Murray, 'A Note on the Origin of Eustace Grenier', pp. 28-30; H. E. Mayer, 'The Wheel of Fortune: Seignorial Vicissitudes Under Kings Fulk and Baldwin III of Jerusalem', *Speculum* 65 (1990), 860-77 (here 870-75).

36. Evremar of Chocques, patriarch of Jerusalem

Evremar, a priest from Chocques (F, Pas-de-Calais, arr. Béthune) in Flanders, began his ecclesiastical career in the bishopric of Thérouanne. In the Holy Land he remained in contact with his former bishop, Lambert (later bishop of Arras) and with his own family in Flanders. Largely on the instigation of Baldwin I, he was chosen to succeed Daibert of Pisa as patriarch in 1102. He had a reputation for piety and charity, and was able enough to carry the True Cross at the Third Battle of Ramla in August 1105. However, he was evidently less well qualified in administrative abilities, and it may be for this reason that Guibert of Nogent describes him as 'simple and illiterate'. These failings led Baldwin to request his deposition from Pope Paschal II, whose legate, Gibelin of Arles, eventually ruled Evremar's election to have been invalid at a church council in Jerusalem (1108). Evremar was translated to the see of Caesarea, where he served as archbishop until his death in 1129.

SOURCES: AA pp. 599-600, 607, 622, 639, 658-59; GN p. 233; *Versus … Tarvanensis*, p. 191; WT XI.4, pp. 500-1; RRH nos. 40, 42, 50, 52a, 65, 69, 76b, 80, 89, 91, 99, 101, 102, 105, 114d, 114e, 126, 134; Hamilton, *The Latin Church*, pp. 56-58, 114-15; Murray, 'Mighty Against the Enemies of Christ', p. 233.

37. Folbert of Bouillon

The crusader *Folbertus, miles egregius, de castello Bullon ortus* figured in an incident during the siege of Antioch, when he and his wife were travelling to Edessa, probably to look for food supplies, and were captured by Turks. Folbert was killed and his wife given to a follower of the Turkish lord of ᶜAzāz. Riley-Smith identifies them with the *Fulcherius de Budelone et Emmelina uxor ejus* who gave a tithe at Orsonville to the abbey of St Martin-des-Champs in Paris before 1096, and evidently came from Bullion (F, Yvelines, arr. Rambouillet).[19] However, this identification seems hazardous, as the name *Folkerus* occurs in only two manuscripts of the chronicle of Albert of Aachen, while no name is given for his wife in any manuscript. Since the crusader is mentioned only by Albert

---

[19] Riley-Smith, *The First Crusaders*, pp. 204, 206; J. Depoin, *Recueil de Chartes et documents de Saint-Martin-des-Champs, monastère parisien*, 5 vols (Paris, 1912-21), no. 69.

rather than any French chronicler, and his place of origin is referred to as a *castellum*, it seems more probable that he was one of the knights known as *Bullonienses*, that is vassals holding fiefs in the allodial territory of Bouillon (B, Luxembourg, arr. Neufchâteau).

SOURCES: AA pp. 435-36.

38. Franco of Maasmechelen

A crusader associated with Godfrey of Bouillon is described as *Franco de Mechela villa, quae est juxta Mosam fluvium*. This full description indicates an origin in Maasmechelen (B, Limburg, arr. Tongeren) on the River Meuse, an area where the Ardennes-Bouillon family held allodial properties.[20] He was accompanied on crusade by his brother *Sigemar. Both are identified by Albert of Aachen as kinsmen of the brothers *Henry and *Godfrey of Esch-sur-Sûre, crusaders from the Ardennes. Franco remained in Palestine after the departure of the majority of crusaders, and was killed at the siege of Arsuf in 1099.

SOURCES: AA pp. 413, 519.

39. Frederick of Corbeil

Fredericus de Corbolio, who witnessed a royal charter in 1104, may be identical with, or a relative of the individual *Fruricus de Curbulo* or *Fredericus de Curbuilo* who appears on charters of Philip I of France in the period 1066/1085, often in the company of Guy I of Montlhéry and Hugh I of Le Puiset, whose son Everard III later married Alice, heiress of the county of Corbeil. His surname probably derives from Corbeil-Essonnes (F, Essonne, arr. Evry) south of Paris.

SOURCES: RRH no. 43; Prou, *Recueil des actes de Philippe Ier*, nos. 24, 30, 50, 116.

40. Fulcher of Chartres, historian

Fulcherus Carnotensis was born in 1059. He was already a cleric in the diocese of Chartres when he attended the Council of Clermont, where he was an eyewitness to the crusade appeal of Urban II. According to his own testimony, Fulcher left the West in the company of Stephen of Blois, but after Stephen deserted from the crusading army at Antioch in 1097, Fulcher joined Baldwin I in Edessa, becoming his chaplain. When Baldwin inherited the throne of Jerusalem in 1100, Fulcher went with him, and until around 1111, when he was

---

[20] Not Mechelen/Malines (B, Antwerpen, arr. Mechelen) in Brabant, as identified by Riley-Smith, *The First Crusade and the Idea of Crusading*, p. 45. J. Newcomer, *The Grand Duchy of Luxembourg: The Evolution of Nationhood, 963 A.D. to 1983* (Lanham, 1984), p. 60, refers to the brothers 'Francis and Sigismund of Grevenmacher'. The placename Grevenmacher (Lux) was often written as *Machera* at this time (Gysseling, *Woordenboek*, 1: 423-24), but it was situated on the Moselle rather than the Meuse.

over fifty years of age, often accompanied the king on campaign. At some point he became a canon of the church of the Holy Sepulchre in Jerusalem. In 1100/1101 he began work on his *Historia Hierosolymitana*, which he subjected to major revision in the period 1124-27; he probably died in the autumn of 1127.

SOURCES: FC I.7, pp. 163-64, I.14, 206-8; Ch. Kohler, 'Un sermon commémoratif de la prise de Jérusalem par les croisés attribué à Foucher de Chartres', *ROL* 8 (1900-1), 158-64; Epp, *Fulcher von Chartres: Studien zur Geschichtsschreibung des ersten Kreuzzuges*.

41. Fulcher of Chartres, lord of Sarūj

Folkerus Carnotensis is mentioned as having commanded a garrison at the town of Sarūj (*Sororgia*) in northern Syria in 1097; he was thus a prominent member of the *comitatus Baldewini*. His surname indicates that he came from Chartres (F, Eure-et-Loir, arr. Chartres). If he was identical with *Fulgerius, frater scilicet Budelli Carnotensis* named by Raymond of Aguilers, he was the brother of Bartholomew Boel of Chartres; both brothers went on crusade as members of the Italian Norman contingent under Bohemund. Fulcher remained with Baldwin in the county of Edessa. When Sarūj was finally wrested from the control of the Turks, he appears to have been given the lordship of the town and its surrounding territory; Matthew of Edessa calls him 'count of Sarūj'. He was killed in battle against Sokman ibn Artuk, the ruler of Diyar Bakr, in 1100/1101.

SOURCES: AA pp. 357, 442, 446; RA p. 251; Matthew of Edessa, trans. Dostourian, pp. 320-21; Riley-Smith, *The First Crusaders*, pp. 100-1, 206.

42. Fulk of Guînes

Fulk was the second son of Baldwin I, count of Guînes († ante 1097). Guînes (F, Pas-de-Calais, arr. Boulogne-sur-Mer) was situated in the *pagus Bononiensis*, between the main part of the county of Boulogne and its detached dependent territory of Marck. The counts of Boulogne and Guînes were related; Lambert of Ardres calls Fulk's sister Alice a *cognata et consanguinea* of Geoffrey, bishop of Paris, brother of Eustace II of Boulogne and uncle of the Bouillon-Boulogne brothers. Fulk was a great-great-grandson of Adelolf of Guînes and Mathilda, daughter of Arnulf I of Boulogne. Although unknown to sources produced in Outremer, Fulk was probably on crusade with Eustace III of Boulogne and Robert II of Flanders. He later obtained the fief of Beirut. The *Versus de viris illustribus de dioecesis Tarvanensis* gives the terse information *Fulco Ghisnensis urbem tenuit Baruth*, which is confirmed by Lambert of Ardres. *Fulconem in terra promissionis comitem apud Baruth, ibique demum sepultum.* Fulk's tenure of Beirut must therefore be dated to between May 1110, when the Franks captured the city, and 1125, when Walter Brisebarre appears as lord of Beirut.

SOURCES: Vanderkindere, *La formation territoriale des principautés belges* 1: 327-29; Longnon, *Etudes sur les pagi de la Gaule*, 1: 25-38; Lambert of Ardres, pp. 574-75; *Versus … Tarvanensis*, pp. 191-92.

43. Garin *de Verno*

Garinus de Verno appears as witness to a royal charter of 1112. He may be identical with the Garin who appears as viscount of Tyre in 1129.

SOURCES: RRH nos. 68a, 127.

44. Geldemar Carpinel

Gaudemarus Carpinellus or *Geldemarus cognomine Carpinel* was a rare case of a crusader from southern France in the Bouillon-Boulogne affinity.[21] Geldemar was on crusade with Raymond of Saint-Gilles, and was an important man who was accompanied by his *gens* or retinue. At some point he entered the service of Godfrey, who promised him the port of Haifa when it should be captured. However, he and his retinue were expelled from the city by *Tancred, and Geldemar evidently received St Abraham as compensation. He was a member of the group of knights that summoned Baldwin from Edessa on the death of Godfrey, although there is no evidence that he was its leader.[22] He regained Haifa by March 1101. At the First Battle of Ramla (September 1101) he commanded the second division of the Frankish army, and was killed in the same engagement. He was buried in the church of the Holy Sepulchre.

SOURCES: AA pp. 507, 521-26, 531, 537-38, 549; PT p. 103; RA, pp. 307-8; RRH nos. 57, 293.

---

[21] A *Galdemarus Carpinellus* witnessed an undated charter for the abbey of Conques (F, Aveyron, arr. Rodez): G. Desjardins, *Cartulaire de l'abbaye de Conques en Rouergue* (Paris, 1879), no. 506. However, the appearance on this document of Humbert, archbishop of Lyon from 1119 to 1128, Gaucher, bishop of Langres from 1113 to 1126, and Bernard, bishop of Macon from 1096 to 1121, would suggest a date of 1119/1121, long after the crusader's death. Thus the two individuals cannot be identical although it is probable that they were related.

[22] The RHC edition of Albert of Aachen (AA p. 526F) says that this act was done in the name of the *milites et princeps regni Iherusalem*. Riley-Smith, 'The Motives', p. 728, concluded that 'the "prince" could only have been Galdemar'. However, this reading is undoubtedly incorrect. The Oxford and Florence manuscripts of Albert's history have *principes* (personal communication from Dr S. Edgington), as does the text edited by Bongars (PL 166: 584).

45. Geoffrey the Chamberlain

Albert of Aachen's listing of members of the *domus Godefridi* in the summer of 1100 includes one *Joffridus camerarius Ducis.*

SOURCES: AA p. 526.

46. Gerard, secretary

Gerard is mentioned as a *familiaris* and *secretarius* of Baldwin from around the time that he left the main army of the crusade in order to conquer the area around Edessa, and the appearance of an office of secretary is probably connected with the establishment of the *comitatus Baldewini* as a separate military force during this period. Gerard seems to have undertaken administrative tasks, as he was employed to send money from Baldwin to the other leaders of the crusade at Antioch. In late 1098 he was captured by troops of Balak, the Turkish lord of Sarūj, and beheaded.

SOURCES: AA pp. 395, 446.

47. Gerard of Avesnes

Gerard *de genere Hainaucorum de praesidio Avennis* or *de castello Avennis* came from Avesnes-sur-Helpe (F, Nord, arr. Avesnes) in southern Hainaut. Therefore although a Lotharingian, he was not originally connected with the Ardennes-Bouillon family, whose suzerainty of Hainaut lapsed on the death of Duke Godfrey III. Gerard must have left Europe in the retinue of *Baldwin II of Mons, count of Hainaut, who marched with Godfrey of Bouillon. However, after Baldwin was killed in an ambush near Nicaea in 1098 Gerard evidently entered the service of Godfrey. In the summer of 1099 he was installed in the Muslim-held port of Arsuf as overseer and receiver of tribute. When the town refused admittance to Godfrey's troops in December he was imprisoned and presumed killed by the Franks. However, he had been transferred to Ascalon and in March 1100 he was released by the Fatimid authorities as a diplomatic gesture, and was granted fiefs at St Abraham (Hebron) as compensation: *cui statim in remunerationem sui grandis laboris maxima terrae beneficia centum marcarum, cum castello quod dicitur ad sanctum Abraham, in praesentia omnium Fidelium qui aderant largitus est.* Gerard was killed at the Second Battle of Ramla (May 1102).

SOURCES: AA pp. 499, 507, 516, 593; Mayer, 'Die Herrschaftsbildung in Hebron', p. 66 n. 13.

48. Gerard the Chamberlain

One *Girardus,* described variously as *camerarius* or *cubicularius* appears in documents from 1108 to 1115. He can probably be identified with the *Gerhardus quidam eques de domo regis Baldewini* who received part of the revenues of Jaffa as a money-fief (*qui partem reditus civitatis Japhet pro militari obsequio obtinebat*) in 1107. He is certainly the only Gerard attested for this period, while Albert's description probably refers to his position as a household officer.

SOURCES: RRH nos. 52, 59, 68a, 76b, 80; AA p. 636.

49. Gerard of Fauquembergues

Gerard was brother of *Hugh of Fauquembergues (F, Pas-de-Calais, arr. Saint-Omer), and therefore a native of the diocese of Thérouanne. He seems to have served in the retinue of his brother, who was lord of Tiberias. He was already ill when Hugh was killed by pursuing Turks and Arabs after a raid against Damascene territory in 1106. Gerard died eight days after this and was buried in Nazareth.

SOURCES: AA pp. 633-34.

50. Gerbod, lord of Scheldewindeke

Gerbodo de castello Winthinc can be identified as Gerbod III, lord of Scheldewindeke (B, Oost-Vlaanderen, arr. Gent), younger son of Gerbod II, lord of Oosterzele and advocate of the abbey of St Bertin at Saint-Omer. This Flemish family, which was known as *de Wentica*, had previously been involved in overseas adventure, as Gerbod II and his brother Frederick took part in the Norman Conquest of England. Gerbod II was given the earldom of Chester by William the Conqueror in 1070, but within twelve months had abandoned it, probably because of the instability in Flanders caused by the death of Count Baldwin VI. His sister, Gundrada, was married to William de Warenne I, first earl of Surrey. According to Warlop, Gerbod III first appears around 1067;[23] however, his first appearance in fact seems to be on a document for St Bertin from 1063 describing a donation made by Gerbod and Gerbod the younger. In 1096 he, his brother Arnulf III of Oosterzele and Arnulf's wife Adelaide sold the allod of Roquetoire (F, Pas-de-Calais, arr. Saint-Omer) to St Bertin for fourteen silver marks. This transaction was probably a fund-raising venture for the crusade and was witnessed by Eustace III of Boulogne. Gerbod was killed at the Second Battle of Ramla (May 1102). His striking physical resemblance to King Baldwin I caused a temporary panic among the Franks when his severed head was displayed by the Egyptians to the garrison of Jaffa.

SOURCES: AA pp. 591, 593; *Monumenta s. Bavonis Gandavensis minora*, MGH SS 15: 598-99; Haigneré, *Les Chartes de St Bertin*, 1, nos. 80 (B. Guérard, *Cartulaire de Saint-*

---

[23] Warlop, *Flemish Nobility*, p. 1024. The existence of the younger Gerbod means that there is no reason to assume that the family had died out in the male line by 1079, as argued by F. Anderson, '*Uxor mea*: The First Wife of the First William of Warenne', *Sussex Archaeological Collections* 130 (1992), 107-29.

Bertin, p. 201 gives the date wrongly as 1084) and 96; A. J. Farrington, 'A Note on Gherbod the Fleming', *Journal of the Chester and North Wales Architectural, Archaeological and Historic Society* 51 (1964), 21-22; C. P. Lewis, 'The Formation of the Honor of Chester, 1066-1100', *Journal of the Chester Archaeological Society* 71 (1991), 37-66.

51. Gervase of Bazoches, lord of Tiberias

Guibert of Nogent mentions the *miles egregius ... isdem Gervasius vocabatur apud castrum Basilicas pagi Suessonici nobiliter oriundus*, while Albert of Aachen gives similar descriptions, although he is less precise as to geographical origins. Gervase was advocate of the church of Mont-Notre-Dame and brother of Hugh, lord of Bazoches-sur-Vesle (F, Aisne, arr. Soissons) and was also related to the lords of Milly in the Beauvaisis. In 1106 he was given the fief of Tiberias on the death of its lord, *Hugh of Fauquembergues. Before that date he seems to have been one of Baldwin I's household officers; he is the *Gervasius dapifer* who witnessed RRH no. 43 (1104). His tenure of Tiberias was brief. In May 1108 his force of 80 knights and 200 footsoldiers was defeated by Tughtikīn, atabeg of Damascus, and Gervase and some of his knights were taken prisoner. Tughtikīn demanded Acre, Haifa and Tiberias for his release, but although Baldwin I offered a large monetary ransom he refused to surrender any cities, and Tughtikīn had Gervase executed. On the strength of a remark of Ibn al-Athir that an unnamed lord of Tiberias executed at Damascus around this time was a son of King Baldwin's sister, Pirie-Gordon concluded that 'either Gerberga or Ida of Bouillon must have married Miles' (i.e. Gervase's father), although he does not identify either lady and gives no documentation. No Gerberga is known in the Ardennes-Bouillon dynasty; a Gerberga of *Boulogne* (daughter of Count Eustace I) is known only to have married Frederick of Luxembourg, duke of Lower Lotharingia, whom she predeceased. Ida of Boulogne, mother of Baldwin I, was married only to Eustace II of Boulogne and had no daughters.[24] Neither Albert of Aachen nor Ibn al-Qalānisī, who identifies Gervase by name (*Jarfas*) and correctly gives the year as AH 501 (22 August 1107-10 August 1108), mention this supposed relationship. It is possible that Ibn al-Athīr, who gives the wrong year (AH 502) and does not actually name Gervase, but who was writing over a century later, confused Gervase with *Godfrey, the *nepos* of Baldwin I killed in battle against Tughtikīn in 1113. His tenure of Tiberias, the descriptions of him given by Albert and Guibert and the high ransom he was able to command all indicate that Gervase had a high status among the nobles of Baldwin I, but it cannot be explained in terms of a relationship with the royal house.

[24] H. Pirie-Gordon, 'The Reigning Princes of Galilee', *English Historical Review* 27 (1912), 445-61 (here 447-48); Renn, *Luxemburger Grafenhaus*, pp. 121-23.

SOURCES: GN pp. 259-60; AA pp. 635 (*vir illuster et nobilissimus, de regno occidentalis Franciae ortus*), 643, 656 (*vir nominatissimus et nobilissimus de regno Franciae*), 657-58; RRH no. 43; Bur, *La Formation du comté de Champagne*, pp. 247, 251; Ibn al-Qalānisī, pp. 86-87; Ibn al-Athīr, pp. 267-69; S. Prioux, 'Gervais de Bazoches, prince et gouverneur de Tiberiade', *Bulletin de la Société historique et archéologique de Soissons* 19 (1865), 351-71 [without references].

52. Gibelin of Arles, patriarch of Jerusalem

Gibelin, archbishop of Arles, came to the Holy Land in 1108 as a legate sent by Paschal II to arbitrate in the case of *Evremar of Chocques, whom Baldwin I had deposed from the patriarchate. At the council held in Jerusalem which eventually translated Evremar to the see of Caesarea, Gibelin was himself elected patriarch. During his period of office he carried out a considerable reorganisation of the Latin church, establishing new bishoprics at Bethlehem, Nazareth and Beirut. He died during Lent 1112.

SOURCES: Hamilton, *The Latin Church*, pp. 57-61.

53. Giselbert of Clermont

Giselbertus de Monte Claro was a member of the *comitatus* formed by Baldwin of Boulogne in Cilicia. He was captured by Tancred during hostilities at Mamistra in 1097. It is likely that he can be identified with Giselbert, count of Clermont-sous-Huy (B, Liège, arr. Huy, also known as Clermont-sur-Meuse), who with his wife Longarde and brother Hermann donated the priory of St. Symphorian to the abbey of Cluny in 1091. He had previously been notorious for despoiling church property and menacing river traffic in the region of Liège, so much so that Bishop Otbert of Liège besieged the castle in June-August 1095 with no success, and thereafter was obliged to purchase the stronghold. It therefore seems probable that Giselbert seized on the crusade to seek new opportunities in the East, although he is not heard of after the Cilician campaign.

SOURCES: AA p. 350; *Cantatorium*, pp. 194-97; Giles of Orval, p. 84; Murray, 'The Army of Godfrey of Bouillon', pp. 304-6.

54. Giselbert of Couvin

It is likely that *Giselbert de castello quod dicitur Cuvin, vir illustris* derived his surname from the castle of Couvin (B, Namur, arr. Philippeville), an allodial possession of the counts of Hainaut which *Baldwin II of Mons sold to Bishop Otbert of Liège in 1095 before departing on crusade. After Baldwin's death at Nicaea in 1098 Giselbert must have entered the service of the

Bouillon-Boulogne brothers. He was killed in battle at Sidon in 1108, and mourned by Baldwin I.

SOURCES: AA p. 655; Bormans, Schoolmeesters and Poncelet, *Cartulaire de l'église de Saint-Lambert,* 1, no. 29.

55. Godehilde (Godevere) of Tosny

Godehilde was a daughter of Ralph II, lord of Tosny and Conches and banner-bearer of Normandy (†1102), and Isabella of Montfort-l'Amaury. Probably between 1086 and 1096 she married Baldwin of Boulogne. After the marriage both partners resided in Normandy until their departure on crusade. Godehilde accompanied her husband when he detached the *comitatus Baldewini* from the main army in 1097, but she died around 15 October at Marash while Baldwin was campaigning in Cilicia and northern Syria. Runciman has claimed that Baldwin and his wife took with them 'their little children', and that after the death of Godehilde, 'their children too, were sick and did not survive'.[25] In fact there is no evidence of any children before or during the crusade. Runciman's erroneous information may derive from an misinterpretation of William of Tyre, who records that Godfrey handed over *dominum Balduinum, ducis fratrem, cum uxore et familia* as hostages to the king of Hungary during his army's crossing of that country. However, since in medieval Latin the term *familia* means 'household' and not 'family', these children should be regarded as phantoms of scholarship.

SOURCES: Orderic Vitalis, 3: 128; AA p. 358; WT II.2, p. 164; Musset, 'Aux origines d'une classe dirigeante: les Tosny, grands barons normands du Xe au XIIe siècle'; Mayer, *Mélanges*, pp. 32-48.

56. Godfrey, *nepos* of Baldwin I

A *Gotefredus nepos regis* is named as a witness on a charter of Baldwin I confirming possessions of the Hospital of Jerusalem, issued on 20 June 1112. The same individual is named by William of Malmesbury as one of the casualties sustained in the defeat of the Franks of Jerusalem by Tughtikīn of Damascus and Mawdūd of Mosul on 28 June 1113 at the battle of al-Sinnabrah: *ceciderunt ibi plures quos ego quoque noram; inter quos Godefridus abnepos ejus nothus, jam inde a pueritia umbram virtutis vultu colorans, veritatem animo spirans.* In his edition of the text Stubbs identifies this Godfrey as a nephew of Godfrey of Bouillon; however, it is clear from the syntax of this passage that *ejus* refers back to Baldwin I of Jerusalem, who is mentioned several sentences previously.[26] Godfrey the *abnepos*

[25] Runciman, *A History of the Crusades*, 1: 147, 200-1.

[26] William of Malmesbury, *De Gestis Regum Anglorum*, ed. W. Stubbs, 2 vols (London, 1887-89), 2: 451.

was thus of illegitimate birth (*nothus*), and somehow related to the king. It is likely that the word *abnepos* does not have the classical meaning of '(great-)great-grandson', but that the prefix *ab-* indicates distance, which in this case could be explained by illegitimate status.[27] There are therefore two likely possibilities for Godfrey's parentage: either that he was a bastard son of Eustace III of Boulogne, who is known to have had other illegitimate offspring, or that he was a (legitimate) son of a bastard of Eustace II of Boulogne. The fact that William of Malmesbury indicates a personal acquaintance with this Godfrey would point to a relationship with the Boulognes, who held extensive estates in England, rather than with the Ardennes-Bouillon ancestry. The relatively late appearance and the absence of any mention of Godfrey in accounts of the First Crusade would suggest that he did not come to the East until some time after the capture of Jerusalem. He was notable for being the sole close male relative of the king present in the kingdom during the reign of Baldwin I. He may have been the origin of the literary character known as the Bâtard de Bouillon who appears in the Old French Crusading Cycle of epics.

SOURCES: *C. Hosp.*, 1 no. 28 (= RRH no 68a); William of Malmesbury, *Gesta regum Anglorum*, ed. Mynors *et al.*, IV.385, pp. 686-88; A. V. Murray, 'A Little-Known Member of the Royal Family of Crusader Jerusalem in William of Malmesbury's *Gesta Regum Anglorum*', *Notes and Queries* 241 (1996), 397-99; Murray, 'Why a Bastard? A Possible Historical Origin for the Illegitimate Hero in the *Bâtard de Bouillon*', *Neuphilologische Mitteilungen* 98 (1997), 179-85.

57. Godfrey of Bures

Godfrey *de Burs et de terra civitatis Parisius* came from Bures-sur-Yvette (F, Essonne, arr. Palaiseau), part of the lordship of Gometz-la-Châtel south of Paris. Knowledge of Godfrey is limited to one passage in the history of Albert of Aachen, which describes his death on a raid across the Jordan in the army of Tiberias commanded by *Joscelin of Courtenay, whose vassal he evidently was. He was greatly lamented by Baldwin I, who 'paid for many masses for his soul' and later bestowed Tiberias on his brother *William of Bures. William apparently had no surviving sons of his own, but some or all of his four documented nephews, Elias, William, Ralph of Yssy and Simon, may have actually been sons of Godfrey. The surname of Ralph, given as *de Ysiaco* (1129) and *de Ysis* (1132) derives from Issy-les-Moulineaux (F, Hauts-de-Seine, arr. Boulogne-Billancourt), now part of greater Paris, which appears in the form *de Issiaco* in 1084.[28]

---

[27] D. C. Jackman, 'Abnepos, pronepos', *Notes and Queries* 245 (2000), 14-16.

[28] A. Dauzat and Ch. Rostaing, *Dictionnaire etymologique de noms de lieux en France* (Paris, 1978), p. 368.

SOURCES: AA pp. 710-12; RRH nos. 115, 131, 142; J. Lair, 'Histoire de la seigneurie de Bures', *Mémoires de la Société de l'histoire de Paris et l'Ile-de-France* 2 (1876), 187-97.

58. Godfrey of Esch

Godefridus de Ascha was the brother of the crusader *Henry of Esch-sur-Sûre (Lux) in the Ardennes. He was a (probably younger) son of Frithelo, advocate of the abbeys of Echternach and Malmédy and a kinsman of Godfrey of Bouillon. Along with Henry, he was present at the sale of Baisy and Genappe to the abbey of Nivelles by Ida and Godfrey of Bouillon. He was evidently closer to the duke than his brother was, which may be a reflection of his junior status and consequent lesser degree of independence. During the march across Hungary he was sent by the duke on a legation to King Coloman, probably because he had personal experience of Hungary from several years before the crusade. He was also one of three envoys sent on the duke's first embassy to the Emperor Alexios.

SOURCES: AA pp. 299, 300, 306-7, 322, 366; *Triumphus s. Remacli de Malmundariensi coenobio*, MGH SS 11: 447-48; Thiofrid of Echternach, *Ex vita s. Willibrordi*, MGH SS 23: 26; MGH DD H.IV, no. 459 (*Henricus de Ase, frater eius Godefridus*); J. Vannérus, 'Les anciens dynastes d'Esch-sur-la-Sûre', *Ons Hémecht* 11 (1905), 434-42, 485-93, 532-40, 12 (1906), 18-23, 51-56, 112-18, 138-42.

59. Gotmann of Brussels

Gutmannus de Brussella is first mentioned at the Second Battle of Ramla (1102). He was undoubtedly a Lotharingian from Brussels (B, Bruxelles) although he can hardly have been connected with Godfrey of Bouillon before the crusade, since the counts of Louvain, in whose territory Brussels lay, were long-standing enemies and rivals of the Ardennes-Bouillon family. Gotmann is attested in Palestine up to 1115. It is therefore doubtful whether he can be identical with the John Gotmann who appears from 1126 to 1161, and who is more likely to have been his son, in which case the surname Gotmann should be understood as a patronymic.[29]

SOURCES: AA pp. 591, 594, 621; RRH nos. 43, 52, 56a, 57, 76a, 76b, 80.

60. Gozelo of Montaigu

The crusader described as *Gozelo filius comitis Cononis de Monte Acuto* was a son of *Cono, count of Montaigu (B, Luxembourg, arr. Marche-en-Famenne), whom he and his brother *Lambert accompanied on crusade. His name Gozelo, which had been borne by Cono's own father, suggests that he was the

---

[29] RRH nos. 115, 164, 299, 326, 366, 368, 369; WT XVIII.14, p. 831.

elder brother and heir. He died of disease at Artah. The *Chanson d'Antioche* gives a more heroic account of a death in battle.

SOURCES: AA pp. 317, 358, 369; *Chanson d'Antioche*, lines 2511, 2525, 2527, 2532, 2537; Roland, 'Les seigneurs et comtes de Rochefort', pp. 63-141.

61. Gunfrid of the Tower of David

The fullest description of this official is given by Albert of Aachen, who names him as *Gunfridus custos ac praepositus arcis et turris Iherusalem*, a title which relates to his office of castellan of the Tower of David, the citadel of Jerusalem. He is known to have had lands in the territory of Jerusalem. He held the casalia of Taret and Tarphin situated between Nablus and Jerusalem, and whose tithes he gave to the abbey of Josaphat. With his wife Ida he sold casalia in the *vallis Suech* to the Hospital. He may be the same person as the *Gumfridus de Cavis* who gave to Josaphat the tithes of Mezerech and Dalfim, which were in the same area as Tarphin (Kh. Tarfin). Gunfrid witnessed a royal charter in 1104, and fought at the Third Battle of Ramla in 1105. He was the commander of the garrison of Chastel Hernaut when it was attacked by the Egyptians in 1107; he was captured and taken to Ascalon. His subsequent fate may be discernable in an eastern source. Two Jacobite monks, Michael of Marash and Romanus of Malatya, writing in 1138, tell of a Frank whose name Martin transliterates as *Gounefar*, who came with the First Crusade. He afterwards took possession of the casalia of *Beith-'Arif* and *'Adecieh*, which were properties of the Jacobite church in Jerusalem, 'seeing that they had no master, and since he was a relative of the king at the time'. However, after some time he was captured by the Arabs and taken to Egypt. The Jacobite patriarch Mar Athanasius and the metropolitan Mar Cyril came to Jerusalem, and producing testimony of ownership, were restored the villages by the king. Approximately thirty-three years later, during the reign of Fulk, *Gounefar* was still alive. An Armenian bishop, who had been promised a village by *Gounefar*'s wife and relatives, interceded with the authorities and obtained his release, dated by Michael to 1137-38. Fulk restored *Gounefar*'s property, which led to a dispute with the Jacobites. In February 1138 a compromise was reached by which he gave up the villages and accepted 200 dinars in compensation. One of the casalia was probably Hadessa (Kh. 'Adasa) north of Jerusalem, whose ownership was mentioned in a document of 1161 as being disputed between the church of the Holy Sepulchre and the Jacobite monastery of St Mary Magdalene in Jerusalem.[30]

[30] Bresc-Bautier, *Le Cartulaire du chapitre du Saint-Sépulcre de Jérusalem*, no. 131. The other casale is less easy to identify. It could possibly be Bet ᶜArif north-east of Lydda (*Atlas of Israel* 3/11 ref. 156/144E).

Belgian and Luxembourgeois historians have identified this *Gounefar* with the crusader *Godfrey of Esch, who was known to be a kinsman of Godfrey of Bouillon, and whose last certain appearance was at the siege of Antioch.[31] However, Godfrey of Esch was not the only kinsman of Godfrey and Baldwin I in the Lotharingian army, and since he is known to have led a legation to Hungary many years before the First Crusade, and was presumably of some experience then, his release in 1137 at the earliest would make him unfeasibly old. All other indications are in favour of the identification with Gunfrid, whose name is phonetically closer to *Gounefar*. Michael's dating would place his capture at around 1105. Gunfrid was taken to Ascalon, which was held by the Egyptians, and he may well have been sent on to Egypt for security. Michael relates that while he languished there several kings unsuccessfully tried to procure his release; as a field commander and castellan of the Tower of David, Gunfrid was clearly a high-ranking personage. Lastly, we have independent evidence that Gunfrid had a wife with him in Palestine, and held possessions around Jerusalem.

SOURCES: AA pp. 621, 637-38; RRH nos. 43 (*Gaufridus de Turre David*), 67 (*Gumfridus de Cavis*), 81a (*Gunfridus de Turri*), 129a (*Gaufridus de Turri*), 245 (*Gumfredus de Turre David*); Michael of Marash, 'Note to the Syriac Breviary', ed. and trans. Abbé Martin, *Journal Asiatique*, ser. 8, 13 (1888), 39-79.

62. Gunter

Gunter was a member of the *domus Godefridi* in 1100. His name indicates a Germanic origin. He may well be identical with the crusader *Gundram* commemorated along with his compatriot *Wicher for their part in the capture of Jerusalem by the Franconian John of Würzburg.

SOURCES: AA p. 526; John of Würzburg, p. 125.

63. Guy of Milly

Guido de Miliaco, documented from 1108 up to 1126, probably came from Milly-sur-Therain (F, Oise, arr. Beauvais) in the Beauvaisis. Guy's frequent appearances as a witness in royal charters can be explained by his status as an important baron of the royal domain with substantial property around Nablus. By his wife Stephanie, presumably the *Estefenie qui fut de Flandre* of the *Lignages d'Outremer,* Guy had three sons: Guy Francigena, whose surname suggest that he

[31] M. F. Nau, 'Le croisé lorrain Godefroy de Ascha d'après deux documents syriaques du XIIe siècle', *Journal Asiatique* ser. 9, 14 (1899), 421-31; Nau, 'Les croisés Henry et Godefroy du château de Ascha', *L'Ancien Pays de Looz* 4-5 (1900), 21-25; Baron de Chestret de Haneffe, 'Les premiers seigneurs d'Esch sur la Sûre à propos des croisés Henri et Godefroid du château d'Ascha', *L'Ancien Pays de Looz* 8-9 (1900), 3-9.

must have been born in France; Philip of Nablus, later Grand Master of the Templars; and Henry *Bubalus* (the Buffalo).[32]

SOURCES: RRH nos. 52, 57, 76a, 80, 90, 91, 101, 102a, 105, 112, 113, 130, 134, 596; Bur, *Formation du comté de Champagne*, pp. 248, 251-52; M-L. Bulst-Thiele, *Sacrae Domus Militiae Templi Hierosolymitani Magistri* (Göttingen, 1974), p. 75.

64. Hartmann I, count of Dillingen and Kyburg

Hartmann, who was born around 1040, was a son of Hupold III (†1074), count of Dillingen in Swabia (Ger, Bayern, Kr. Dillingen an der Donau). Around 1065 he married Adelheid, heiress of Adalbert of Winterthur-Kyburg, one of the Udalrichinger dynasty, and succeeded to her vast estates in the Thurgau. During the Investiture Contest Hartmann was a supporter of the papacy and one of the most bitter enemies of Henry IV; along with his allies Hermann of Salm and Welf I of Bavaria he won a victory over the imperialists at Höchstadt in 1081. In 1095 he founded a Benedictine monastery at Neresheim on allodial possessions near Nördlingen. Since Ernest, the first abbot, is known to have been on crusade, it is likely that his benefactor was identical with the *Hartmannus comes Alemanniae* mentioned on three occasions by Albert of Aachen. Certainly the description *dives et nobilissimus et unus de praepotentibus in terra Alemanniae* (i.e. Swabia) accords well with his landed wealth, as does the fact that at Nicaea he was able to pay for the construction of a siege engine along with *Henry of Esch. It is an indication of the privation suffered by many crusaders that by the winter of 1097-98 Hartmann had been forced to sell his horse and armour to pay for food, and was reduced to riding an ass and fighting with a captured Turkish sword and shield. As a result he was obliged to become a dependent of Duke Godfrey who allotted him a daily ration of food. His straitened circumstances, which were quite incommensurate with his status in the West, as well as his pro-papal loyalties may account for his lack of prominence in Godfrey's contingent, and consequently in the sources. He evidently returned to Germany soon after the completion of the crusade. He died on 16 April 1121.

SOURCES: AA pp. 290, 322, 427; *Annales Neresheimenses*, MGH SS 10: 20-21; *Necrologii Neresheimensis*, ed. F. L. Baumann, MGH Necrologii Germaniae 1 (Berlin, 1888), pp. 95-98; N. von Salis-Soglio, 'Das Dillinger Grafenhaus und seine Stiftung Neresheim', *Benediktinische Monatsschrift* 3 (1921), 197-214, 269-89; A. Layer, 'Die Grafen

[32] *Lignages d'Outremer*, p. 462; RRH nos. 308, 332. As Stephanie must have been married to Guy before 1108 and married Baldwin of Ramla after his death problems are caused by the Elisabeth who is referred to as Guy's wife on RRH no. 80 (1115). For discussion see Mayer, 'Carving Up Crusaders', pp. 101-18.

von Dillingen-Kyburg in Schwaben und in der Schweiz', in *Die Grafen von Kyburg*, ed. H. Müller *et al.* (Olten, 1981), pp. 31-38.

65. Henry of Esch

Henricus de Ascha castello ... filius Fredelonis, unus de collateralibus ducis Godefridi, accompanied on crusade by his brother Godfrey, belonged to the family which held the castle of Esch-sur-Sûre/Esch an der Sauer (Lux) in the Ardennes. Their father can be identified with one Frithelo, sometime advocate of the abbeys of Echternach and Malmédy. It is unclear how they were related to Godfrey of Bouillon. Both brothers were present at the sale of Baisy and Genappe to the abbey of Nivelles by Ida and Godfrey of Bouillon. The fact that he is usually mentioned first in sources, and is given greater prominence than Godfrey, suggests that Henry of Esch was the elder brother, although he does not seem to have been as close to the duke as his brother was. He left the army along with *Baldwin II of Hainaut during the march through Thrace in order to reach Constantinople early in the hope of profiting from the expected generosity of the Emperor Alexios. He could afford to finance the construction of a siege machine together with *Hartmann of Dillingen at Nicaea. Later he was recognised by a nun from the convent of St Mary *ad Horreas* in Trier who had been captured by the Turks. All this suggests that Henry was a fairly important, well-known and financially independent man in the Ardennes/Mid-Moselle area when he left the West. By the time of the siege of Antioch, however, his circumstances were so reduced that he was obliged to accept the charity of the duke. He died of plague at Turbessel in late summer 1098 and was buried there.

SOURCES: AA pp. 299, 305, 307, 322, 369, 413, 422, 424, 427, 435; *Triumphus s. Remacli de Malmundariensi coenobio*, MGH SS 11: 447-48; Thiofrid of Echternach, *Ex vita s. Willibrordi*, MGH SS 23: 26; MGH DD H.IV, no. 459 (*Henricus de Ase*); Vannérus, 'Les anciens dynastes d'Esch-sur-la-Sûre'.

66. Heribrand of Bouillon

The crusader *Heribrandus de Buillon* or *Herebrandus de Bullon* can be identified as castellan of the stronghold of Bouillon (B, Luxembourg, arr. Neufchâteau). It is likely that he was the son of the castellan Heribrand known in the period 1049-69. Heribrand the crusader was particularly renowned for having killed Ricuin, a cousin of Count Arnulf II of Chiny, in one of the many hostilities between Chiny and Bouillon (1070/1079). As castellan he was one of the most important members of the household of the lords of Bouillon, and as such he witnessed the donation of Assenois to the abbey of Saint-Hubert by Duke Godfrey III as well as two important transactions of Godfrey IV and his mother on the eve of the crusade: the sale of allods to the abbey of Nivelles and donations to the abbey of Saint-Hubert. On crusade he was known as the owner of an exceptionally fine helmet and hauberk, which he was obliged to surrender to be used as a present for the Muslim ruler of ᶜAzāz when Godfrey made a treaty of friendship with him in the late summer of 1098.

SOURCES: AA pp. 317, 440; *Cantatorium*, pp. 38 (*Heribrandus Bulloniensis*), 53, 64-65 (*consilio tamen Heribrandi castellani aliorumque fidelium suorum*), 105; Kurth, *Chartes de l'abbaye de St. Hubert*, 1, no. 48, pp. 59-62; MGH DD H.IV, no. 459 (*Heribrandus ... de Bulon*); G. Despy, 'La Formation de la "Terre de Hierges" du XIe au XVe siècle', *PSHIGDL* 102 (1986), 13-30 (here p. 17).

67. Hubert of Pacy

Hubertus de Paci appears once as a witness to a royal charter (1108), and is also known to have held the casale of Akhzhiv near Ascalon. He may have come from Pacy-sur-Eure (F, Eure, arr. Evreux) in Normandy, although this identification is uncertain as variants of the placename Pacy are common in France.

SOURCES: RRH nos. 52, 101, 134, 281.

68. Hugh Botuns

Hugo Botuns accompanied Baldwin I at the Second Battle of Ramla (May 1102) and was killed there.

SOURCES: AA pp. 591-93.

69. Hugh of Bourcq

Hugo de Burg is recorded as having fought at the Second Battle of Ramla. He was probably originally a follower of *Baldwin of Bourcq (F, Ardennes, arr. Vouziers), whose surname was generally written as *de Burch*, *de Burg* or *de Burgo* in narrative sources.

SOURCES: AA p. 593.

70. Hugh *de Brulis*

Hugo de Brulis was one of the handful of knights who broke out of Egyptian encirclement along with Baldwin I in the first engagement in the Second Battle of Ramla (17 May 1102). He is otherwise unknown.

SOURCES: AA p. 593.

71. Hugh of Cassel

Hugo de Cassel, egregius miles of Baldwin I, was killed at Hebron in 1107. His surname probably relates to Cassel (F, Nord, arr. Dunkerque) in Flanders.

SOURCES: AA p. 647.

72. Hugh Chostard

Ugo Chostard dapifer is known only from his appearance as witness on a royal charter issued in 1112. He is the first recorded royal seneschal after the appearance of *Gervase of Bazoches in this office.

SOURCES: RRH no. 68a.

73. Hugh of Fauquembergues, lord of Tiberias

The surname of *Hugo de Falchenberch* or *Falkenberc* derived from the village of Fauquembergues (F, Pas-de-Calais, arr. Saint-Omer) in the diocese of Thérouanne. He must have joined the *comitatus Baldewini* in northern Syria, since his first appearance occurs in July 1100, when he accompanied Baldwin I from Edessa to claim the throne of Jerusalem: along with *Robert, bishop of Ramla, he was sent in advance of the main army to secure the Tower of David. After Tancred left the kingdom in 1101 to assume the regency in Antioch, his vast fief of Tiberias was given to Hugh, with the exception of the port of Haifa, which was restored to *Geldemar Carpinel. The responsibility placed in Hugh, as well as his rapid rise suggest that he was already one of Baldwin's most trusted followers when the latter was still count of Edessa. Although Hugh must have come east with Robert II of Flanders he probably joined Baldwin's company in the autumn or winter of 1097-98. In 1106, when returning from a raid in the Hauran, Hugh and his troops were ambushed by Turks. Hugh was killed by an arrow, and later buried at Nazareth, while his brother *Gerard died eight days later.[2] There are no definite indications of any other relatives. On the authority of the *Lignages*, which call him castellan of Saint-Omer, Du Cange and Rey identify him with Hugh, lord of Fauquembergues, the son of William II, castellan of Saint-Omer, and Melisende of Picquigny, and therefore brother of the Walter of Saint-Omer who was prince of Galilee between 1159 and 1170. However, apart from the impossible difference in ages between the two supposed brothers, we know that the latter Hugh of Fauquembergues was alive in 1146 and died around 1175. Neither can he be identified with Hugh, nephew of William I of Saint-Omer, who was still living in 1121/1123.[33] Thus we have no evidence of how, if at all, Hugh of Tiberias was related to the family of the castellans in Flanders. William of Tyre

[33] *Lignages d'Outremer*, pp. 450-51; Du Cange, *Les Familles d'Outremer*, pp. 443-44; A. Giry, 'Les châtelains de Saint-Omer 1042-1386', *Bibliothèque de l'Ecole des Chartes* 35 (1874), 325-55; Warlop, *Flemish Nobility*, pp. 1106-9.

calls him Hugh *de Sancto Aldemaro* but the contemporary Albert of Aachen only uses the name Fauquembergues.[5]

SOURCES: AA pp. 531, 538, 591, 633-35; RRH no. 43 (*Ugo de Tabaria*); WT X.9, p. 464, X.23, p. 480, XI.5, pp. 502-3; FC II.36, p. 509 (*Hugo, qui Tiberiadem urbem tunc possidebat*); *Versus … Tarvanensis*, p. 190 (*Falkemberga suum dedit Hugonem dominum, qui obtinit totam regionem Tyberiadis*).

74. Hugh (II) of Le Puiset

Hugh, also known as Hugotin, was a son of Hugh I Blavons, lord of Le Puiset (F, Eure-et-Loir, arr. Chartres), and Alice, daughter of Guy I of Montlhéry. He acted as guardian to his nephew Hugh III from 1097 to 1106, but then came to the East with his wife Mabel of Roucy, appearing as witness to a royal charter of 1110. According to William of Tyre, he was given the lordship of Jaffa by his cousin Baldwin II shortly after the latter's accession (1118) but died soon after, at which point Mabel married Albert, son of Count Albert III of Namur. Mayer has argued that Jaffa was in fact given to Hugh in 1106 and on his death to Albert, who held the fief from 1112 until he died in the 1120s. Certainly Jaffa was in the possession of Hugh's son (also called Hugh), before 1123. Yet apart from the objection that Baldwin I would not likely have given the principal port of the kingdom to a member of a dynasty that had contested his brother's Lotharingian inheritance for years, the evidence for Hugh's tenure of Jaffa in the reign of Baldwin I is slight. A charter in favour of the order of the Hospital of 1112, RRH no. 68a (= *C. Hosp.* 1, no. 28), lists an *Albertus* as a witness. However, this name has no additional designation such as *Joppensis* or *Namucensis* that would permit a positive identification as Albert of Namur. It is unlikely that one of the few holders of one of the major lordships in the kingdom would be listed after minor personages such as *Johannes interpres* and the otherwise unknown *Otto Aegidius*. The absence of Albert from any other documents is consistent with a short tenure of Jaffa between the death of Hugh after the accession of Baldwin I, and the succession of Hugh II by 1123. This all suggests that Hugh of Le Puiset had a fairly lowly status before 1118, rising to prominence only on the accession of Baldwin II.

SOURCES: RRH no. 57; WT XIV.15-16, pp. 651-53; Dion, 'Le Puiset au XIe et XIIe siècles', pp. 20-21; La Monte, 'The Lords of Le Puiset on the Crusades', pp. 100-18; H. E. Mayer, 'The Origins of the County of Jaffa', *Israel Exploration Journal* 35 (1985), 35-45.

75. Hugh of Rebecques, lord of St Abraham

Ugo de S. Habraam first appears in Palestine in a document of 1104 and is mentioned once by Albert of Aachen, referring to the year 1105. He is identified as a Fleming by the *Versus de viris illustribus dioecesis Tarvanensis*, which says of him: *Et castrum quoddam, quod Sancti dicitur Abraham, / Hugo Rebeccensis tenuit, miles generosus.* Hugh's surname derives from Rebecques (F, Pas-de-Calais, arr. Saint-Omer) just outside Thérouanne. He is probably the same *Hugo de Resbeca* who witnessed an undated charter of Gerard, bishop of Thérouanne, issued some time before the crusade. He seems to have died or have been removed from the lordship by 1107, when it was known to have been held by *Walter Mahomet.

SOURCES: AA p. 621; RRH nos. 43, 983; *Versus ... Tarvanensis,* p. 192; Th. Duchet and A. Giry, *Cartulaire de l'église de Terouane* (Saint-Omer, 1881), no. 5; Mayer, 'Die Herrschaftsbildung in Hebron', pp. 67-68.

76. Hugh II, count of Saint-Pol

Hugo comes de sancto Paulo ex regno Franciae or *Hugo Grandaevus de Sancto Paulo* was Hugh II, count of Saint-Pol (F, Pas-de-Calais, arr. Saint-Pol-sur-Terncise), in Artois. He was a vassal of Count *Eustace III of Boulogne, whom he and his son *Engelrand probably accompanied on crusade. Hugh and Engelrand had a retinue which was substantial enough to form the core of raids on the Turkish forces at the siege of Antioch in 1097, and both acquired fame as military leaders. Hugh is characterised as being aged (*longaevus*, *grandaevus*) He is last mentioned on crusade at the siege of Jerusalem (summer 1099).

SOURCES: AA pp. 315, 372, 373, 422, 463; BD pp. 28, 33; RA pp. 276-77; Orderic Vitalis, 5: 34; Feuchère, 'Les origines du comté de Saint-Pol', pp. 125-49.

77. Hugh, viscount in Transjordan

This official is known only from a fragmentary inscription from the castle of Montréal in the Transjordan. In 1867 it was recorded as reading UGO VICE .... QVI ..... MCXVII. As Mayer has argued, the only possible completion for the second word is *vicecomes*. It would therefore seem that this otherwise unknown Hugh was royal viscount for those areas of Transjordan under Frankish control around the year 1118.

SOURCES: H. E. Mayer, *Die Kreuzfahrerherrschaft Montréal (Šōbak): Jordanien im 12. Jahrhundert* (Wiesbaden, 1990), pp. 68-69.

78. Humphrey of Toron

Umfredus de Torum, ancestor of a famous Frankish dynasty, derived his surname from the castle of Toron in Galilee. He first appears as a vassal of *Joscelin of Courtenay in 1115, although as Toron was constructed in 1105 he may have held the fief from around that time.

SOURCES: RRH nos. 79, 90a, 105, 121; WT XI.5, pp. 502-3.

79. Joscelin of Courtenay, lord of Tiberias

Joscelinus videlicet de Cortenay, vir nobilis de Francia, de regione quae dicitur Gastineis came from Courtenay (F, Loiret, arr. Montargis) in the Gâtinais. He was the second son of Joscelin, son of Atho, castellan of Châteaurenard; and Isabella, daughter of Guy I of Montlhéry and Hodierna of Gometz. Joscelin was thus not only related to Guy's male descendants, the lords of Montlhéry-Bray and Rochefort-Crecy, but he was also first cousin of King Baldwin II, son of Guy's daughter Melisende and Count Hugh of Rethel; and of Everard III of Le Puiset and his brothers, sons of Guy's daughter Alice and Hugh I Blavons. The Courtenay family fiefs were inherited by the eldest son, Milo; Joscelin went to Syria after the First Crusade (possibly on the crusade of 1101), as did a third brother, Geoffrey Chatpalu, at a much later date. Although he had 'neither lands nor wealth on his arrival', Joscelin clearly profited from his family connections; Baldwin, then count of Edessa, granted him the fief of Turbessel, although after a dispute in 1113 Joscelin was deprived of the fief and went to Jerusalem where he was granted the lordship of Tiberias. However, the importance of this quarrel should not be exaggerated; on the death of Baldwin I, Joscelin headed the party which supported the candidature of his cousin, and in return received the county of Edessa in 1119. He died before 1 October 1131. Joscelin was thus a member of the Jerusalem nobility for a period of seven years at the most. Nevertheless his origins and family connections help to explain the presence of men from the Ile-de-France as vassals in Galilee.[34]

SOURCES: AA pp. 615, 648-49, 710; WT X.23, pp. 482-83, XI.22, pp. 527-29, XII.4, pp. 550-51; *Ex continuatione historii Aimonii monachi Floriacensis*, Recueil des historiens des Gaules et de la France 11: 276; Nicholson, *Joscelyn I, Prince of Edessa*; Rheinheimer, *Das Kreuzfahrerfürstentum Galiläa*, pp. 44-45.

80. Lambert

Godfrey of Bouillon had a military follower called *Lambertus* who along with *Gerard of Avesnes had been installed in the Muslim-held port of Arsuf as overseer in the summer of 1099, and was threatened by its inhabitants when Godfrey's troops besieged the town in the autumn. This means that he cannot be identified with *Lambert of Montaigu, who returned home to Lotharingia with his father *Cono in the summer of that year, although it is possible that he was the *Lambertus* who donated a casale near the *flumen Diaboli* to the abbey of Josaphat, as recorded in a pancart of 1115.

SOURCES: AA p. 510; Delaborde, *Chartes de Terre Sainte provenant de l'abbaye de N.-D. de Josaphat*, no. 6 (= RRH no. 80).

---

[34] For example, *Drogo of Brie, *Godfrey of Bures and *William of Bures.

81. Lambert of Montaigu

Lambertus filius comitis Cononis de Monte Acuto was a son of Cono, count of Montaigu and Huy (B, Luxembourg, arr. Marche-en-Famenne), whom he accompanied on crusade. The precise identity of Lambert and his role during the crusade have caused much confusion in scholarship. Several of the narrative sources agree that one of the infamous deserters from the army at Antioch in June 1098 was a crusader named *Lambertus Pauper*, who is often glossed in source editions as count of Clermont-sur-Meuse (also known as Clermont-sous-Huy or Clermont-lez-Nandrin) near Liège. Yet unambiguous references to the son of Cono in the chronicles only use the surnames *Clarimontensis* or *de Monte Acuto*, and not *Pauper*; this suggests that he was a quite different person from the deserter at Antioch. It was only after the crusade that he received the county of Clermont from Bishop Otbert of Liège, who in 1095 had purchased the castle and its lands from its previous owner, the crusader *Giselbert of Clermont. After the siege of Antioch Lambert went on to Jerusalem, being given greater prominence in the sources after the death of his brother *Gozelo, and along with his father, he fought at the battle of Ascalon (August 1099). It has been claimed that Lambert settled in the kingdom of Jerusalem on the basis of a mention of a *Lambertus* at the siege of Arsuf, and a donation by one *Lambertus* to the abbey of Josaphat of a casale near the *flumen Diaboli*.[35] Yet neither occurrence has a surname which would allow an identification with Lambert of Montaigu. By contrast, Alberic of Troisfontaines relates that he returned home with his father; he was undoubtedly back in the West by 3 September 1104, when he and Cono were present at the feast of St Remaclus at Stavelot. He succeeded his father as count of Montaigu in 1106 and died sometime after 1140.

SOURCES: AA pp. 317, 422, 464, 495; Alberic of Troisfontaines, pp. 804, 815; *Chanson d'Antioche*, lines 1397 (*Lambert, le fil Quenon*), 2536, 8988; *Cantatorium*, pp. 208, 254; Roland, 'Les seigneurs et comtes de Rochefort', pp. 63-141, esp. pp. 117-23; Murray, 'The Army of Godfrey of Bouillon', pp. 304-6.

---

35 Riley-Smith, 'The Motives', pp. 724-26, citing AA p. 510 and Delaborde, *Chartes de Terre Sainte provenant de l'abbaye de N.-D. de Josaphat,* no. 6 (= RRH no 80). Lambert was a common Christian name, especially in the diocese of Liège where many of the crusaders came from. The exact wording of the charter for Josaphat is *Lambertus dedit Deo et Sancte Marie de valle Josaphat casale nomine Soesme situm super flumen quod vulgo Diaboli nuncupatur, laudantibus Goscelino principe Tyberiadis et Willelmo de Buris qui hoc ipsum casale eidem Lamberto prebuerat.* According to these terms the donation could not have been made until 1113, when Joscelin became lord of Tiberias.

82. Letold of Tournai

The crusader known as *Letaldus*, *Lietoldus* or *Litholfus* was regarded by most chroniclers of the crusade as having been the first to mount the walls of Jerusalem on the day that the city was captured, 15 July 1099. He and his brother *Engelbert were described by Albert of Aachen as *ortos de civitate Tornacio*, i.e. the town of Tournai (B, Hainaut, arr. Tournai), which at the time of the crusade was a lordship of its bishop. It is likely that both brothers had left the West in the contingent of Robert of Flanders, but by the time of the siege of Jerusalem they had joined that of Godfrey of Bouillon, whose forces mounted the successful assault.

SOURCES: AA pp. 472, 477; *GF* p. 91; PT p. 108; Robert the Monk, p. 867; GN p. 226; BD p. 102; Metellus von Tegernsee, *Expeditio Hierosolymitana*, ed. P. C. Jacobsen (Stuttgart, 1982), p. 128.

83. Lithard of Cambrai

Lithardus vero Cameracensis or *de Cameraco civitate Galliae* is identified by Albert of Aachen as originating from the episcopal territory of Cambrai (F, Nord, arr. Cambrai) in the extreme west of Lower Lotharingia. He was present at the Second Battle of Ramla (May 1102) and commanded a garrison of 300 men in Jaffa during the major Fatimid invasion of 1105. He was probably identical with the *Lethardus vicecomes* who gave land in the *casali Huberti de Paci, Siph vocato* (Akhzhiv) to the abbey of Josaphat, and the *Litardus tertius vicecomes Joppitarum* described by Bartolf of Nangis. Thus, although the function he exercised in Jaffa was similar to that of a castellan, as Mayer has argued, it would seems that his title was viscount.

SOURCES: AA, pp. 593, 621-22; RRH no. 134; Bartolf of Nangis, *Gesta Francorum expugnantium Iherusalem*, RHC Occ. 3: 534; Mayer, 'The Origins of the County of Jaffa', pp. 38-39.

84. Louis, count of Mousson

The crusader called *Ludovicus comes de Montione* or *Ludowicus de Monzunz filius comitis Tirrici de Muntbiliarht*, can be identified as Louis of Mousson (F, Meurthe-et-Moselle, arr. Nancy), a son of Theoderic II, count of Bar and Montbéliard, and Ermentrude, daughter of William the Great, count of Burgundy. Theoderic had taken a crusading vow but had been released from it because of illness. Louis was the grandson of Sophia of Bar, the daughter of Frederick II of Upper Lotharingia and sister of Beatrix, wife of Godfrey III of Lower Lotharingia. It was on Theoderic that Bishop Richer of Verdun conferred the county of Verdun after Baldwin of Boulogne had refused it. This affiliation to a lineage with claims on some of the Bouillon lands may explain

Louis's lack of prominence in Godfrey of Bouillon's army during the crusade, and he returned to the west by 1102. He was killed by some of his own ministerials in the same year.

SOURCES: Alberic of Troisfontaines, p. 804; AA p. 317, 422, 464; LL p. 492; *Chanson d'Antioche*, line 8975 (*Looïs de Mosson*); M. Grosdidier de Matons, *Le Comté de Bar des origines au Traité de Bruges (vers 950-1301)* (Bar-le-Duc, 1918), pp. 103-23; Grosdidier de Matons, *Catalogue des actes des comtes de Bar 1022-1239* (Paris, 1922), no. 35; J. Choux, *Recherches sur le diocèse de Toul au temps de la réforme. L'épiscopat de Pibon (1069-1107)* (Nancy, 1952), pp. 102-5; G. Poull, *La Maison ducale de Bar, 1: La maison ducale de Haute-Lorraine (942-1033), Les premiers comtes de Bar (1033-1239)* (Rupt-sur-Moselle, 1977), pp. 51-72; Parisse, 'Généalogie de la Maison d'Ardenne', pp. 9-42 (here 36); Parisse, 'Les possessions des ducs de Haute-Lotharingie (959-1033)', *PSHIGDL* 95 (1981), 241-57 (here 249-51); *Annales Einsidlenses*, MGH SS 3: 146.

85. Louis, archdeacon of Toul

A *quidam Tullensis Ecclesiae archidiaconus, nomine Ludewicus* is known only from an episode during the siege of Antioch, when he went foraging for food in a group of 300 pilgrims, but was killed by the Turks. It is likely that this archdeacon of Toul (F, Meurthe-et-Moselle, arr. Toul) had come on crusade with *Rainald III, count of Toul.

SOURCES: AA pp. 375-76.

86. Manasses of Haifa

Manasses de Caiphas appears as witness to documents of 1115 and 1120. he thus appears to have held the fief of Haifa between the tenures of *Pagan and Vivian, and to have survived the change of regime in 1118.

SOURCES: RRH nos. 80, 90, 91.

87. Martin of Nazareth

Martinus vicecomes witnessed a charter of *Bernard, bishop of Nazareth, in 1115, and is undoubtedly the *Martinus de Nazareth* who witnessed a royal charter of 1130/1131. It is likely that for at least part of this time he was viscount of Nazareth under the lord of Tiberias.

SOURCES: RRH nos. 81a, 137 (= Bresc-Bautier, *Cartulaire du chapitre du Saint-Sépulcre*, no. 31); Rheinheimer, *Das Kreuzfahrerfürstentum Galiläa*, pp. 172-73, 193-94.

88. Matthew the Seneschal

Matthaeus dapifer was a member of the group which summoned Baldwin I from Edessa on the death of Godfrey.

SOURCES: AA p. 526.

89. Milo of Clermont

Milo de Claro Monte fought at the siege of Haifa in June-July 1100, and is described as a knight of the *domus Godefridi*. He was probably originally connected with *Giselbert, count of Clermont-sous-Huy (B, Liège, arr. Huy, also known as Clermont-sur-Meuse), who went on crusade with Godfrey and is last mentioned as a member of the *comitatus Baldewini* in Cilicia in 1097.

SOURCES: AA pp. 350, 522, 526.

90. Otto Altaspata

Otto cognomine Altaspata was a Lombard, nephew of Count Albert of Biandrate (I, Piemonte, prov. Novara). He came to Palestine on the crusade of 1101 in the Lombard army led by Anselm, archbishop of Milan, and remained there. He was killed in September 1104 as a member of the Frankish garrison defending Jaffa from an attack by Fatimid forces from Ascalon.

SOURCES: AA pp. 559, 568, 591, 603, 608.

91. Pagan, chancellor

Paganus cancellarius appears in 1115 as first chancellor of the kingdom. He was a Norman by origin, and may have come from southern Italy in 1113 in the entourage of *Adelaide del Vasto. He emerged from the change of regime of 1118 with enhanced influence, attending the Council of Nablus in January 1120 and accompanying Baldwin II to northern Syria during his regency. By September 1129 he had left office to become archbishop of Caesarea, and must have died before 19 October 1129 when Gaudentius appears as archbishop.

SOURCES: RRH nos. 76b, 79, 90, 90a, 91, 100a, 102, 105, 109, 121; WT XII.13, pp. 563-64; Mayer, *Die Kanzlei der lateinischen Könige*, 1: 59-71.

92. Pagan, lord of Haifa

In 1109 Baldwin I sent *Paganum de Cayphas* along with *Eustace Granarius as envoys to Tancred of Antioch and William of Cerdagne during the dispute over the succession to the county of Tripoli. In view of the weightiness of the mission and the chronology, it is likely that Pagan was actually lord of Haifa, having been given the fief in succession to *Rorgius, who died in 1107. Pagan is otherwise known only from a donation made to the Hospital of Jerusalem before 1110. It is possible that he was related to Vivian of Haifa, who is known to have had a son called Pagan, who first appears in 1161.[36]

SOURCES: AA pp. 666-67; RRH no. 57.

---

[36] RRH nos. 366, 418.

93. Peter of Dampierre, count of Astenois

The crusader known as *Petrus de Stadeneis* or *de Staneis* has repeatedly been identified as originating from Stenay (F, Meuse, arr. Verdun) on the Meuse, which was a possession of Godfrey of Bouillon before the crusade.[37] However, Peter was the same person who is called *Petrus de Dunperrun*, after the castle of Dampierre-le-Château (F, Marne, arr. Sainte-Menehould). He was count of the *pagus Stadunensis* (Astenois), a district of Champagne in the extreme east of the kingdom of France, and was a younger son of Frederick I, count of Astenois, and Gertrude, daughter of Count Rainald II of Toul. Several sources allude to a blood relationship between Godfrey III of Lower Lotharingia and Frederick's brother Henry of Verdun, bishop of Liège, and it is likely that Count Baldwin, the father of Henry and Frederick, had married a woman of the Ardennes-Bouillon dynasty. Peter and his brother *Rainald III of Toul were thus kinsmen of Godfrey of Bouillon, although Peter also had ties with Godfrey's enemies: as a vassal of the bishop of Verdun (*unus de baronibus episcopi*), he commanded the bishop's forces during his campaigns against Godfrey. Despite this he seems to have played a fairly prominent part in Godfrey's army on crusade. He joined Baldwin of Boulogne in the conquest of Edessa, but thereafter returned to the main army, and returned to the West in the summer of 1099.

SOURCES: AA pp. 299, 310, 317, 365-66, 422, 424; LL pp. 494, 497; *Chanson d'Antioche*, lines 2260, 8188 (*Pieres d'Estaenor*), 8205; A. de Barthélemy, 'Le comté d'Astenois et les comtes de Dampierre-le-Château', *Revue de Champagne et de Brie* 16 (1888), 401-16, 17 (1889), 177-91, 18 (1890), 801-7, 19 (1891), 691-99; Ch. Aimond, 'La nécrologe de la cathédrale de Verdun', *JGLGA* 21 (1909), 132-314 (here 185); Parisse, *La Noblesse lorraine*, pp. 879-82.

94. Peter *Langobardus*

A *Petrus Langobardus* is known only from his participation at the siege of Arsuf by Godfrey's forces in autumn 1099. His surname suggests that he was a Lombard from southern Italy.

SOURCES: AA p. 509.

---

37 Röhricht, *Geschichte des Ersten Kreuzzuges*, p. 62; Chalandon, *Histoire de la première croisade*, p. 112; Grousset, *Histoire des croisades et du royaume franc de Jérusalem*, 2 vols (Paris, 1934-36), 1: 12; Lobet, *Godefroid de Bouillon*, p. 71; H. Hardenberg, *De Nederlanden en de kruistochten* (Amsterdam, 1944), pp. 57-58; Runciman, 'The First Crusade: Constantinople to Antioch', in *A History of the Crusades*, ed. Setton, 1: 296; Knoch, *Studien zu Albert von Aachen*, pp. 167-69, 171-73, 188; Runciman, *History of the Crusades*, 1: 147.

95. Peter of Lens

Peter is known only from his donation to the Hospital of the casale of Dirberham on the eastern shore of Lake Tiberias, sometime before 1110. Richard suggests that he was a follower of the Artesian *Gervase of Bazoches, lord of Tiberias from 1106 to 1108,[38] but it is more probable that he was originally a vassal of the counts of Boulogne, who had held Lens (F, Pas-de-Calais, arr. Lens) from 1054 onwards.

SOURCES: RRH nos. 57, 293.

96. Philip of Bouillon

Philippus de Bulon was in the Frankish army at the Second Battle of Ramla (May 1102). His surname suggests he was originally a Lotharingian knight from the territory of Bouillon (B, Luxembourg, arr. Neufchâteau).

SOURCES: AA p. 593.

97. Pisellus, viscount of Jerusalem

Pisellus appears between 1104 and 1119; from 1108 at the latest he held the office of viscount of Jerusalem. He may well be identical with the *Pisellus de Tuorna* who fought at the Third Battle of Ramla in 1105, [39] and may also have been related to Pisellus, a nephew of Udelrard of Wissant (F, Pas-de-Calais, arr. Boulogne-sur-Mer) who died during the crusade. From records of donations made by him, his wife Gisla and his (unnamed) brother to the abbey of Josaphat, the order of the Hospital and the episcopal church of Bethlehem, it can be deduced that he and his family had considerable land holdings concentrated in central Judaea: (1) Meschium, on the road to Nablus near Montjoie, and the unidentified Delescu and Micheel between Jerusalem and the Jordan, (2) Bethamis near Jerusalem, (3) Cadichinos between Jerusalem and Bethlehem, (4) Bessura in Transjordan.[40] Pisellus's tenure of the viscountship

---

[38] Richard, *Royaume latin*, p. 82.

[39] Albert of Aachen's *Tuorna* could be meant to represent Tournai in Hainaut, in which case Pisellus could have been a Lotharingian, but elsewhere the chronicler uses the more standard form *Tornacium*, as in the case of Engelbert and Letold *de civitate Tornacio* (AA p. 472)

[40] Mayer, *Die Kreuzfahrerherrschaft Montréal*, pp. 86-91 argues that after 1115 Pisellus was moved to the office of viscount of Transjordan. His evidence for this is RRH no. 134 (= Delaborde, *Chartes de Terre Sainte provenant de l'abbaye de N.-D. de Josaphat*, no. 18), a charter of Baldwin II of 1130 which mentions a previous confirmation by Roman of Le Puy for the abbey of Josaphat: *Romanus vero de Podio et Richildis uxor sua et heredes eorum concesserunt eidum ecclesie supradicte in terra Belcha casalia Bessura et La cum omnibus pertinentiis eorum.* Mayer concludes that if Roman as lord of Transjordan

explains his frequent appearances as witness on charters of the reign, more than any other layman.

SOURCES: RRH nos. 43, 52, 56a, 57, 59, 76a, 79, 80, 87, 134, 291, 983; AA p. 621. Mayer, *Die Kreuzfahrerherrschaft Montréal*, pp. 69-91.

98. Pisellus of Wissant

Pisellus … filio sororis Udelardi, praeclaris militis et nobilissimi de Wizan was a member of Baldwin of Boulogne's *comitatus* in late 1098, when he was taken prisoner by troops of Balak, the Turkish lord of Sarūj, and later executed. He was evidently on crusade with his uncle, *Udelrard of Wissant (F, Pas-de-Calais, arr. Boulogne-sur-Mer) and therefore probably originally a vassal of Eustace III of Boulogne.

SOURCES: AA pp. 358, 446.

99. Rainald III, count of Toul

Rainald was the elder son of Frederick I, count of Astenois, who had been given the county of Toul (F, Meurthe-et-Moselle, arr. Toul) by its bishop in 1069 and had married Gertrude, daughter of Rainald II, a previous count. Rainald III and his brother *Peter of Dampierre were kinsmen of Godfrey of Bouillon. Rainald joined Baldwin of Boulogne in the conquest of Edessa, but thereafter returned to the main army, commanding a division at the Great Battle of Antioch. He returned to Upper Lotharingia after the crusade, and was dead by 1124, when a charter names his son Frederick as count of Toul.

SOURCES: AA pp. 299, 301, 317, 343, 365-66, 398, 422, 424; BD p. 77; LL p. 494; Alberic of Troisfontaines, p. 804; Barthélemy, 'Le comté d'Astenois et les comtes de Dampierre-le-Château'; Parisse, *La Noblesse lorraine*, pp. 879-82.

100. Rainier Brus

Reinerus de Bruso or *Brus, miles imperterritus* was killed in battle against Tughtikīn, atabeg of Damascus, during the latter's great invasion across the Jordan in 1113. On the basis of the similarity of forename and surname it is likely that he was the father (or another male relative) of the better documented *Rainerius de Bruso* or *Rainerius cognomine Brus*, first mentioned in May 1125, who became lord of Banyas after its capture by the Franks in 1129.

---

confirmed a donation of Pisellus, he must have been his successor (*Rechtsnachfolger*), while admitting that the possession of Bessura was not necessarily connected with the administration of the area. It would seem much more plausible that when he became lord of Transjordan, Roman confirmed various previous donations in the al-Balqā hills to Josaphat, and that Pisellus's donation comprised Bessura (Beit-Zira'ah) only, while the nearby La (al-ᶜAl) evidently came from a different donor.

SOURCES: AA p. 696; RRH nos. 105, 174, 181; WT XIV.17, p. 631; Mayer, 'Angevins versus Normans', p. 12.

101. Ralph of Aalst

Rodulfus de castello Alos, quod est in Flandria was the second son of Ralph, advocate of St Peter's Abbey at Ghent, and Gisela of Luxembourg, sister-in-law of Count Baldwin IV of Flanders. His elder brother was Baldwin I, also advocate of St Peter's and lord of Aalst (B, Oost-Vlaanderen, arr. Aalst), Waas and Drongen. Ralph belonged to the foremost rank of the Flemish nobility, and was chamberlain of Flanders. His last appearance in Flanders was in September or October 1096. Warlop questions his participation on the crusade; however his early appearance in Palestine makes it likely that he accompanied Robert II of Flanders along with his nephews Gilbert, who subsequently returned home, and Baldwin II of Aalst, who was killed at Nicaea on 13 June 1097. Ralph himself evidently remained in the kingdom of Jerusalem and was killed at the Second Battle of Ramla in May 1102.

SOURCES: AA p. 591, 593; Vercauteren, *Actes des comtes de Flandre 1071-1128*, nos. 12, 20, 23; *Chronicon monasterii Watinensis*, MGH SS 14: 168-69; Warlop, *The Flemish Nobility*, pp. 587-91.

102. Ralph of La Fontanelle

This crusader is first mentioned in the company of Everard III of Le Puiset at the siege of Antioch, when he temporarily deserted from the crusading army. The descriptions *Radulfus de Fontanellis et alii Andegavorum* and *de Fontenella Radulphus, et is Turonensis* point to a placename derived from a diminutive of Latin *fontanum* situated in Touraine or Anjou. This suggests as a place of origin La Fontanelle (F, Loir-et-Cher, arr. Vendôme) in an area held by the counts of Anjou from the counts of Blois. Ralph probably came to Palestine in the army of Stephen, count of Blois and Chartres. A bull of Gregory IX for the church of Bethlehem mentions the donation of the casale of Bechfassa, probably Beit Fajjar south of Bethlehem, *ex feudo Radulfi de Fontaneto*. The possession of a substantial fief in the royal domain explains the frequency with which he witnessed royal and patriarchal charters. However, from 1133 up to his last appearance in 1145 he is known only from documents issued in the principality of Antioch and the county of Tripoli. At the beginning of this period King Fulk went to Antioch to act as regent, yet Ralph does not appear on either of the charters issued by Fulk in this capacity. In January 1133 he witnessed a charter of Princess Alice of Antioch at Laodicea, and that same month a charter of Walter of Sourdeval, which was confirmed by Alice, who was a focus of opposition to the rule of Fulk. In 1134 Ralph was again at Laodicea with Alice and Hugh, count of Jaffa, who had been exiled as a result of his revolt against Fulk in the kingdom of Jerusalem. Clearly Ralph was not in Antioch in royal service, but rather was associated with those who were opposed to the king. These connections go back beyond 1133. Ralph came from the same area in France as the Le Puiset family, and later witnessed a charter of Hugh's constable Barisan in 1127. His son-in-law Geoffrey *de Parenti* was also associated with Hugh, and like Ralph disappears from Jerusalem documents around 1131/1134. Taken together, this evidence suggests that both Ralph and Geoffrey were dispossessed or exiled for supporting Hugh.[41]

SOURCES: AA p. 410; Radulph of Caen, p. 662; BD p. 65; RRH nos. 52, 59, 76b, 80, 87, 105, 120, 148, 149, 150, 151a, 157, 212, 236, 982.

103. Ralph of Montpinçon

Rodulfus de Montpinzon is described by Albert of Aachen as one of the *milites de domo ducis Godefridi*. He belonged to the Norman family of Montpinçon (F, Calvados, arr. Lisieux), several members of which bore the name Ralph. One of these was the steward to William I of England and benefactor of the abbey of Saint-Evroul who died around 1103. According to Orderic Vitalis, this Ralph had two sons: Hugh, and Ralph the Younger, *qui in via Ierusalem peregrinus obierat*. However, this does not necessarily mean that he died on the way to Jerusalem, as Chibnall translates the phrase in her edition of Orderic; it could also mean that he died in the Holy Land, before he could return to Normandy. If so he is probably the knight mentioned by Albert; it would also explain why he is known in Palestine only from this one reference.

SOURCES: AA p. 531; Orderic Vitalis, 3: 164-67.

104. Ralph of Mousson

Rodulfus de Monzon or *Mozon* was a member of Godfrey's household and belonged to the group that invited Baldwin I to Jerusalem in July 1100. Riley-Smith gives his place of origin as Menonville, which he does not identify and which is hardly justified by the forms of the name.[42] It is far more likely that Ralph was a follower of the crusader *Ludowicus comes de Montione* or *Ludowicus de Monzunz filius comitis Tirrici de Muntbiliart* who can be identified as *Louis of Mousson (F, Meurthe-et-Moselle, arr. Nancy), a son of Theoderic, count of Bar and Montbéliard.

[41] Richard, *Comté de Tripoli*, p. 78 claims that Ralph was a Tripolitan noble. This is clearly not the case, although his presence on RRH nos. 212 (1142) and 236 (1145) suggests that Ralph was unable to return to Jerusalem and was obliged to spend the latter part of his exile in Tripoli.

[42] Riley-Smith, 'The Motives', p. 725.

SOURCES: AA pp. 317, 526.

105. Reinard of Hemmersbach

Reinardus de Hamersbach is mentioned as being in Godfrey's company in 1098. His probable place of origin was Hemmersbach (Ger, Nordrhein-Westfalen, Kr. Bergheim) approximately 25 km west of Cologne. In the late summer of 1098 he died of plague and was buried in the church of St Peter at Antioch.

SOURCES: AA pp. 422, 426, 435. E. Meuthen, review of Knoch, *Studien zu Albert von Aachen*, in *Zeitschrift des Aachener Geschichtsvereins* 78 for 1966-67 (1967), 347-51 (here 348-49); Lohrmann, 'Albert von Aachen und die Judenpogrome des Jahres 1096', p. 133 n. 12.

106. Reinard of Verdun

Albert of Aachen describes this knight among the losses among King Baldwin's forces at the Third Battle of Ramla in 1105: *de cujus comitatu tantummodo centum perierunt cum milite egregio Reinardo Virdunense.* This Reinard of Verdun would thus seem to have been the most prominent casualty in this engagement. There was a placename Verdun in western Normandy (F, Manche, cant. Pontorson), from which a prominent Anglo-Norman family took its name.[43] However, the name Reinard does not seem to occur in it, and the Germanic ending *-(h)ard*, as well as the fact that its bearer is recorded only by Albert of Aachen, suggests that Reinard's place of origin was the major settlement of this name, Verdun (F, Meuse, arr. Verdun) in Upper Lotharingia. Godfrey of Bouillon had been count of Verdun before the crusade, but in view of his fairly tenuous hold over the county it is likely that Reinard was not originally in Godfrey's own retinue but in that of *Peter of Dampierre or his brother *Rainald of Toul, who were both barons of the bishop of Verdun.

SOURCES: AA p. 623.

107. Reinold, master of archers

A *Reinoldus quidam miles Regis, arte sagittandi peritissmus*, is mentioned as being with Baldwin I at the siege of Acre in 1103. His designation as *magister sagittariorum* implies the organisation of a separate force of archers in the army of Jerusalem under a specialist commander. He was killed during this same engagement and was buried at the abbey of Mount Thabor.

Sources. AA p. 602.

---

[43] R. Dace, 'Bertran de Verdun: Royal Service, Land, and Family in the Late Twelfth Century', *Medieval Prosopography* 20 (1999), 75-93; Keats-Rohan, *Domesday People, 1*: 168.

108. Robert, chancery official

The *Robertus sacerdos* who figured as the scribe of a charter of Baldwin I for the Hospital of Jerusalem in 1112 has been identified by Mayer as a Lotharingian who had probably come to the East in the entourage of Godfrey of Bouillon. He served as the principal official in the royal chancery between 1102 and 1114, and seems to have been replaced before 1115 on the nomination of a chancellor, *Pagan.

SOURCES: RRH no. 68a; Mayer, *Die Kanzlei der lateinischen Könige*, 1: 373-421.

109. Robert *Anglus*

According to William of Malmesbury, the English prince Edgar the Ætheling made a pilgrimage to Jerusalem *cum Roberto filio Godewini*, a journey which can be dated to 1102. Robert was a son of one Godwine of Worcester, but his Continental-Germanic name suggests that he was born after the Norman Conquest. Robert accompanied Edgar to Scotland and held land in Lothian in 1099. He evidently remained in Palestine; he can be identified with the *Robertus Anglus* who fought at the Second Battle of Ramla (May 1102), where he was killed at the side of Baldwin I while attempting to break out of Egyptian encirclement.

SOURCES: William of Malmesbury, ed. Mynors *et al.*, III.251, pp. 464-66, IV.384, pp. 684-86; R. L. G. Ritchie, *The Normans in Scotland* (Edinburgh, 1954), p. 95; N. Hooper, 'Edgar the Ætheling: Anglo-Saxon Prince, Rebel and Crusader', *Anglo-Saxon England* 14 (1985), 197-214 (here 210-11).

110. Robert of Apulia

Robertus miles … de Apulia, as he is named by Albert of Aachen, was one of Godfrey's military commanders after the capture of Jerusalem. Along with *Warner of Grez he commanded a force of 140 knights which ambushed the garrison of Arsuf in March 1100. After the town offered submission Godfrey assigned him its revenues as a money-fief. He was a member of the group which mounted the coup in favour of Baldwin I on Godfrey's death. Since his surname indicates that he was of southern Italian origin he must have been a crusader in the contingent of Bohemund; it is conceivable that he was identical with *Robertus de Ansa civitate*, a Norman who had settled in Anzi (I, Basilicata, prov. Potenza), and who served with Bohemund on crusade, and is last recorded under this name as a witness to a treaty between Bohemund and the Genoese of 14 July 1098.

SOURCES: AA pp. 514-15, 526; *GF* pp. 7, 20; Jamison, 'Some Notes on the *Anonymi Gesta Francorum*', pp. 202-3; Hagenmeyer, *Epistulae*, no. 13.

111. Robert FitzGerard of Buonalbergo

Robertus filius Gerardi was a Norman from southern Italy, the second son of Gerard, count of Buonalbergo (I, Campania, prov. Benevento), who was a nephew of Alberada, mother of Bohemund. Robert went on crusade with his cousin Bohemund, whom he served as banner-bearer and constable, distinguishing himself at the Lake Battle of Antioch in February 1098. At some point he transferred his allegiance to Godfrey, possibly having come to Jerusalem in Tancred's company, and belonged to the group that summoned Baldwin I to Jerusalem in July 1100. It is uncertain how long he remained in Palestine; he was back in Italy by 1112, when he received land from Count Jordan, the son of his brother Herbert. He was murdered in 1121 and buried in the abbey of St Sophia in Benevento.

SOURCES: BD p. 47; AA p. 316, 526; PT p. 44; GN p. 178; *GF* p. 36; Falco of Benevento, *Chronicon Beneventanum*, ed. E. D'Angelo (Florence, 1998), pp. 60-62; Jamison, 'Some Notes on the *Anonymi Gesta Francorum*', pp. 201-2.

112. Robert Giffard

Robertus Giffarz appears as a witness to a charter of Baldwin I of 1115 confirming donations of William of Bures to the abbey of Josaphat. His name is given in fifth place among the first group of witnesses who are distinguished from the *testes Jocelini* (i.e. witnesses of Joscelin of Tiberias, William's lord), suggesting that Robert was in royal service. He was probably a member of the Norman family of Giffard which originally came from Longueville-la-Gifart, now Longueville-sur-Scie (F, Seine-Maritime, arr. Dieppe). A Robert Giffard is known to have been in England in the late 1070s, but evidently went to Apulia with William of Grandmesnil and fought at Durazzo in 1081. As William himself later went on crusade it is possible that Robert accompanied him and that he or his son should be identified with this individual.

SOURCES: RRH no. 79; L. C. Loyd, *The Origins of Some Anglo-Norman Families* (Leeds, 1951), pp. 129-47; *Regesta Regum Anglo-Normannorum* 1, ed. H. W. Davis, nos. 114, 192; Orderic Vitalis, 4:16.

113. Robert, bishop of Lydda

When the army of the First Crusade reached the town of Ramla in early June 1099, its leaders installed a cleric called Robert as bishop of the nearby settlement of Lydda, with the shrine of St George as his cathedral. William of Tyre records that he was a Norman from the bishopric of Rouen (*quendam Robertum, Normannum genere, de episcopatu Rotomagensi*). He was given Lydda and Ramla to be held as an ecclesiastical lordship, although Ramla was subsequently removed from it. The bishop appears to have strongly fortified his church, and had a *clientela* to assist him in its defence. Although he owed his initial promotion to the leadership of the crusade as a whole rather than to the Bouillon-Boulogne brothers, Robert clearly identified himself with the interest of the latter; he was instrumental in the group which appealed to Baldwin I to take the throne on the death of Godfrey, and acted as one of its envoys to Baldwin in Edessa. Between the unconfirmed election of Arnulf of Chocques as patriarch in July 1099 and the election of Daibert of Pisa at Christmas Robert was the only universally recognised Latin bishop in Palestine, and it was he who consecrated Daibert. He must have died by 1112, when *Roger appears as bishop of Lydda.

SOURCES: AA pp. 512, 526, 531, 591, 592, 599; BD p. 110; WT VII.22, pp. 372-74; RRH no. 52; Mayer, 'The Origins of the Lordships of Ramla and Lydda', pp. 537-52.

114. Roger, bishop of Lydda

Roger followed the Norman *Robert as bishop of Lydda (from around 1112), holding office until at least 1125. His origins are unknown. In March-April 1118 he took part in Baldwin I's expedition against Egypt.

SOURCES: RRH nos 68, 68a, 69, 76b, 80, 89, 91, 102, 105; RHC Occ. 4: 543.

115. Roger of Rozoy

A *dominus Roger de Rosoit* was present at the foundation of the priory of St Peter at Bouillon by Godfrey II of Lower Lotharingia in 1069. It was probably he or his son who was the crusader called *Rotger de castello Roiset* or *Roseit*, or in the vernacular *Rogiers del Rosoi*, who is first mentioned at the siege of Artah in 1097. His place of origin was Rozoy-sur-Serre (F, Aisne, arr. Laon), among whose lords Roger was a favourite name. The crusader was in Jerusalem by at least Easter 1102, and fought at, and escaped from, the Frankish defeat at the Second Battle of Ramla (May 1102). Thereafter he seems to have risen in status. He was in command of the Frankish forces in Jaffa, probably as castellan, when it was attacked by the Egyptians in 1106. He witnessed a charter of Baldwin I in 1108, and evidently had property *in Monte Betherico*, which can be deduced from the donation of a *villanus* to the abbey of Josaphat before 1115.

SOURCES: G. Despy, 'Un fragment d'une *cronica monasterii Sancti Huberti in Ardenna*', *Bulletin de la Commission Royale d'Histoire* 121 (1956), 171-73; AA pp. 358, 591, 593, 636-37, *Chanson d'Antioche*, lines 1179, 2680, 2680, 8996; RRH nos. 52, 80; 'Feoda Campaniae', in A. Longnon, *Documents relatifs au comté de Champagne et de Brie 1172-1361* (Paris, 1901-14), 1: 22, 140, 168; Mayer, 'The Origins of the County of Jaffa', pp. 39-40.

116. Roman of Le Puy

Romanus de Podio was in Palestine before 1110 and last appears in 1133. Although placenames corresponding to Latin *Podium* were common in France, his most likely place of origin was Le Puy in the Auvergne (F, Haute-Loire, arr. Le Puy); he was probably a follower of Adhemar, bishop of Le Puy, and his brothers William-Hugh and Francis-Lambert of Monteil who were with the Provençal army of Raymond of Saint-Gilles.[2] Roman was made lord of Transjordan in the reign of Baldwin II, but was dispossessed by 1126, when Pagan the Butler appears as holder of the lordship.

SOURCES: RRH nos. 68a, 79, 91, 105, 121, 147; Riley-Smith, 'The Motives', p. 729.

117. Rorgius, lord of Haifa

Rorgius is first mentioned as having been given the lordship of Haifa by 1102 (*Rorgius, qui civitatem Cayphas in beneficio acceperat et obtinebat*) and still held it at the time of his death (*qui dono Regis civitati Cayphas praeerat*). He fought alongside Baldwin I at the Third Battle of Ramla (August 1105). He died after an illness in 1107 and was buried in the church of the Holy Sepulchre.

SOURCES: AA pp. 593, 621, 639, 646.

118. Rothold

A *Rotholdus*, described as *miles acerimus*, is known only from his participation at the siege of Arsuf by Godfrey's forces in autumn 1099.

SOURCES: AA p. 509.

119. Sigemar of Maasmechelen

Brother of the crusader *Franco of Maasmechelen (*Franco de Mechela*) and a kinsman of the brothers *Henry and *Godfrey of Esch-sur-Sûre.

SOURCES: AA p. 413; above, Franco of Maasmechelen.

120. Simon the Constable

Simon or *Symon constabularius* is attested as witness to royal charters in 1108 and 1115. He was evidently the first constable of the kingdom. In two cases he is given a surname: *Simon dux* and *Symon ducis filius*. His relatively high ranking in the witness lists is a reflection of his position as senior military official. It is possible that he can be identified with one *Σιμουντος* who is recorded by Anna Komnene as having been sent by Baldwin I to Tripoli to receive Greek ambassadors in 1108, and who is described by her as a cousin (*εξάδελφος*) of the king. This relationship and the description *ducis filius* have caused him to be identified as a son (otherwise unknown) of Count Henry of Limburg (†1119) who held the title of duke of Lower Lotharingia between 1101 and 1106.[44] Henry was indeed the son of Waleran of Arlon-Limburg and Judith, daughter of Frederick of Luxembourg and Gerberga, daughter of Eustace I of Boulogne.[45] This would make Simon a very distant kinsman of King Baldwin, assuming that Anna Komnene's *Σιμουντος* is indeed identical, although it is perhaps doubtful as to how well she would be informed about such a relationship.

SOURCES: RRH nos. 52, 59, 68a, 76b, 79; Anne Comnène, *Alexiade*, trans. Leib, 3: 150.

121. Stabelo the Chamberlain

Stabelo camerarius ducis Godefridi is first mentioned as a member of Godfrey's household during the march across Hungary in 1096, during which he took part in a legation to King Coloman. He was killed at the Second Battle of Ramla (May 1102). He was a *familiaris* of Godfrey before the crusade, when he was supposed to have experienced a vision which was later interpreted as referring to the duke's pilgrimage. In view of this long service, it is likely that he was a Lotharingian by origin. His name seems to be the basis for the erroneous Baldwin of 'Stabelo' or 'Stavelot' mentioned as one of Godfrey's followers by Andressohn and Runciman.[46]

SOURCES: AA pp. 300, 481-83, 593.

122. Tancred, lord of Tiberias

Tancred was a Norman from southern Italy, son of Odo 'the Good Marquis' (Odobonus) and Emma, daughter of Robert Guiscard, duke of Apulia and Calabria. He came to the East in the army of his uncle Bohemund I, later prince of Antioch, but on the final part of the march to Jerusalem seems to have joined Godfrey. After the capture of Jerusalem he established himself as lord of Tiberias, which he ruled until March 1101 when he left to assume the regency of Antioch. Tiberias was restored to him by Baldwin I in 1109 as part of a general settlement also involving the succession to the county of Tripoli,

---

[44] RHC Grecs 2: 113-14; Röhricht, *Geschichte des Königreichs Jerusalem*, p. 95; Mayer, *Die Kreuzfahrerherrschaft Montréal*, p. 70; Mayer, *Die Kanzlei der lateinischen Könige* 2: 888.

[45] Mohr, *Geschichte des Herzogtums Lothringen*, 2; 74-76; Parisse, 'Généalogie de la Maison d'Ardenne', p. 32. The editors of the RHC wrongly state that Henry, rather than his father, was married to Jutta (Judith). Röhricht compounds this error of generations by referring to Simon's mother as Baldwin's niece ('Sohn seiner Nichte Juntha und des Herzogs Heinrich von Limburg', p. 95).

[46] Andressohn, *The Ancestry and Life of Godfrey of Bouillon*, p. 53; Runciman, *History of the Crusades*, 1: 147.

although he seems to have remained in northern Syria up to his death in December 1112.

SOURCES: R. L. Nicholson, *Tancred: A Study of His Career and Work in Their Relation to the First Crusade and the Establishment of the Latin States in Syria and Palestine* (Chicago, 1940), pp. 1-4, 20-21, 103-21; Rheinheimer, *Das Kreuzfahrerfürstentum Galiläa*, pp. 39-41, 64-66, 102-7.

123. Theobald of Nivelles

Teobaldus Nivellensis appears as a witness to a charter of *Bernard, bishop of Nazareth, for the abbey of Josaphat in 1115. He can be identified with the *Teobaldus de Nigella* who had previously given the casale of Zebezeb to Josaphat. Taking the witness form of the name rather than that of the pancarts as the more correct, his surname would suggest that he originated from Nivelles in Brabant (B, Brabant Wallon, arr. Nivelles), which appears under the forms *Nivialensis*, *Niviellensis* and *Nivigellensis* in the seventh to twelfth centuries.[47] The Ardennes-Bouillon family held lands in the vicinity of Nivelles before the crusade, which may indicate a connection with Godfrey of Bouillon. The casale which Theobald donated to Josaphat lay in the *Terre de Suète* south-east of Bosra, and the accumulated evidence indicates that he was a rear-vassal in the lordship of Tiberias, holding land from *William of Bures, at that time a vassal of Joscelin of Courtenay.

SOURCES: RRH nos. 80, 81a, 90, 134; Mayer, *Bistümer, Klöster und Stifte*, pp. 323-35.

124. Thoros, lord of Edessa

The ruler of Edessa when Baldwin I led his expedition towards that city and, for a short time afterwards his adoptive father, was an Armenian chief named T(h)oros, son of Hethoum. He was probably a lieutenant of Philaretos, a former commander in Byzantine service who became effective ruler of Cilicia in the aftermath of the Byzantine defeat at Manzikert (1071). Thoros bore the Greek title of *κουροπαλατης* which had evidently been awarded as a diplomatic honour by the Byzantine government during this period. By 1094 he was a military commander in service of Tutush, brother of the sultan Malik Shāh, and during the struggles over the Seljuk succession in the aftermath of Malik Shāh's death Thoros was installed as governor of Edessa. On the arrival of the crusaders he allied himself with Baldwin to throw off Turkish rule. As the price for this assistance, Thoros and his wife were obliged to adopt Baldwin as their son and heir (February 1098). The Latin sources do not name him, but William of Tyre calls him *natione Graecus*, while the Armenian Matthew of Edessa describes him

[47] Gysseling, *Woordenboek*, 2: 743. Another possible (but less likely) place of origin might be Nivelles-sur-Meuse (B, Liège, arr. Liège).

as a Roman prince, both indicating that Thoros belonged to that minority of Armenians, primarily among the nobility, who belonged to the Chalcedonian (i.e. Melkite or Greek orthodox) church, unlike the majority who were adherents of the Monophysite faith.[48] Because of this and his collaboration with the Turks he was hated by the majority Armenian population, and during Baldwin's absence on campaign Thoros was overthrown by a revolt of notables of the city and murdered after his capitulation (8 March 1098). It would seem that Thoros's decision to share government was a reluctant one, and Baldwin may well have been privy to the plot against him, as claimed by Matthew of Edessa.

SOURCES: Matthew of Edessa, ed. Dostourian, pp. 287, 289-92, 298-305; AA pp. 352-53, 355; C. J. Yarnley, 'Philaretos, Armenian Bandit or Byzantine General', *Revue des études arméniennes* n.s. 9 (1972), 331-53; J. Laurent, 'Des Grecs aux croisés. Etude sur l'histoire d'Edesse entre 1071 et 1098', *Byzantion* 1 (1924), 367-449.

125. Udelrard of Wissant

Udelrardus ... de Wizan is described as being a member of the *domus ducis Godefridi*. His surname would seem to derive from the port of Wissant (F, Pas-de-Calais, arr. Boulogne-sur-Mer).[49] He and his nephew *Pisellus were probably originally vassals of Eustace III of Boulogne. Udelrard seems to be an example of the service of knights being shared by all three of the Bouillon-Boulogne brothers, since he was in the company of Baldwin's wife *Godehilde when he died at Marash in October 1097.

SOURCES: AA pp. 358, 446.

126. Ulric of Nablus

Ulric appears with the office of viscount of Nablus between 1115 and 1152. He is known to have had a brother Peter and a son Baldwin, who held extensive properties in this part of the royal domain.

SOURCES: RRH nos. 90, 121, 133, 134, 137, 137a; G. Beyer, 'Neapolis und sein Gebiet in der Kreuzfahrerzeit', *Zeitschrift des Deutschen Palästinavereins* 63 (1940), 155-70.

---

[48] On this socio-religious group, see V. A. Arutyunova-Fidanyan, 'The Ethno-Confessional Self-Awareness of Armenian Chalcedonians', *Revue des études arméniennes* n.s. 21 (1988-89), 345-63.

[49] Various men with the surnames *de Wissand, de Witsant* or *de Wissant* are known as tenants in Domesday Book, and are often associated with the Boulogne family. Keats-Rohan, *Domesday People, 1*: 212.

127. Walter Bigod

Galterius Bigotus is known only from his appearance as witness to a charter of Baldwin I from 1108. He was probably a member of the Norman family called Bigot or Bigod, whose principal lands (*Le fief Bigot*) were situated at Courvaudon (F, Calvados, arr. Caen), and which had several connections with the crusade. Roger Bigod (†1107), lord of Les Loges and Savenay, married Alice, daughter of Robert of Belvoir (Leicestershire), a cadet of the Anglo-Norman Tosny family who were relatives by marriage of Baldwin I. In 1103/1104 he also founded a priory at Thetford, evidently in lieu of a pilgrimage to the Holy Land. An Ilger Bigod was on crusade with Tancred and became Bohemund's *magister militum*.

SOURCES: RRH no. 52; Loyd, *The Origins of Some Anglo-Norman Families*, pp. 14-15; Musset, 'Les Tosny', pp. 65-66; Orderic Vitalis, 5: 168-70.

128. Walter of Bouillon

In 1148 *Barisan, lord of Ibelin, gave to the order of St Lazarus ten carrucates of land *in territorio casalis quod Galteri de Bulion nuncupatur*. The Walter who gave his name to the village is otherwise unknown in Palestine, although it is likely that he was a vassal from the territory of Bouillon (B, Luxembourg, arr. Neufchâteau). He can most readily be identified with the Walter of Bouillon who was present at the sale of allods to the abbey of St Gertrude at Nivelles by Godfrey and Baldwin in 1096 and may have come on crusade with *Heribrand, castellan of Bouillon, who was in Godfrey's army and also at the transaction at Nivelles.[50]

SOURCES: Comte de Marsy, 'Fragment d'un cartulaire de l'ordre de Saint-Lazare en Terre-Sainte', *Archives de l'Orient latin* 2 (1884), 121-57, no. 5 (= RRH no. 252); MGH DD H.IV, no. 459.

129. Walter of Domart

Walterus de Domedart and his son Bernard first appear at the siege of Nicaea in 1097. Later he is mentioned along with other known companions of Godfrey in an order of battle at the siege of Antioch. The form of his locative surname indicates a toponym deriving from the saint's name *domnus Medardus*. The most probable place of origin is Domart-en-Ponthieu (F, Somme, arr. Amiens) for which corresponding forms are attested from *c.* 1110 onwards.[51] Walter and

---

[50] The Walter of Bouillon who witnessed a document of the chapter of St Lambert of Liège in 1116 could have been a relative of the crusader. Bormans, Schoolmeesters and Poncelet, *Cartulaire de l'église de Saint-Lambert*, 1, no. 32.

[51] Gysseling, *Woordenboek*, 1: 276; E. Nègre, *Toponymie général de la France*, 3 vols (Geneva, 1990), 1: 415; C. Brunel, *Recueil des actes des comtes de Pontieu* [*sic*] *1026-1279*

Bernard are probably identical with the *Gualterius de Sancto Gualterico et Bernardus filius eius* mentioned by Orderic Vitalis, which would identify Walter as lord of Saint-Valéry-sur-Somme. They probably left the West in the company of Robert of Normandy.

SOURCES: AA pp. 316, 422, 424; Orderic Vitalis, 5: 34, 58; Keats-Rohan, *Domesday People, 1*: 453-54.

130. Walter Mahomet

Galterius Mahomet or *Walterus cognomine Mahumeth* first appears in a royal charter of 1104 and is attested until 1115. In 1107/1108 he became lord or castellan of St Abraham (Hebron). In 1111 he accompanied the king on the expedition to join the Franks of the north in a campaign against Shaizar. From donations made by him he is known to have held land at Gemerosa and Sussia. His dual name suggests that Walter was a converted Muslim, as it was usual for converts to assume the Christian name of their baptismal sponsor.[52] A fragmentary anonymous account of the First Crusade relates that when Baldwin I led an expedition into Arabia in 1112 the city of Jerusalem was left in the charge of a certain *Machomus* [variant for *Mahomet*] *aliquando a Christianis captus adolescens baptismumque adeptus*, whose knowledge of Arabic enabled him to discover a Saracen plot to capture the city. It is tempting, therefore, to identify Machomus with Walter, whose status as lord of St Abraham would warrant the responsibility accorded to him in the fragmentary account.

SOURCES: RRH nos. 43, 52, 57, 76b, 80, 134; AA pp. 646-47, 682-83; RHC Occ. 3: 261-63; Mayer, 'Die Herrschaftsbildung in Hebron', p. 68-69.

131. Walter of Verviers

Walterius de Verveis is mentioned at the siege of Nicaea along with others known to have been in Godfrey's army. A possible place of origin would be Verviers (B, Liège, arr. Verviers) in the northern Ardennes, a placename whose early recorded forms were *Verviers* or *Vervies*.[53]

SOURCES: AA p. 317.

(Paris, 1930), no. 9, p. 18 (*de Domedardo*). Another, but less likely possibility (i.e. with fewer early attestations) would be the nearby Domart-sur-la-Luce.

[52] For example, the former Muslim in the service of Baldwin I, *in domini regis comitatu, eius familiaris et quasi cubicularius, quidam Balduinus* (WT XI.14, pp. 517-18). Another case of a dual name like Walter's can be found in 1141, when Roger II of Sicily confirmed a donation of the convert Roger Achmet: F. Chalandon, *Histoire de la domination normande en Italie et Sicilie*, 2 vols (Paris, 1907), 2: 107.

[53] Gysseling, *Woordenboek*, 1: 1007.

132. Warmund of Quierzy

Warmundus de Cerisi appears in a pancart of 1115 which records his donation of the casale of Lichorat to the abbey of Josaphat, and also witnessed a charter of *Joscelin, lord of Tiberias, in 1119. He was the son of *Ado of Quierzy (F, Aisne, arr. Laon) and like him appears to have been a vassal of Joscelin.

SOURCES: RRH nos. 80, 87.

133. Warner, count of Grez

Warnerus de Greis was one of Godfrey of Bouillon's most prominent associates during the crusade and the first year of the Frankish settlement. Albert of Aachen stresses his close relationship with the duke, mentioning him first after Godfrey and Baldwin in his list of departing crusaders, and describing him as *cognatus ipsius Ducis* and *vir nobilissimus et propinquus ejus*. Runciman refers to 'the Burgundian count, Warner of Gray',[54] but documentary evidence indicates that Warner was in fact a Lotharingian, undoubtedly from Grez-Doiceau (B, Brabant Wallon, arr. Nivelles). In late 1095 *Garnerus de Greis* sold the allod of Vaux (B, Liège, arr. Huy) which he had received in the division of his inheritance with his brother Henry (*allodium quoque in comitatu Hoyensi, quod Vallis dicitur, quod in divisione patrimonii cum fratre suo Henrico in partem susceperat*) to the church of Fosses in order to raise funds to go to Jerusalem with Duke Godfrey. Both Warner and Henry were present at the sale of the allods of Baisy and Genappe by Ida and Godfrey to the abbey of Nivelles, and Warner appeared immediately after Rainer, the advocate of Liège, among the *laici nobiles* who witnessed the purchase of the castle of Couvin by Bishop Otbert on 14 June 1096. It is therefore likely that Warner was a vassal of the bishop of Liège, particularly since Vaux was situated within the county of Huy, held from the prince-bishop by *Cono of Montaigu. In Palestine Warner apparently held lands in Samaria; he was the *comes Guarnerius* who gave the casale of Aschar (Askar) east of Nablus to the abbey of Josaphat. Along with *Robert of Apulia he was made commander of a force sent to attack Arsuf, which led to the tribute from the city being bestowed on Robert. Nevertheless, Warner clearly had the higher status of the two, and he went on to act as Godfrey's deputy during the monarch's last illness and to command the army sent to besiege Haifa. Warner's ties of kinship with the duke as well as his comital status, unique among Godfrey's retinue at this time, explain why he was accorded leadership of the household knights who mounted the coup in favour of Baldwin of Edessa after Godfrey's death. However, soon after seizing the

[54] Runciman, *History of the Crusades*, 1: 313.

Tower of David, Warner himself died on 22 July 1100. He was buried in the abbey of Josaphat.

SOURCES: AA pp. 299, 300, 301, 310, 383, 514, 520-24; 'Documents extraits du cartulaire du chapitre de Fosses', no. 1, pp. 396-98; Bormans, Schoolmeesters and Poncelet, *Cartulaire de l'église de Saint-Lambert*, 1, no. 29, pp. 46-48; MGH DD H.IV, no. 459; Miraeus, *Opera diplomatica et historica*, 1: 670-71; *Chanson d'Antioche*, line 1163 (*li quens Garniers de Griés*); RRH nos. 80, 134, 291; Mayer, *Bistümer, Klöster und Stifte*, pp. 342-48.

134. Wicher the Swabian

Wicherius Alemannus was in Godfrey's army during the march to Jerusalem. He was prominent in the sieges of Jerusalem in June-July 1099 and Haifa in 1099 and 1100. He was celebrated by numerous writers for deeds of valour such as killing a lion and cutting a Turk in two. Du Cange and Rey claimed him as a member of a Provençal family.[55] This cannot be the case, in light of descriptions applied to him, particularly by German and Lotharingian authors, who commemorated his deeds longest. As even the Rhinelander Albert of Aachen uses the surname *Alemannus* this term is probably meant in the particular sense of 'Swabian' rather than simply 'German'; this is confirmed by the poet Metellus of Tegernsee, who describes him as *Suevus* and *Fuldanus ... pauper minister*. He was therefore originally one of the *ministeriales* of the abbey of Fulda (Ger, Hessen, Kr. Fulda), which under its abbot Ruthard (1075-96) was strongly imperialist in sympathy.[56] He may have left the West on one of the earlier German expeditions, joining Godfrey between Nicaea and Jerusalem; in a passage referring to 1098, one of the manuscripts of Baldric of Dol describes him explicitly as *Guischerius ... miles ducis Godefridi*. He died of fever at Jaffa in August 1101. In the mid-twelfth century the German pilgrim John of Würzburg claimed to have seen his tomb in the church of the Holy Sepulchre, complaining that the epitaph of a Frenchman had been placed over the original. John may have been in error, since Albert of Aachen reports that Wicher was buried at Jaffa.

SOURCES: AA pp. 507, 522, 526, 531, 553; BD pp. 47, 50, 92; Robert the Monk, p. 867; Alberic of Troisfontaines, p. 811; Gilo of Paris, in *The Historia Vie Hierosolimitane of Gilo of Paris and a Second, Anonymous Author*, ed. C. W. Grocock and J. E. Siberry (Oxford, 1997), pp. 246-47; *Chanson d'Antioche*, lines 1021 (*Guigiers l'Alemans*), 1189, 3232, 3650 (*Hungiers l'Alemans*), 4443, 5096, 6381, 8690, 8669, 9000, 9080,

[55] Du Cange, *Les Familles d'Outremer*, p. 503.

[56] K. Lübeck, *Die Fuldaer Äbte und Furstäbte des Mittelalters. Ein geschichtlicher Überblick* (Fulda, 1952), pp. 110-12.

9129, 9200; John of Würzburg, p. 125; *Die Kaiserchronik eines Regensburger Geistlichen*, p. 382; Metellus von Tegernsee, pp. 125-26, 128.

135. William of Bures

Willelmus de Buris was in the kingdom of Jerusalem before 1115, and during the reign of Baldwin I he and his brother Godfrey appear to have been rear-vassals of Joscelin of Courtenay in Tiberias, although the two brothers were important enough to command separate divisions of Joscelin's army during the great raid across the Jordan in 1119, while William certainly had vassals of his own. Pirie-Gordon claimed William was a Norman although he gave no evidence for this assertion,[57] a claim which can be easily dismissed since Albert of Aachen gives the brothers' place of origin as *Burs et de terra civitatis Parisius*, now Bures-sur-Yvette (F, Essonne, arr. Palaiseau) south-west of Paris. Bures formed part of the lordship of Gometz-la-Châtel; towards the end of the eleventh century Hodierna, daughter and heiress of William of Gometz, married Guy I of Montlhéry, and the lordship passed to their son Guy the Red of Rochefort, seneschal of France. These connections explain the appearance of William as vassal of *Joscelin of Courtenay, son of Hodierna's daughter Isabella. When Joscelin succeeded Baldwin II as count of Edessa, William was granted Tiberias. This rise to the tenure of the kingdom's greatest fief seems to be another reflex of the wide-ranging Montlhéry-Courtenay-Le Puiset-Rethel family network, as Baldwin was another grandson of Guy and Hodierna. William was very much a favourite of Baldwin II's regime, becoming constable and regent for the captive king in 1123 in succession to *Eustace I Granarius. In 1128-29 he was entrusted with the mission to select a husband in France for Baldwin's daughter and heiress Melisende. He must have died after 1 February 1147, his last documented appearance.

SOURCES: RRH nos. 79, 80, 87, 89, 90, 92, 93, 102, 115, 131, 137c, 142, 244; AA pp. 710-12; FC III.22, pp. 674-75; WT XIII.24, pp. 618-19; Marquis d'Albon, *Cartulaire general de l'Ordre du Temple* (Paris, 1913-22), 1, nos. 8, 12; Lair, 'Histoire de la seigneurie de Bures', pp. 187-97; Rheinheimer, *Das Kreuzfahrerfürstentum Galiläa*, pp. 46-51; H. E. Mayer, 'The Crusader Principality of Galilee between Saint-Omer and Bures-sur-Yvette', in *Itinéraires d'Orient: Hommages à Claude Cahen* (Bures-sur-Yvette, 1994), pp. 157-67.

136. William, count of Dülük

Matthew of Edessa records that a William, count of Dülük (*Tulupa*) in northern Syria, was killed in battle in 1101/1102 while fighting for Baldwin I of Edessa. He had a surname which transliterates from Armenian as *Sancawel*

[57] Pirie-Gordon, 'The Reigning Princes of Galilee', pp. 450-51.

or *Santzavel*; since William was obviously a Frank this may be an Armenian rendering of a French name. Among the so-called People's Crusades there was family group led by one Walter *de Pexeio*, whose surname the narrative sources render variously as *Senzavohir* or *Sine Habere*. It is likely that the surname relates to Boissy-Sans-Avoir (F, Yvelines, arr. Rambouillet), about forty km west of Paris. In this case William of Dülük would be identical with Walter's documented brother William; he travelled east with Walter and Peter the Hermit, and was involved in the defeats of Peter's troops near Kibotos in Bithynia in September/October 1096. Thereafter, presumably having lost arms and baggage, he joined Godfrey and Baldwin, and was given a substantial lordship in the county of Edessa.

SOURCES: Matthew of Edessa, ed. Dostourian, p. 335; Orderic Vitalis, 5: 28; AA pp. 274, 286; BD p. 20; Murray, 'Walther Duke of Teck', pp. 35-54.

137. William of Normandy

In August 1108 a major Frankish raid into Damascene territory was led by one *Wilhelmum ... filium Roberti Normannorum*, who must be identical with the *Willelmus filius comitis* who witnessed a royal charter (RRH no. 52) in the same year. Runciman mistakenly identifies him with William Clito, son of Robert Curthose, duke of Normandy, and Sibylla of Conversano. However, at this time Clito, who was still a boy, was at the court of his kinsman Baldwin VII of Flanders, where he had been sent after the capture of his father by Henry I of England in 1106. When Baldwin's successor Charles the Good was murdered, Clito himself became a claimant to the county of Flanders and was killed, still a young man, at the siege of Aalst in 1128.[58] The William who appears in Outremer was actually an illegitimate son of Robert Curthose born during his exile in France. William and his brother Richard were acknowledged by Robert after their mother, formerly a priest's concubine, underwent a judicial ordeal to prove paternity. When Curthose was defeated by Henry I of England in 1106 William left for Jerusalem. He seems to have served Baldwin I as a military commander, but was not installed as lord of Tiberias, as was assumed by Pirie-Gordon.[59] By 1111 William had become lord of the city of Tortosa in the county of Tripoli.

SOURCES: AA p. 653, 682 (*Willelmus ... filius comitis Nortmanorum, dominium habens civitatis Tortosae*); RRH no. 52; Orderic Vitalis 5: 282; Rheinheimer, *Das Kreuzfahrerfürstentum Galiläa*, pp. 43-44.

---

[58] Runciman, *History of the Crusades*, 2: 97; Hermann of Tournai, *De restauratione s. Martini Tornacensis*, MGH SS 14: 284.

[59] Pirie-Gordon, 'The Reigning Princes of Galilee', p. 448.

138. William of Tincques

Guillelmus de Tenches, known only from a donation to the Hospital, possibly came from Tincques (F, Pas-de-Calais, arr. Arras) in Flanders which appeared in the forms *Tenches*, *Tenkes* and *Tenques* before 1226.[60]

SOURCES: RRH no. 57.

139. William *de Wanges*

Willelmus de Wanges, miles gloriosus et nobilis was killed at the siege of Tyre in 1111.

SOURCES: AA p. 691.

140. Wirich the Butler

The *Wiricus pincerna Ducis* who belonged to Godfrey's household in July 1100 is also described with the adjective *Flandriense* by Albert of Aachen. It is thus likely that he was originally in the army of Robert II of Flanders and only entered Godfrey's service in the course of the crusade. He fought at the siege of Haifa in June-July 1100.

SOURCES: AA pp. 522, 526.

---

[60] Gysseling, *Woordenboek*, 2: 969.

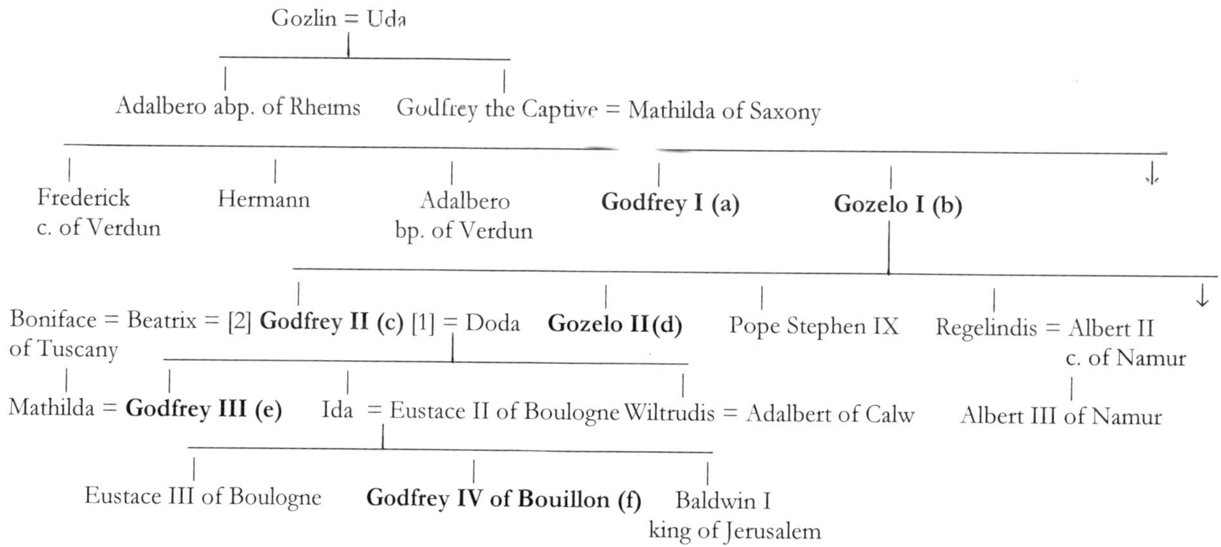

Bold = dukes of Lower and/or Upper Lotharingia. Tenures as follows:
(a) Lower Lotharingia 1012-23 (b) Upper and Lower Lotharingia 1023-44 (c) Upper Lotharingia 1044-46, Lower Lotharingia 1065-69 (d) Lower Lotharingia 1044-46 (e) Lower Lotharingia 1069-76 (f) Lower Lotharingia 1087-1100

Genealogical Table 1. The Ardennes-Bouillon Dynasty (simplified)

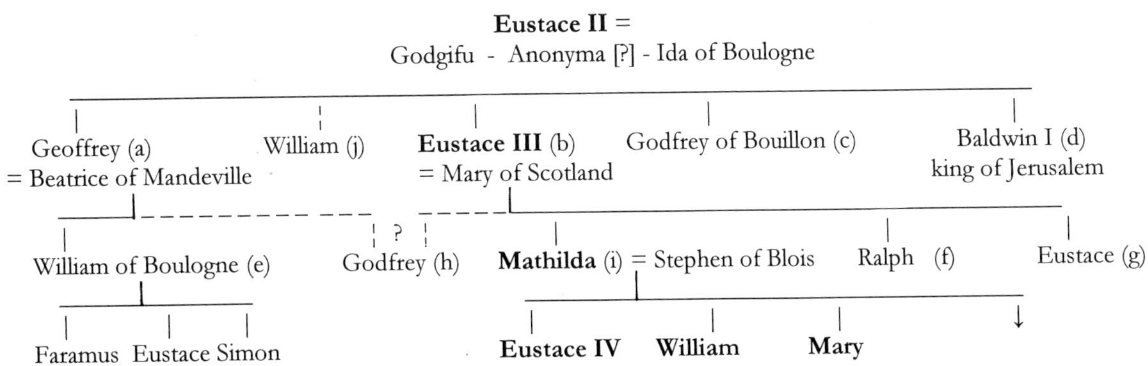

Bold = counts and countesses of Boulogne
Broken lines denote conjectural descent

Letters after each name refer to Appendix A, 'The Descendants of Eustace II of Boulogne'.

Genealogical Table 2. The Descendants of Eustace II of Boulogne

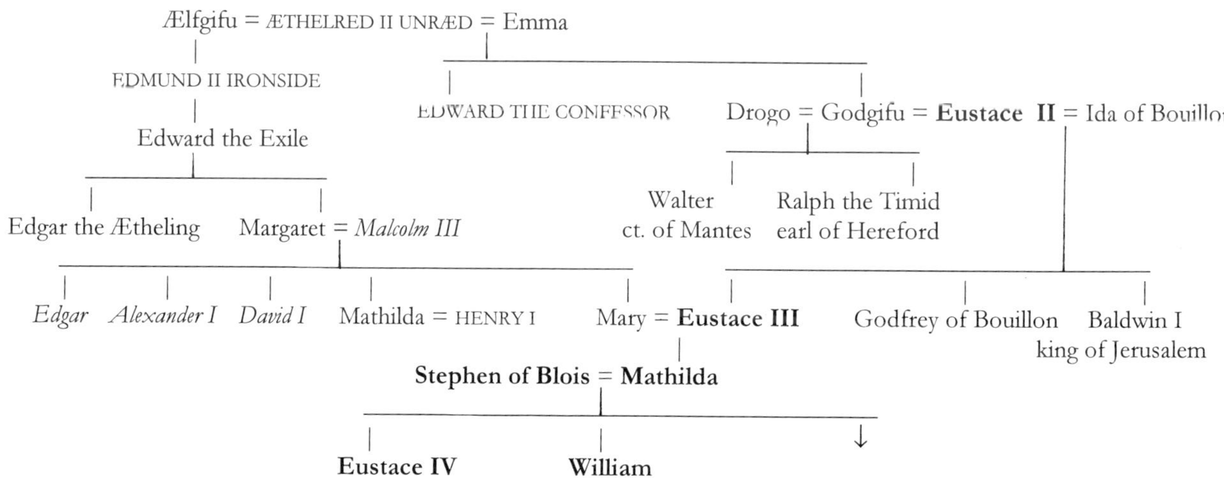

Bold = counts and countesses of Boulogne
Italic = kings of Scotland
CAPITALS = kings of England

Genealogical Table 3.
The Counts of Boulogne and the Kings of England and Scotland

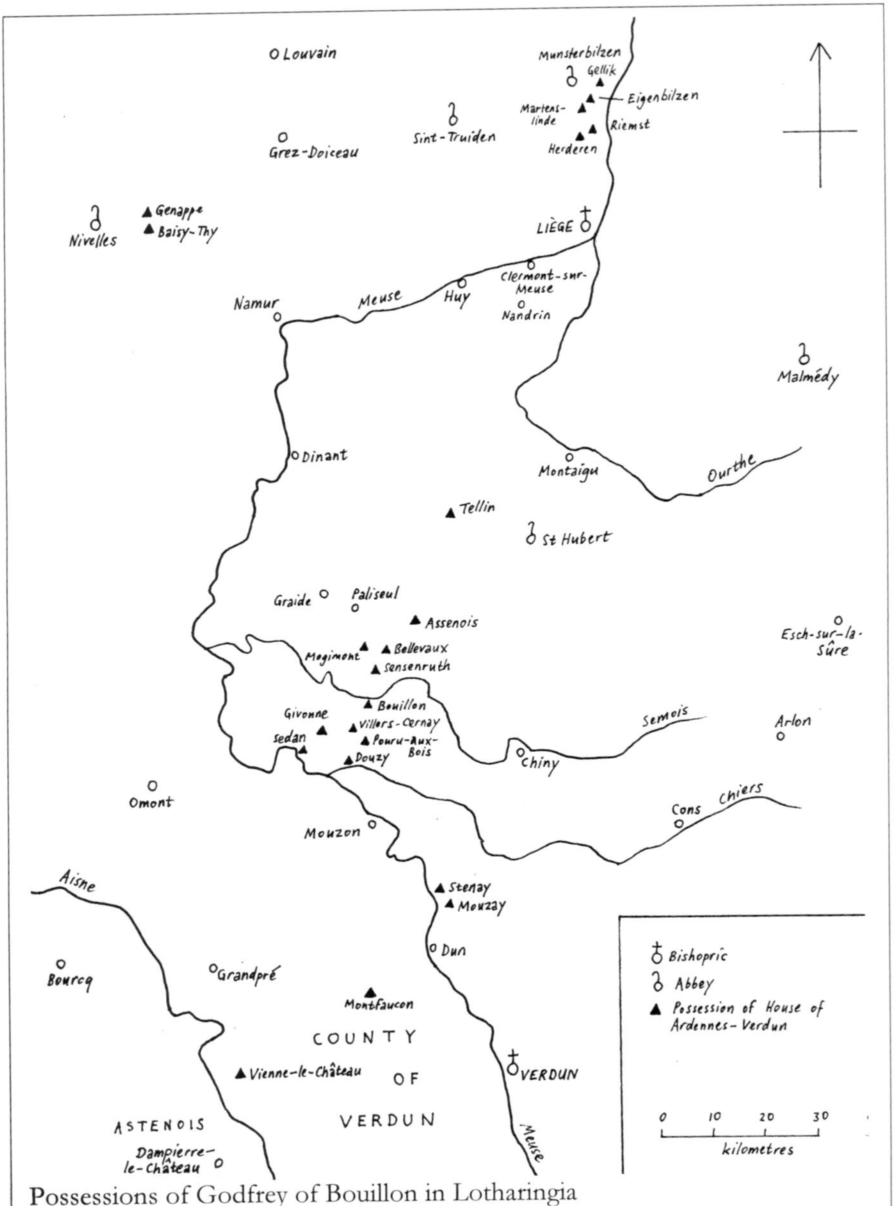

Possessions of Godfrey of Bouillon in Lotharingia

Bibliography

Manuscript Sources

Arlon, Archives de l'Etat, fonds Saint-Hubert 10.A.4.

Stuttgart, Württembergische Landesbibliothek, Cod. Don. 580 and 581.

Printed Primary Sources

Achard of Arrouaise, 'Poem on the Templum Domini', *Archives de l'Orient latin* 1 (1881), 562-79.

Adam of Bremen, 'Gesta Hammaburgensis ecclesiae pontificum', in *Quellen des 9. und 11. Jahrhunderts zur Geschichte der hamburgischen Kirche und des Reiches*, ed. Werner Trillmich and Rudolf Buchner, Freiherr vom Stein-Gedächtnisausgabe 11 (Darmstadt, 1961), pp. 137-496.

Aimond, Charles, 'La nécrologe de la cathédrale de Verdun', *JGLGA* 21 (1909), 132-314.

Alberic of Troisfontaines, *Chronica*, ed. P. Scheffer-Boichorst, MGH SS 23: 631-950.

Albert of Aachen, *Alberti Aquensis Historia Hierosolymitana*, RHC Occ. 4: 265-713.

d'Albon, Marquis, *Cartulaire général de l'ordre du Temple* (Paris, 1913-22).

Anglo-Saxon Chronicle, ed. B. Thorpe, Rolls Series 23, 2 vols (London, 1861).

Anna Comnena, *The Alexiad of Anna Comnena*, trans. E. R. A. Sewter (Harmondsworth, 1969).

Anne Comnène, *Alexiade*, ed. Bernard Leib, 4 vols (Paris, 1937-76).

Annales Altahenses maiores, ed. W. von Giesebrecht, MGH SS 20: 772-824.

Annales Laubienses, ed. G. Pertz, MGH SS 4: 8-28.

Annales Mosomagenses, ed. Georg Heinrich Pertz, MGH SS 3: 160-66.

Annales Neresheimenses, ed. O. Abel, MGH SS 10: 20-34.

Annales s. Iacobi Leodiensis, ed. L. C. Bethmann, MGH SS 16: 632-50.

Annals s. Vitoni Virdunensis, ed. Georg Waitz, MGH SS 10, 525-30.

Anne Comnène, Alexiade, trans. Bernard Leib, 4 vols (Paris, 1937-76).

Anonymous Syriac Chronicle, 'The First and Second Crusades from an Anonymous Syriac Chronicle', ed. and trans. A. S. Tritton and Hamilton A. R. Gibb, *Journal of the Royal Asiatic Society* 92 (1933), 69-102, 273-306.

Anselm, *Gesta episcoporum Leodiensium*, ed. Rudolf Köpke, MGH SS 7: 189-234.

Anselm of Canterbury, *S. Anselmi Cantuarensis archiepiscopi opera*, ed. F. S. Schmitt (Edinburgh, 1949).

Baldric of Dol, *Baldrici episcopi Dolensis Historia Jerosolimitana*, RHC Occ. 4: 1-111.

Bar Hebraeus, *The Chronography of Gregory Abu'l Faraj ... Commonly Known as Bar Hebraeus*, trans. Ernest A. Wallis Budge, 2 vols (London, 1932).

Bartolf of Nangis, *Gesta Francorum expugnantium Iherusalem*, RHC Occ. 3: 492-543.

Benzo of Alba, *Benzonis episcopi Albensis Ad Heinricum IV imperatorem libri VII*, ed. K. Pertz, MGH SS 11: 591-681.

Bernard Maragone, *Annales Pisani*, ed. C. Pertz, MGH SS 19: 236-266.

Bernold of St Blasien, *Chronicon*, ed. Georg Heinrich Pertz, MGH SS 5: 385-467.

Bloch, Hermann, 'Die älteren Urkunden des Klosters S. Vanne zu Verdun', *JGLGA* 10 (1898), 338-449, 14 (1902), 48-150.

Bormans, Stanislas, E. Schoolmeesters and Edouard Poncelet, *Cartulaire de l'église de Saint-Lambert à Liège*, 6 vols (Brussels, 1893-1933).

Bresc-Bautier, Geneviève, *Le Cartulaire du chapitre du Saint-Sépulcre de Jérusalem*, Documents relatifs à l'histoire des croisades publiés par l'Académie des Inscriptions et Belles-Lettres 15 (Paris, 1984).

Brunel, Clovis, *Recueil des actes des comtes de Pontieu [sic] 1026-1279* (Paris, 1930).

Calixtus II, *Epistolae et privilegia*, PL 163.

Cartulaire du prieuré de Nôtre-Dame de Longpont (Lyon, 1879).

Cartularium Monasterii Sancti Johannis Baptiste de Colecestria, ed. Stuart A. More, 2 vols (London, 1897).

The Cartulary of the Knights of St John of Jerusalem in England: Secunda Camera, ed. Michael Gervers (Oxford, 1982).

La Chanson d'Antioche. Edition du texte d'après la version ancienne, ed. Suzanne Duparc-Quioc, Documents relatifs à l'histoire des croisades publiés par l'Académie des Inscriptions et Belles-Lettres 11 (Paris, 1976).

Chibnall, Marjorie, *Select Documents of the English Lands of the Abbey of Bec*, Camden Third Series 73 (London, 1951).

'Chronicle of Solomon bar Simson', in Eidelberg, *Chronicles*, pp. 15-72.

Chronicon Affligemense, ed. Georg Heinrich Pertz, MGH SS 9: 407-17.

Chronicon monasterii Watinensis, ed. Oswald Holder-Egger, MGH SS 14: 161-175.

Chronik der Grafen von Zimmern: Handschriften 580 und 581 der Fürstlich Fürstenbergischen Hofbibliothek Donaueschingen, ed. Hansmartin Decker-Hauff *et al.*, 7 vols (Konstanz, 1964-)

Chronique de Saint-Hubert dite Cantatorium, ed. Karl Hanquet (Brussels, 1906).

Concilium Remense, in Recueil des Historiens des Gaules et de la France 11, ed. D. Bouquet (Paris, 1878).

Daris, Joseph, *Notices historiques sur les églises du diocèse de Liège*, 17 vols (Liège, 1867-99).

Delaborde, Henri-François, *Chartes de Terre Sainte provenant de l'abbaye de N.-D. de Josaphat*, Bibliothèque des Ecoles Françaises d'Athènes et de Rome 19 (Paris, 1880).

Delaville Le Roulx, Joseph, *Cartulaire générale de l'Ordre des Hospitaliers de Saint-Jean de Jérusalem, 1100-1310*, 4 vols (Paris, 1894-1906).

——, 'Chartes de Terre-Sainte', *ROL* 11 (1905-8), 181-91.

Depoin, Joseph, *Recueil de Chartes et documents de Saint-Martin-des-Champs, monastère parisien*, 5 vols (Paris, 1912-21).

De Sandoli, Sabino, *Corpus inscriptionum crucesignatorum Terrae Sanctae 1099-1291* (Jerusalem, 1974).

Desjardins, G., *Cartulaire de l'abbaye de Conques en Rouergue* (Paris, 1879).

Despy, Georges, 'Un fragment d'une *cronica monasterii Sancti Huberti in Ardenna*', *Bulletin de la Commission Royale d'Histoire* 121 (1956), 171-73.

'Documents extraits du cartulaire du chapitre de Fosses', *Analectes pour servir à l'histoire ecclésiastique de la Belgique* 4 (1867), 396-98.

Duchet, Th., and A. Giry, *Cartulaire de l'église de Térouane* [*sic*] (Saint-Omer, 1881).

Eidelberg, Shlomo, *The Jews and the Crusaders: The Hebrew Chronicles of the First and Second Crusades* (Madison, 1977).

Ekkehard of Aura, *Frutolfs und Ekkehards Chroniken und die Anonyme Kaiserchronik. Frutolfi et Ekkehardi Chronica necnon Anonymi Chronica Imperatorum*, ed. and trans. Franz-Josef Schmale and Irene Schmale-Ott, Freiherr vom Stein-Gedächtnis-ausgabe 15 (Darmstadt, 1972).

Evrard, Jean-Pol, 'Les actes des évêques de Verdun jusqu'à 1156' (unpublished doctoral dissertation, Univ. of Nancy, 1973).

Ex continuatione historii Aimonii monachi Floriacensis, Recueil des Historiens des Gaules et de la France 11, ed. D. Bouquet (Paris, 1876), 274-76.

Falco of Benevento, *Chronicon Beneventanum*, ed. E. D'Angelo (Florence, 1998).

Fragment of a History of the Crusades, RHC Occ. 4: 261-263.

Fragmenta necrologii Neresheimensis, ed. Franz Ludwig Baumann, MGH Necrologii Germaniae 1 (Berlin, 1888), 95-98.

Fulcher of Chartres, *A History of the Expedition to Jerusalem 1095-1127*, trans. Frances S. Ryan, ed. Harold S. Fink (Knoxville, 1960).

Fulcher of Chartres, *Fulcheri Carnotensis Historia Hierosolymitana (1095-1127)*, ed. Heinrich Hagenmeyer (Heidelberg, 1913).

Fundatio ecclesiae s. Albani Namucensis, ed. Oswald Holder-Egger, MGH SS 15: 962-64

Galbert of Bruges, *The Murder of Charles the Good, Count of Flanders*, trans. James B. Ross (New York, 1960).

Galbertus notarius Brugensis, *De multro, traditione, et occisione gloriosi Karoli comitis Flandriarum*, ed. Jeff Rider, Corpus Christianorum, Continuatio Mediaevalis 131 (Turnhout, 1994).

Genealogia comitum Buloniensium, ed. L. Bethmann, MGH SS 9: 300-1.

Genealogia ex stirpe s. Arnulfi descendentium Mettensis, ed. I. Heller, MGH SS 25: 381-84.

Genealogiae scriptoris Fusniacensis, ed. Georg Waitz, MGH SS 13: 251-56.

Gesta abbatum Lobbiensium, ed. W. Arndt, MGH SS 21: 307-33.

Gesta episcoporum Cameracensium, ed. L. C. Bethmann, MGH SS 7: 393-489.

Gesta Francorum et aliorum Hierosolimitanorum (The Deeds of the Franks and Other Pilgrims to Jerusalem), ed. and trans. Rosalind Hill (London, 1962).

Gesta Treverorum, ed. Georg Waitz, MGH SS 8: 111-200.

Gesta triumphalia per Pisanos facta, ed. L. A. Muratori, Rerum Italiarum Scriptores 6/2 (Bologna, n.d.), 89-96.

Gibbs, Marion, *Early Charters of the Cathedral Church of St. Paul, London*, Camden Third Series, 58 (London, 1939).

Giles of Orval, *Aegidii Aureaevallensis Gesta episcoporum Leodiensium*, ed. J. Heller, MGH SS 25: 1-129.

Giselbert of Mons, *Chronicon Hanoniense*, ed. Léon Vanderkindere (Brussels, 1904).

Godefridi Bullionis Epistolae ac Diplomata, PL 155: 389-98.

Grosdidier de Matons, Marcel, *Catalogue des actes des comtes de Bar 1022-1239* (Paris, 1922).

Guérard, Benjamin, *Cartulaire de Saint-Bertin* (Paris, 1840).

Guibert of Nogent, *Historia quae dicitur Gesta Dei per Francos*, RHC Occ. 4: 113-263.

Guillaume de Tyr, *Chronique*, ed. Robert B. C. Huygens, Corpus Christianorum, Continuatio Mediaevalis 63, 2 vols (Turnhout, 1986).

Gysseling, Maurits, and A. C. F. Koch, *Diplomata Belgica ante annum millesimum centesimum scripta*, 2 vols (Brussels, 1950).

Hagenmeyer, Heinrich, *Epistulae et chartae ad historiam primi belli sacrae spectantes: Die Kreuzzugsbriefe aus den Jahren 1088-1100* (Innsbruck, 1901).

Haigneré, Daniel, *Les chartes de St Bertin*, 2 vols (Saint-Omer, 1886).

Haverkamp, Eva, 'Hebräische Berichte über die Judenverfolgungen während des Ersten Kreuzzuges' (unpublished doctoral thesis, Univ. of Konstanz, 1999).

Henry of Huntingdon, *Historia Anglorum*, Rolls Series 74 (London, 1879).

D'Herbomez, A., *Cartulaire de l'abbaye de Gorze: Ms. 826 de la Bibliothèque de Metz* (Paris, 1898).

Herman of Tournai, *De restauratione monasterii s. Martini Tornacensis*, ed. Georg Waitz, MGH SS 14: 274-317.

Hermann of Reichenau, *Chronicon*, ed. Georg Heinrich Pertz, MGH SS 5: 67-133.

Hiestand, Rudolf, 'Zwei unbekannte Diplome der lateinischen Könige von Jerusalem aus Lucca', *Quellen und Forschungen aus italienischen Archiven und Bibliotheken* 50 (1971), 1-57.

The Historia Vie Hierosolimitane of Gilo of Paris and a Second, Anonymous Author, ed. C. W. Grocock and J. E. Siberry (Oxford, 1997)

Ibn al-Athīr, *Extrait de la chronique intitulée Kamel-Altevarykh par Ibn-Alatyr*, RHC Or. 1: 187-800, 2: 1-180.

Ibn al-Qalānisī, *The Damascus Chronicle of the Crusades, extracted and translated from the Chronicle of Ibn al-Qalanisi*, trans. Hamilton A. R. Gibb, University of London Historical Series 5 (London, 1932).

Imperiale di Sant'Angelo, C., *Codice Diplomatico della Repubblica di Genova*, 1 (Rome, 1936).

Indiculus loricatorum, in MGH Const. 1, ed. Ludwig Weiland (Hannover, 1893), pp. 632-33.

Infeodatio comitatus Hanoniense, in MGH Const. 1, ed. Ludwig Weiland (Hannover, 1893), 649-50.

John of Ibelin, *Livre*, RHC Lois I

Die Kaiserchronik eines Regensburger Geistlichen, ed. Edward Schröder, MGH Deutsche Chroniken 1/1 (Hannover, 1892), 1-392.

Kohler, Ch., 'Chartes de l'abbaye de Notre-Dame de la Vallée de Josaphat (1108-1291)', *ROL* 7 (1900), 108-222.

Kurth, Godefroid, *Chartes de l'abbaye de St Hubert en Ardenne* (Brussels, 1903-).

Lambert of Ardres, *Lamberti Ardensis Historia comitum Ghisnensium et Ardensium dominorum*, ed. I. Heller, MGH SS 24: 550-642.

Lambert of Hersfeld, *Annales*, ed. L. F. Hesse, MGH SS 5: 134-263.

Laurence of Liège, *Laurentii de Leodio Gesta episcoporum Virdunensium et abbatum s. Vitoni*, ed. Georg Waitz, MGH SS 10: 486-516.

Le Glay, A. J. G., *Revue des opera diplomatica de Miraeus* (Brussels, 1856)

Lignages d'Outremer, RHC Lois 2: 435-74.

Longnon, Auguste, *Documents relatifs au comté de Champagne et de Brie (1172-1361)*, 3 vols (Paris, 1901-14).

Luchaire, Achille, *Louis le Gros. Annales de son vie et de son règne (1081-1137)* (Paris, 1890).

Mabille, E., *Cartulaire de Marmoutier pour le Dunois* (Châteaudun, 1874).

Marsy, Comte de, 'Fragment d'un cartulaire de l'ordre de Saint-Lazare en Terre-Sainte', *Archives de l'Orient latin* 2 (1884), 121-57.

Matthew of Edessa, *Chronicle*, trans. Ara. E. Dostourian, 2 vols (Ann Arbor, 1972).

Merlet, L., and L. Jarry, *Cartulaire de l'abbaye de la Madeleine* (Châteaudun, 1896).

Metellus von Tegernsee, *Expeditio Hierosolymitana*, ed. Peter C. Jacobsen, Quellen und Untersuchungen zur lateinischen Philologie des Mittelalters 6 (Stuttgart, 1982).

Michael of Marash, 'Note to the Syriac Breviary', trans. Abbé Martin, *Journal Asiatique*, ser. 8, 13 (1888), 39-79.

Michael the Syrian, *Chronique de Michel le Syrien, patriarche jacobite d'Antioche (1166-1199)*, ed. and trans. J-B. Chabot, 4 vols (Paris, 1899-1910).

Miraeus, Aubraeus, *Opera diplomatica et historica*, ed. Jean-François Foppens, 4 vols (Brussels, 1723-48).

Monumenta Germaniae Historica, Diplomata Regum et Imperatorum Germaniae (Hannover, 1879-): 1. *Conradi I, Heinrici I, et Ottonis I Diplomata*, ed. Theodor Sickel (1879-84). 2/1. *Ottonis II Diplomata*, ed. Theodor Sickel (1888). 2/2. *Ottonis III Diplomata,* ed. Theodor Sickel (1893). 3. *Heinrici II et Arduini Diplomata*, ed. Harry Bresslau *et al.* (1900-3). 4. *Conradi II Diplomata*, ed. Harry Bresslau *et al.* (1909). 5. *Heinrici III Diplomata*, ed. Harry Bresslau and Paul Kehr (1926-31). 6. *Heinrici IV Diplomata*, ed. Dietrich von Gladiss and Alfred Gawlik (1941-78). 8. *Lotharii III Diplomata nec non Richenzae Imperatricis Placita*, ed. Emil von Ottenthal and Hans Hirsch (1927). 11. *Friderici I Diplomata*, ed. Heinrich Appelt *et al.* (1975-90)

Monumenta s. Bavonis Gandavensis minora, ed. Oswald Holder-Egger, MGH SS 15: 589-620.

'Narrative of the Old Persecutions', in Eidelberg, *Chronicles*, pp. 95-116.

Newman, W. M., *Les seigneurs de Nesle en Picardie*, 2 vols (Philadelphia, 1971).

Orderic Vitalis, *The Ecclesiastical History of Orderic Vitalis*, ed. and trans. Marjorie Chibnall, 6 vols (Oxford, 1969-81).

Orderici Vitalis Anglicenae coenobii Uticensis monachi Historiae Ecclesiasticae, ed. Auguste Le Prevost, 5 vols (Paris, 1838-55).

Ordines für die Weihe und Krönung des Kaisers und der Kaiserin, ed. Reinhard Elze, MGH Fontes iuris Germanici antiqui 9 (Hannover, 1960).

Otto von Freising, *Chronica sive historia de duabus civitatis. Chronik oder Die Geschichte der zwei Staaten*, ed. Walther Lammers, trans. Adolf Schmidt, Freiherr vom Stein-Gedächtnisausgabe 16 (Darmstadt, 1960).

Peregrinationes Tres: Saewulf, John of Würzburg, Theodericus, ed. Robert B. C. Huygens, Corpus Christianorum, Continuatio Mediaevalis 139 (Turnhout, 1994).

Peter Tudebode, *Petri Tudebodi seu Tudebovis sacerdotis Sivracensis historia de Hierosolymitano itinere*, RHC Occ. 3: 1-117.

Prou, Maurice, *Recueil des actes de Philippe Ier, roi de France (1059-1108)*, Chartes et documents relatifs à l'histoire de France 1 (Paris, 1908).

Quantin, Maximilien, *Cartulaire général de l'Yonne*, 3 vols (Auxerre, 1854-73).

Radulph of Caen, *Gesta Tancredi in expeditione Hierosolymitana ... auctore Radulfo Cadomensi*, RHC Occ. 3: 587-716.

Ralph of Saint-Trond, *Gesta abbatum Trudonensium*, ed. R. Köpke, MGH SS 10: 215-317.

Raymond of Aguilers, *Raimundi de Aguilers canonici Podiensis historia Francorum qui ceperunt Iherusalem*, RHC Occ. 3: 231-309.

Regesta Regum Anglo-Normannorum, 1066-1154, 1: Regesta Willelmi Conquestoris et Willelmi Rufi, 1066-1100, ed. H. W. C. Davis and R. J. Whitwell (Oxford, 1913).

Regesta Regum Anglo-Normannorum, 1066-1154, 2: Regesta Henrici Primi, 1100-1135, ed. Charles Johnson and H. A. Cronne (Oxford, 1956).

Regesta Regum Anglo-Normannorum: The Acta of William I (1066-1083), ed. David Bates (Oxford, 1998).

Renier of St Laurence, *Triumphale Bulonicum*, ed. W. Arndt, MGH SS 20: 583-92.

Robert the Monk, *Roberti Monachi historia Iherosolimitana*, RHC Occ. 3: 717-882.

Robert, G., *Documents relatifs au comté de Porcien* (Monaco, 1935).

Röhricht, Reinhold, *Regesta Regni Hierosolymitani* (Innsbruck, 1893), and *Additamentum* (Innsbruck, 1904).

Rosières, François de, *Stemmatum Lotharingiae ac Barri ducum* (Paris, 1580).

Rousseau, Félix, *Actes des comtes de Namur de la première race 946-1146*, Commission royale d'histoire: Recueil des actes des princes belges (Brussels, 1937).

Saige, Gustave and Henri Lacaille and L.-H. Labande, *Trésor des chartes du comté de Rethel*, 5 vols (Monaco, 1902-16).

Saxo Annalista, ed. Georg Waitz, MGH SS 6: 542-777.

Self and Society in Medieval France: The Memoirs of Abbot Guibert of Nogent (1064?-1125), ed. J. F. Benton (New York, 1970).

Sigebert of Gembloux, *Chronica*, ed. L. C. Bethmann, MGH SS 6: 300-74.

Suger, *Vie de Louis le Gros*, ed. and trans. Henri Waquet, Les Classiques de l'histoire de France au Moyen Age 11 (Paris, 1964).

Suger, *The Deeds of Louis the Fat*, trans. Richard Cusimano and John Moorhead (Washington, 1992).

Tafel, G. L., and G. M. Thomas, *Urkunden zur älteren Handels- und Staatsgeschichte der Republik Venedig mit besonderer Berücksichtigung auf Byzanz und die Levante*, Fontes rerum Austriacum, 2. Abteilung 12-14, 3 vols (Vienna, 1856-57).

Thiofrid of Echternach, *Ex vita s. Willibrordi*, ed. L. Weiland, MGH SS 23: 13-30.

Tractatus de reliquiis s. Stephani Cluniacum delatis, RHC Occ. 5: 317-20.

Triumphus s. Lamberti Leodiensis de castro Bullonio, ed. W. Arndt, MGH SS 20: 497-511.

Triumphus s. Remacli de Malmundariensi coenobio, ed. W. Wattenbach, MGH SS 11: 433-61.

Tudebodus imitatus et continuatus, *Historia peregrinorum euntium Jerusolymam ad liberandum Sanctum Sepulcrum de potestate ethnicorum*, RHC Occ. 3: 165-230.

Vercauteren, Fernand, *Actes des comtes de Flandre 1071-1128*, Commission Royale d'Histoire: Recueil des actes des princes belges (Brussels, 1938).

Versus de viris illustribus dioecesis Tarvanensis qui in sacra fuere expeditione, in Charles Moeller, 'Les flamands du Ternois au royaume latin de Jérusalem', *Mélanges Paul Fredericq* (Brussels, 1903), pp. 189-202.

Vita Balderici episcopi Leodiensis, ed. Georg Heinrich Pertz, MGH SS 4: 724-38.

Vita Beatae Idae auctore monacho Wastensi coaevo, PL 155: 437-52.

Walter of Thérouanne, *Vita Karoli comitis Flandriae*, ed. Rudolf Köpke, MGH SS 12: 537-61.

Walter the Chancellor, *Galterii Cancelarii Bella Antiochena*, ed. Heinrich Hagenmeyer (Innsbruck, 1896).

Wauters, Alphonse, *Table chronologique des chartes et diplômes imprimés concernant l'histoire de la Belgique* (Brussels, 1866-).

Weigle, F., *Die Briefsammlung Gerberts von Reims*, MGH Briefe der deutschen Kaiserzeit 2 (Berlin, 1966).

William of Malmesbury, *De Gestis Regum Anglorum*, ed. William Stubbs, Rolls Series 90, 2 vols (London, 1887-89).

William of Malmesbury, *Gesta Regum Anglorum: The History of the English Kings*, ed. and trans. Roger A. B. Mynors, Rodney M. Thomson and Michael Winterbottom (Oxford, 1998).

William of Poitiers, *The Gesta Guillelmi of William of Poitiers*, ed. and trans. R. H. C. Davis and Marjorie Chibnall (Oxford, 1998).

Secondary Sources

Albrecht, Günter, *Das Münzwesen im niederlothringischen und friesischen Raum vom 10. bis zum beginnenden 12. Jahrhundert*, Numismatische Studien 6 (Hamburg, 1959).

Amouroux-Mourad, Monique, *Le comté d'Edesse, 1098-1150*, Institut français d'archéologie du Proche Orient: Bibliothèque archéologique et historique 128 (Paris, 1988).

Anckaer, Jan, 'Boudewijn van Heestert, een onbekend Vlaams kruisvaarder', *De Leiegouw* 40 (1998), 105-7.

Anderson, Freda, 'Uxor mea: The First Wife of the First William of Warenne', *Sussex Archaeological Collections* 130 (1992), 107-29.

Andressohn, John C., *The Ancestry and Life of Godfrey of Bouillon,* Indiana University Publications: Social Sciences Series 5 (Bloomington, 1947).

Appleby, John T., *The Troubled Reign of King Stephen* (London, 1969).

Arutyunova-Fidanyan [Arutjunova-Fidanjan], Viada A., 'The Ethno-Confessional Self-Awareness of Armenian Chalcedonians', *Revue des études arméniennes*, n.s. 21 (1988-89), 345-63.

Asbridge, Thomas, 'The Principality of Antioch and the Jabal as-Summaq', in *The First Crusade: Origins and Impact,* pp. 142-52.

Atlas of Israel, publ. Survey of Israel, Ministry of Labour (Jerusalem, 1970)

Aubé, Pierre, *Godefroy de Bouillon* (Paris, 1985).

Barlow, Frank, *Edward the Confessor* (London, 1970).

Barthélemy, Anatole de, 'Le comté d'Astenois et les comtes de Dampierre-le-Château', *Revue de Champagne et de Brie* 16 (1888), 401-16; 17 (1889), 177-91; 18 (1890), 801-7; 19 (1891), 691-99.

Bates, David, 'Lord Sudely's Ancestors: The Family of the Counts of Amiens, Valois, and the Vexin in France and England During the Eleventh Century', in *The Sudelys, Lords of Toddington*, ed. Robert Smith (London, 1987).

Baumgart, Hans, 'Studien zur Zimmerschen Chronik des Grafen Froben Christoph und zur Mainzer Bistumschronik des Grafen Wilhelm Werner von Zimmern' (unpublished doctoral thesis, Univ. of Freiburg, 1923).

Becker, Alfons, *Papst Urban II. (1088-1099*), Schriften der MGH 19, 2 vols (Stuttgart, 1964-88).

Bertholet, Jean, *Histoire ecclésiastique et civile du duché de Luxembourg et du comté de Chiny*, 8 vols (Luxembourg, 1743).

Beumann, Jutta, *Sigebert von Gembloux und der Traktat de investitura episcoporum*, Vorträge und Forschungen: Sonderband 20 (Sigmaringen, 1976).

Blumenthal, Uta-Renate, *The Investiture Controversy: Church and Monarchy from the Ninth to the Twelfth Century* (Philadelphia, 1988).

Boeren, Pieter Cornelis, 'Overzicht der dynastie van Wassenberg-Gelre en verwante geslachten gedurende de elfde eeuw', *Bijdragen en Mededelingen van de Vereeniging Gelre* 41 (1938), 1-23.

Boeren, Pieter Cornelis, *De oorsprong van Limburg en Gelre en enkele naburige heerschappijen* (Maastricht, 1938).

Boshof, Egon, 'Lothringen, Frankreich und das Reich in der Regierungszeit Heinrichs III', *Rheinische Vierteljahrsblätter* 42 (1978), 63-127.

Brandt, Coenraad D. J., *Kruisvarders naar Jeruzalem: Geschiedenis van de eerste kruistocht* (Utrecht, 1950).

Brassat, H., *Die Teilnahme der Friesen an den Kreuzzügen ultra mare vornehmlich im 12. Jahrhundert* (Berlin, 1970), pp. 17-32.

Breysig, Kurt, 'Gottfried von Bouillon vor dem Kreuzzuge', *Westdeutsche Zeitschrift für Geschichte und Kunst* 17 (1898), 169-201.

Bulst-Thiele, Marie-Luise, *Sacrae Domus Militiae Templi Hierosolymitani Magistri* (Göttingen, 1974).

Bur, Michel, *La formation du comté de Champagne 950-1150*, Mémoires des Annales de l'Est 54 (Nancy, 1977).

Calmet, Augustin, *Histoire de la Lorraine*, 3 vols (Nancy, 1728).

Caspar, E., *Roger II und die Gründung der Normannisch-Sicilischen Monarchie* (Innsbruck, 1904).

Cauchie, Alfred, *La querelle des investitures dans les diocèses de Liège et de Cambrai* (Louvain, 1890).

Chalandon, Ferdinand, *Histoire de la domination normande en Italie et Sicilie*, 2 vols (Paris, 1907).

——, *Histoire de la première croisade jusqu'à l'élection de Godefroi de Bouillon* (Paris, 1925).

Charles, J. L., *La ville de Saint-Trond en Moyen Age* (Paris, 1965).

Chazan, Robert, *European Jewry and the First Crusade* (Berkeley, 1987).

Chestret de Haneffe, Baron, 'Les premiers seigneurs d'Esch-sur-la-Sûre', *L'Ancien Pays de Looz* 4 (1900), 47-48.

Choux, Jacques, *Recherches sur le diocèse de Toul au temps de la réforme grégorienne: L'episcopat de Pibon (1069-1107)* (Nancy, 1952).

Cognasso, Francesco, *La genesi delle crociate* (Torino, 1934).

Cohen, Jeremy, 'The Hebrew Crusade Chronicles in Their Christian Cultural Context', in *Juden und Christen zur Zeit der Kreuzzüge*, pp. 17-34.

Le Concile de Clermont de 1095 et l'appel à la croisade: Actes du Colloque Universitaire International de Clermont-Ferrand (23-25 juin 1995), Collection de l'Ecole française de Rome 236 (Rome, 1997).

Cowdrey, H. E. John, 'The Latin Kingdom of Jerusalem', *History* 57 (1972), 228-34.

——, 'Pope Urban II and the Idea of Crusade', *Studi Medievali*, ser.3, 36 (1995), 721-42.

Crouch, David, *The Reign of King Stephen, 1135-1154* (Harlow, 2000).

Crusade and Settlement: Papers Read at the First Conference of the Society for the Study of the Crusades and the Latin East and presented to R.C. Smail, ed. Peter W. Edbury (Cardiff, 1985).

The Crusades and Their Sources: Essays Presented to Bernard Hamilton, ed. John France and William G. Zajac (Aldershot, 1998).

Dace, Richard, 'Bertran de Verdun: Royal Service, Land, and Family in the Late Twelfth Century', *Medieval Prosopography* 20 (1999), 75-93.

Dajani-Shakeel, Hadia, 'Diplomatic Relations Between Muslim and Frankish Rulers, 1097-1153 A.D.', in *Crusaders and Muslims in Twelfth-Century Syria*, ed. Maya Shatzmiller, The Medieval Mediterranean 1 (Leiden, 1993), pp. 190-215.

Danzer, André, 'La querelle des investitures dans les évêchés de Metz, Toul, et Verdun de 1075 au 1122', *Annales de l'Est* 16 (1902), 85-100.

Dauzat, A., and Ch. Rostaing, *Dictionnaire etymologique de noms de lieux en France* (Paris, 1978).

David, Charles W., *Robert Curthose, Duke of Normandy*, Harvard Historical Studies 25 (Cambridge, Mass., 1920).

Davis, R. H. C., *King Stephen 1135-1154,* 3rd edn (London, 1990).

Deprez, René, 'La politique castrale dans la principauté de Liège du Xe au XIVe siècle', *Le Moyen Age* 65 (1959), 501-38.

Despy, Georges, 'La Formation de la "Terre de Hierges" du XIe au XVe siècle', *PSHIGDL* 102 (1986), 13-30.

——, 'Godefroid de Bouillon, mythes et réalités', *Academie Royale de Belgique, Bulletin de la Classe des Lettres et des Sciences morales et politiques*, ser.5, 71 (1985), 249-75.

——, 'La date de l'accession de Godefroid de Bouillon au duché de Basse-Lotharingie', *RBPH* 36 (1958), 1275-84.

——, 'La fonction ducale en Lotharingie, puis en Basse-Lotharingie de 900 à 1100', *Revue du Nord* 48 (1966), 107-9.

——, 'Les actes des ducs de Basse-Lotharingie du XIe siècle', *PSHIGDL* 95 (1981), 65-132.

Dion, A. de, 'Le Puiset au XIe et XIIe siècles', *Mémoires de la Société archéologique d'Eure-et-Loir* 9 (1889), 1-34, 71-85.

Dodu, Gustave, *Histoire des institutions monarchiques dans le royaume latin de Jérusalem* (Paris, 1894).

Dorchy, H., 'Godefroid de Bouillon, duc de Basse-Lotharingie', *RBPH* 26 (1948), 961-99.

Douglas, David, 'The Domesday Tenant of Hawling', *Transactions of the Bristol and Gloucestershire Archaeological Society* 84 (1965), 28-30.

Du Cange, Charles du Fresne, *Les Familles d'Outremer*, ed. Emmanuel-Guillaume Rey, Collection des documents inédits sur l'histoire de France 18 (Paris, 1869).

Duncalf, Frederic, 'The Peasants' Crusade', *American Historical Review* 26 for 1920-21 (1921), 440-53.

Dupont, Christian, 'Les domaines des ducs en Basse-Lotharingie au XIe siècle', *PSHIGDL* 95 (1981), 217-40.

Dupont, Etienne, 'Le château de Brix en Normandie', *Scottish Historical Review* 2 (1905), 424-28.

Dupréel, Eugène, *Histoire critique de Godefroid le Barbu* (Uccle, 1904).

Dussaud, René, *Topographie historique de la Syrie antique et médiévale* (Paris, 1927).

Edbury, Peter W., and John Gordon Rowe, *William of Tyre: Historian of the Latin East,*

Cambridge Studies in Medieval Life and Thought ser. 4, 8 (Cambridge, 1988).
Edgington, Susan B., 'Albert of Aachen Reappraised', in *From Clermont to Jerusalem: The Crusades and Crusader Societies, 1095-1500*, ed. Alan V. Murray, International Medieval Research 3 (Turnhout, 1998), pp. 55-67.
——, 'The First Crusade: Reviewing the Evidence', in *The First Crusade: Origins and Impact*, pp. 57-77.
Eichmann, Eduard, *Die Kaiserkrönung im Abendland* (Würzburg, 1942).
Epp, Verena, *Fulcher von Chartres: Studien zur Geschichtsschreibung des ersten Kreuzzuges*, Studia humaniora: Düsseldorfer Studien zu Mittelalter und Renaissance 15 (Düsseldorf, 1990).
Ernst, Simon Pierre, *Histoire du Limbourg*, 7 vols (Liège, 1837-52).
Der Erste Kreuzzug 1096 und seine Folgen: Die Verfolgung von Juden im Rheinland, Schriften des Archivs der Evangelischen Kirche im Rheinland 9 (Düsseldorf, 1996).
Evrard, Jean-Pol, 'Les comtes de Verdun aux Xe et XIe siècles', *PSHIGDL* 95 (1981), 153-82.
Farrington, A. J., 'A Note on Gherbod the Fleming', *Journal of the Chester and North Wales Architectural, Archaeological and Historical Society* 51 (1964), 21-22.
Favreau-Lilie, Marie-Luise, *Die Italiener im Heiligen Lande vom ersten Kreuzzug bis zum Tode Heinrichs von Champagne (1098-1197)* (Amsterdam, 1989).
Feuchère, P., 'Essai sur l'évolution territoriale des principautés français (Xe-XIIIe siècles)', *Le Moyen Age* 58 (1952), 85-117.
——, 'Les origines du comté de Saint-Pol (Xe siècle – 1205)', *Revue du Nord* 35 (1953), 125-49.
Ficker, Julius, *Vom Reichsfürstenstande*, 2 vols (Innsbruck, 1866-1911).
The First Crusade: Origins and Impact, ed. Jonathan P. Phillips (Manchester, 1997).
Flesch, Stefan, 'Die Verfolgung und Vernichtung der jüdischen Gemeinde von Köln während des Ersten Kreuzzugs', in *Der Erste Kreuzzug 1096 und seine Folgen*, pp. 77-94.
Fliche, Augustin, *La chrétieté médievale* (Paris, 1929).
——, *Le règne de Philippe Ier, roi de France* (Paris, 1912).
Flori, Jean, *La première croisade: l'Occident chrétien contre l'Islam* (Paris, 1992).
——, *Pierre l'Ermite et la Première Croisade* (Paris, 1999).
France, John, 'The Election and Title of Godfrey de Bouillon', *Canadian Journal of History* 18 (1983), 321-29.
——, *Victory in the East: A Military History of the First Crusade* (Cambridge, 1994).
Frech, Gustl, 'Die deutschen Päpste – Kontinuität und Wandel', in *Die Salier und das Reich, 2: Die Reichskirche in der Salierzeit*, ed. Stefan Weinfurter and Frank Martin Siefarth (Sigmaringen, 1991), pp. 303-32.
Friedman, Yvonne, 'The Ransom of Captives in the Latin Kingdom of Jerusalem', in *Autour de la Première Croisade: Actes du Colloque de la Society for the Study of the Crusades and the Latin East (Clermont-Ferrand, 22-25 juin 1995)*, ed. Michel Balard (Paris, 1996), pp. 177-89
Genicot, Léopold, *Etudes sur les principautés lotharingiennes*, Université de Louvain,

Recueil de Travaux d'Histoire et de Philologie, ser.6, 7 (Louvain, 1975).

Giese, Wolfgang, 'Untersuchungen zur *Historia Hierosolymitana* des Fulcher von Chartres', *Archiv für Kulturgeschichte* 69 (1987), 62-115.

Giry, A., 'Les châtelains de Saint-Omer 1042-1386', *Bibliothèque de l'Ecole des Chartes* 35 (1874), 325-55.

Goetz, Hans-Werner, 'Das Herzogtum im Spiegel der salierzeitlichen Geschichtsschreibung', in *Die Salier und das Reich*, 1: *Salier, Adel und Reichsverfassung*, ed. Stefan Weinfurter and Helmut Kluger (Sigmaringen, 1991), pp. 253-71.

Goffinet, Hippolyte, 'Les comtes de Chiny, étude historique', *Annales de l'Institut archéologique de Luxembourg* 8 (1874), 255-356; 9 (1875), 17-109.

Grabois, Aryeh, 'Charlemagne, Rome and Jerusalem', *RBPH* 59 (1981), 792-809.

Grossman, Avraham, 'The Cultural and Social Background of Jewish Martyrdom in Germany in 1096', in *Juden und Christen zur Zeit der Kreuzzüge*, pp. 73-86.

Grosdidier de Matons, Marcel, *Le Comté de Bar des origines au Traité de Bruges (vers 950-1301)* (Bar-le-Duc, 1918).

Grousset, René, *Histoire des croisades et du royaume franc de Jérusalem*, 2 vols (Paris, 1934-36).

Gysseling, Maurits, *Toponymisch woordenboek van België, Nederland, Luxemburg, Noord-Frankrijk en West-Duitsland (vóór 1226)*, 2 vols (Brussels, 1960).

Hagenmeyer, Heinrich, 'Chronologie de la première croisade 1094-1100', *ROL* 6 (1898), 214-93, 490-549; 7 (1899), 275-399, 430-503; 8 (1900-1), 318-82.

——, 'Der Brief der Kreuzfahrer an den Pabst und die abendländische Kirche im Jahre 1099 nach der Schlacht bei Askalon', *Forschungen zur deutschen Geschichte* 13 (1873), 400-12.

——, 'Etude sur la Chronique de Zimmern: Renseignements qu'elle fournit sur la première croisade', *Archives de l'Orient latin* 2 (1884), 20-36.

——, *Peter der Eremite: Ein kritischer Beitrag zur Geschichte des ersten Kreuzzuges* (Leipzig, 1879).

——, *Le Vrai et le faux sur Pierre l'Hermite* (Paris, 1883).

Hagspiel, Gereon, *Die Führerpersönlichkeit im Kreuzzug*, Geist und Werk der Zeiten 10 (Zürich, 1963).

Hamilton, Bernard, 'Women in the Crusader States: The Queens of Jerusalem 1100-1190', in *Medieval Women*, Studies in Church History, Subsidia 1, ed. Derek Baker (Oxford, 1978), 143-74.

——, *The Latin Church in the Crusader States: The Secular Church* (London, 1980).

Hamm, Stefanie, 'Regentinnen und minderjährige Herrscher im normannischen Italien', in *Roma, magistra mundi: Itineraria culturae medievalis – parvi flores*, ed. Jacqueline Hamesse, Fédération Internationale des Instituts d'Etudes Médiévales: Textes et études du Moyen Age 10/3 (Louvain-la-Neuve, 1998), pp. 123-39.

Hansay, A., 'L'inféodation du comté de Hainaut à l'église de Liège en 1071', *Bulletin de la Société de l'art et l'histoire du diocèse de Liège* 13 (1902), 45-58.

Hansen, Joseph, *Das Problem eines Kirchenstaates in Jerusalem: Ein Beitrag zur Geschichte der Kreuzzüge* (Luxembourg, 1928).

Hardenberg, Herman, *De Nederlanden en de kruistochten* (Amsterdam, 1944).
Héliot, Pierre, *Histoire de Boulogne et du Boulonnais* (Lille, 1937).
Hiestand, Rudolf, 'Der Erste Kreuzzug in der Welt des ausgehenden 11. Jahrhunderts', in *Der Erste Kreuzzug 1096 und seine Folgen*, pp. 1-36.
——, 'König Balduin und sein Tanzbär', *Archiv für Kulturgeschichte* 70 (1988), 343-60.
A History of the Crusades, ed. Kenneth M. Setton et al., 2nd edn, 6 vols (Madison, 1969-89).
Hooper, Nicholas, 'Edgar the Ætheling: Anglo-Saxon Prince, Rebel and Crusader', *Anglo-Saxon England* 14 (1985), 197-214.
Houben, Hubert, 'Adelaide "del Vasto" nella storia del Regno di Sicilia', in *Bianca Lancia d'Agliano: Fra il Piemonte e il Regno di Sicilia. Atti di Convegno (Asti-Agliano, 28/29 aprile 1990)*, ed. Renato Bordone, Ricerche di storia locale 4 (Alessandria, 1992), pp. 121-45.
——, *Roger II. von Sizilien: Herrscher zwischen Orient und Okzident* (Darmstadt, 1997).
Huyghebaert, Nicolas, 'La mère de Godefroid de Bouillon: La comtesse Ide de Boulogne', *PSHIGDL* 95 (1981), 43-63.
——, 'Pourquoi l'église a-t-elle besoin d'avoués?', *PSHIGDL* 98 (1984), 33-42.
Jackman, Donald C., 'Abnepos, pronepos', *Notes and Queries* 245 (2000), 14-16.
Jamison, E. M., 'Some Notes on the *Anonymi Gesta Francorum*, with Special Reference to the Norman Contingent from South Italy and Sicily in the First Crusade', in *Studies in French Language and Medieval Literature presented to Professor Mildred K. Pope*, Publications of the University of Manchester 268 (Manchester, 1939), pp. 195-204.
Jenny, Beat Rudolf, *Graf Froben Christoph von Zimmern: Geschichtsschreiber, Erzähler, Landesherr. Ein Beitrag zur Geschichte des Humanismus in Schwaben* (Konstanz, 1959).
Jensen, Jørgen Steen, 'A Maastricht Coin Representing the Investiture of Bishop Otbert of Liège by the Emperor Henry IV in 1091', *Spink Numismatic Circular* 98 (1990), 310-11.
Joris, André, 'Le Triomphe de Saint-Lambert à Bouillon (1141)', *PSHIGDL* 95 (1981), 183-200.
——, 'Remarques sur les clauses militaires des privilèges urbains liégeois', *RBPH* 37 (1959), 297-316.
——, *La ville de Huy au Moyen Age*, Bibliothèque de la Faculté de Philosophie et Lettres de l'Université de Liège 152 (Paris, 1959).
Juden und Christen zur Zeit der Kreuzzüge, ed. Alfred Haverkamp, Vorträge und Forschungen 47 (Sigmaringen, 1999).
Keats-Rohan, K. S. B., *Domesday People. A Prosopography of Persons Occurring in English Documents, 1066-1166, 1: Domesday Book* (Woodbridge, 1998).
——, 'The Prosopography of Post-Conquest England: Four Case Studies', *Medieval Prosopography* 14 (1993), 1-52.
Keats-Rohan, K. S. B., and David E. Thornton, *Domesday Names: An Index of Latin Personal Names in Domesday Book* (Woodbridge, 1997).
Kedar, Benjamin Z., *Crusade and Mission: European Approaches toward the Muslims*

(Princeton, 1984).
Kern, Fritz, *Gottesgnadentum und Widerstandsrecht im früheren Mittelalter: Zur Entwicklungsgeschichte der Monarchie* (Münster, 1954).
Knappen, Marshall M., 'Robert II of Flanders in the First Crusade', in *The Crusades and Other Historical Essays presented to Dana C. Munro by his Former Students*, ed. Louis J. Paetow (New York, 1928), pp. 79-100.
Knoch, Peter, *Studien zu Albert von Aachen: Der Erste Kreuzzug in der deutschen Chronistik*, Stuttgarter Beiträge zur Geschichte und Politik 1 (Stuttgart, 1966).
Kohler, Charles, 'Un sermon commémoratif de la prise de Jérusalem par les croisés attribué à Foucher de Chartres', *ROL* 8 (1900-1), 158-64.
Krey, August C., 'Urban's Crusade, Success or Failure?', *American Historical Review* 53 (1948), 235-50.
Kupper, Jean-Louis, 'La Maison d'Ardenne-Verdun et l'Eglise de Liège. Remarques sur les origines d'une principauté épiscopale', *PSHIGDL* 95 (1981), 201-15.
——, *Liège et l'église imperiale, XIe-XIIe siècles*, Bibliothèque de la Faculté de Philosophie et Lettres de l'Université de Liège 228 (Paris, 1981).
——, '*Mulier nobilissima Ermengardis nomine*: Contribution à l'histoire de la seigneurie rurale en Basse-Lotharingie', *PSHIDL* 102 (1986), 69-74.
——, 'Otbert de Liège: les manipulations monétaires d'un évêque d'Empire à l'aube du XIIe siècle', *Le Moyen Age* 86 (1980), 353-85.
La Monte, John L., 'The Lords of Caesarea in the Period of the Crusades', *Speculum* 22 (1947), 145-61.
——, 'The Lords of Sidon in the 12th and 13th Centuries', *Byzantion* 17 (1944-45), 183-211.
——, 'The Lords of Le Puiset on the Crusades', *Speculum* 17 (1942), 100-18.
——, *Feudal Monarchy in the Latin Kingdom of Jerusalem*, Monographs of the Mediaeval Academy of America 4 (Cambridge, Mass., 1932).
Lair, Jules, 'Histoire de la seigneurie de Bures', *Mémoires de la Société de l'histoire de Paris et l'Ile-de-France* 2 (1876), 187-97.
Laret-Kayser, Arlette, 'La fonction et les pouvoirs ducaux en Basse-Lotharingie au XIe siècle', *PSHIGDL* 95 (1981), 133-52.
Lauranson-Rosaz, Christian, 'Le Velay et la croisade', in *Le Concile de Clermont de 1095 et l'appel à la croisade* (Rome, 1997), 33-64.
Laurent, J., 'Des Grecs aux croisés: Etude sur l'histoire d'Edesse entre 1071 et 1098', *Byzantion* 1 (1924), 367-449.
Läwen, Gerhard, *Stammesherzog und Stammesherzogtum. Beiträge zur Frage der Rechtstellung von Herzog und Stamm im Mittelalter*, Neue Deutsche Forschungen: Abteilung Mittelalterliche Geschichte 1 (Berlin, 1935).
Layer, Adolf, 'Die Grafen von Dillingen-Kyburg in Schwaben und in der Schweiz', in *Die Grafen von Kyburg: Kyburger-Tagung 1980 in Winterthur*, ed. Heinz Müller *et al.*, Schweizer Beiträge zu Kulturgeschichte und Archäologie des Mittelalters 8 (Olten, 1981), pp. 31-38.

Lestocquoy, J., *Histoire des territoires ayant formé le département du Pas-de-Calais* (Arras, 1946).

Lewis, C. P., 'The Formation of the Honor of Chester, 1066-1100', *Journal of the Chester Archaeological Society* 71 (1991), 37-66.

Leyser, Karl, 'Money and Supplies on the First Crusade', in Leyser, *Communications and Power in Medieval Europe: The Gregorian Revolution and Beyond*, ed. Timothy Reuter (London, 1994), pp. 77-95.

Lobet, Marcel, *Godefroid de Bouillon: Essai de biographie antilégendaire* (Brussels, 1943).

Lohrmann, Dietrich, 'Albert von Aachen und die Judenpogrome des Jahres 1096', *Zeitschrift des Aachener Geschichtsvereins* 100 for 1995-96 (1996), 129-51.

Loisne, A. de., *Dictionnaire topographique du Pas-de-Calais* (Paris, 1907).

Longnon, Auguste, *Etudes sur les pagi de la Gaule*, 2 vols (Paris, 1869-72).

Lotter, Friedrich, 'Tod oder Taufe. Das Problem der Zwangstaufen während des Ersten Kreuzzugs', in *Juden und Christen zur Zeit der Kreuzzüge*, pp. 107-52.

Loyd, L. C., *The Origins of Some Anglo-Norman Families*, Harleian Society Publications 103 (Leeds, 1951).

Lübeck, Konrad, *Die Fuldaer Äbte und Furstäbte des Mittelalters. Ein geschichtlicher Überblick*, Veröffentlichungen des Fuldaer Geschichtsvereins 31 (Fulda, 1952).

La Maison d'Ardenne, Xe-XIe siècles: Actes des Journées Lotharingiennes, 24-26 octobre 1980, Centre Universitaire, Luxemburg = *PSHIGDL* 95 (1981).

Martin, Abbé, 'Les premiers princes croisés et les Syriens jacobites de Jérusalem', *Journal Asiatique* 133-34 (1888-89), 471-90.

Mathieu, Jean-Noël, 'Sur les comtesses de Rethel au XI siècle: contribution à l'histoire des comtes de Rethel et des comtes de Porcien', *Revue historique ardennaise* 32 (1997), 3-19.

Matzke, Michael, *Daibert von Pisa. Zwischen Pisa, Papst und erstem Kreuzzug*, Vorträge und Forschungen, Sonderband 44 (Sigmaringen, 1998).

Maurer, Helmut, *Der Herzog von Schwaben: Grundlagen, Wirkungen und Wesen seiner Herrschaft in ottonischer, salischer und staufischer Zeit* (Sigmaringen, 1978).

Mayer, Hans Eberhard, 'Angevins versus Normans: The New Men of King Fulk of Jerusalem', *Proceedings of the American Philosophical Society* 133/1 (1989), 1-25.

——, *Bistümer, Klöster und Stifte im Königreich Jerusalem*, Schriften der MGH 26 (Stuttgart, 1977).

——, 'Carving Up Crusaders: The Early Ibelins and Ramlas', in *Outremer: Studies in the History of the Crusading Kingdom of Jerusalem presented to Joshua Prawer*, ed. Benjamin Z. Kedar, Hans Eberhard Mayer and R. C. Smail (Jerusalem, 1982), pp. 101-18.

——, 'The Crusader Principality of Galilee between Saint-Omer and Bures-sur-Yvette', in *Itinéraires d'Orient: Hommages à Claude Cahen* (Bures-sur-Yvette, 1994), pp. 157-67.

——, 'Die Herrschaftsbildung in Hebron', *Zeitschrift des Deutschen Palästinavereins* 101 (1985), 64-82.

——, *Jérusalem et Antioche au temps de Baudouin II*, Comptes-rendus de l'Académie des Inscriptions et Belles-Lettres, Nov.-Déc. 1980 (Paris, 1980).

——, *Die Kanzlei der lateinischen Könige von Jerusalem*, Schriften der MGH 40, 2 vols (Hannover, 1996).

——, *Die Kreuzfahrerherrschaft Montréal (Šōbak): Jordanien im 12. Jahrhundert*, Abhandlungen des Deutschen Palästinavereins 14 (Wiesbaden, 1990).

——, *Mélanges sur l'histoire du royaume latin de Jérusalem*, Mémoires de l'Académie des Inscriptions et Belles-Lettres n.s. 5 (Paris, 1984).

——, 'The Origins of the County of Jaffa', *Israel Exploration Journal* 35 (1985), 35-45.

——, 'The Origins of the Lordships of Ramla and Lydda in the Latin Kingdom of Jerusalem', *Speculum* 60 (1985), 537-52.

——, *Das Siegelwesen in den Kreuzfahrerstaaten*, Bayerische Akademie der Wissenschaften: Philosophisch-historische Klasse, Abhandlungen n.s. 83 (Munich, 1978).

——, 'Studies in the History of Queen Melisende of Jerusalem', *Dumbarton Oaks Papers* 26 (1972), 93-183.

——, 'The Succession to Baldwin II of Jerusalem: English Impact on the East', *Dumbarton Oaks Papers* 39 (1985), 139-47.

——, 'The Wheel of Fortune: Seignorial Vicissitudes Under Kings Fulk and Baldwin III of Jerusalem', *Speculum* 65 (1990), 860-77.

The Medieval Nobility: Studies on the Ruling Classes of France and Germany from the Sixth to the Twelfth Century, ed. Timothy Reuter, Europe in the Middle Ages 14 (Amsterdam, 1979).

Mentgen, Gerd, 'Die Juden des Mittelrhein-Mosel-Gebietes im Hochmittelalter unter besonderer Berücksichtigung der Kreuzzugsverfolgungen', in *Der Erste Kreuzzug 1096 und seine Folgen,* pp. 37-75.

Menzel, Michael, 'Gottfried von Bouillon und Kaiser Heraclius', *Archiv für Kulturgeschichte* 74 (1992), 1-21.

Moeller, Charles, 'Godefroid de Bouillon et l'avouerie du Saint-Sépulcre', in *Mélanges Godefroid Kurth: Recueil de mémoires relatifs à l'histoire, à la philologie et à l'archéologie*, 2 vols (Liège, 1908), 1: 173-83.

——, 'Les flamands du Ternois au royaume latin de Jérusalem', in *Mélanges Paul Fredericq* (Brussels, 1903), pp. 189-202.

Mohr, Walter, *Geschichte des Herzogtums Lothringen*, 3 vols: 1. *Geschichte des Herzogtums Groß-Lothringen*. 2. *Niederlothringen bis zu seinem Aufgehen im Herzogtum Brabant (11.-13. Jahrhundert)*. 3. *Das Herzogtum der Mosellaner (11..-14. Jahrhundert)* (Saarbrücken, 1976-79).

Möhring, Hannes, 'Graf Emicho und die Judenverfolgungen von 1096', *Rheinische Vierteljahrsblätter* 56 (1992), 97-111.

Monier, R., *Les institutions centrales du comté de Flandre de la fin de la XIe siècle à 1384* (Paris, 1943).

Müller-Kehlen, Helga, *Die Ardennen im Frühmittelalter* (Göttingen, 1973).

Munro, Dana C., 'The Speech of Pope Urban II at Clermont, 1095', *American Historical Review* 11 (1905-6), 231-42.

Murray, Alan V., 'The Army of Godfrey of Bouillon, 1096-1099: Structure and

Dynamics of a Contingent on the First Crusade', *RBPH* 70 (1992), 301-29.
——, 'Baldwin II and his Nobles: Baronial Factionalism and Dissent in the Kingdom of Jerusalem, 1118-1134', *Nottingham Medieval Studies* 38 (1994), 60-85.
——, 'The Chronicle of Zimmern as a Source for the First Crusade: The Evidence of Ms. Stuttgart, Württembergische Landesbibliothek, Cod. Don. 580', in *The First Crusade: Origins and Impact*, pp. 78-106.
——, 'Dynastic Continuity or Dynastic Change? The Accession of Baldwin II and the Nobility of the Kingdom of Jerusalem', *Medieval Prosopography* 13 (1992), 1-28.
——, 'A Little-Known Member of the Royal Family of Crusader Jerusalem in William of Malmesbury's *Gesta Regum Anglorum*', *Notes and Queries* 241 (1996), 397-99.
——, 'Mighty Against the Enemies of Christ: The Relic of the True Cross in the Armies of the Kingdom of Jerusalem', in *The Crusades and Their Sources: Essays Presented to Bernard Hamilton*, ed. John France and W. G. Zajac (Aldershot, 1998), pp. 217-38.
——, 'A Note on the Origin of Eustace Grenier', *Bulletin of the Society for the Study of the Crusades and the Latin East* 6 (1986), 28-30.
——, 'The Origins of the Frankish Nobility of the Kingdom of Jerusalem, 1100-1118', *Mediterranean Historical Review* 4 (1989), 281-300.
——, 'The Title of Godfrey of Bouillon as Ruler of Jerusalem', *Collegium Medievale* 3 (1990), 163-78.
——, 'Walther Duke of Teck: The Invention of a German Hero of the First Crusade', *Medieval Prosopography* 19 (1998), 35-54.
——, 'Why a Bastard? A Possible Historical Origin for the Illegitimate Hero in the *Bâtard de Bouillon*', *Neuphilologische Mitteilungen* 98 (1997), 179-85.
Musset, Lucien, 'Aux origines d'une classe dirigeante: les Tosny, grands barons normands du Xe au XIIe siècle', *Francia* 5 (1977), 55-80.
Nau, M. F., 'Le croisé lorrain Godefroy de Ascha d'après deux documents syriaques du XIIe siècle', *Journal Asiatique* ser. 9, 14 (1899), 421-31.
——, 'Les croisés Henry et Godefroy du château de Ascha, Assche, Asch, Esch ou Aix d'après les historiens occidentaux et deux notes syriaques du XIIe siècle', *L'Ancien Pays de Looz* 4 (1900), 21-25.
Nègre, Ernest, *Toponymie général de la France*, 3 vols (Geneva, 1990).
Nellman, Eberhard, *Die Reichsidee in deutschen Dichtungen der Salier- und frühen Stauferzeit* (Berlin, 1963).
Newman, W. M., *Les seigneurs de Nesle en Picardie* (Philadelphia, 1971).
Nicholson, Robert L., *Joscelyn I, Prince of Edessa*, Illinois Studies in the Social Sciences 34/4 (Urbana, 1954).
——, *Tancred: A Study of His Career and Work in Their Relation to the First Crusade and the Establishment of the Latin States in Syria and Palestine* (Chicago, 1940).
Nickerson, Mary E., 'The Seigneurie of Beirut in the 12th Century and the Brisebarre Family of Beirut-Blanchegarde', *Byzantion* 19 (1949), 141-85.

Nielen-Vandevoorde, Marie-Adélaïde, 'Un livre méconnu des *Assises de Jérusalem*: Les *Lignages d'Outremer*', *Bibliothèque de l'Ecole des chartes* 153 (1995), 103-30.

Nonn, Ulrich, *Pagus und comitatus in Niederlothringen: Untersuchungen zur politischen Raumgliederung im früheren Mittelalter*, Bonner historische Forschungen 49 (Bonn, 1983).

Pagny, Raymond, 'Les seigneurs et la seigneurie de Cons-la-Grandville', *Bulletin de l'Association 'Les Amis du Vieux Longwy'* 5 (1962), 3-9, 74-78.

Parisot, R., *Les origines de la Haute-Lorraine et sa première maison ducale 959-1033* (Paris, 1909).

Parisse, Michel, 'Les ducs et la duché de Lorraine au XIIe siècle, 1048-1206', *Blätter für deutsche Landeskunde* 111 (1975), 86-102.

——, 'Généalogie de la Maison d'Ardenne', *PSHIGDL* 95 (1981), 9-42.

——, *Noblesse et chevalerie en Lorraine médiévale. Les familles nobles du Xie au XIIIe siècle* (Nancy, 1982).

——, *La noblesse lorraine, XIe-XIIIe siècle*, 2 vols (Lille, 1976).

Phillips, Jonathan P., *Defenders of the Holy Land: relations Between the latin east and the West, 1119-1187* (Oxford, 1996).

——, 'Hugh of Payns and the 1129 Damascus Crusade', in *The Military Orders: Fighting for the Faith and Caring for the Sick*, ed. Malcolm Barber (Aldershot, 1994), pp. 142-47.

Pirie-Gordon, Harry, 'The Reigning Princes of Galilee', *English Historical Review* 27 (1912), 445-61.

Poncelet, Edouard, 'Les droits souverains de la principauté de Liège sur le duché de Bouillon', *Bulletin de la Commission royale d'histoire* 108 (1943), 157-258.

Pontieri, E, 'La madre di Re Ruggiero, Adelaide del Vasto, contessa di Sicilia, regina di Gerusalemme', in *Atti del Convegno internazionale di studi ruggeriani*, 2 vols (Palermo, 1955), 2: 322-432.

Porteous, John, 'Crusader Coinage with Greek or Latin inscriptions', in *A History of the Crusades*, ed. Setton, 6: 354-420.

Poull, Georges, *La Maison ducale de Bar, 1: La maison ducale de Haute-Lorraine (942-1033), Les premiers comtes de Bar (1033-1239)* (Rupt-sur-Moselle, 1977).

Prawer, Joshua, *Crusader Institutions* (Oxford, 1980).

——, *Histoire du royaume latin de Jérusalem*, 2 vols (Paris, 1969).

——, *The Latin Kingdom of Jerusalem: European Colonialism in the Middle Ages* (London, 1972).

——, 'La noblesse et le régime féodal du royaume latin de Jérusalem', *Le Moyen Age* 65 (1959), 41-74.

——, 'The Settlement of the Latins in Jerusalem', *Speculum* 27 (1952), 490-503.

——, 'Social Classes in the Latin Kingdom: The Franks', in *A History of the Crusades*, ed. Setton, 5: 117-92.

Renn, Heinz, *Das erste Luxemburger Grafenhaus*, Rheinisches Archiv 39 (Berlin 1941).

Rheinheimer, Martin, *Das Kreuzfahrerfürstentum Galiläa*, Kieler Werkstücke, Reihe C: Beiträge zur europäischen Geschichte des frühen und hohen Mittelalters 1 (Frankfurt am Main, 1990).

Richard, Jean, *Le comté de Tripoli sous la dynastie toulousaine*, 1102-1187 (Paris, 1945).
——, 'Guy d'Ibelin OP, évêque de Limassol et l'inventaire de ses biens', *Bulletin de correspondance hellénique* 74 (1950), 98-133.
——, *Histoire des croisades* (Paris, 1996).
——, *The Latin Kingdom of Jerusalem*, Europe in the Middle Ages 11, 2 vols (Amsterdam, 1969).
——, 'Note sur l'archidiocèse d'Apamée et les conquêtes de Raymond de Saint-Gilles en Syrie du Nord', *Syria* 25 (1946-48), 102-8.
——, 'The Political and Ecclesiastical Organisation of the Crusader States', in *A History of the Crusades*, ed. Setton, 5: 193-250.
——, *Le royaume latin de Jérusalem* (Paris, 1953).
Rigaux, E., *Recherches sur les premiers comtes de Boulogne* (Boulogne-sur-Mer, 1896).
Riley-Smith, Jonathan S. C., *The First Crusade and the Idea of Crusading* (London, 1986).
——, *The First Crusaders, 1095-1131* (Cambridge, 1997).
——, 'The Latin Clergy and the Settlement in Palestine and Syria, 1098-1100', *Catholic Historical Review* 74 (1988), 539-57.
——, 'The Motives of the Earliest Crusaders and the Settlement of Latin Palestine, 1095-1100', *English Historical Review* 98 (1983), 721-36.
——, 'Raymond IV of St Gilles, Achard of Arles and the Conquest of Lebanon', in *The Crusades and Their Sources*, pp. 1-8.
——, 'The Title of Godfrey of Bouillon', *Bulletin of the Institute of Historical Research* 52 (1979), 83-86.
Ritchie, R. L. G., *The Normans in Scotland* (Edinburgh, 1954).
Röhricht, Reinhold, *Die Deutschen im Heiligen Lande* (Innsbruck, 1894).
——, *Geschichte des Ersten Kreuzzuges* (Innsbruck, 1901).
——, *Geschichte des Königreichs Jerusalem* (Innsbruck, 1898)
Roland, C. G., 'Les seigneurs et comtes de Rochefort', *Annales de la Société archéologique de Namur* 20 (1893), 63-141.
Round, John Horace, *Studies in Peerage and Family History* (Westminster, 1901), pp. 147-80.
Rowe, John Gordon, 'Pascal II and the Relations Between the Spiritual and Temporal Powers in the Kingdom of Jerusalem', *Speculum* 32 (1959), 470-501.
Rüdt de Collenberg, Wipertus Hugues, 'Les premiers Ibelins', *Le Moyen Age* 71 (1965), 433-74.
Runciman, Steven, 'The First Crusade: Constantinople to Antioch', in *A History of the Crusades*, ed. Setton, 1: 280-304.
——, *A History of the Crusades*, 3 vols (Cambridge, 1951-54).
Russell, Josiah C., 'The Population of the Crusader States', in *A History of the Crusades*, ed. Setton, 5: 295-314.
Sabourin, Pascal, 'Baudoin [*sic*] de Bourcq, croisé, comte d'Edesse, roi de Jérusalem. Proposition de lecture d'un itinéraire peu ordinaire', *Revue historique ardennaise* 31 (1996), 3-15.

Salis-Soglio, Nikolaus von, 'Das Dillinger Grafenhaus und seine Stiftung Neresheim', *Benediktinische Monatschrift* 3 (1921), 197-214, 269-89.

Saur, Léon, 'Entre Bar, Namur et Liège: Bouillon: place stratégique', *PSHIGDL* 95 (1981), 258-82.

Schlotterose, B. S., *Die Besetzung der deutschen Herzogtümer bis zum Jahre 1125* (Halle, 1912)

Schramm, Percy Ernst, *Herrschaftszeichen und Staatssymbolik: Beiträge zu ihrer Geschichte vom dritten bis zum sechzehnten Jahrhundert*, Schriften der MGH 13, 3 vols (Stuttgart, 1954-56).

——, *Kaiser, Rom und Renovatio* (Bad Homburg, 1962).

——, 'Die Ordines der mittelalterlichen Kaiserkrönung', *Archiv für Urkundenforschung* 11 (1930), 285-390.

La Seigneurie rurale en Lotharingie. Actes des 3es Journées Lotharingiennes = PSHIGDL 102 (1986).

Slack, Corliss K., 'Royal *Familiares* in the Latin Kingdom of Jerusalem, 1100-1187', *Viator* 22 (1991), 15-67.

Smail, Raymond C., *Crusading Warfare, 1097-1193*, Cambridge Studies in Medieval Life and Thought n.s. 3 (Cambridge, 1956).

Somerville, Robert, 'The Council of Clermont (1095) and Latin Christian Society', *Archivum Historiae Pontificiae* 12 (1974), 55-90.

Sproemberg, Heinrich, 'Eine rheinische Königskandidatur im Jahre 1125', in *Aus Geschichte und Landeskunde: Forschungen und Darstellungen. Franz Steinbach zum 65. Geburtstag gewidmet*, ed. Max Braubach *et al.* (Bonn, 1960), pp. 50-70.

Stein, Henri, *Dictionnaire topographique du département de Seine-et-Marne* (Paris, 1964).

Struve, Tilman, 'Kaisertum und Romgedanke in salischer Zeit', *Deutsches Archiv für Erforschung des Mittelalters* 44 (1988), 424-54.

——, 'Die Stellung des Königtums in der politischen Theorie der Salierzeit', in *Die Salier und das Reich*, 3: *Gesellschaftlicher und ideengeschichtlicher Wandel im Reich der Salier*, ed. Stefan Weinfurter and Hubertus Seibert (Sigmaringen, 1991), pp. 217-44.

Tanner, Heather J., 'Between Scylla and Charybdis: The Political Role of the Comital Family of Boulogne in Northern France and England (879-1159)' (unpublished Ph.D. dissertation, Univ. of California at Santa Barbara, 1993).

——, 'The Expansion of the Power and Influence of the Counts of Boulogne Under Eustace II', in *Anglo-Norman Studies, XIV: Proceedings of the Battle Conference, 1991*, ed. Marjorie Chibnall (Woodbridge, 1992), pp. 251-86.

Tellenbach, Gerd, 'From the Carolingian Imperial Nobility to the German Estate of Imperial Princes', in *The Medieval Nobility: Studies on the Ruling Classes of France and Germany*, pp. 203-42.

Tourneur, Victor, 'Un denier de Godefroid de Bouillon frappé en 1096', *Revue Belge de numismatique* 83 (1931), 27-30.

Twellenkamp, Markus, 'Das Haus der Luxemburger' in *Die Salier und das Reich*, 1: *Salier, Adel und Reichsverfassung*, ed. Stefan Weinfurter and Helmut Kluger (Sigmaringen, 1991), pp. 475-502.

Van Rey, M., *Die Lütticher Gaue Condroz und Ardenne im Frühmittelalter*, Rheinisches Archiv 102 (Bonn, 1977).

Vanderkindere, Léon, *La formation territoriale des principautés belges au Moyen Age*, 2 vols (Brussels, 1902).

Vanderlinden, Herman, 'La date de la nomination de Godefroid de Bouillon comme duc de Lotharingie (1087)', *Bulletin de la Commission Royale d'Histoire* 90 (1926), 189-92.

——, 'Le tribunal de la Paix de Henri de Verdun (1082) et la formation de la principauté de Liège', in *Mélanges Henri Pirenne*, 2 vols (Brussels, 1926), 2: 589-96.

Vannérus, J., 'Les anciens dynastes d'Esch-sur-la-Sûre', *Ons Hémecht* 11 (1905), 434-42, 485-93, 532-40, 12 (1906), 18-23, 51-56, 112-18, 138-42.

Vaughn, Sally N., 'St. Anselm and Women', *Haskins Society Journal* 2 (1990), 83-93.

Vogtherr, Thomas, 'Die Regierungsdaten der lateinischen Könige von Jerusalem', *Zeitschrift des Deutschen Palästinavereins* 110 (1994), 51-81.

Waas, Adolf , *Geschichte der Kreuzzüge* (Freiburg im Breisgau, 1956).

——, *Vogtei und Bede in der deutschen Kaiserzeit*, 2 vols (Berlin, 1919-23).

Waeger, Gerhart, *Gottfried von Bouillon in der Historiographie* (Zürich, 1969).

Warlop, Ernest, *The Flemish Nobility before 1300*, 4 vols (Kortrijk, 1975).

Werner, Karl Ferdinand, 'Die Nachkommen Karls des Großen bis um das Jahr 1000', in *Karl der Große: Das Nachleben*, ed. W. Braunfels and P. E. Schramm (Düsseldorf, 1967), pp. 403-79.

——, 'Liens de parenté et noms de personne', in *Famille et parenté dans l'occident mediéval*, ed. Georges Duby and Jacques Le Goff (Rome, 1977), pp. 13-34.

Werner, Matthias, 'Der Herzog von Lothringen in salischer Zeit', in *Die Salier und das Reich*, 1: *Salier, Adel und Reichsverfassung*, ed. Stefan Weinfurter and Helmut Kluger (Sigmaringen, 1991), 367-473.

Yassif, Eli, 'Rashi Legends and Medieval Popular Culture', in *Rashi 1040-1990: Hommages à Ephraïm E. Urbach*, ed. Gabrielle Sed-Rajna (Paris, 1993), pp. 483-92.

Yewdale, Ralph B., *Bohemond I, Prince of Antioch* (Princeton, 1924).

Zoller-Devroey, C., 'Féodalité et économie rurale dans les Ardennes médiévales: le fief de Bouillon en Sedanais', in *Centenaire du Seminaire d'histoire de l'Université libre de Bruxelles 1876-1976*, ed. Georges Despy (Brussels, 1977), pp. 21-57.

Zöllner, Walter, *Geschichte der Kreuzzüge* (Berlin, 1977).

Index